Analysis through Action for Actors and Directors

CW01501598

Analysis through Action for Actors and Directors is a comprehensive view of an innovative and exciting process for making new theatre.

As well as an understanding of how Analysis through Action has developed over time, this book also demonstrates how it can be put into practice in today's theatre. The first part of this book traces the exciting genealogy from Stanislavsky's unfinished experiments, through the insights of geniuses Maria Knebel and Georgii Tovstonogov, down to today's avant-garde auteurs. The second part is a practical manual based on extensive field testing by the author and colleagues. Here, two key components of the process are elucidated: Text Actions – ten interwoven text analysis steps – to be twinned with the thrilling rehearsal process using focused and joyful improvisations called Études.

Written for new or experienced theatre students and practitioners, this book will enrich the technique of any theatre artist and anyone else interested in the theatre and its future.

David Chambers is a director, writer, and producer of theatre and opera. His work has been seen in New York from basements to Broadway, in theatres throughout the US, as well as Europe, Russia, and Asia. He taught acting and directing at the Yale School of Drama for three decades. Since then he has been on the faculties of The New School for Drama, The Stella Adler Studio, and Harvard University. He currently teaches in the department of Theatre, Dance, and Performance Studies at Yale University, USA.

Analysis through Action for Actors and Directors

From Stanislavsky to Contemporary Performance

David Chambers

Routledge
Taylor & Francis Group

LONDON AND NEW YORK

Designed cover image: © Cover photograph courtesy of photographer Ken Reynolds

First published 2024
by Routledge
4 Park Square, Milton Park, Abingdon, Oxon OX14 4RN

and by Routledge
605 Third Avenue, New York, NY 10158

Routledge is an imprint of the Taylor & Francis Group, an informa business

© 2024 David Chambers

The right of David Chambers to be identified as author of this work has been asserted in accordance with sections 77 and 78 of the Copyright, Designs and Patents Act 1988.

All rights reserved. No part of this book may be reprinted or reproduced or utilised in any form or by any electronic, mechanical, or other means, now known or hereafter invented, including photocopying and recording, or in any information storage or retrieval system, without permission in writing from the publishers.

Trademark notice: Product or corporate names may be trademarks or registered trademarks, and are used only for identification and explanation without intent to infringe.

British Library Cataloguing-in-Publication Data
A catalogue record for this book is available from the British Library

ISBN: 978-1-138-78212-9 (hbk)
ISBN: 978-1-138-78213-6 (pbk)
ISBN: 978-1-003-47557-6 (ebk)

DOI: 10.4324/9781003475576

Typeset in Times New Roman
by SPi Technologies India Pvt Ltd (Straive)

To my Russian friends and colleagues, whether still there or recently departed

and

To my family, especially Christine, Jessica, and Dmitri who will delighted by the completion of TFB

Contents

SECTION A
Text Actions   183

SECTION B
Études   269

To The Reader

Welcome! Here are a few words to assist you in reading *Analysis through Action*.

This book is intended for all actors, directors, related teachers, and theatre aficionados. It is in two parts. Part I, 'A Genealogy of Analysis through Action,' traces the evolving lineage of Analysis through Action from the originators, starting with Stanislavsky's last experiments, through selected historical and current-day practitioners. Part II, 'The Practice of Analysis through Action,' covers the intwined aspects of (1) a close reading text analysis process – here called "Text Actions" – and (2) 'The practice of Études,' meaning focused improvisations pointed toward the exploration and theatrical realization of a text.

Part I covers some basic Russian theatre history and theory and is aimed toward a new reader in this field, someone seeking practical knowledge readily applicable in today's Western theatre. Part II is a kind of manual, with a progression of text analysis steps – ten Text Actions - followed by strategies for implementing Études. While an impatient reader could leap immediately into Part II, there are critical underlying ideas and important references to be found in Part I. So, think of the entire volume as an introductory handbook to this creatively exciting and highly productive rehearsal and training process.

Some tips: The book cites examples from well-known plays, most often from Chekhov and regularly from *The Cherry Orchard*. I strongly advise reading or re-reading that play. I recommend the Paul Schmidt translation used in this volume or the Laurence Senelick edition, generally considered to be closer to the Russian original with an extensive introduction and valuable notes. Other Chekhov dramas will come into play now and again; while they do not play a critical role, they are always worth a read. Also cited periodically are *Hamlet* and *Romeo and Juliet*, where basic knowledge is assumed.

A reader unfamiliar with Russian nomenclature will run into a common problem: pronunciation of names, places, and terms. The general rule of thumb for non-Russian readers is to first sound out the name or word phonetically so that you don't completely stumble when it comes up again. The Senelick single-play Chekhov editions offer a pronunciation guide for characters and locations. For further help, enter the word into Google Translate for a recording. Best yet, a two-minute audio of *Cherry Orchard* (and other Chekhov plays) names and places can be found at https://www.dialectsarchive.com/the-cherry-orchard.

A simple guide to how Russian names work – 1. given name, 2. patronymic (a middle name derived from the father's given name), 3. surname, and 4. affectionate names (nicknames), as well as masculine and feminine endings - can be found at https://en.wikipedia.org/wiki/Eastern_Slavic_naming_customs

On translation: The translations are mine unless otherwise noted. I also relied heavily on Yulia Kleiman in Russia and Ilya Khodosh in the US, for translation and consultation.

On spelling: I have used the most common transliterations, except inside quotations where different spellings may appear. I use the 'y' ending on Russian names – Stanislavsky, not Stanislavski - except where the subject uses a different ending when they write in English.

On capitalization: As one can already see on these prefatory pages, throughout the book I capitalize words that are important to Analysis through Action: for instance, here you have seen 'Text Actions' and 'Études.' Many more uppercase examples will follow, including (following Maria Shevtsova and others) "System" for Stanislavsky's decades-long attempt to codify the components of stage acting. Non-Stanislavsky uses of the word 'system' will remain in lower case.

On acronyms and place names: Russians are as devoted as any culture to acronyms for official organizations. But Russian acronyms and place names can be thorny because of numerous government reformations. As an example, the city Saint Petersburg became Petrograd in 1914 (Petersburg was considered too German), then Leningrad in 1924, and then back to Saint Petersburg in 1991. Such changes were similarly reflected in the names of governmental and artistic institutions and their acronyms.

The Moscow Art Theatre opened in 1898 as The Moscow Public-Art Theatre, then became The Moscow Art Theatre, then The Moscow Art Academic Theatre. Then, for political reasons in 1987, it split into The Gorky Moscow Art Theatre, with a separate new home and resident company, and The Chekhov Moscow Art Theatre, the traditional one we shall follow. To avoid confusion, in this book we shall simply refer to this institution as the Art Theatre or sometimes use the general acronym MAT, regardless of era.

The two major drama schools that trained almost all the Russian theatre artists we shall meet in this book went through similar changes. We shall refer to the Moscow school as GITIS (The State Institute for Theatre Arts), the name it has held since 1923. Since 2015, the main Petersburg theatre school has been called RGISI (The Russian State Institute of Performing Arts). Prior incarnations were colloquially known as the Institute (The Leningrad State Institute of Theatre, Music, and Cinema, LGITMiK) from 1962 to 1992, and The Saint Petersburg State Theatre Arts Academy (SPbGATI), or simply the Academy from 1993 to 2014.

Acronyms found in this book are:

BDT: the Large (Bolshoi) Dramatic Theatre, Leningrad/Saint Petersburg

CCT: Central Children's Theatre (Moscow home of Knebel and Efros)

KGB: the State Security Committee (secret police)

MDT: Maly (Small) Drama Theatre, Saint Petersburg (home of Lev Dodin's company)

Narkompros: People's Commissariat for Enlightenment (the cultural ministry of the USSR)

NEP: New Economic Policy (a 1920s attempt to jump-start Russian post–Civil War economy)

USSR: Union of Soviet Socialist Republics (aka the Soviet Union)

Finally but importantly, Analysis through Action is the term I use here and elsewhere. I believe this translation to be more accurate to the Russian (Действенном Анализе per Maria Knebel) and more descriptive: a process that activates Analysis – meaning embodied knowledge – through or by means of psychophysical Action: hence Analysis through Action. More common usages elsewhere include Active Analysis, Action Analysis, or the Method of Active Analysis.

By whatever name, Analysis through Action is a recent arrival in the anglophone world. Articles and chapters have begun to appear regularly, often in the online journal *Stanislavsky Studies*. Moreover, two recent books, James Thomas' *A Director's Guide to Stanislavsky's Active Analysis: Including the Formative Essay on Active Analysis by Maria Knebel* (2016) and Sharon Carnicke's *Dynamic Acting through Active Analysis: Konstantin Stanislavsky, Maria Knebel, and Their Legacy* (2023) have recently entered the conversation, a dialogue long needed in the American theatre. Readers familiar with Katie Mitchell's *The Director's Craft: A Handbook for the Theater* (2009) will notice some similarities between this book and hers (Mitchell studied with a Lev Dodin–trained actor). Each of these authors have their own style, emphases, and foci; each broaches the topic in a distinct manner leading to a diversity of options and opinions in this new field of study and practice.

And there will be more books and articles. As James Thomas said to me: "It's becoming a cottage industry."

As we enter a challenging new era in our art – the *Washington Post* describes the American theatre as being in "freefall" – innovations are an urgent necessity. Certainly the institutional leaders have a lot of soul-searching to do to remain relevant – or just to keep their doors open. But the artists who make theatre can also look at what they are making, whom they are making it for, and *how* they are making it.

May this book, and the articles and volumes cited above, be instrumental in creating a lively, unexpected, and vividly exciting theatre that will draw audiences young and old, new or experienced, back into the increasingly empty spaces – there to find a theatre created by passionate actors and directors trained in an innovative, vigorous, and surprising approach to making inspiring and significant theatre.

Part I

A Genealogy of Analysis through Action

Introduction

A Journey Begins

I stumbled onto Analysis through Action[1] and Études through a back door. As co-director of The Meyerhold Project, a mid-1990s collaboration between the Yale School of Drama and The Saint Petersburg State Academy of Theatre Arts that was dedicated to reconstructing Vsevolod Meyerhold's landmark 1926 production of *Revizor* (Gogol's *The Inspector General*), I made several trips to "Piter." It was immediately apparent that something very different was going on in actor and director training there. Much of the rigor, ferocity, and intensity of the instruction I observed in their classrooms would likely be branded as 'unsafe' or 'inappropriate' at an American institution.

But in contrast to the arduous intensity of the classrooms, the Russian student performances were alive with an imaginative, buoyant, and emotional *joie de jouant* I had not seen at home. This was something different; an unpredictable cascade of spontaneity, whimsy, playfulness, and psychophysical danger was released through astonishingly flexible bodies and voices, all coached to the hilt. Yes, Vsevolod Meyerhold's *commedia* and biomechanical researches were somehow encoded inside the cultural DNA of these actors and directors…but I sensed that something else was up, some process that allowed for this theatrical freedom in rehearsal and performance, that encouraged this deeply soulful, highly physical action-based theatre.

However, I was there on a mission that required a singular focus: tending to our bi-national "production about Meyerhold's production" which would ultimately play in Saint Petersburg, Amsterdam, and New Haven. I had neither physical energy nor psychic capacity to pursue anything else.

Nonetheless, it did not escape my notice that in the hallways of the Academy there were austere Soviet-era photographs of departed master teachers. The sepia ghosts of an extraordinary team of 1950s to late 1980s acting and directing teachers – Georgii Tovstonogov, Arkady Katsman, Mar Sulimov, Boris Zon, Zinovy Korogodsky, and others we shall meet later – were still smoking their long cigarettes and monitoring their students from the vapors. My docent in this gallery, Academy graduate and now Professor Sergei Tcherkasski, taught me

DOI: 10.4324/9781003475576-2

the recurring student question: "Who was your teacher's teacher?" I soon learned that one or another of this Tovstonogov-era cohort had taught all my current colleagues on the Academy directing faculty.

Unlike the other names, Tovstonogov's was distantly familiar to me: a translated book of his, *The Profession of the Director*, lay unread on some shelf back home. I vaguely recalled that he had directed a unique *Uncle Vanya* at Princeton's McCarter Theater in the 1980s. My own mentor, Russophile Zelda Fichandler, famed founder of Washington's Arena Stage, had spoken of him with great respect – and had given me that unread book long ago. I learned from Tcherkasski that Tovstonogov taught something called Analysis through Action. I knew that to some people this towering figure was a god – but probably not my god: Stanislavsky's pedagogical descendants were not my interest. Stanislavsky was Satan, as far as I was concerned.

Instead, my god Meyerhold called me back to work, and in I went.

A decade later, I taught a mask workshop at a university in Romania. The head acting and directing teacher there was a lively Bulgarian named Maria Ganeva, who had studied with Tovstonogov at the Petersburg Academy for eight years in the 1980s. It was she who first outlined to me Tovstonogov's core ideas on Analysis through Action and then spoke of her own interest in Maria Knebel, who had independently developed her own related but distinct methodology in Moscow.

Now having time to listen, I sensed that somewhere in what Professor Ganeva was telling me there might be some common ground between Russian and American actor director training. Despite my ongoing enthusiasm for Meyerhold, I had sadly concluded that his work was too aesthetically distant, too extreme, and too specialized for most American actors' careerist interests (though directors loved it).

I needed to know more about this Analysis through Action, the roots of which could be traced directly to Stanislavsky, certainly a familiar if misunderstood icon in American theatre whom I had perennially discarded as obsolete and counter-theatricalist, despite American actor training's continual embracement. Perhaps there was some key in Analysis through Action, an outgrowth of Stanislavsky's little known (in the West) final experiments that could unlock the high-spirited Russian freedom-within-form that I so rarely saw back home.

Supported by a Likhachev Foundation Fellowship in 2012, I returned to a greatly changed Petersburg. With my close colleague and co-producer of the Meyerhold Project Nikolai Pesochinsky translating, I first interviewed Irina Malochevskaya, who had been Tovstonogov's principal associate for many years, joined by her PhD student Andrei Smolko with whom I had already corresponded; (ergo Andrei's teacher's teacher was Tovstonogov himself). After her mentor's death in 1989, Malochevskaya had authored *The Directing School of Georgii Tovstonogov*, a detailed appraisal of his four-year directing course including an in-depth chapter on Analysis through Action. We shall be citing passages of this invaluable book ahead.

One conversation in Petersburg always led to another; soon I was talking to world-renowned director Lev Dodin, scholar-director Veniamin Filshtinsky, master of vocal expression Valery Galandeev. This should be the spelling throughout and Dodin's associate director, and other experts of Tovstonogov's mode of Analysis through Action and Maria Osipovna Knebel's 'Étude Method' of Rehearsal.

Numerous Petersburg artists, all rightfully proud of their theatrical legacy, at that time was generally unknown in the West, generously came forward to help: Tcherkasski led me through a chronological introduction to the genealogy of Analysis through Action, from Stanislavsky to today. Fluently bilingual (and very funny) Dina Dodina, Lev Dodin's niece and gatekeeper, set up crucial interviews, and translated them live. Academy faculty member Yulia Kleiman photocopied numerous early articles and chapters and translated some of them as later did the remarkable Yale dramaturgy student, Russian/American Ilya Khodosh. Over time, I became familiar with the people in the fading sepia Academy portraits – Georgii Tovstonogov, Arkady Katsman, Mar Sulimov, Boris Zon, Zinovy Korogodsky – as well as Maria Knebel, who, as she hailed from a competing institute in Moscow called GITIS, did not have a picture on the wall, but nonetheless was justifiably highly regarded by her Petersburg legatees.

I now had a new list of teachers about whom I could say to my directing and acting students: "These artists have become your teacher's teachers."

Maria Knebel

Early in the journey I was shown a few words by Maria Knebel that encapsulated what I had started looking for – a succinct definition of Analysis through Action and the central role of Études:

> The idea of this technique…is that at an early stage of work, the play chosen for staging is not rehearsed as usual at the table, but subsequent to a certain preliminary analysis it is analyzed in action through études with improvised text. These études serve as steps leading the actor to the creative assimilation of the text of the play.[2]

I am now embarrassed to admit this, but at that time the name Maria Knebel was barely known to me. In my student study of the canon formation of directing, she had never come up. Allusions to her had drifted by me later in life but only faintly.

Maria Osipovna Knebel: I remembered there was a link to Stanislavsky's last years, about which I then knew nothing other than Toporkov's *Stanislavski in Rehearsal*, in which she is not mentioned. I also knew that an American scholar I greatly respected, Sharon Carnicke, had started to write about Knebel. That was about it. (Even today, despite the untiring work of Carnicke, Bella Merlin, James Thomas and a few others, it is the rare North American professional theatre practitioner who could identify this remarkable director, artistic director, and deeply influential teacher at GITIS. Bob Falls, the long-time artistic director of Chicago's Goodman Theatre is a notable exception.)

But in Russia I soon found that if Tovstonogov was a god to some, Knebel was a god to all. In a conversation with Valery Galandeev, Lev Dodin's key associate at the Maly Drama Theatre and renowned teacher at the Academy, he started with: "I think that in the Russian theatre of the Soviet period no one has ever had such a life story to tell as M.O. Knebel did." Galandeev finished two hours later with: "I was once shown a note written in Knebel's hand. It was obviously from some sort of public discussion where somebody wrote her a note from the auditorium, asking 'What is the essence of the Analysis through Action Method?' She wrote back "I don't know. Nor does anyone."[3]

I have since grasped that Knebel's perplexing reply *is* the essence of Analysis through Action, that is: no one can *definitively* say what its essence is or catalogue its practical design; there are many variants. But every young Russian director knows what their teacher's teacher taught their teacher and how their teacher teaches their lessons today, always urging their students to consider what they will do with it tomorrow. Hence there is a generational and individualistic evolution.

In very simplistic form: Stanislavsky taught Knebel, who adapted his last experiments into Analysis through Action (her term), with an emphasis on Études; Knebel then taught Anatoly Efros, Lev Dodin, Anatoly Vasiliev, and others; they in turn taught the next generation of students, and so forth. More or less concurrently, in Leningrad Tovstonogov created his rigorous text analysis process drawn from Stanislavsky; he taught Kama Ginkas and Genrietta Yanovskaya; today Ginkas teaches his students his own variant, his wife, Yanovskaya, teaches her variant, and Maria Ganeva, who sat in the same classes with them, teaches her own variant. Their students will in turn make their own adaptation.

Once the student becomes a professional, their task is not to reiterate what their teacher did but to transform it for their own generation through their distinctive cultural personality and life experience. Consequently there are many branches in the family tree emanating from the rootstock of Stanislavsky up to today's avant-garde such as Yuri Butusov and Dmitry Krymov – neither of whose works look at all Stanislavskian. I soon recognized that Analysis through Action is not a doctrine, not a tick-list of mandatory obligations. It is an individually deployed interactive process of text analysis (called 'Reconnaissance of the Mind') and Étude rehearsal technique ('Reconnaissance of the Body').

It also became clear to me that just as "the étude form reveals the actor's individuality especially vividly"[4] so too will Analysis through Action 'especially vividly' reveal the director or teacher's individuality. Analysis through Action is not a dogma; it is an open-ended suite of practices with some basic underlying principles that re-invents itself generation-to-generation, director-to-director, rehearsal-to-rehearsal.

Back Home

My first-year graduate directing students at Yale – Cole Lewis, Katie McGerr, and Dustin Wills – and I now had translations of Knebel's *Analysis through Action of the Play and the Role*; Malochevskaya's manual on Tovstonogov's course and my notes from a lengthy interview with her; an essay by her PhD student Andrei Smolko; Maria Ganeva's detailed class notes; two essays on Analysis through Action in practice by Tovstonogov; two lengthy interviews with Lev Dodin; two equally long interviews with Dodin's colleague Valery Galandeev; two with scholar of Études, insert comma Academy Professor Veniamin Filshtinsky; and several transcribed conversations with my friends Sergei Tcherkasski and Nikolai Pesochinsky. In English, along with Carnicke and Merlin essays, we had the following pertinent books: Tovstonogov's *The Profession of the Stage* Director, now dusted off from my shelves of unread books; Irina and Igor Levin's instructive *Working on the Play and the Role*; Kama Ginkas' provocative *Provoking Theater* (as interviewed by John Freedman); and Katie Mitchell's *The Director's Craft*.[5] Later many more interviews would come, most notably with directors Yuri Butusov and Dmitry Krymov and several more with the prodigious scholar Anatoly Smeliansky.

In class, we began to forge our own step-by-step version of Reconnaissance of the Mind, the text analysis side of Analysis through Action, also known as 'the Director *Tête-à-Tête* with the Play.'[6] With crucial contributions from then-student Katie McGerr, we created a preliminary workflow of analytical 'Text Actions.' Over time these became a staple of the Yale School of Drama's introductory directing seminar, encompassing the entire semester of the first year. Each of my trio of directing students had their own Chekhov play to break down sequentially: *The Three Sisters, Uncle Vanya*, and *The Seagull. The Cherry Orchard* served as the master text from which examples were created. By the end of the semester, they had scrupulously interrogated their text à la Tovstonogov, gone into the 'poetic heart' of their play, and formulated distinctive initial ideas of how to generate their own production, presumably to be explored with actors serving as "co-authors."

It was time for Études.

Into the Lab

Words from celebrated Academy master teacher and expert on Études Veniamin Filshtinsky became our principle guideline as the trio of directors prepared to work with their peer actors: "The theater of co-authorship is our postulate…The director is not a boss nor a judge, but the primary 'ringleader.' This person is only a powerful spur, they choose the text and help the actors fall in love with it."[7]

Co-authorship. Could young directors forgo their dreams of being a brilliant *auteur* to being a generous and inspiring co-author of a production?

Could the actors, often a self-protective lot through negative past experiences, trust this unstated directorial offering: 'come co-author with me?' Or conversely, did some directors and some actors not want the responsibilities of co-authorship? Given the debilitating brief amount of rehearsal time in the US was co-authorship a romantic fantasy? And as professional drama schools and conservatories are vocational training centers, not research institutions, of what use would all this Analysis through Action be once the student has graduated into 'the industry?'

Fortunately, we had a laboratory in which we could attempt to bring flesh to these inconvenient ideas. An actor-director practicum class using Chekhov plays as source material which I co-taught with renowned acting teacher Ron Van Lieu had been born a few years earlier out of a desire to find a common ground for our respective first-year participants. In student rehearsals on new and classic plays I had observed vague terminology that was frequently obstructive: many terms common to the rehearsal hall – objectives, action, beats, rhythm, and the like– meant different things to different people. An over-reliance on *naming* things in lengthy table sessions, particularly pre-identifying so-called objectives, seemed to lead most students to a schematic approach to acting, with concomitant results. These rambling tablework negotiations, at best expedient for general collective knowledge, rarely seemed to generate dynamic stage life, idiosyncratic characters, or stimulating theatrical possibilities.

On a deeper level, the actor-director, labor-management struggle so common in the American theater – who 'owns' what share of the creative enterprise? – often created actor resistance and/or an overly aggressive directorial manner – or, worse yet, director confusion or passivity when trying to appease an assertive actor. At the table and then later on the floor tension between these two camps was routinely present, if sometimes subliminal; at worst it was paralytic and soul-crushing.

These were the concerns our "Chekhov Lab" was born to address. Perhaps the Étude method could be the mainspring that could release these tensions. Forging ahead with no experiential precedent to rely on, the directors and I drew up an Étude protocol for our laboratory experiment in co-authorship (a revised version can be found in Part II of this book). Our Étude guidelines were aggregated from ideas and insights drawn from numerous sources referenced above, particularly Boris Zon, Maria Knebel, Zinovy Korogodsky, Sharon Carnicke, and Bella Merlin. Always recalling wise words I had heard from Professor Tcherkasski – "Whatever you would talk about at the table, we do on the floor"[8] – we ambitiously if innocently began our embodied research into Analysis through Action. That first year the Études ranged from tiresome to exhilarating but those of the latter kind were truly revelatory, showing us that we were on the right track. Over the years, the students consistently improved as did we faculty, and a similar course exists to this day at that school.

The Research Continues

Much has happened since those first years of synthesizing Analysis through Action at the Yale School of Drama. We have subsequently developed our version of this process in classes and rehearsals at Yale College's Theatre, Dance, and Performance Studies Department; Harvard College's Theatre, Dance, and Media concentration; The New School of Drama's MFA Acting and Directing Programs; and The Stella Adler Studio. I say 'our version' because I was blessed over the years with fantastic teaching associates. In chronological order they are: Angie Tennant (The New School); Aida Rocci (Harvard); Annelise Lawson (New School and Adler); Sara Holdren (New School); Mikaela Boone (Yale); and Evelyn Giovine (Adler). All of them were keen lab co-teachers and idea generators. Additionally, the numerous bold and talented acting students who joined our ongoing experiments at these institutions are emblazoned on my memory – they are the unsung heroes of this book. My former student directors, now working professionally in US and Canadian theatres and universities, are implementing their own variants of this exciting process. Thanks to those associates and the scores of students who have participated over time, what I can guarantee you is: Analysis through Action *works*, the onstage results can be unexpectedly breath-taking, and it's a fabulously exciting thing to do for all. It makes for a complete "joy of rehearsal" to quote a brilliant student of Knebel's, director Anatoly Efros.[9]

To encourage you to partake in this joy, the Text Action process – Reconnaissance of the Mind, and the Étude process – Reconnaissance of the Body – are the subjects of Part II of this book. In Part I, I shall trace (necessarily all too briefly) the Russian genealogy of Analysis through Action from Stanislavsky to today. I recommend reading the book in its order. Part I serves as a crucial artistic chronology preceding the practical how-to "manual" of Part II. Many ideas and references in the second part will be established in the first.

Why do this? I won't hide it: my project is to break the chokehold of imagination with which American directors and actors have too often suffocated Chekhov, Shakespeare, and so many other authors, classical and contemporary, domestic and foreign, whom they dutifully say they want to 'serve.' The pages that follow have a passionate personal motivation. As Yuri Butusov says, "I want to "knock the spectators out of their chairs"[10] to "shake the conscience of the audience"[11] and jump-start the artistic lassitude of American theatremakers and their shrinking audiences. The need to jolt the American theatre forward has never been more compulsory than now.

Accordingly I close this introduction with a poetic vision I treasure from William Butler Yeats: "What is there left for us…but to rediscover an art of the theatre, which shall be joyful, fantastic, extravagant, whimsical, beautiful, resonant, and altogether reckless."[12]

Notes

1 The technically correct and to me more helpful English translation of *МЕТОДЕ ДЕЙСТВЕННОГО АНАЛИЗА* is "The Method of Analysis Through Action," a.k.a. Analysis through Action. In English this approach has also been called Action Analysis or Active Analysis. This book will use Analysis through Action throughout except where quoted otherwise.
2 Knebel, Maria, *О том, что мне кажется особенно важным статьи, очерки, портреты [About What Seems Especially Important to Me]*, trans. Ilya Khodosh (Москва: Искусство, 1971), p. 44.
3 Valery Galandeev, author interview, Maly Drama Theatre, Saint Petersburg May 23, 2011.
4 Maria Knebel, *Poeziia Pedagogiki [The Poetry of Pedagogy]*, trans. Khodosh (Moskva: Vserossiiskoe teatral noe obshchestvo, 1976), 358.
5 As a young London director, Katie Mitchell had observed Dodin's teaching in Russia and later studied with an actor from his company. Readers of directing books will notice some parallels between her book *The Directors Craft* (Routledge, New York, 2009) and this one.
6 Malochevskaya, I.В. *Режиссерская Школа Товстоногова [The Directing School of Tovstonogov]*, Trans. Khodosh (Акад. Театрального Искусства, Sankt-Peterburg, 2003), p. 32.
7 Filshtinsky, Venjamin, Interview with author, Saint Petersburg, May 26, 2012. stanislavskistudies.org Issue #4, May 2014 p. 115.
8 Tcherkasski, author interview, Saint Petersburg, March 9, 2011.
9 Director Anatoly Efros' book *Репетиция - любовь моя [Rehearsal – My Love]* is translated by James Thomas as *The Joy of Rehearsal* (Peter Lang, New York, 2006).
10 Butusov Interview with Ludmila Gromyko, November 10, 2016, https://gromykotheatre.org/author/gromykotheatre/ as of June 2023.
11 Butusov Interview with author, June 6, 2014, Saint Petersburg.
12 W.B. Yeats *The Collected Works in Verse and Prose of William Butler Yeats, Vol. 4*, (Shakespeare Head Press, Stratford-on-Avon, 1908), 174.

1 An Anatomy of Stanislavsky's System

Introduction

I once asked a Jesuit priest, what does a Jesuit do? "We wrestle with the God problem" he replied. After many years of evasion I realized that to move forward with Analysis through Action I finally had to wrestle with the Stanislavsky problem. While the match may have been a near draw: he won, but (like a good Jesuit) I still have real doubts and questions. But in the end I developed an appreciation for this god of modern acting's dogged efforts to articulate the elements of good acting as he saw it, if often ineptly expressed. I now think the problem is not only Stanislavsky's tangled writing, it's also what we Americans did to him.

Partway through my own encounter, another longtime System denier, the brilliant Russian director and my teaching colleague Dmitry Krymov, was concurrently having his first bout with KS.[1] Comparing notes, Krymov said: "If you read Stanislavsky like Newton, he will disappoint you. But if you read him like Einstein, he is brilliant."[2] Meaning if you are looking for the "laws" of acting in the manner of Newton's laws of motion, you will come away discouraged. But if one reads Stanislavsky's System[3] as an attempt at a unified field theory – an open line of research with many valuable propositions but destined to be incomplete as was Einstein's search – there are some surprising spiritual rewards, creative possibilities, and practical offerings amid the oft-jumbled verbiage.

What This Chapter Is and Is Not

Caveat emptor: the following pages are not an exhaustive survey or critique of Stanislavsky's System. Numerous more worthy anglophone scholars than I have taken on those daunting tasks: England's polymathic Maria Shevtsova and erudite Rose Whyman, Jonathan Pitches, and, of course, the prolific translator/author, albeit prone to mistranslation, Jean Benedetti. Americans include Sharon Carnicke, Bella Merlin (UK born), and the doyen of American Russian theatre scholarship, Laurence Senelick (his *Stanislavsky: A Life in Letters*[4] is the best biography there is, alongside his numerous other books and essays).

DOI: 10.4324/9781003475576-3

Possibly the clearest of them all for System newcomers is the late Professor Burnet Hobgood's excellent though unpublished PhD thesis, which can be found online.[5]

But even in Russia, much less the anglophone world, grasping what the System actually *is* proves difficult. About KS's works the Russian Stanislavsky sage Anatoly Smeliansky quips: "the problem [with reading Stanislavsky] is not to translate from Russian into English but the equally complex problem of translating Russian into Russian."[6] The brilliant director Kirill Serebrennikov said on the 150th anniversary of Stanislavsky's birth: "Not even professionals can explain what the 'Stanislavsky system' is."[7]

That said, this book, intended for theatre students, teachers, and professional practitioners, is about Analysis through Action, and not about deciphering the myriad complexities and cultural contexts of the System by diligent and laudable authors such as those listed above. However, Analysis through Action is a rehearsal methodology and a teaching program that is inextricably rooted in the System. Maria Knebel herself wrote about Analysis through Action: "One cannot view this part of his work [Analysis through Action] separately from the entire Stanislavsky system. That is precisely why I believe it is essential to touch upon especially important elements of the Stanislavsky system."[8] Following Knebel's lead, in this chapter I put forth a modest and selective overview of the System, concentrating on some key ideas and propositions that will materialize through the practice of Analysis through Action.

While both Stanislavsky and Knebel attempted to record their ideas in numerous published volumes and private notebooks, the poetic heart, the ethereal spirit of what they laboriously delineated on paper, can only be truly known, truly *felt*, through extensive psychophysical Experience. And, as we shall see, Experience (переживание, pronounced *perezhivanie*) is one of the cardinal words of Stanislavsky's System and therefore of Knebel's Analysis through Action. How to best achieve deep psychophysical Experiencing through the practice of Analysis through Action is the subject of Part II of this book.

Helpful Hint: The System Is Not a System

Although it was he who first coined the term "System" in 1909 to describe his then-nascent acting methodology, Stanislavsky was perennially ambivalent about the word. Throughout his life he regularly shrouded the word System in quotation marks, sometimes further diminishing it further as "my so-called System." His hesitancy suggests that he was never fully satisfied with his tireless rehearsal research, studio classes, and consequent writing – writing he found agonizing (unlike his letters and speeches, which are more fluid). He must have felt that his thirty-two years, 1906 to 1938, of manuscript to nail the System were never comprehensive or precise enough to merit the status of a concrete system.

Or he simply felt that the word itself was misleading. System implies something, well, systematic: a weather system, a school system, the solar system.

A car is a system composed of many systems: fuel system, electrical, mechanical, and so forth.

Stanislavsky's "System" is not an all-inclusive 'thing,' materially, mathematically, or philosophically. Instead, it is a set of often clumsily written chapters – Maria Shevtsova calls them "baggy"[9] – based on his observations of the underlying components of acting, good acting and bad acting. Given his changeable mind and importunate experiments, Stanislavsky's System was perpetually evolving; it was still being formulated, not tweaked but formulated, up to a few days before his death. For the coup de grâce, on the final page of Stanislavsky's epic opus *An Actor's Work: Years One and Two* (a more recent and revised translation of the topics covered in *An Actor Prepares* and *Building a Character*) the master teacher tells us: "There is no 'system.' There is nature."[10]

Herein lies the reason behind Stanislavsky's ambivalence about his own term: he must have recognized that his System is not actually a system; it is a set of hypotheses about human nature in search of a unified field theory. As Laurence Senelick has written:

> It would be a mistake to take Stanislavsky as a systematic thinker, and there is something ironic that his articulated thoughts on acting have been labelled variously the System and the Method. System suggests a coherent and organized body of material or principles; method an orderly arrangement of ideas based on Cartesian logic. On the other hand, *The Actor Works on Himself* is configured as the narrative of classroom études, goal-oriented but open-ended, closer to Platonic dialogues than metaphysical treatises.[11]

So, does this mean we should then ignore the System, write it off as a suite of lofty but incomplete drafts? Or perhaps consult it for periodic divine guidance through chance readings, like, say, the *I Ching*? Of course not. For any serious theatre-maker of any artistic inclination, KS's attempts to create a System provides a humanist, quasi-scientific if incomplete approach to theatre, to acting, to directing – and to creative life. If Stanislavsky did not write a "manual" or a "grammar" of acting as he hoped to, it's because he couldn't verbalize what he intuitively felt. Senelick has said: "Much of what seems contradictory in KS comes from his trying to reconcile an essentially supernal concept with a scientific or positivist one."[12]

Nonetheless, he did write, or overwrite, substantial books about theatre with human insight and some valuable practical theatre advice. No one has left us so much on the topic of achieving artistic freedom and discipline onstage. No one has tried so thoroughly to grapple with life in rehearsal and performance. No one has championed collective artistry and deep training so ardently. Will reading the major works of Stanislavsky make you a better actor or director? Probably not; at best maybe a little. But you will gain some insight to what you are doing on stage or in rehearsal. Reading his works, you will inevitably experience moments when something meaningful will leap out at you, a sentence or a paragraph, or possibly a chapter that explains or even inspires you (and might leave someone else cold). There will be pages you will skim or just give up on. Then some passage will unexpectedly snag you, make you stop and think. Yes, Stanislavsky still asks to be wrestled with, especially today when many students and more than a few teachers consider his ideas old and in the way.

From Newton to Einstein

To revivify the System, we need to experience it holistically. This is where the above quotation from the director Dmitry Krymov echoes: If you are looking for a taxonomic concordance of systematic laws about how to act, direct, or teach, Stanislavsky will disappoint you. But if you are eager to explore a unified field theory of creativity, art, and human nature – the very things theatre exists for – Stanislavsky at his best can inspire, provoke, and challenge you.

Isaac Newton, the principal progenitor of modern systems theory, became known for his "laws," for example, the Third Law of Motion: "For every action there is an equal and opposite reaction."[13] Such scientific laws of the physical world are observable, measurable, reliable, and often mathematically captured in formulae, as Newton did. But Stanislavsky's restless soul insistently strove for something beyond the cold scientific rationality of Newtonian maxims. Rose Whyman states:

> Although Stanislavsky may have subscribed to the view that science would eventually define the laws of nature, at the same time he viewed human nature as having *mysterious hidden depths* (emphasis added) (*AWHE*, p. 61). As these are not accessible directly, he states on many occasions that the conscious psychotechnique of the artist…is the ground for the growth of the subconscious creative processes of our organic nature.[14]

'Mysterious human depths.' Therein lies Stanislavsky main fixation. Depths that yield sudden intuitions, impulses, affective memories, and communal spirit.

For thirty years Stanislavsky worried his problem daily: how can we access what he called the subconscious by conscious means? Unfortunately, the word he chose to organize his conclusions under – "System" – has led many to believe that there is an efficient system for acting that one can master as an electronics engineer would master computer systems or a plumber HVAC systems. Not the case. Stanislavsky "so-called System" is best seen as a *theory* dedicated to exploring the mysteries of acting. This theory is akin to Einstein's vain struggle with his unified field theory of the universe, which yielded many valuable ideas but was never consummated.

So, theory, yes; "System," not so much. While in this book we will continue to use Stanislavsky's term "System," it will be helpful for the reader to mind-whisper "Theory" every time you see it.

The Books and the Spirit

As should be clear by now, attempting to decode Stanislavsky's writings requires accepting a certain amount of perplexity. Joseph Roach writes: "Stanislavsky's theories defy tidy summation."[15] And Jean Benedetti, the most recent translator of Stanislavsky's main works says: "You can see what he means but the words get in the way."[16]

In the anglophone world we are further bedeviled by two translators writing in two different time periods from two different countries, the US and the UK, therefore employing slightly differing languages. These two, American Elizabeth Reynolds Hapgood and British Jean Benedetti, spent much of their lives converting Stanislavsky's elusive Russian words into hopefully intelligible English. Their two translation sets, while more or less sharing the basic structure of Stanislavsky's writings, exhibit some key differences.

Hapgood's volumes, which became the American gold standards for decades, are based on pages that Stanislavsky or others passed on to her. They appeared with wide chronological gaps in publication as *An Actor Prepares* (1936), *Building a Character* (1949), and *Creating a Role* (1963). The first two were highly redacted by the American publishing house which deleted a third to half of both books. The second volume, which Stanislavsky had not completed before his death, was based on disordered fragments sent by Stanislavsky's son. The third volume, *Creating a Role*, is a dog's breakfast of essays and incomplete notebook entries that Stanislavsky wrote between 1916 and 1937, these selected and edited by biased Soviet editors. The long hiatuses in publication left much of the US actor market thinking that *An Actor Prepares* was the complete Stanislavsky bible, not knowing that it was (*a*) highly redacted and (*b*) lacking its crucial companion volume on the necessity of physical and vocal expressive technique.

Jean Benedetti's unredacted versions were published almost simultaneously by Routledge Press as a package: Stanislavsky's first book, *My Life in Art* (2008), which Hapgood did not translate; then came *An Actor's Work on Himself: A Student's Diary* (2008); followed by *An Actor's Work on a Role* (2009). As Stanislavsky originally intended, Benedetti's doorstop volume *An Actor's Work on Himself* (henceforth *AWH*) contains two parts, "Year One" (*AWH1*) and "Year Two" (*AWH2*). This 600+ page volume generally follows the path of Hapgood's highly condensed pair: *An Actor Prepares* and *Building a Character* but is much longer. Benedetti's *AWH* tome includes revisions that Stanislavsky made after Hapgood's *An Actor Prepares* appeared; it is as close to a "final" volume as there is – close, but not conclusive, given the absence of a crucial pedagogical event found in the Hapgood edition, to be discussed later.

One can fall deep down a rabbit hole comparing any two translations of anything (try Chekhov plays, for instance); limited space prohibits comprehensive comparison here. But for those who do wish to take a peek down the rabbit hole, and thereby enhance their understanding of the System, I heartily recommend two articles: Bella Merlin's "Where's the spirit gone: The complexities of translation and the nuances of terminology in *An Actor's Work*"[17] and Maria Shevtsova's "*My Life in Art* and *An Actor's Work* (review)."[18] Both focus on Benedetti's failed translation choices about spirituality and the actor, a conception that is central to Experiencing the System and therefore to Analysis through Action. About Benedetti's translation of *AWH* Shevtsova writes that "it does not quite fully convey the emotional principle embedded in Stanislavski's research."

> Thus, too frequently, he uses "mind" for Stanislavski's *dusha* (meaning both "heart" and "soul") as well as for *dukh* ("spirit"). "Mental," then, covers the adjectives *dushevnoe* and *dukhovnoe* from the corresponding two nouns. Benedetti's choices might be tidy, but they suggest that Stanislavski envisaged the actor as more rationally driven and in-the-head in his/her practice than is implied by his continual emphasis on the actor as a constantly developing emotional and spiritual being.[19]

Merlin quotes actor/teacher Benjamin Lloyd:

> Why has spirituality been excised from the transmission of Stanislavski's work, when so much else which came from him has shaped Western actor training?…There is a tremendous urge in our modern era to remove the mysterious, the spiritual, the inexplicable from the study of acting.[20]

As Shevtsova reinforces with clarity and wisdom in her illuminating 2020 book *Rediscovering Stanislavsky*, one cannot truly experience the man and therefore his System without incorporating Stanislavsky's profound spirituality, both as a devotee of the Russian Orthodox religion and as a practicing artist. In the Preface she cuts right to her argument:

> Much has been written in English about Stanislavsky's System and here is to be found another perspective – that of the worldview which underpins the System's practical purpose and is rooted in Russian Orthodoxy. Stanislavsky's religious outlook shapes the worldview that envelops his search for the organic actor-creator for whose benefit he elaborated the System until his dying day.[21]

Citing Russian scholar Tatiana Bachelis, Senelick states matters succinctly: KS was "a mystic rather than a scientist."[22]

Recognizing Stanislavsky's deep spiritual 'worldview,' and his lifelong devotion to a theatre as a spiritual space, a "cathedral" as he often called it, turns us away from Newtonian formulae, dollar-book Freudian psychology, and toward the inner spiritual world of the actor and the audience. When in Hapgood's words Stanislavsky writes "soul," he means *soul*. When he writes "spirit" he means *spirit*. Hapgood got that part right.

The Plan of 1935: Overview

As we have said, Stanislavsky never was able to write a definitive summary of his System. The diagram Figure 1.1[23] is probably the most concise and useful synopsis he left behind, but it did not make it into any of the English-language translations. This detailed specimen, which both Sharon Carnicke and Rose Whyman have previously exhibited, was drawn under Stanislavsky's supervision

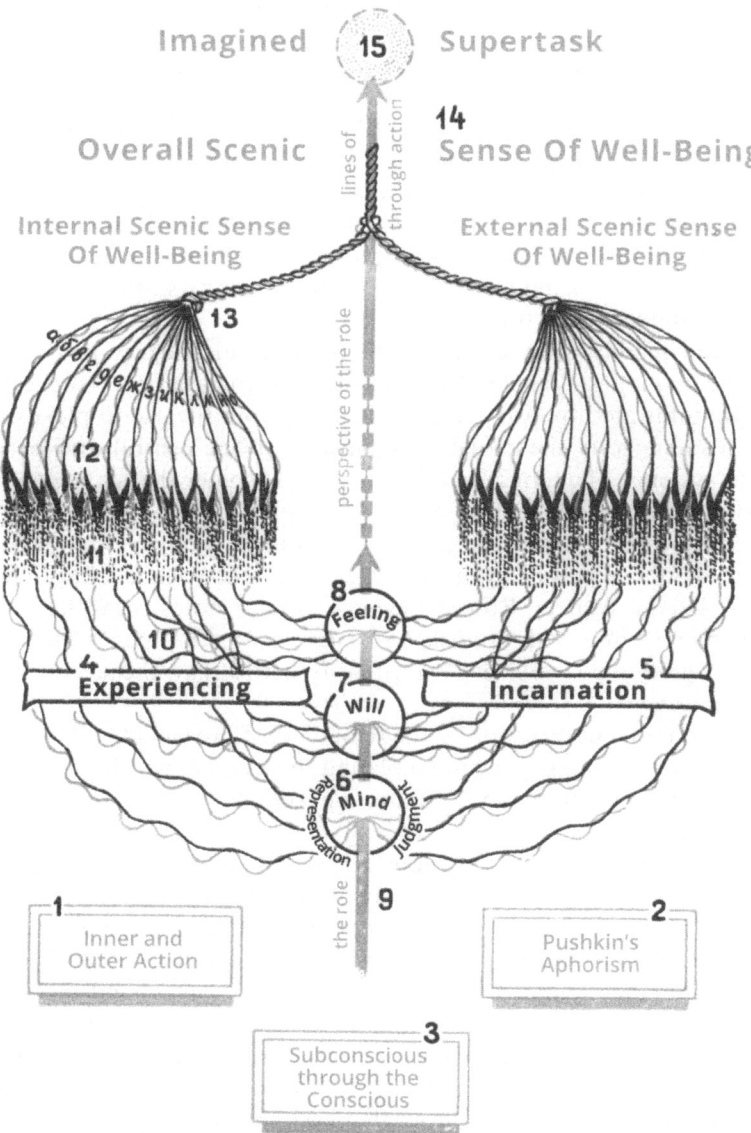

Figure 1.1 The Plan of the System 1935.

during the mid-1930s. Designed to be an all-inclusive visual summary of the first-year actor lessons in Experiencing, it was originally intended to be placed at the end of *AWH1*, then at the end of *AWH2* – which Stanislavsky never finished. Consequently, it was not published until 1955 in the first set of Stanislavsky's collected works.[24] Stanislavsky wrote: "The drawing illustrates and summarizes the course of our first-year program…Now you know what the so-called 'system' is."[25] (N.B.: As we will cite Figure 1.1 throughout the remainder of this chapter, I strongly advise bookmarking or photocopying the image for easy reference.)

While regularly declaring that he was no scientist, Stanislavsky opportunistically appropriated whatever scientific sources might inspire or support his theories, what Senelick describes as "a lazy Susan of concepts: Ribot, Freud, Dalcroze, Duncan, yoga, *I tutti quanti.*"[26] Accordingly his Plan of 1935 was presumably influenced by the exquisitely detailed drawings in Henry Gray's *Anatomy: Descriptive and Surgical* (1858). This landmark medical text with over 1,200 detailed anatomical illustrations is still in print today as *Gray's Anatomy* – yes, it's the punning source for the TV show's title – and remains a staple of global medical training.

One can readily infer some specific anatomical imagery in the Plan of 1935: the two lobes – labeled Experiencing and Incarnation – suggest lungs; these are infiltrated by wavy lines emanating from the sacral plexus region, which also suggests the radiating pathways of the central and peripheral nervous systems. The lungs are bifurcated by a "spine" that charts the actor's ascending journey of creating a role. The spine carries inside it the spinal cord, which transmits nerve signals throughout the body. Simultaneously we can also associate this diagram with a chart of the yogic chakras. (Another System chart, drawn by Robert Lewis, following notes from Stella Adler's 1934 Paris meetings with Stanislavsky, suggests organ pipes perhaps unconsciously signifying the System's spirituality better than the scientism of the 1935 rendering.[27])

From an initial observation of the Plan of 1935, we can identify two fundamental principles crucial to contemplating the System, which as Knebel says above is inseparable from Analysis through Action.

First off, Stanislavsky conceived his System as an organically unified entity, pulsing with energy passing through two primary pathways: psychic (**4.** *Experiencing*) and physical (**5.** *Incarnation*); these two are regularly compounded as "psychophysical." Joseph Roach asserts that "at every stage of the development of his system [Stanislavsky] accepted the premise of dual-aspect monism."[28] Roach then quotes from *An Actor Prepares*: "The bond between body and soul is indivisible…In every physical act there is a psychological element and a physical one in every psychological act."[29] This indivisible correspondence between body and soul, soma and psyche, is *the* central premise of the System, and crucial for us to understand during the physicality of Analysis through Action.

Second, the Plan of 1935 addresses two interrelated programs: (1) the process of training an actor and (2) the actor's work in creating a role. The Plan illustrates both agendas dynamically: an actor's journey of role creation necessitates activating the System, and vice-versa. The actor's journey to creation of the role is founded from a base of three maxims – particularly maxim **3**, the "Subconscious through the Conscious" – and passes through "Experiencing" and "Incarnation" to finally reach (**15**)...the "Imagined Supertask?" All that psychophysical energy to come up with a proposed Supertask?

A Contradictory Plan

To understand the Plan more fully, we must make an essential digression. German scholar Karin Jansen informs us that the Plan of 1935 is noticeably different from a 1930 System plan sketched by Stanislavsky which she displays in her book.[30] Crucially, at the pinnacle of the 1930 plan lies *not* "Imagined Supertask" as in 1935: the apex in 1930 is labeled "The Unconscious." Jansen denotes "The Unconscious" in the 1930 plan as the "summation of the system, therefore at the top."[31]

Why would Stanislavsky change something so critical as the very peak, the ultimate goal of the System? Most likely Stanislavsky's replacement of 'The Unconscious' at the pinnacle of the Plan of 1935 was bowing to advisers, particularly his Russian colleague, first reader, and editor Liubov Gurevich, who repeatedly urged him to avoid any suspect European psychological terms in the 1930s Soviet era of reflexology per native Russians Sechenov and Pavlov. (Stanislavsky inexplicably retained the word 'Subconscious' at the base of The Plan of 1935 [**3**] but nonetheless stopped short of applying it at the pinnacle.)

As always, Stanislavsky's experience of an actor's creative process had more to do with his own *intuitive* reflexes, not Pavlovian reflexology; his lifelong religious faith necessarily clandestine by this time (he kept a shrine secreted in a cupboard);[32] and his own experiences as an actor, than it did with the finer points of Pavlovian psychology or Marxist ideology – he was uneducated and uninterested in both. Going forward with the Plan of 1935, we shall recognize that "The Imagined Supertask" should read "The Subconscious."

An Actor's Journey: Ascending the Plan of 1935

We begin this section with another fair warning: what follows is an attempt to comprehend the System and how it functions in the process of creating a role, using this visual guide. In real life, role creation by an actor is far more instinctual, haphazard, and disordered, whatever the rehearsal process. While the

Plan of 1935 attempts to track an ideal progression numerically ascending from the base to the Subconscious, it is improbable, nor recommended in this book, that an actor should (or even could) follow this order, albeit the way stations it illustrates will likely be familiar to the working actor and director. That said, let us follow the sequential Plan as KS charted it.

So far we have identified the starting point and the pinnacle: maxim **3**, at the root of the spine – the "Subconscious through the Conscious" – to **15**, the pinnacle which should read "The Subconscious." Elsewhere, Stanislavsky calls "the subconscious through the conscious" the "basic principle of our school of acting,"[33] and indeed entering into the subconscious by conscious means is the very raison d'être and purpose of the System.

To make this latter point, let us for now circumvent the numbered stations ascending along and beside the "spine" and jump to the region above the lobes, the upper target zone of the whole process. Here we find two Scenic Senses of Well-Being, Internal and External. These two states or conditions then merge into the Overall Sense of Well-Being (**14**).

A definition of a state of "well-being" – sometimes translated as "health" – is crucial to our actor's journey upward. Today, we might think of this as a "flow state," a state of heightened awareness of self and environment, opening to a virtually supernatural ease at achieving the task at hand. This is a term created by Hungarian-American psychologist Mihaly Csikszentmihalyi who writes that the flow state is:

> the holistic sensation that people feel when they act with total involvement…In the flow state, action follows upon action according to an internal logic that seems to need no conscious intervention by the actor. He experiences it as a unified flowing from one moment to the next, in which he is in control of his actions, and in which there is little distinction between self and environment, between stimulus and response, or between past, present, and future.[34]

The author then quotes a dancer describing this state:

> Your mind isn't wandering, you are not thinking of something else; you are totally involved in what you are doing. Your body feels good. You are not aware of any stiffness. Your body is awake all over. No area where you feel blocked or stiff. Your energy is flowing very smoothly. You feel relaxed, comfortable, and energetic.[35]

This dancer's recollection of being in a fully alive and self-confident state echoes Stanislavsky's Overall Scenic Sense of Well-Being: all the psychophysical elements of the System, psychic (Experiencing) and physical (Incarnation), are in full flow with total harmony as they pursue an Action, in the dancer's case dancing. But the dancer, like the actor in a flow state, is aware of their sensory self being 'relaxed, comfortable, and energetic.'

In the flow state we are standing "On the Threshold of the Subconscious," the title of the concluding chapter of *An Actor Prepares*. Stanislavsky via Hapgood – but surprisingly nowhere else to be found in English or Russian – narrates this state, beginning with the actor standing on the shoreline of an ocean: "Sometimes the tide of the subconscious barely touches an actor, and then goes out. At other times it envelops his whole being, carrying him into its depths until, at length, it casts him up again on the shore of consciousness."[36]

But before our actor was cast back to the shore of consciousness, where were they? What was this ocean that enveloped their whole being? Obviously in quasi-scientific terms the ocean is the subconscious, though others might call it divine or spiritual inspiration, terms Stanislavsky could not employ. Our actor in this example did indeed, at least for a time, fulfill the promise of the System: through conscious means – that is, through activating the psychotechnique of Experience – he reaches the subconscious, thereby "flowing," even if briefly, into the ocean of intuitive creation and spiritual wholeness. It is into this ocean that Stanislavsky wants us to submerge. Rose Whyman confirms this: "For Stanislavsky, the unconscious is the source of inner experience and truth."[37]

But we have no surety about what Stanislavsky specifically meant by unconscious or subconscious – these are vernacular terms we must take at a laymen's level. However, Stanislavsky did give us a term that speaks to the state of the "healthy" or "self-confident" actor's body and soul just before the ocean envelops them, the state just prior to subconsciousness. Teacher Tortsov – the Stanislavsky avatar in his books – speaks to his pupils of a certain state.

> "Your head spins with the number of moments when the life of the character and your own unexpectedly and totally fuse. You will feel parts of yourself in the role and of the role in you."
> "And after that?"
> "What I told you. Truth, belief, '*I am being*' [emphasis added] puts you in the control of nature and the subconscious."[38]

Ya yesm: "I am" (or "I am being")

While "flow state" is a contemporary term invented in the 1970s by a Hungarian-American academic psychologist, a key System term, я есм (pronounced 'yah yesm'), was used by the more mystically inclined Stanislavsky. *Ya yesm*, generally translated as "I am" ("I am being" by Benedetti), is virtually unknown in English-speaking theatre classrooms and non-existent in Western acting studios and rehearsal halls. Certainly attention has been paid by Professors Carnicke, Whyman, Benedetti, and most extensively by Maria Shevtsova, who fully grasps and celebrates Stanislavsky's spirituality. But the term remains obscure in anglophonic practice: try asking an English-speaking actor if they have ever experienced *ya yesm*.

The most prevalent notion of its derivation is that *ya yesm* originates in an ancient language known as Old Church Slavonic and still can be heard in certain Russian Orthodox services. At an impressionable age, young Konstantin Sergeevich Alekseev (he later adopted the pseudonym Stanislavsky) a lifelong believer, surely heard the term *ya yesm* intoned during the family Sunday visitations to their Orthodox church: hours of standing (no sitting, except for the elderly), women in prayer shawls men with heads bare, amid colorful religious wall paintings, watchful eyes of icons, droning bass voices from above mixed with prayer chanting below, jewel-colored light from stained-glass windows beaming through the dense smoke of pungent incense, lighting of votive candles for the deceased, shared bread, and the mysterious movement of the clergy passing through their inner and outer sanctums – a religious *gesamtkunstwerk* (total theatre work). One does not go to an Orthodox service to worship God, one goes to be in the *presence* of God: to transcend into the state of *ya yesm*. Certainly, all of this ritual would have made a profound impression on young Kostya Alekseev, spiritually and theatrically.

But what *ya yesm* means in the anglophone world is vague because it does not translate nimbly; the term imparts deep religious meaning but is mystifying to a Western rationalist mind. *Ya yesm* is a state of wholeness – of *holiness*; a state of preparedness of the soul; a state of the self in the presence of God and the presence of God in the self. In the Old Testament's Exodus 3:14, God tells Moses to say to the Israelites: "I am" – using the similar sounding word *Yahweh* – "has sent me to you."

Fortunately, Stanislavsky provided us with his definition of *ya yesm* pertinent to the actor and the System. "And what is 'I am being?' That means, I am, I live, I feel, I think as one with the role. In other words, 'I am being' leads to emotion, to feeling, to *experiencing*. 'I am being' is distilled, almost absolute truth onstage."[39]

So, *ya yesm* is the pre-pinnacle state, the flow state of creativity. *Ya yesm*, or "I am," is what should be written near the top of the Plan of 1935, where it reads "Overall Scenic Sense of Well-Being"; this is an experiential condition just prior to reaching the Subconscious. Whyman confirms this idea: "What Stanislavsky wants…is for the actor to *experience*, to be in the state of *I am* (*Ia yesm'*)." She then adds that Stanislavsky's use of Old Church Slavonic *ya yesm* indicates Stanislavsky's vision of the highest actor's art as "a spiritual state."[40]

Shevtsova elaborates on this state:

> Stanislavsky knew from church services, purification rituals and other such religious observances that "*ya yesm*" means nothing less than "I am in God and God is in me" in spirit and body; and the attitude underpinning "*ya yesm*" is "I am attentive to my state of oneness with God."…By saying (or thinking) "*ya yesm*," the actor acknowledges his/her acceptance of the "sacred task" of art and his/her readiness to inhabit its "human form divine."[41]

Thus Hapgood's title for Chapter 16 of *An Actor Prepares* – "On the Threshold of the Subconscious" – is accurate: *ya yesm* is the threshold, the creative *flow state* or a "divine state of grace"[42] in which "an actor stands on the ocean shore, a spiritual liminal space where the actor and the ocean of the subconscious merge. One wave wets his foot, a second rises to his knees, a third – higher, a fourth seizes him and sweeps him away."[43] Having been swept into the ocean of the Subconscious (or divine inspiration), the actor and the role are now ideally fused into a dual entity called actor/role, ideally mutually creating stage action within the full state of Experiencing. I am Hamlet; Hamlet is I; *we* are Hamlet, and together *we* create our Hamlet.

But what exactly happens when one is immersed in this sea of the subconscious? During a class late in the students' first year of study – again, only found in Hapgood, not Benedetti or any Russian edition – director Tortsov guides his prized pupil Kostya through an exercise:

> "He is out in the ocean of the subconscious now," said the Director. Then he leaned over the footlights and said softly to me [Kostya who is 'in the ocean']: "Don't hurry, go through to the very end."
>
> He turned to the other students again and pointed out that, although I was motionless, you could feel the storm of emotions inside of me. I heard all these remarks, but they did not interfere with my life on the stage or draw me away from it. At this point my head was swimming with excitement because my part [role] and my own life were so intermingled that they seemed to merge. I had no idea where one began or the other left off. My hand ceased wrapping the string around my fingers and I became inert.
>
> "That is the very depth of the ocean," explained Tortsov.
>
> I do not know what happened from then on. I know only that I found it easy and pleasant to execute all sorts of variations.[44]

On the threshold Kostya slips from a split consciousness – in his divine state of *ya yesm* he remains aware of Tortsov's voice – into a state of hypnotic subconsciousness while submerged at the 'very depth of the ocean.' There, he loses all self-cognizance. He is unaware of what is happening to him, where he is, or what he is doing. Nonetheless he executes 'all sorts of variations' with ease and pleasure. Kostya is experiencing the ultimate destination of the System – full immersion into the ocean of the subconscious (divine inspiration). A state of *ya yesm* preceded this submergence. "The readiness is all," quoth Hamlet.

But we don't get any news about what actually transpired in student Kostya's underwater odyssey; the student seems not to recall what he did in the depths of the subconscious. All we get from him is a terse report about his submergence: 'I do not know what happened from then on.' This, of course, raises questions about efficacy of this process: if the actor can't recall the many 'easy and pleasant' variations he executed while immersed in the deep, of what use is the journey? But later we are told that over time a trained actor will develop a dual consciousness: we learn this in Hapgood's *Building a Character* (the long-delayed companion volume of *An Actor Prepares*). Here the now second-year acting student Kostya tells us: "I divided myself, as it were, into two personalities. One continued as an actor, the other was an observer. Strangely enough this duality not only did not impede, it actually promoted my creative work. It encouraged and lent impetus to it."[45]

Back to the Base (Plan of 1935 1, 2, and 3)

Now that we know the ultimate goal of a System-trained actor – entry into the state of *ya yesm* (**14**: Overall Scenic Sense of Well-Being), then into the ocean of the subconscious (**15**) – it's time to go back to Figure 1.1, The Plan of 1935, and look at the foundation blocks of the System, maxims **1**, **2**, and **3**.[46]

Number **1** is **Inner and Outer Action** – also translated as Activeness (Whyman) and Dynamism (Carnicke) – and it refers to inner psychic action and outer physical action. Inner action can include motionless intense observation, listening, and relevant thought, all of which are Actions. External action may be physical – gestural or movement – and/or verbal – speech or sounds. In all cases, *Action is energy expended toward a specific goal* – even if that goal is at the moment unrecognized by the character or the actor. Indeed, in Analysis through Action, energy expended may well precede knowledge of a specific goal or task; physical and verbal Études are a means for *discovering* (or discarding) a Task. But whether silent or verbal, motionless or kinetically hyperactive, the actor must be in Action every milli-moment onstage – *doing* something active.

Number **2** is **Pushkin's Aphorism**: "The truth of the passions, the verisimilitude of the feelings in supposed circumstances – this is what our minds require of the dramatic author"[47] was appropriated by Stanislavsky from poet/dramatist Alexander Pushkin's review of a play with the dubious title *Martha, the Governor's Wife*.[48] It is the source for Stanislavsky's crucial tenet Given Circumstances, a fundamental component of the System and Analysis through Action.

At the very base sits number **3 Subconscious through the Conscious**. As we now know, this is the entire goal of everything above this pillar. It is the primary hypothesis of the System: the subconscious can be reached through conscious means.

Experiencing and Incarnation 3 and 4

Moving upward there are two are essential regions of the Plan: **4 Experiencing** and **5 Incarnation**.[49] These are the two "platforms" (KS's word) through which the dynamic processes of the psychotechnique and external technique are brought to life. While for demonstration and training purposes they are separated in the Plan of 1935 and elsewhere, in practice they are biologically and dynamically interwoven, like lungs. The pair vigorously exchange energy in a psychosomatic-somatopsychic convergence.

4 Experiencing is a complex term – Carnicke, Whyman, Merlin, Mollica, and others have written about it extensively; these authors are recommended for those seeking further exploration of this complex subject. For our purposes, let us start with two sentences from Sharon Carnicke's glossary:

> The Russian root of "experiencing" conveys many different nuances: "to experience," "to feel," "to live through," "to survive." The System generates a synonym for "experiencing" in "I am" (*ia esm'*), which stresses the actor's immediacy and presence on stage.[50]

So, *peak* Experiencing, or *perezhivanie*, is *ya yesm.*

Other definitions for the root words of experiencing (*perezhivat, perezhivanie, perezhivaniia*) are given by visual artist and author Dale Pesmen in her book *Russia and Soul*: "living through things, pouring your soul into them, intuiting, suffering, caring."[51] Stanislavsky initially drew his idea of Experiencing from his marked copy of Leo Tolstoy's *What Is Art*:

> To call up in oneself a feeling once experienced and having called it up, to convey it by means of movements, lines, colors, sounds, images expressed in words, so that others express the same feeling – in this consists the activity of art. Art is that human activity which consists in one man's consciously conveying to others, by certain external signs, the feelings he has experienced, and in others being infected by those feelings and also experiencing them.[52]

It became imperative for Stanislavsky that the actor's task is to call up in oneself and convey what Tolstoy identifies as 'a feeling once experienced.' In Benedetti's *AWH2*, Tortsov identifies this area as "*Re*-experiencing."[53] In the Russian edition of *AWH1* (though not in Benedetti's translation) we find: "In our art of experiencing, every moment of playing a role must be *re-experienced* and *reincarnated* every time" (emphasis added).[54] Re-experience – in Europe sometimes called "re-living" or "revivification" – signifies what Stanislavsky first called "affective memory" from Ribot,[55] then changed it to Emotional (or Emotion) Memory when Soviet censors proscribed Western psychological terms. As translated by Hapgood in *AAP*, Tortsov tells his students that Emotion Memory is:

> That type of memory, which makes you relive the sensations you once felt when seeing Moskvin [a famous Russian actor] act, or when your friend died, is what we call emotion memory. Just as your visual memory can reconstruct an inner image of some forgotten thing, place or person, your emotion memory can bring back feelings you have already experienced.[56]

Recently in many anglophone quarters, Emotional Memory has been avoided, even vigorously discredited. But it is alive and well in Russia: it is taught in the major Russian conservatories and applied professionally. The main drama school in Moscow, GITIS, includes the following description of Emotional Memory in their *Dictionary of Theatrical Terminology*, used by all acting and directing students and faculty:

> The more extensive the emotional memory, the more material for internal creativity with it, the richer and more complete the actor's work. The experienced feelings and emotional impressions become the exciters of new processes; they stimulate the imagination...In the process of working on the character and in the performance as a whole, the role of these sensations, impressions, including those beyond conscious experience, is immense.[57]

Robert Ellermann, the American acting teacher and walking encyclopedia of the Stanislavsky System, contends that Emotional Memory, Re-experiencing, is *the* fundamental postulate in practicing the System. But Re-experiencing must be subtly teased out through Sense Memory, that is, recalling a corporeal "re-*feeling*" through sight, hearing, touch, smell, or taste – a recalling and re-experiencing of certain sensory impressions that preceded, surrounded, or attended the actual emotional memory. These Sense Memories are what Stanislavsky called "lures" with which to arouse a submerged emotional memory: Was it a hot day? What color was the room you were in? Can you remember the sound of the waves? and so forth.

Tortsov speaks to his students in the *AWH1* chapter *Emotion Memory* about "the close link and interaction between our five senses and their influence on the recollections of the emotional memory. So, the artist needs not only emotional memory but also the memory of our five senses."[58] Thus, for example, from one simple taste of a *madeleine* (a small butter cake) dipped in tea, French novelist Marcel Proust evoked a deeply hidden involuntary memory (this is now known as a "madeleine moment") which instigated his seven-volume memoir *Remembrance of Things Past*.

Number **5 Incarnation** is simpler to grasp because it is more corporeal than Experience. Incarnation is composed of the practical components of the System discussed in *Building a Character* and *AWH2*. This includes what we know as "technique" or "skills" training, including a chapter on Physical Education – movement, dance, gymnastics – and another on Voice and Speech. There is a lengthy chapter on a subject Stanislavsky sermonized on for his entire life: "Ethics and Discipline." While The Plan of 1935 intentionally focused only on Experience, a few components of Incarnation will appear when we look further into Elements.

The Actor's Odyssey Begins

Now that we know the foundation stones **1**, **2**, and **3**, the Platforms **4** and **5** and the goals **14** and **15**, it is time to attend to the spine, which starts at **9**. But our caveat again: the System is not a system; there is no absolute formulaic 1-2-3 procedure to creating a role. Creating a role is necessarily *un*systematic, even messy, whatever the rehearsal process.

Opposite the numeral **9** we see "the role." This demarks the start of the journey of the actor and the role. Stanislavsky's key to the Plan explains that when first encountering a new role, the actor will initially *randomly* throw "seeds" of perception and inspiration into the "engines" above: **6 Mind, 7 Will,** and **8 Feeling** – stimulating "creative desire" to Experience the role. Numbers **6, 7,** and **8**, located in the sacral plexus region, inject oxygen into the lungs; or, if you will, discharge energy into the peripheral nervous system. In yoga, this energy center is known as the sacral, or second, chakra, and is associated with emotions, sensations, imagination and creativity, and the expression of our sensual and sexual selves – all good things for an actor to be animated by. Stanislavsky calls this trio "the three engines of psychic life,"[59] motive forces that excite the elements of inner and outer action.

Different actors will begin differently, usually favoring either Mind or Feeling at first. But once the actor has ignited Mind (**6**) and/or Feeling (**8**), then the Will (**7**) to perform the actions of the role is aroused. The Will is the actor's *desire*, the drive to activate body and soul toward achieving their task or goal in a scene and ultimately throughout the life of the play. Stanislavsky rated Feeling as "the most capricious," Will less so, and Mind the least, which is why they are ordered as they are. Early on, these three indivisible motors radiate or discharge creative energy into the regions of **4**. Experience and **5**. Incarnation.

That creative energy is first indicated by the squiggly lines we see at the bottom half of both lobes (**10**). Stanislavsky calls these intersecting wavy lines "lines of aspiration," ideas and impulses aspiring to be evaluated and clarified. As these energy waves discharge into the lobes we see that the lines of aspiration are "haphazard, patchy, disordered, and chaotic" – the muddled feelings and thoughts we have all experienced in rehearsal. Those are to be welcomed as part of the journey.

From this confusion of impulses and ideas at **10**, we gradually ascend to a kind of refinery zone, number **11**. Stanislavsky writes that this is: "The inner region of our soul, or creative apparatus with all its properties, capacities, talents, natural gifts, artistic skills, psychotechnical methods." In **11** the jumbled lines in **10** begin to clarify themselves due to talents and gifts in the actor's soul and the actor's training in the psychotechnique. This process of fusion and purification impels the actor's energy into an even higher region, **12**, where earlier chaotically fluctuating lines of aspiration, initially generated by the motors of Mind, Will, and Feeling, are further clarified, straightened out, simplified, and fortified. Here, as rehearsals progress, things are getting clearer, cleaner, and more direct as we go upward. Decisions are being made.

At **13** we see a "knot" where the now-clarified lines of aspiration bind together as a braided unity. At this point we have achieved the **Internal Scenic [Stage] Sense of Well-Being** (self-confidence, fullness). Meanwhile, although not illustrated here, a symbiotic and similar process has been going on in the Incarnation lobe; thus, the body reaches its External Scenic Sense of

Well-Being as well. The two plaits then rise together and coil around the arrow, the actor's "spine." Now the actor and the role are fusing, as we ascend to **14**, the **Overall Sense of Well-Being**, what we now know as the Threshold of the Subconsciousness: *ya yesm*.

Finally we arrive at the problematic number **15**, the **Imagined Supertask**, a phrase we can assume is there to appease the censor's eye. Of course, this is where we should find The Subconscious (or Unconscious, per the 1930 plan); the region that student Kostya passed into. When we look up Stanislavsky's key for number **15** we read "The as yet spectral, not fully-defined proposed super task." The word spectral – elsewhere translated as "ghostly" – leaps out. Does this suggest some apparition from the other side, the other side of consciousness, the mystical spirit of divine grace? Stanislavsky's broken-line circumference and tiny stipples around numeral **15** seem to indicate that the so-called Imagined Supertask is at least elusive and provisional. These anomalies provoke us to ask what else Stanislavsky might be trying to tell us behind the censors' backs.

The Spine: Overview

To finish off decoding the Plan, we have two matters to resolve: the ascending central "spine" of the actor/role and the famous Elements.

Let us look for a moment at the simple visual image of the spine with its pointed peak; we might call this an ascending arrow. Stanislavsky continually phrased the actor's journey as an *ascension*, an elevation to a higher plane. The associations with religious transcendence are not to be ignored or belittled. He yearned for actors to be "priests" in a "theatre-church."[60] Their holy task was to lift the congregants (the audience) to a higher level of perception and human spirituality.

Thus, while we can certainly read the "spine" of the Plan of 1935 as a corporeal design – solar plexus, vertebrae, neck – it is also a religious image – an arrow pointing to the realm of the spiritual, toward the divine. From Mind, Will, and Feeling, the trio which generates the "soul" of the actor, the arrow ascends through the responsive body, then transcends metaphysical spiritual and creative states into the subconscious and the celestial world of inspiration.

The System is not a system. It is a spiritual ascension to divinely-inspired creativity.

The Spine: Perspective and the Throughline Action

We have already touched on several components of this ascending arrow. But there are three important notations alongside the shaft. Between number **8** and the braided plaits of internal and external **Scenic Well-Being**, lie the "vertebrae" and the words **perspective of the role**. "Perspective of the Role" was a late arriver to the System. Marianna Stroyeva notes its appearance in rehearsals for *The Ardent Heart*, which opened in 1926.[61] By this time, Stanislavsky's focus was increasingly absorbed by Incarnation, the actor's mental and physical management of work discovered through the psychotechnique.

For the actor, Perspective conveys two meanings: (1) From their *character*'s point of view Perspective contributes to the attempt to realize their life goal, their deepest desire, or as director/pedagogue Georgii Tovstonogov put it, the "character's idea of happiness: what we call the character's supertask";[62] (2) Perspective also means the organized distribution of an actor's energetic expenditures, scoring their creative actions in order to play the role with variety and unpredictability. To illustrate Perspective, Hamlet is Stanislavsky's example in *AWH2*, from his first appearance in Act I to his death five acts later.

Moving up the spinal arrow, we come to text that reads: "lines of through action." Throughline Action (aka Through-action, Cross-cutting action, etc.) can have a meaning for both the play and the actor. For the play, the Throughline Action is what the audience witnesses visually and aurally. A character's Throughline Action is what the character says and does within the play. Stanislavsky likened the Throughline Action to a thread upon which the actor puts beads, one by one, each bead being an Action. Ultimately, the actor will construct a psychophysical Throughline Action which is at once emotional, personally stimulating, and in the end coherent, but unpredictable.

Which brings us to the all-important Supertask.

The Supertask: Gogol's Nail

In the embryonic days of the System, 1908, while researching for an upcoming production of Nikolai Gogol's *The Inspector General*, Stanislavsky reviewed the author's instructions for acting in his play, which Gogol laid out after suffering painful disappointment at the 1836 premiere. Gogol insisted that the actor must "observe the main, the chief concern of each character, on which his life is supported, which is the constant subject of his thoughts, the eternal nail sitting in his head."[63] Stanislavsky appropriated this idea (as he did Pushkin's aphorism), and soon was urging his bewildered actors to find their character's "nail" and then hammer it into their heads. In a notebook Stanislavsky wrote his own instructions on "How to Prepare for a Performance:"

> The creative process of experiencing gets its development when the artist feels the nerve of the role, which, like a leitmotif, accompanies the character in all situations. Gogol calls this main concern a nail, which the artist must drive into his head before entering the stage…Until such a nail, or an emotional chord, is found, the created character is devoid of wholeness and essence. Without it, the individually experienced pieces of the role do not bind into one common, viable organism…A nail, or soul chord, of a role is that key with the aid of which you can penetrate the recesses of the

soul of the created character. The actor should deeply cherish and be in-extricably related to this nail, the spiritual chord of the role.[64]

Over time in Stanislavsky-speak, the "nail" became the Supertask (Superobjective in Hapgood) – and the more transcendent phrase 'soul chord' sadly disappeared in favor of something more materialist. The term Supertask can be applied to three specific interwoven lines: The Supertask of the Play (or Supertask of the Author); the Supertask of the Actor/Role; and the Supertask of the Production – called by one Russian pedagogue "The Scream of the Director."[65]

The Supertask of the Play has many kindred terms: the "main idea"; the "kernel"; "the idea for which the author picked up their pen"; "the suffering of the author"; "what the play is *about*"; and my personal favorite: "the poetic heart" of the play.[66] It is critical to Stanislavsky that whatever goes on, the Supertask, the author's main idea, must be the core principle in the artistry of making the production. Like a main artery, the Supertask of the Play pumps lifeblood to the actors, the director, the creative team, the artisans, and finally to the audience.

It is incumbent upon the actor to discover their own Supertask of the Role. As the actor explores the Given Circumstances in event after event, they must search for their own bespoke Supertask, one that excites their personal imagi-nation, creativity, psyche, and body – *and* contributes to the Supertask of the Play. Lydia Novitskaya, a lead teacher in Stanislavsky's Opera-Dramatic Studio (the subject of the next chapter), wrote about the Supertask:

> The [Super]task must be sought not only in the role, but also in the soul of the artist himself…It is necessary to search for responses in the artist's soul, so that both the super-task and the role become alive, trembling, shining with all the colors of genuine human life. It is important that the attitude to the role of the artist does not lose their sensual individuality and, at the same time, does not disagree with the writer's intentions."[67]

And here is a primary goal of Analysis through Action for each actor: to dis-cover the Tasks and their Supertask that personally 'tremble with all the colors of human life' and are connected to the poetic heart of the play. We will cover the Supertask of the Role and the Supertask of the Play, and the Supertask (Scream) of the Production in Part II of this book.

The Elements

Finally we come to the Elements, the all-important components of both the psychotechnique (Experiencing) and external technique (Incarnation). Tucked into the very top of the Experiencing lobe, adjacent to **13**, lies a sequence of tiny lower-case letters, the Cyrillic equivalent of "a" through "n." In Rose Whyman's translation from Stanislavsky's key, the fourteen letters enumerate the following Elements of the System:

a. Imagination and its inventions ("if," the Given Circumstances of the role)
b. Bits and tasks
c. Attention and objects
d. Action
e. The feeling of truth and belief
f. Internal tempo-rhythm
g. Emotional memories
h. Communion
i. Adaptation
j. Logic and consistency
k. Internal characterization
l. Internal stage charm
m. Ethics and discipline
n. Control and finish[68]

In Stanislavsky's Plan, these are the Elements fully activated by stage **13**, the crucial inner region of the soul where the play, the role, and the actor begin to unify and clarify. But the diminutive size and secreted placement of the fourteen letters seems to diminish the importance and practical value of the Elements, making them a kind of postscript, an afterthought – odd, as they are integral structural components that he describes so thoroughly in his two main books. Furthermore, at least three of them – Internal stage charm; Ethics and discipline; Control and finish – would correctly be placed in the realm of Incarnation; this is where they appear as chapters in both Hapgood's and Benedetti's books.

Like so many things in his struggle to specify the System, Stanislavsky never finalized his catalog of Elements. The fourteen listed in the 1935 Plan is just one specimen, and brief at that. In the schematic graph of the System drawn by Robert Lewis and shown in his *Method or Madness*, we see thirty Elements.[69] So, Stanislavsky is dictating thirty Elements to Adler in 1934 but one year later in the Plan of 1935 he lists just fourteen. Tcherkasski suggests that there are "twenty-five or something elements" and that "the most crucial thing is that the list of elements will never be finished."[70] He likens it to Mendeleev's Periodic Table of Elements, which has grown from 28 elements to 118. The core Experiencing elements can be found in the first two Hapgood volumes – *An Actor Prepares* and *Building a Character* – and Benedetti's *AWH1* and *AWH2*. In both, the elements listed in the chapter titles tend to be self-explanatory as far as they go. In *An Actor Prepares* and *AWH1* we find more or less the same catalog of Elements:

HAPGOOD	BENEDETTI
III. Action	3. Action, "if," Given Circumstances
IV. Imagination	4. Imagination
V. Concentration of Attention	5. Concentration and Attention
VI. Relaxation of Muscles	6. Muscular Relief
VII. Units and Objectives	7. Bits and Tasks
VIII. Faith and a Sense of Truth	8. Faith and a Sense of Truth
IX. Emotion Memory	9. Emotion Memory
X. Communion	10. Communication
XI. Adaptation	11. An actor's adaptations and other elements, qualities, aptitudes, and gifts

But a couple of matters deserve attention as we progress toward Analysis through Action. First, Benedetti's "Bits and Tasks" is a more accurate and useful rendition than Hapgood's "Units and Objectives." Unit is indefinite. Stanislavsky used the Russian word бит (be-YIT), or "bit." A bit is a distinct part of something larger, such as an Event or a "beat" in a play. (Americans tend to say "beat," due to early Russian promulgators of the System in the US, mispronouncing "bit" as "beat.")

Moreover, "Task" is a more action-inciting idea than "Objective." A task is something, possibly difficult or resistant, that must be achieved now and requires work and a directed expenditure of energy. Task is translated from задача, (za-DAH-cha). While "Objective" is a viable alternate translation, задача more actively also denotes a goal (to be achieved) or a problem (to be solved). The last is useful: the actor/role must solve the problem in front of them that the opposite character is presenting. Henceforth we will use Task and Problem, occasionally Goal.

One further note. In Bella Merlin's "Where's the Spirit Gone,"[71] her excellent inquiry into Benedetti's terminological translations in *AWHI*, she focuses on the word "concentration" which both Benedetti and Hapgood link with "attention." Merlin quotes from Declan Donnellan's must-read book, *The Actor and the Target*, on his distinction between these two words: "concentration destroys attention. You cannot pay attention to something and concentrate on it at the same time…Attention is about the target [the person you are trying to effect]; concentration is about me."[72]

This valuable insight is critical to the Étude work in Analysis through Action: all psychophysical energy expended onstage must be focused on the "target" – that is, the other person(s) onstage – not yourself. While you may have Gogol's nail in your head, that is not your concern at the moment; the Supertask nail is an energy-source which you involuntarily draw from as you direct action(s) toward your target(s).

The last thing to look at here is the vast difference between Hapgood's "Communion" and Benedetti's "Communication." Communication can mean anything from sending an e-mail to delivering a lecture to chit-chat. Communion expresses "The sharing or exchanging of intimate thoughts and feelings, especially when the exchange is on a mental or spiritual level."[73] Surely this is what Stanislavsky intended; communal interaction between partners onstage and the spiritual overtone of the word *communion* moves us deeper into the heart of the System than communication.

Incarnation Elements, while not fully attended to in the Plan of 1935, are evidenced in *Building a Character and AWH2*. Here there are more noticeable differences.

Hapgood	*Benedetti*
iv. Making the Body Expressive	18. Physical Education
v. Plasticity of Motion	19. Voice and Speech
vi. Restraint and Control	20. Perspective of the Actor and the Role
vii. Diction and Singing	21. Tempo-rhythm
viii. Intonations and Pauses	22. Logic and Sequence
ix. Accentuation: The Expressive Word	23. Physical characteristics
x. Perspective in Character Building	24. The Finishing Touches
xi. Tempo-Rhythm in Movement	25. Charisma
xii. Speech Tempo-Rhythm	26. Ethics and Discipline
xiii. Stage Charm	
xiv. Toward an Ethics for the Theatre	

Going by chapter titles, Hapgood's seem more descriptive and active. Benedetti's table of contents reads like a syllabus of "technique" classes at Western theatre conservatories (minus combat and the obligatory "industry showcase"). Indeed, the researcher/translator/historian Jean Benedetti was also the Principal of Rose Bruford College, a respected drama school south of London. Hapgood, who was fluent in Russian, knew little about the theatre. But she did know Stanislavsky personally and they wrote frequently and fondly. (He closed one letter with: "I get down on one knee, bow to the ground and kiss your slipper.")[74]

Conclusion

In this chapter we have surveyed Stanislavsky's System through his Plan of 1935 and touched on his two major System books, Benedetti's *AWH* combining both into one large volume as Stanislavsky had hoped. These volumes are his never-quite-finished thoughts after three decades of examining and often castigating his own acting, observing genius actors, experimenting on wary older actors, experimenting with eager younger actors, writing, rewriting, starting over, writing more, giving sporadic lectures and classes, and sitting in dark rooms smoking.

The System itself was almost fully developed from 1906 up to the 1917 Bolshevik Revolution, a watershed for everyone in Russia, certainly for Stanislavsky and The Moscow Art Theatre. Much of the System was developed in MAT studios, particularly the First Studio, which opened in 1912, led by a Stanislavsky protégé the genius Leopold Sulerzhitsky. By 1917, through much trial and error, the fundamental precepts of the System had been made if not fully refined; the rest up to the 1930s was tinkering and moving toward Physical Action.

But among the many wish-list things unfinished at Stanislavsky's death in 1938 was an ideal rehearsal methodology with which to deploy and activate the System and its core Elements. A dedicated search for a new rehearsal practice was not to come until Stanislavsky's Opera-Dramatic Studio of 1935–1938 and the laboratory workshop of *Tartuffe* in 1937–1938. But Stanislavsky died before his experiments were completed – and realistically he might never have been satisfied. However, The Opera-Dramatic Studio, the subject of the next chapter, is profoundly important to us as it was the research laboratory that ultimately produced Analysis through Action due to the presence of actor/director/teacher Maria Osipovna Knebel.

Notes

1 Konstantin Sergeevich Stanislavsky, regularly referred to in Cyrillic by Russian theatre aficionados as кс, therefore in English KS.
2 Krymov, Dmitry. Author Interview, February 12, 2018, New York City.
3 Following scholar Maria Shevtsova and others I will capitalize "System" to differentiate it from other uses of the word and quotations where lower case is appropriate.
4 Senelick, Laurence. *Stanislavsky: A Life in Letters*. London: Routledge, 2014.
5 https://www.proquest.com/docview/302123481?pq-origsite=gscholar&from openview=true
6 Smeliansky, A. "Afterword" in *Stanislavsky: An Actor's Work*, trans. J. Benedetti, Routledge, London/New York, 2008, p. 690.
7 Serebrennikov, Kirill interview January 14, 2013, https://www.vashdosug.ru/msk/theatre/article/69716/
8 Knebel, M. 1961. *О Действенном Анализе Пьесы И Роли; В Помощь Коллективам Театральнои Самодеиательности*, M: Iskusstvo. Knebel M. 1961. *On the Analysis through Action of the Play and the Role; In Aid to Theatrical Self-Determination Collectives*, Moscow: Iskusstvo, 2.
9 Shevtsova, Maria. *Rediscovering Stanislavsky*. Cambridge, United Kingdom; New York, NY: Cambridge University Press, 2020, p. 11.
10 Stanislavsky Konstantin and Jean Benedetti. 2008. *An Actor's Work: A Student's Diary*. London: Routledge, p. 612.
11 Senelick, Laurence. "The Ever-Widening Contexts of Konstantin Stanislavsky." *Stanislavski Studies* 8, no. 1 (2019), 7.
12 Senelick, e-mail to author, August 3, 2023.
13 Newton, Isaac. *The Mathematical Principles of Natural Philosophy. The Science Classics Library*. New York: Philosophical Library, 1964.
14 Whyman, Rose. *The Stanislavsky System of Acting: Legacy and Influence in Modern Performance*. Cambridge, UK; New York: Cambridge University Press, 2008, p. 12.
15 Roach, Joseph R. *The Player's Passion: Studies in the Science of Acting. Theater–Theory, Text, Performance*. Ann Arbor: University of Michigan Press, 1993, p. 206.
16 Stanislavsky/Benedetti. *An Actor's Work* 2008.
17 Merlin, Bella, "Where's the Spirit Gone: The complexities of translation and the nuances of terminology in An Actor's Work, *Stanislavsky Studies* 1:1 (English version), pp. 43–63.
18 Shevtsova, Maria, Shevtsova, Maria. "Review of My Life in Art, and: An Actor's Work" *TDR: The Drama Review* 54, no. 1 (2010): 172–174.
19 Shevtsova *Rediscovering Stanislavsky* 173.

20 Merlin in "Where's the Spirit Gone" cites Lloyd, Benjamin "Stanislavsky, Spirituality, and the Problem of the Wounded Actor," *New Theatre Quarterly*, February 2006, p. 74.

21 Shevtsova, *Rediscovering Stanislavsky*, p. xi.

22 Senelick, Lawrence; "The Stanislavsky Colloquium at the Theatre de Chaillot" *Soviet and East - European Drama, Theatre, and Film*; New York, Vol. 8, no. 2–3 (Fall 1988): 26.

23 Stanislavsky Konstantin Sergeevich and M. N. Kedrov. 1954–61. *Собрание Сочинений Т.3* [Collected Works Vol. 3] Art, Moscow, 1955, color plate facing 361.

24 There are two sets of Собрание Сочинений [Collected Works], the first containing eight volumes published from 1954 to 1961. The second consists of nine volumes published from 1989 to 1998, containing new introductions and many things that had been censored by Soviet editors in the first set. In both sets the first three volumes contain *My Life in Art, AWH1* and 2. The fourth volume contains essays, some found in *Creating a Role* and *An Actors Work on a Role*. The remaining volumes contain KS's speeches, notes, diaries, memoirs, and correspondence. In many ways these untranslated volumes are more interesting and illuminating than those that were published in English.

25 Sergeevich and Kedrov, p. 362.

26 Senelick, e-mail to author, August 3, 2023.

27 Lewis, Robert. *Method – or Madness?* With an Introd. By Harold Clurman. New York: French, 1958. Facing, p. 34.

28 Roach, *Player's Passion 206; Actor Prepares 132,136*.

29 Stanislavsky, Konstantin, Elizabeth Reynolds Hapgood, *An Actor Prepares* New York: Theatre Arts, 1936, pp. 132, 136.

30 Jansen Karin. *Stanislawski-Theaterarbeit Nach System: Kritische Studien Zu Einer Legende* (Frankfurt am Main: Lang, 1995), pp. 113–114.

31 Ibid., p. 111.

32 Shevtsova, *Rediscovering Stanislavsky*, p. 95.

33 Ibid., p. 209.

34 Csikszentmihalyi, Mihaly "A Theoretical Model for Enjoyment," in Caines, Rebecca, and Ajay Heble. *The Improvisation Studies Reader: Spontaneous Acts.* London; New York: Routledge, 2015, pp. 151–152.

35 Ibid., p. 152.

36 Stanislavsky/Hapgood, *Actor Prepares*, 269.

37 Whyman *Stanislavsky System* 67.

38 Stanislavsky/Benedetti *AWH* 331–332.

39 Stanislavsky/Benedetti *AWH* 186.

40 Whyman, Stanislavsky System of Acting, 254.

41 Shevtsova *Rediscovering Stanislavsky* 101.

42 Senelick, e-mail to author, August 3, 2023.

43 Stanislavsky, Konstantin Собрание Сочинений Т.6, 1994, p. 519 quoted in Shevtsova *Rediscovering Stanislavsky* 117.

44 Stanislavsky/Hapgood, *An Actor Prepares*, 275.

45 Stanislavsky/Hapgood, *An Actor Prepares*, p. 19.

46 All references to Stanislavsky's key in this section come from Stanislavsky Собрание Сочинений Т.3 (*Collected Works v 3*) pp. 360–361.

47 Pushkin, Aleksandr Sergeevich, and Tatiana Wolff. *Pushkin on Literature.* London: Methuen, 1971, 265. Found in Whyman Stanislavsky System, 44.

48 A translation of this play titled "Martha the Seneschal's Wife" can be found in Senelick, Laurence. 1981. *Russian Dramatic Theory from Pushkin to the Symbolists: An Anthology.* 1st ed. Austin: University of Texas Press.

49 We choose the more spiritual "Incarnation," per Whyman, over the more common "Embodiment"; both are legitimate translations.

50 Carnicke, Sharon Marie. *Stanislavsky in Focus: An Acting Master for the Twenty-First Century*. Routledge Theatre Classics. 2nd ed. London; New York: Routledge, 2009, 218.

51 Pesmen, Dale. *Russia and Soul: An Exploration*. Ithaca: Cornell University Press, 2000, xii.

52 Tolstoy, Leo, *What Is Art?* trans. Richard Pevear and Larissa Volokhonsky (New York: Penguin Books, 1995), pp. 39–40.

53 Stanislavsky/Benedetti AWH2, 582.

54 Stanislavsky Собрание Сочинений Т.2, (*Collected Works v 2*) 1989, 68.

55 Théodule Ribot (1839–1916) was an early psychologist whose main works preceded Freud's. His *Psychology of Emotions* greatly influenced Stanislavsky. In English: Ribot, Th. *The Psychology of the Emotions. The Contemporary Science Series*. London/New York: W. Scott Pub. Co.; C. Scribner's, 1897.

56 Stanislavsky/Hapgood Actor Prepares, 158.

57 Н. А. Зверева, Д. Г. Ливнев, Словарь Театральных Терминов ГИТИС; Н. А. Zvereva, Д.G. Livnev Dictionary of Theatrical Terms, GITIS, Moscow 2007, 34.

58 Stanislavsky/Benedetti. *An Actor's Work*, 285.

59 Stanislavsky K. S. Собрание Сочинений Т. 6; *Collected Works*: In 9 vols. M.: Art, 1994. V. 6, 61–62.

60 Shevtsova, *Rediscovering*, 11.

61 Строева М. Н. Режиссерские искания Станиславского: 1917–1938. М.: Наука, 1977; Stroyeva, M.N., The Directing Quest of Stanislavsky, Moscow: Science, p. 106.

62 Tovstonogov, Georgii, Stenographic class notes sent to author by former Tovstonogov student Maria Ganeva, translation Ganeva, caps hers.

63 Nikolai Gogol, *Polnoe Sobranie Sochinenii*, vol. 4 (Leningrad: AN SSR, 1951), pp. 112–13; in Whyman, Stanislavsky System, 100.

64 Станиславский К. С. Собрание сочинений: В 9 т. М.: Искусство, 1993. Т. 5. Кн. 1. Статьи. Речь. Воспоминания. Художественные записи; Stanislavsky K.S. Collected Works: V 9 t. M.: Art, 1993. V. 5. Book. 1. Articles. Speech. Memories. Artistic Records, 630.

65 М.В Сулимов. Посвящение В Режиссуру. Sankt-Peterburg: Изд. дом С.-Петербургского гос. Университета, 2004; M.V. Sulimov. *Dedication to Directing*, Publishing house of St. Petersburg State University, Saint-Peterburg, 2004, Translation Ilya Khodosh 531.

66 This phrase was spoken by the late eminent scholar/translator Paul Schmidt at a colloquium after a Wooster Group performance of *Brace Up*, their irreverent mixed media adaptation of Schmidt's translation of *The Three Sisters*. About the production he said that "it captured the poetic heart of Chekhov's play better than any American or British production he had ever seen. I have used this phrase instead of Supertask ever since.

67 Л.П Новицкая 1984. *Уроки Вдохновения: Система К.С. Станиславского В Действии*. Moskva: Всероссийское театральное общество; L. P. Novitskaya. *Lessons of Inspiration: The System of K. S. Stanislavsky in Action*. Moskva: All-Russian Theatrical Society, 1984, 16S.

68 Whyman, *Stanislavsky System*, pp. 41–42.

69 Lewis *Method*, facing, p. 34.

70 Tcherkasski, Sergei Lecture at "Stanislavski on Stage" exhibition, Pushkin House, London, January 29, 2013. Pushkin House transcript sent to author by Tcherkasski.

71 See Note 13 above.

72 Donnellan, Declan. *The Actor and the Target*. London: Nick Hern, 2002, 28.

73 "communion." Oxford Dictionaries. Oxford University Press. https://premium-oxforddictionaries-com/us/definition/american_english/communion (accessed June 18, 2023).

74 Senelick *Letters* 605.

2 The Opera-Dramatic Studio

Prelude: October 1928

Stanislavsky was exhausted from a recent Moscow Art Theatre tour of Europe, where he had been regularly fêted until the early morning hours. On his return to Moscow he was immediately met with a pressing workload including making plans for the Thirtieth Anniversary Jubilee of the theatre he had co-founded. During the opening night celebration, Stanislavsky erred dangerously by extemporaneously praising a deceased Moscow capitalist baron who had provided substantial personal funds to construct the Art Nouveau Moscow Art Theatre building. The tribute was spoken to an audience that included the General Secretary of the Communist Party of the Soviet Union, Joseph Stalin, and ranking members of his Politburo. Apprehension about this treacherous, even potentially fatal gaffe kept Stanislavsky sleepless that night and the next.

Two evenings later a presentation of the first act of *The Three Sisters* was the main feature of the evening's celebration. Offstage, Stanislavsky twisted into his original woolen military costume originally worn in somewhat trimmer days, by now a bit constricting and, as always under stage lights, stiflingly warm. On cue "the lovesick major" Vershinin strode onto the set of the Prozorov family parlor, greeted by a lengthy standing ovation from the audience. Then, with his customary aplomb, Stanislavsky took command of the stage, soon speaking his famous lines:

> True, no one will remember us. That's fate; there's nothing you can do about it. Things that seem important to us, serious and significant things...the time will come when they'll all be forgotten – or they won't seem so important anymore.

Toward the end of the act, Stanislavsky felt a sharp stab in his chest. He continued to play onstage but as the piercing pain intensified he nearly collapsed. He managed to finish the act and supported by fellow actors, made two company bows but could not make the remainder. A pair of Stanislavsky's personal doctors were hastily summoned from the audience. In the wings they found Stanislavsky lying on a divan in cardiac shock, his pulse weak, the uniform

DOI: 10.4324/9781003475576-4

soaked in sweat. He was rushed to his home on nearby Leontiev Lane, diagnosed with angina pectoris and myocardial infarction and kept under 24-hour surveillance for days.

He later wrote to one of the doctors:

> I remember that fatal night of the anniversary play after which you drove me home in an auto. I remember you, in your tuxedo, taking care of me, looking inquisitively and lovingly in my eyes to see if I was sick or if I was already dying.[1]

That Thirtieth Jubilee night proved to be the last time Konstantin Stanislavsky acted on the stage of the Moscow Art Theatre or any other stage. A week later Stanislavsky, feeble and confused, was struck with a second heart attack.

Thus, began the final decade of Konstantin Sergeevich Stanislavsky's life. Of this final period renowned director Lev Dodin has written:

> The last years of Stanislavsky's life are still very little described and little deciphered, those years when he rediscovered his system. From rather rigid methods, which to many is the Stanislavsky system…he came to the logic of a free search for a free life of a free human spirit.[2]

The Zon Interviews

In April 1933, a partially recovered Stanislavsky granted an interview to Boris Zon, an inquisitive young director from a Leningrad youth theatre. Prior to the interview, Zon observed an opera rehearsal that was not at all what he anticipated. He watched Stanislavsky guide two young singers through improvisations about their first date. Some improvisations were accompanied by music, none of it from the score; the singers sang impromptu ta-ta-ta sounds or made up their own words None of the vocal improvisations referred to the specific text of the libretto. Zon took notes:

> "No feelings!" – declares Stanislavsky polemically seeking to direct the actor's thought to action, to physically overcoming an obstacle…the performers, through improvisation, recall their real life using impromptu text…The most remarkable thing here is that the director is not a bystander for a single second, he is constantly, even silently, living together with the actors.[3]

After the rehearsal ended, Zon, who had previously studied everything he could find about the System, awkwardly admitted to his idol: "I must confess all my ideas about the 'Stanislavsky system' have been shaken a lot today"[4] Finally, the apprehensive pupil collected himself and asked:

Zon: Do you work at the table for a long time now, and when do you move to the next period?

KS: We read the play today and it's possible to perform it tomorrow. If it's not enough to read it once, we can read it a second time.

Zon: Does it mean that actors don't know anything?

KS: They don't know the words but they know what to do. If they forget, I would remind them. If a question arises, we would look into the text: "Something is written about that in the third act"...we find it...etc.

Zon: Does it mean that in the beginning you even don't need text of the role?

KS: We will come to it step by step, but according to a logical way, through action.

Zon: Does it mean that there is no need in sitting at the table at all?

KS: Here and there they may sit...Always with new efforts the actors may want a table.

But, Stanislavsky quickly added:

> Our ardor for the table led us to 'indigestion.' If a capon is fed too many nuts its stomach can't digest the food anymore; so it is with the actor who is burdened by 'table food' and can't use even a small part of what was served...My new method is a development of my previous one.[5]

Zon continued with questions prompted by the rehearsal he had just witnessed:

Zon: As far as I understand from today's rehearsal, do you lead the actor to the involuntary emergence of a character from the action itself and necessarily from the actor himself?

KS: Absolutely

Zon: When and how are bits and tasks set now?

KS: We play the play and we see that it turns out that we've played a bit [unit, event], and so then a new one begins. You and I have played, say, 'meeting,' and now, it seems, we are playing 'getting to know each other.' The tasks appear involuntarily.[6]

After four hours Stanislavsky concluded the interview by looking over Zon's copious notes. He cautioned the eager apprentice: "I want as much as possible to be taken from me, but until my book comes out not a line can be printed."[7]

But time was running short. Two years later, Stanislavsky said to his last set of students, those of the Opera-Dramatic Studio:

> I will be dying soon and you have to understand: What I offer you here, is the fruit of my whole creative life, the quintessence of my many years

of theatre experience. If you grasp it, you are saved, the art of the theatre will make a leap forward. If you dismiss it or don't grasp it – the art of theatre will go downhill.[8]

The Opera-Dramatic Studio, 1935–1938: Brief Overview

Stanislavsky's Opera Dramatic Studio (ODS) was ostensibly an academy founded with Soviet government funding to train a post-revolutionary generation of student actors. In actuality this last studio was an open-ended laboratory in which Stanislavsky grappled with his ideas about physical actions and attempted to conceive an entirely new rehearsal process. Ideally, after matriculation from their four-year course, 1935 to 1939, the ordained students – 30 were chosen from 3,000 applicants – would go out into Russian cities and hinterlands as collectives or independent proselytizers, teachers, and actors. Their mission, Stanislavsky and his government agency hoped, would be to build a new theatre for the new Russia. That didn't happen: Stanislavsky died in 1938. After their valediction in 1939 many of the students drifted out of theatre or held mid-tier positions at small venues.

But what the ODS did do was deliver into the Russian theatre world a disparate group of Stanislavsky's assistants and instructors. If you have been looking for women in the Stanislavsky story, here they are. Along with sister Zinaida Sokolova (who ran the Studio on a daily basis), Stanislavsky's wife, Maria Petrovna (called Lilina), the teacher/author Lydia Novitskaya, and of course Maria Knebel, who ultimately had a massive influence on the Russian theatre.

The entire program of the school was dedicated to the study and practice of Stanislavsky's 'new development': physical actions.

ODS Terminology 1: What Are Physical Actions?

Let's look again at our definition of action itself: 'Action is a living organic process directed to the realization of a specific goal.'[9] Prepending the word 'physical' gives us 'physical action,' specifying that this particular energy is expended by the human body: the body of the actor.

But the definition of physical actions goes further. The inexhaustible Russian chronicler of Stanislavsky's life, Irina Vinogradskaya, summarized physical actions succinctly: "By physical actions, KS meant a material basis from which the actor could start creating a role. But the physical is inseparable from the spiritual. Actions contain an actor's internal work."[10]

Thus, in both System and related Analysis through Action terms, it is understood that a physical action is not merely some simple physical motion that you accomplish with your body, such as opening a door, or speaking to Yorick's skull, or standing silently onstage. To achieve what Stanislavsky called a 'correct' physical action, there must be a found a specific *goal, 'goal'* being yet another translation of *zadacha*, along with 'task,' and 'problem (to solve).' So, to achieve a 'correct physical action,' the energy expended by an actor opening a door must be intended for, or intended to *discover*, 'the recognition of a specific goal'; the energy expended by the actor speaking to Yorick's skull must be intended for, or to discover, the realization of a specific goal; the energy of the silent actor standing still must be expended for a specific goal (for instance, observing or pondering 'what should I do next?').

A physical action must be truthful, emotionally infused, and theatrically exciting, as action was earlier. But the process of *getting* to the goal is now reversed. It used to be:

• Predetermine Goal through Mind or Feeling→Activate imagination, emotional memory, physical and or verbal energy, Will etc.→Execute Action

It is now:

• Execute simple physical action→Make Études stimulating given circumstances, imagination, emotional memory, physical and or verbal energy, etc.→Discover Goal

Hours and hours of speculative 'table food' and isolated homework are gone; indeed, the table itself is abandoned for most or even all of the rehearsal period. Instead we now have: start creating a role, right away, on stage, no script in hand. Start by *doing* things, simple physical actions with the body that the play suggests. Do the simple thing – open the door, talk to the skull, stand still – and then, primarily through Études, discover *why* you are opening the door, talking to the skull, or standing still. A cardinal rule: always start an Étude with two key given circumstances questions: Where have I just been? Where am I going now?

Don't read and discuss the play and the role endlessly at the table, don't pre-program objectives: Improvise the play on its feet in a focused and intentional way and thereby *discover* the play and the role, *discover* the 'specific goal.'

The physical action process, in time formulated into Analysis through Action by Maria Knebel, does not necessarily lead to some new form of acting or an innovative style of performance. But it does lead to a richer, rawer, more energetic, more imaginative, more 'dangerous' (in the right way) rehearsal process and performances, by activating Incarnation and Experience – body and soul – and numerous Elements from the very outset of rehearsals.

Alternatively, through Études, it is possible, as some choose, to 'explode' the play and the roles, thereby creating innovative and vivid contemporary productions, in which the text is a pretext, a springboard for unorthodox performance.

'We read the play today and it's possible to perform it tomorrow.' Simple but powerful thought, that.

ODS Terminology 2: Exercises, Improvisations, Études

These three words are vital to understanding the student experience at Stanislavsky's Opera-Dramatic Studio and the underlying premises of Analysis through Action. Rather than classifying these terms as we go along, let's investigate them here.

The following Venn diagram (Figure 2.1) displays the overlap between three central ODS training techniques. The lines below the rings denote that an exercise can evolve into an improvisation and an improvisation can evolve into an Étude. Thus, over time, a mere larval exercise can mature into a full-fledged Étude. Or, each can be done independently, full stop, with no further evolution.

There are not necessarily bright lines between these three training components, they are inter-related and porous, and the three nouns may vacillate in use. But we can determine some general notions for each.

ODS Terminology 2a. Exercises

There were numerous types of exercises at the ODS, but all were designed to prepare the psychophysical apparatus of the ODS actor for creativity through training the actor to respond *psychically* to simple *physical* actions. There were myriad solo 'objectless' physical action exercises – sweeping the floor, kneading bread, fishing at a pond, lighting a cigarette – all done with great intricacy but with no objects or props of any kind in hand. These were known as 'invisible object' exercises, or 'objectless' exercises. There were no words, no events, just simple physical actions, scores and scores of them. There were also 'animal exercises': go the zoo, study an animal, learn to move like a panda, hop like a deer, and over time achieve a kind of *ya yesm* with your animal: Through extended physical research and exploration I *experience* the panda.

In addition, teacher Lydia Novitskaya taught hundreds of exercises in key Elements of the System, a process that was called 'training and drill,' about which more soon.

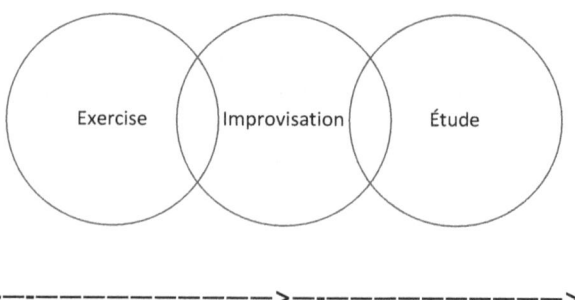

Figure 2.1 From Exercise to Étude.

ODS Terminology 2b. Improvisations

This word has Latin roots – *improvisus* – and translates as 'sudden,' and/or 'unexpected.' Improvisations are as old as theatre by the campfire, and have long been associated with traveling players, clowns, and commedia dell'arte troupes.

Zon witnessed improvisations at the opera rehearsal in 1933. There, Stanislavsky guided the two young singers through improvisations on a theme: falling in love on the first date. There was no plot as such, no character conflict, no dramatic event; the absence of these are hallmarks of an improvisation. There was a simple premise – two people meet and fall in love on their first date – after that, anything can happen.

It was common at the ODS for successful exercises to be developed into improvisations by complicating the given circumstances. What happens if a rival fisherman arrives at the pond? What happens if a stranger begs a precious cigarette from the first? What happens if the panda and the deer escape from the zoo? What happens if a betrothed partner accidentally spies the first-date couple falling in love? What happens *if...*

Improvisations of this kind had no script, no hard-and-fast story, or even mandatory events. They are open to whatever actions the actors create. But, like the first-date improvisation Zon witnessed, there is a shared actor postulate – 'our first date' – which inspires but does not determine the resultant physical actions. Successful versions of these improvisations were sometimes urged by Stanislavsky to expand, progressively adding increasingly problematic given circumstances. Thus, former improvisations would evolve into full-scale Études.

ODS Terminology 2c. Études

It is our misfortune that this French word, in Russian этюд (é-tyood), did not transfer into the English-language translations of Stanislavsky's books. In the final Russian edition of Stanislavsky's *AWH1* the word этюд appears 135 times. But 'Étude' is not to be found in Hapgood's *An Actor Prepares* nor Benedetti's *AWH1*; both translators dance around the word, indeterminately utilizing 'exercise,' and 'improvisation,' in places where Stanislavsky wrote этюд. Two key recurring *AWH1* examples – 'the burning money' and 'the madman' – are repeatedly referred to in the Russian edition as этюды (Études). Not so in the two English-language versions of the same book.

The reasons for our Anglo translators to avoid 'Étude' are unclear. Too French? Too grandiose? Already claimed by the music department (where Études – training exercises on an instrument – are commonplace)? This quibbling can be dismissed as translation-shaming until we take a look at the actual French meanings of the word Étude as Stanislavsky adopted it. In the French dictionary, *Le Larousse*, we find these definitions of *Étude* [edited for brevity and annotated by author]:

1. Effort oriented toward the observation and *understanding of beings*, things, *events*, etc. which applies itself to knowing, to deepening something. [emphasis added; here, we can cite KS: 'to know is to feel']
2. Thorough preparatory examination of something; analysis, for development or research. [KS calls Étude analysis 'not a mental analysis, but emotional analysis.' Analysis through Action "is a matter of the heart" said one director.]
3. Drawing, painting or modeling carried out from nature, in order to capture reality as *preparation for a more complicated work*. [emphasis added][11]

As we shall see, at the Opera-Dramatic Studio, Études were undertaken tirelessly in every phase of the students' work. Stanislavsky delighted in watching an exercise evolve through improvisations into a full-fledged étude.

Written dramatic texts were introduced at the ODS only after one-and-one-half years of physical action and System Elements training. Longwinded discussions at the table were of course banished – Stanislavsky had virtually rejected his own table work by 1929, when he outlined a complicated score of physical actions for *Othello*.[12] The entire approach to 'analyzing' the chosen ODS texts was through on-the-floor Études. But the actors did not start speaking the actual words of the author for several months; indeed, in some cases, actors were forbidden to even read the play until halfway through the process. The play was learned through Action, not discussion.

ODS Terminology 3: Episodes and Events (Action-Facts)

By the time of the Opera-Dramatic Studio, Stanislavsky had (mostly) disavowed *kuski*: units, bits, segments, pieces – which became in the US 'beats.' Formerly, a play had been partitioned into many discrete bits (per Benedetti; 'units' to Hapgood) which, like beads strung onto a string, would ultimately compose the entire play. There might be forty or fifty of these bits/units/beads/beats in a typical act of a typical four-act Chekhov play, +/- two hundred for the whole play. In the early days of the System, for each individual bit the actor had to strive to fulfill an immediate specific task, a desire that needed to be realized forthwith.

But, by 1925–1926, while preparing the Russian edition of *My Life in Art*, KS admitted that he had made a mistake by dividing the role into the smallest pieces possible.

> If we take a chicken and cut it into very small pieces it will be impossible to understand by just one of those pieces that it is a chicken. If, however, we take larger pieces: the wing, the thigh, the head – it's immediately clear what it is.[13]

In the new Opera-Dramatic Studio syntax, the larger recognizable parts of the chicken (to pound this unfortunate metaphor even further) become *Episodes*. An

Episode is a sizable sector of an act which incorporates several smaller units, bits, or beats. Novitskaya cites Stanislavsky's list of episodes for Act I of *The Three Sisters*, each of which incorporates its own group of 'Action-Facts' or Events:

Episode 1 – Waiting for the birthday breakfast.
Episode 2 – The sisters meet Vershinin – an interesting person, close to them in spirit.
Episode 3 – With Kulygin's entrance the prose of life bursts in, breaking the bright atmosphere of dreams.
Episode 4 – The birthday breakfast.
Episode 5 – A declaration of love by Andrei and Natasha.[14]

The fact that these episodes emulate 'movements' in an orchestral score is no accident. Each episode is a distinct movement forward, a dynamic progression of the actions of the play. Each has its own timbre, basic tempo-rhythm, and featured 'players.' Stanislavsky was eternally envious of the unique power of concrete musical notation, which in artistic hands could lead to inspiring artistry. The division of the play by episodes became the new normal for defining convenient rehearsal modules.

The ODS Curriculum – Year One: 1935–1936

The goal of the first year was for the students to experience subconscious creation through exercising the Elements of the psychotechnique (mostly with Novitskaya) and executing simple physical actions. Words from dramatic texts were not read nor spoken in the first year; real objects – hand or costume props – were not permitted.

But as noted above, there were those countless imaginary-object exercises – aka 'invisible object' or 'objectless' – simple action exercises. Assistant Grigori Kristi, who, along with others, taught these exercises and later wrote about them. Kristi recalls:

- Objectless exercises demand utilization of specific System elements, in this case concentration (attention), imagination, observation, emotional memory, logic and sequence, and finally faith and belief. Executing the exercise 'precisely' summons those elements, without pre-ordaining them.
- This absolute precision in turn leads to the subconscious mind and the process of creativity for the actor.[15]

The precision demanded necessitates dividing the larger action into a series of smaller physical actions. Kristi itemizes a progression of seventeen simple sub-actions for the basic action of lighting a cigarette with a match:

1) Feel the matchbox in your pocket.
2) Grasp and pull it out.

3) Turn the label up so that when you open the box, the matches don't fall out.
4) Push the inner box out of the case with your finger, while holding the case with another two fingers and your thumb.
5) Separate one match with the fingers of the other hand.
6) Grasp the match with two fingers and pull it out of the box.
7) Turn the match head downward.
8) Grasp the end of the match so as not to burn yourself when ignited.
9) Turn the side plane of the case so that it is underneath the sulfur end of the match.
10) Strike the match.
11) Turn the match upward so that the flame ignites.
12) If the action is happening on the street or in a draft, then block the flames with your hand or the whole body.
13) Bring the match to the cigarette.
14) Light up or consider what is needed.
15) Blow out the match or extinguish it with a sharp movement of the hand.
16) Figure out where to put the burnt match.
17) Throw it away, or put it in an ashtray, or back into the box.[16]

Try this, first with no props, then do it with real props (we are not recommending lighting the cigarette), repeat cycle – no props, with props – until perfected with no props. It'll take a while.

Year One: Training and Drill – the Elements

Lydia Novitskaya seems to have been a favored assistant – perhaps because of her father's high status at Narkompos, the equivalent of a ministry of culture and the agency which approved and funded the ODS. Can we speculate that it was she who pressed her father to support the dream of an acting conservatory which her own teacher Zinaida Sokolova, Stanislavsky's sister, would share with her illustrious brother? Possible, but we'll never know.

Nepotism or no, Novitskaya appears to have been trusted and very good at what she did. It was she who led classes on the psychotechnique, called Training and Drill, one Element at a time. Stanislavsky suggested many of these exercises/improvisations himself and Novitskaya created dozens more. The second half of her invaluable but regrettably untranslated book, *Lessons of Inspiration*, is a recounting of her ODS Training and Drill program using a progression of Elements, presumably co-determined with Stanislavsky. (The first half is a lively and detailed memoir of the ODS itself, the best record we have.) Novitskaya writes:

For many years of directing and pedagogical work, I have made sure that the study of the internal elements of stage well-being [health, confidence, security] should be built in a certain sequence. I followed approximately the scheme below, but it cannot be considered to be unalterable and obligatory:

Muscle release
Action, "if," given circumstances
Imagination:
Stage attention:
A sense of truth, logic and consistency:
Faith and stage naivety:
Emotional memory:
Communication:
Tempo-rhythm:
Characteristics [or Characterization]:
Mise-en-scène
From étude to performance:
Supertasks and Throughline action[17]

The grand total of her psychotechnique exercises is in the hundreds. Note the correlations with Hapgood and Benedetti's primary books (Benedetti repeats some of these exercises in his *Stanislavsky and the Actor.*) But a full English-language translation of the *Training and Drill* section of *Lessons of Inspiration* would be an invaluable asset to American acting training, which for the most part today relies heavily on training in one element, Units and Objectives (Hapgood)/Bits and Tasks (Benedetti). But note that this ubiquitous US training and rehearsal tactic is not mentioned by Novitskaya.

By the time of the ODS, units and bits were 'shreds of larger chicken parts' but the students were being taught employing full Episodes. While Units and Objectives appeared in Hapgood's 1936 *AAP*, in actual practice Stanislavsky had rejected this approach at the ODS. As Professor Sergei Tcherkasski points out, by the mid-1930s Stanislavsky was writing something he no longer endorsed:

> Confined to a small room and often bedridden, the terminally ill Stanislavsky faces a choice of almost Shakespearean tragedy. Either he has to write his book anew to reflect his fundamental inability to separate the psychic from the physical in the process of developing a creative sense of well-being, or he has to publish a book that does not reflect his current understanding of the essence of the actor's work...He sends to [Hapgood] chapters of the book, written according to the old plan of the mid-1920s, and in the classroom he does things that contradict his own manuscript.[18]

Stanislavsky knew that he could not go back to the beginning and revise his book. As he said to his students at the Opera-Dramatic Studio: 'I will be dying soon...' That he was unable to reverse field in his last written testaments is our huge loss.

The ODS Curriculum – Year Two: 1936–1937

In the summer of 1936, Stanislavsky was in failing health. Sister Zina wrote that she did not think he would live.[19] He was taken to Barvikha, an exclusive sanitorium outside Moscow, luxuriantly designed for the highest-ranking government officials (it remains so today). Back on Leontiev Lane, Zina was now in full charge of the ODS.

Initially, the program for Year Two was more of the same, albeit accelerated and expanded. Voice, speech, dance, movement, acrobatics, and academic courses continued from where they left off but with increased rigor and complexity. Certain successful exercises were expanded into improvisations and some of those expanded into complex full-class narrative Études such as 'The Puppet Shop' and 'Flying to the Moon.'

Vocal work, formerly limited to breathing and vocalizing, now turned toward the spoken word – no dramatic texts yet, but 'artistic readings' of poetry and short stories – 'verbal expression' which is where Maria Knebel, appointed to the faculty toward the end of Year One, was focused.

But a surprising and significant mid-course correction at the ODS occurred a little over halfway through Year Two. Stanislavsky was still sequestered at Barvikha, regularly informed about matters ODS by visits from his wife, Lilina, sister Zinaida, and others. When his health improved slightly in February of 1937, he summoned Zina and two of her top assistants, Valentina Vyakhireva and Lydia Novitskaya, to the sanatorium. Rehearsals of full plays had been originally planned for Year Three, but Stanislavsky, doubtless sensing his own mortality, abruptly decided to advance the timetable. This meant starting full-bore rehearsals of full-length plays – literally tomorrow.

Novitskaya remembers Stanislavsky's reasoning for this revision of his curriculum: "It is necessary to find out what links in the method are missing, whether there are any superfluous or non-essential points…He invited us to work in the Studio on performances using the new method – under his leadership, of course."[20] Stanislavsky had determined that the best way to scrutinize his 'new method' was working on 'the classics,' at first, specifically Shakespeare.

Novitskaya was assigned *Romeo and Juliet*, Vyakhierva *Hamlet*. They were not to work on the full text, not on individual' fragments' (isolated 'beats'), but on (through) 'lines' of the play, chunks not bits. These lines would focus on a central character's progression on through a subdivision, aka Episode, of the play. In *Hamlet* this meant going from the coronation of Claudius (I-2) to Hamlet's encounter with the Ghost (I-4, I-5).

Toward the end of the Barvikha session, Novitskaya started to summarize how she understood Stanislavsky's new rehearsal process:

1. Tomorrow, when we get together, I will first tell the students the line of events (event-facts) of the play.
2. Then I will ask each of them – what would they do here, now, under the given circumstances?

"Of course," Stanislavsky answered; [he then continued his list]:

3. And they should tell you their line of physical actions. I emphasize only tell you, in no case should they perform yet!
4. Make sure that the performers do not do anything with their feet and hands – let them "sit on their hands." [more on this technique later, but it means what it says]
5. Solely on the basis of emotional memories from their own lives they must clearly outline what they would do in the given circumstances.
6. You will have to repeat the line of physical actions more than once, not two, not three times – the logic of actions requires a long time to be clarified.
7. All actions found must be recorded [written out in sequence by the actor]. As a result, each performer will have their own entire line – a whole list of physical actions, not of others', but of their own, taken from their own life.
8. The moment will come when, having clarified and spoken this 'list' several times, while 'sitting on their hands,' your charges will feel like ripened chickens in a shell, they will feel confined, they will need to break out to the freedom of action.
9. Then take the list of recorded physical actions and do everything on stage.[21]

Novitskaya writes:

> We asked Konstantin Sergeevich, how long will it take for us to disassemble the play by physical actions, and when do we move on to language and further stages? To this he replied: "Once you play the physical action role correctly, it's almost done. If a play is staged for a year, then physical actions must be worked on for six months...Our independent rehearsal work was to begin the next day. Naturally, both of us – Vyakhireva and I – were in a state of some anxiety.[22]

But, the work did indeed begin the next day, presumably after a sleepless night for the two instructors.

From her notes Novitskaya later recorded a work plan drawn from Stanislavsky's instructions at Barvikha[23]:

a) determine at least an approximate super-task of the play;	WORK OF THE DIRECTOR WITHOUT THE ACTOR
b) division of the play into the largest episodes (major events), finding in the episode the creative task, that is, the main action of each participant of the episode;	WORK OF THE DIRECTOR WITHOUT THE ACTOR
c) division of episodes into smaller event-facts, presence of the main action in those;	WORK OF THE DIRECTOR WITHOUT THE ACTOR

d) pass through the organic processes of the plot of the whole play, while "sitting on hands":	WORK OF THE DIRECTOR WITH THE ACTOR
e) after the elementary description of the given circumstances – then pass through the whole play along the line of physical action: the analysis and recording of the physical action line, each actor telling his line of physical action (the creative task of the episode) separately and with his partner, mentally acting, arousing "urges" to action ("sitting on hands").	WORK OF THE DIRECTOR WITH THE ACTOR

While much of the second-year work continued as before – Études, physical actions, verbal expression, Training and Drill, albeit more complex – the dominant foci for many students was *Romeo and Juliet* and *Hamlet*. Sometime in late February or early March, Stanislavsky returned home and visited his ODS students to consider their work. Stenograms, which we would call transcripts, were recorded on most of the days when Stanislavsky appeared.

The Rozanova Transcripts, 1937–1938

(The following section is annotated from the *Hamlet* transcripts from Vinogradskaya's *Станиславский Репетирует* [Stanislavsky Rehearsing]; Novitskaya's account of *Hamlet* rehearsals in her *Lessons*, a chapter in Maria Ignatieva's superb *Stanislavsky and Female* Actors, and other sources as noted.)

Setting: The 'Onegin Room,' a modest ballroom/concert hall in Stanislavsky's Leontiev Lane home, where students brought Stanislavsky their work that had been rehearsed elsewhere under the supervision of their instructors.

Date: shortly after Stanislavsky's return from Barvikha, March 1937. In the room sit the students of the *Hamlet* project, including the acknowledged star of the class, Irina Rozanova. A classmate recalled her charisma: "Her face was forever memorable. An even, somewhat Gogolian straight nose…The right angles and straight lines [of her hair] gave her face a stern and masculine expression…[her] pronounced personality attracted like a magnet, it was interesting to look at her and listen to her."[24]

Maria Knebel recalled Rozanova as: "Thin, big-eyed, in some kind of black velvet tunic and black leotard, she wandered around the studio. Bangs, shoulder-length-smooth hair, chain with a medallion around the neck. Without the slightest fear, she rehearsed with Stanislavsky. Despite her seventeen or eighteen years of age, she understood him with remarkable subtlety."[25]

In March of 1937 Stanislavsky returned from Barvikha. When he felt well enough he caught up with the student work.

MARCH 1937

At one of the classes, studio student Ira Rozanova asked Konstantin Sergeevich if she could work on Hamlet.

– On Ophelia? K.S. asked.
– No. Hamlet.

      K.S. looked at Rozanova. Ira's trembling look, her pale serious face caused K.S. not a smile, not surprise, but rather a desire to understand this strange girl...

– Well then, work on it. You will hardly ever play it, but it is very useful to do the work. Hamlet is a whole university. If you work properly on Hamlet, to get to the depths of it, to the truth of human feelings and thoughts, you can become a real artist. Hamlet will help to reveal all your spiritual riches. Work on it – this is very interesting..."[26]

The classmate:

> Stanislavsky "treated Irina very well, he was attentive and kind. He was interested in her life. Irina told me that sometimes during class, he looked at her with such kind eyes that she could not help but tear up. Sometimes KS's eyes, in Irina's words, became so unfathomable that they scared her.[27]

April 21, 1937

Stanislavsky asks Irina to read her line of action. After she does:

KS:	It should be much simpler. What is your goal here? [in scene I-2, the coronation]
Irina:	To understand what is happening.
KS:	Good, I have to understand, to observe...What will you do to achieve that, under the given circumstances? Here is a specific given circumstance: I was gone for a long time. Then I returned and saw that everything had changed. Father died; Mother married someone else. You see Mother as a different woman – cheerful, coquettish. What would you do in that case?
Irina:	I would ask Mother for the reason of the change.
KS:	Good, but you don't have an opportunity to speak to Mother. Then what would you do?
Irina:	I would start following her.
KS:	So then write these actions down, write: to follow. In the word "follow," is there one action or many?

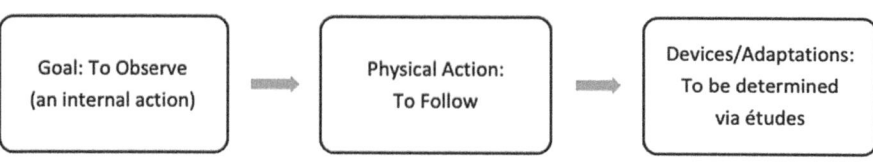

Figure 2.2 Action Plan for Irina.

Everyone: Many.
KS: Then divide this action [to follow] into its component parts....[28]

The 'component parts' are the 'hows' of the physical action: 'follow,' for example, trailing her, peeking through her window, and so forth. But identification of these 'hows,' which Stanislavsky called 'devices,' or 'adaptations,' are not to be pre-ordained. They will be discovered in Études, Irina's process so far looks like this as shown in (Figure 2.2).
     KS continues:

KS: What would you do to understand the metamorphosis that occurred in your mother? What process is going on in your soul?
Irina: A process of bewilderment. I don't understand what is happening with Hamlet's mother.
KS: There is no Hamlet, there is only you! Project everything onto yourself.
Irina: Can I visualize my own mother?
KS: If you please, let this be your real mother. Proceed from your emotional memory. What must you do to sort out this situation?
Irina: I am peering into my mother to understand why she is behaving like that.
KS: That's it? Imagine that you return, expecting to see your mother in grief and tears, and suddenly instead, you find her cheerful, and besides that, married to a scoundrel, a bastard. Imagine the person you hate the most and imagine him next to your mother. What would you do in that situation?

                                                            (Irina thinks.)
Irina: I would remember my mother. My mother was so affectionate! How she served my father tea, how attentive she was!
KS: That's right, you have your own images and visualizations. Now, on the basis of the emotional memories of your life, paint me a bigger picture. In the bigger picture, include affectionate mother, loves you, loved her husband, imagine her bedroom, and suddenly...a completely different picture: you see your mother married to a bastard! She is happy and satisfied.
Irina: This is all flickering in my mind.

KS: It should not flicker. You must thoroughly imagine your whole life
from childhood to your father's death. What does it amount to? It
consists of your own emotional memories, of small episodes that are
especially dear to you...The first condition of art is as follows: as
soon as I receive a role, for example, Hamlet, from then on, Hamlet
does not exist separate from me. I exist in Hamlet's given circumstances. Take everything from your emotional memories.[29]

Stanislavsky repeatedly stresses that Irina must 'imagine' and employ her own
personal emotional memories. He encourages Irina to visualize her own
mother in her bedroom with someone other than her father. The term 'emotional memory' means the same as the earlier 'affective memory,' albeit ad-
justed to a different political era. It's important to stress that here and elsewhere
lie ample evidences that Stanislavsky did *not* abandon emotional memory as
some would later claim, although it may not have held the highest priority it
once did.

May 13, 1937

Three weeks later, Stanislavsky visits the *Hamlet* group again. He asks Irina
about her progress:

Irina: I look at my mother [the student playing Gertrude], but she doesn't
look at me, or she looks cheerful and not sad. How should I play
it – sad or happy?

KS: You are playing the result. Today Mother is like this, so I will behave
like that, but tomorrow it could be completely different. You should
always consider the state of your partner *today*; if you play the same
line of devices continually, without considering the state of your
partner, then this line will be illogical and clichéd. It begins with the
fact that you put the tentacles of your eyes into the eyes of your
mother, in order to understand why she is like she is today.

Irina: Today I look at Olga [Gertrude] and she is one way, but tomorrow
she is a different way?

KS: This is valuable. Act as you need to act today, now. Yesterday she
was gentle, loving, but today she is coquettish. Look and see how she
is now, and don't miss anything. Always proceed from today...You
must develop this habit in yourself, and the first step for this will be
the line of physical actions and the organic process that forces you to
communicate with the object. Is this clear to everyone?

Students: Everyone.

KS: Do you understand the organic process of feeling your partner's soul
with the tentacles of your eyes? It's a simple organic communication
process. Understand that your work in the organic process is '*Today –
here – now.*'[30]

The session concludes with Irina worrying about an upcoming Event in her line of action.

Irina: I just can't imagine the Ghost, whether it is big or small. I can't feel it, but I need to be afraid.

KS: You want to know how to feel, and then secure that feeling. This is impossible. No matter what Ghost you can imagine, you must nevertheless ask yourself: what would I do?

Irina: But what can I do when I have imagined a Ghost, and I see a student instead?

KS: As soon as he enters, ask yourself: if this were the Ghost, what would I do? An actor must be able to, at any moment in his life, turn a lever that shifts everything to the side of imagination.[31]

May 25, 1937

This transcript is mostly devoted to a *Romeo and Juliet* rehearsal. But Irina continues to obsess about the Ghost:

Irina: What do I do with my father's Ghost? I cannot imagine it for myself. Must it be scary, terrifying?

KS: I can't tell you anything about that. You are asking me about the realm of your subconscious life. The only thing you can do is not to interfere with that realm. You can stir it up, tickle it, tease it, rock the subconscious, but no one else can interfere with it. Try only to see your partner and focus all your attention on them...After all, you cannot secure feelings, you can only secure physical actions. But so that you don't do physical actions for their own sake, I must lead you along the organic line of communion. I need you to transmit your visualizations to your partner. When you do this, physical actions, your visualizations, and your attention will all be for your partner, which is most important.

Visualizations are images from the imagination and/or emotional memory. They are personal inner source materials, 'my life till now,' – not images of what to do in a scene. Recall from an earlier transcript: 'You must thoroughly imagine your whole life from childhood to your father's death.' Later in the century 'images' will evolve into 'the film reel,' or 'the movie tape.'

October 26, 1937

Irina: I want to find the uninterrupted line of the role for Hamlet. The line is interrupted when I lose the logic of thought. It's difficult for me. I want to set down paths for an uninterrupted line.

(Irina talks about the line of her role.)[32]

Vinogradskaya inserts a second account of this class, one from the classmate quoted earlier, who was not in the *Hamlet* group. This account provides an excellent report of one phase of the ODS work on physical actions.

> Hamlet will be telling his [*sic*] line of action from the very beginning of the play, sequentially and logically constructing it, trying to weave a continuous thread. He will have to lock eyes with partners who, helping him and accepting his ideas, must remain in contact with him, enter into communication with him, each person existing in their own behavioral logic. The partners must act without moving from their seats, only with their eyes. A condition of this assignment was a ban on using the text of the role. As soon as Rozanova accidentally said, "Then I tell him..." Stanislavsky interrupted her immediately: "I have read the play and I know what you say. Tell me what you do, and what you are thinking about in that moment.

The second classmate continues:

> Over two or three hours, Irina was able to unravel in front of us an uninterrupted line of action, or if you will, a line of life and behavior for Hamlet, his intentions and ruminations, without reaching the end of the first act. This was the result of a lengthy and laborious preparation. She did this very actively. Analyzing the line of her character, she was constantly observed by her partners, who, without saying a word, existed in the logic of their own action. Sometimes, getting carried away by the exposition, she said, "Here he starts thinking." Stanislavsky would correct her: "Not he, but you. Understand that this is fundamentally important."
>
> Rozanova went on, living through the role, sitting on a chair with her hands under her knees.
>
> I intensely followed the development of events in the play. I saw the production in my mind's eye, saw people's characterizations, saw mise-en-scenes and even the set. Tension gripped my hands and feet, and at the end, my jaws were hurting from my clenched teeth.[33]

Irina spent 'two or three hours,' to speak her 'line of actions, – without reaching the end of the first act. She was occasionally interrupted by Stanislavsky, with corrections – or sometimes with encouragement, as recounted in that day's transcript:

KS: What do you do when you lose the line of the role?
Irina: I go back and try to see and imagine everything.
KS: Be careful not to imagine some separate Hamlet. Could Hamlet's story happen in our time? It could. Imagine that Hamlet is today, here, now...If you understand that, you will understand that I have

penetrated your soul in the simplest and most direct way and force you to act like I need.

(Irina resumes speaking.)

KS: (To the students) You feel that she is starting to speak from herself: I feel, I want. That is her will and her feeling.[34]

The above 'today, here, now' – an everyday dictum in ODS training – is a cornerstone of Analysis through Action as well. It means that all Experiencing must happen in the present (today), in this place (here), at this moment (now). Everything is different today: your partner, the environment, the people in the room. Simply repeating what you did yesterday is not experiencing the present moment; it must be alive *here, now, today*.

June 13, 1938

Stanislavsky had been very ill and primarily at Barvikha in the several months between *Hamlet* transcripts. Meanwhile, after fourteen months of sitting on their hands in chairs while verbally describing their physical actions, then doing Études, then returning to sitting on their hands but now speaking the common gibberish called 'Ta-ta-ta' instead of text to express their thoughts and feelings, they finally got up on their feet, speaking the actual (translated) words of Shakespeare. At the finish of their run-through of Act I for Stanislavsky, Irina appears to be disconsolate.

KS: How did it feel? What worked, what didn't? What was unpleasant? Prince, how are you?

Irina: It varies…I have a lot of trouble with that monologue. [*O, that this too too solid flesh would melt*]

KS: In this monologue, you have nothing to do because you've already played everything beforehand. Instead of beginning to hate, you should merely be orienting yourself – how to live, where to go…But you've found everything out before the play began, you already explored everything…Do you feel how the play is written? All action is contained in the words. You do not yet have verbal action…Dozens of words and thoughts did not reach me. In terms of diction, in terms of constructing phrases, you have not done any work. We haven't spoken about verbal action, but your diction is quite weak…I remember when you spoke in your own words, you communicated thoughts quite well…It should be simple. But as soon as you convey simplicity, you become vulgar and petty. Try to speak the text simply, with attention to the thought. (*Pause*) What are you doing now? Let me hear how the words sound.

Irina: I am gathering my focus.

KS: You are gathering the feeling you want. Against your consciousness, you are getting ready to play feeling. You should not do this. I am asking you only to say the thought, and you will see that the right meaning of the words will draw you into feeling. But if you try to communicate feeling, it will run away from you.

Irina attempts to start the monologue:

Irina: "Oh, if this too, too solid flesh would melt…"

KS: Explain your thought. What does that mean? You are rushing, but you should be painting a picture.

Irina tries again:

Irina: "Oh, if this too, too solid flesh would melt…"

KS: What is that? What happened?

And again:

Irina: "Oh, if this too, too solid flesh would melt…"

KS: This is a huge picture. "Thaw and resolve itself into a dew" – this is all connected. What are you emphasizing? You are rushing again. When you say a big phrase, you cannot disconnect the subject from the predicate. They must be smoothly connected, without stepping on each other. They must have form. There cannot be a second identical note.

This time she gets a little further:

Irina: O, that this too too solid flesh would melt/Thaw and resolve itself into a dew!

KS: Why do you give so much emphasis to the word "resolve"? You are not proceeding along the proper path, you are going by breath, by pronunciation. "resolve into a dew" – this must be a concluded phrase. Going further, construct a new phrase.

Irina: "Or that the Everlasting had not fix'd. His canon 'gainst self-slaughter!"

KS: Two adjectives, two nouns, the genitive tense. You are rushing these words. Where is the difficulty?…If your voice doesn't vibrate or resonate, then you will look for what will make it sound better. So you start with all these tricks. Where does this foul pathos come from? It's just that the voice isn't placed correctly.[35]

Toward the end of the session, an unflagging Irina wants more feedback.

Irina: But tell me what was bad. At least in general terms.
KS: There were good things in it, but there was little action. When you be-
            gin taking action, you fall into pathos. There was no verbal action; but
            when it burst forth accidentally, that was very good. Through this work,
            you must understand the importance of verbal action. If you act with-
            out rhythm, it will be comical. You must play Shakespeare completely
            simply. If you make a gesture, you must follow it through to the end.[36]

Days later, the Opera-Dramatic Studio came to the end of its third year. On
August 7, 1938, Konstantin Sergeevich Alekseev Stanislavsky died in his bed, a
few steps from the Onegin Room.

Irina Rozanova: Coda

In the course of Stanislavsky's final criticisms, Konstantin Stanislavsky and
Irina Rozanova exchanged these words:

KS: You must not mind that I am critiquing you like this. After all, you
            took on a role that actors should be ending their careers with. The
            greatest challenge in our art is Hamlet. But I gave it to you...You
            were assigned Hamlet because you have a good temperament for it.
Irina: Of course, I am not stopping here. I realize I have a tremendous
            amount of work ahead of me.[37]

After Stanislavsky's death, Irina did not give up her dream of playing Hamlet.
She left the Opera-Dramatic Studio, acted here and there, but soon it was wartime
and jobs were scarce. She took a position at the Maly Theater, but often seemed
despondent. Then, a former Meyerhold actor, Nikolai Okhlopkov, was made
Artistic Director of the Theatre of the Revolution, a large and famous theatre in
central Moscow. He immediately contacted Irina, offered her the role of Hamlet,
and asked to meet with her. The evening following that call, Irina joined her close
friend, Vladimir Fromgold, who had played the Ghost in the ODS *Hamlet*.

> Irina was rejuvenated. She became the same Irina we had remembered
> from the Studio, inspired and enthusiastic. The meeting with Okhlopkov
> was supposed to happen the next day. We went to the dorms where I
> lived. During the whole day and evening all she talked about was Hamlet.
> At 11 p.m., we suddenly remembered about the curfew. It was 1943. I
> walked her to the subway, but halfway she sent me back to the dorms. It
> was late. Later I found out that while crossing the street the same night,
> she ran in front of a trolleybus, not noticing the car driving behind it.
> Trying to escape the car, she moved back and was run over by the trolley-
> bus. She died instantaneously.[38]

Three Legacies of Leontiev Lane

Shortly after the final session with Irina, Stanislavsky gathered his ODS teaching staff, all of whom thought Year Three had been a success. Stanislavsky did not: "Everything now is lost...The technique and all the rest. I don't see any foundation, any ground, any more. You should now start with a critique of the method I have been experimenting on."[39] This was to be the work ahead. But Stanislavsky died before Year Four classes began. Over time, the students scattered, one of them later wondering:

> How did it happen that not even a single even moderately significant actor came out of Stanislavsky's studio?...We were the cream of the crop, the chosen few, the lucky ones, envied by the students of all the other theatrical schools. I think the answer is a simple one. No one really cared whether or not we would become actors...were only wooden pawns on a chessboard grandly called "The Theater as Temple." We were the guinea pigs on whom Stanislavsky tested his latest theory, the so-called theory of physical actions.[40]

But while the legacy of the ODS did not flourish under the actors (certainly not if compared with the First Studio), it was nonetheless a crucial test site that launched the future of the Russian theatre through associates who had observed or participated in the work. But Stanislavsky, always searching along many avenues, had said different thing to different people at different times in different rooms. Thus, during his 1930s era of 'physical actions,' various practitioners left Leontiev Lane with varying interpretations of what they had learned, taught, or witnessed.

In his book *Открытая Педагогика* (*Open Pedagogy*),[41] director and scholar Veniamin Filshtinsky proposes three methodological techniques that emanated from Leontiev Lane, each with its own 'disciples.'

Legacy 1: The Étude Method

Let us recall the shocked Boris Zon's first questions and Stanislavsky's answers in 1933: 'How long do you work at the table now? Today we read the play, tomorrow we get up and act.' Or consider this from a December 1936 letter to Elizabeth Hapgood from the sanitorium Barvikha:

> This is how we do it now: today I read a new play, and tomorrow we are to act it. What can be acted?...Do you know how to enter a room? Then, make an entrance...You don't know the words? Never mind, speak your own words.[42]

Or, perhaps most significantly, what Stanislavsky wrote in a 1937 notebook at the peak of the Opera-Dramatic Studio period (his fictive characters, teacher Tortsov and student Kostya, are back):

Kostya! Do you remember Gogol's *The Government Inspector?*' Tortsov asked, suddenly turning to me.

Yes, but not very well, only in general outline.

Good. Go up on stage and play Khlestakov's entrance in Act Two.

How can I when I don't know what to do?', I objected in surprise.

You don't know everything, but you know something. Play that something. In other words, perform the smallest physical actions in the life of the role that you can play sincerely, truthfully, as yourself.

...

But I don't know the words and I have nothing to say', I said stubbornly.

You don't know the words, but do you remember the drift of the conversation?

More or less.

Then give us that in your own words.[43]

Later in the *Government Inspector* draft Stanislavsky/Tortsov replaces Kostya playing Khlestakov. He concludes by evaluating his own classroom demonstrations of how to approach the role:

For a time I guarded against the writer's views and deliberately did not open the book. I did all that to stay free and independent, so as to approach the role in my own way, prompted by my own creative nature, my subconscious, intuition and human experience, etc....when no real base has been established, on which I can rely, I am wary of anything that will distract me from the point at hand and complicate my work.[44]

The writer is seen as an obstacle, to be 'guarded against.' Tortsov/Khlestakov is wary of distractions, such as the author's precise text, until he is 'more deeply into the role' and has established a 'real base.'

This process – forgoing looking at the author's words until well into rehearsals – was most fully utilized in the ODS *Cherry Orchard*, which began work in 1937, the last of the five ODS 'classics' projects to go into rehearsal. The students were led by Stanislavsky's wife, Lilina, who before each rehearsal consulted with her husband. Per KS's instructions, there was not even a table reading of the play – so much for 'today we read the play, etc.' Indeed, the students were forbidden to look at or hear a text at all; they were not told what play they were working on (although presumably some must have guessed). Lilina would give detailed descriptions of the act or the scene in the beginning of the rehearsal, after which students would improvise. This was meant to be "the artistic proof of his theory."[45] Would it be possible to rehearse the play without its text and to apply the text at the very end of the process? After several months of productive Études, a teaching assistant read the full text of *The Cherry Orchard* to the student cast.

The specific term 'Étude method' – the method in which Études proceed without consulting the text until a 'real base' has been established – does not appear until years later, when it is taught and written about by a former student of Zon's and Knebel's, Zinovy Korogodsky. In turn, Korogodsky mentored Veniamin Filshtinsky, who proselytizes the Étude method in his own prolific directing, writing, and teaching. This is one genealogic line that emerged from the Opera-Dramatic Studio.

Legacy Two: The Method of Physical Actions

In his office adjacent to the Onegin Room, Stanislavsky carried out a rehearsal experiment quite apart from *The Cherry Orchard*. The play was Molière's *Tartuffe*, with Mikhail Kedrov playing the title role and serving as company director under Stanislavsky's supervision. The cast was composed of established Art Theatre actors, including veterans Lilina and Knipper-Chekhov and younger members, most prominently Vasily Toporkov, who played Orgon and later wrote about these rehearsals.[46]

Unlike Lilina's *Cherry Orchard* or the Tortsov-Kostya *Government Inspector* Études, the text of *Tartuffe* was very much in evidence throughout rehearsals. It was read in full and discussed at Kedrov's first rehearsal – although Stanislavsky forbid him from making an advance director's plan.

On twenty dates from January 1937 to April 1938, Kedrov brought individual scenes or full acts to Leontiev Lane for Stanislavsky's review. Once again, Stanislavsky had ordered the actors not to memorize the lines or speak aloud any of Molière's (translated) verse; the actors were to create their own words, and not permit those to ossify into repetitively recited 'text.'

For *Tartuffe*, as with other Stanislavsky projects of this era, Molière's dialogic text served as a catalog of prompts, its purpose being to 'indicate the line of physical actions.' But unlike Lilina's *Cherry Orchard*, situations and characters of the scene were discussed and debated. Toporkov writes that Stanislavsky initially focused on the line of physical actions, then gave scrupulous attention to the spoken verse as verbal action. Then, on a boiling hot August 7, 1938, the initiator and artistic director of the *Tartuffe* project and head of the ODS died in his bed.

But Stanislavsky's death did not end work on *Tartuffe*. Kedrov, with his fellow actors' assent, overrode Stanislavsky's dictum that there was never to be a public performance of the Molière play. After showing scenes to the directorate of the Art Theatre, and hailing *Tartuffe* as a tribute to Stanislavsky, actor/director Kedrov was granted a full production replete with elaborate sets. While the production was only a modest popular success, it nonetheless was the beginning of Mikhail Kedrov's ascension to the highest levels of the Art Theatre. Toporkov writes:

> It can't be said that Stanislavski brought anything completely new to his final work with us, or anything contrary to his previous teachings about the system, as will be evident from my description of the rehearsals for *Tartuffe*. But now Stanislavski's method was richer, more practical, and that was expressed in the definition, the 'Method of Physical Action.'[47]

This is a dodgy passage. Toporkov intimates that Stanislavsky's 'new approach' was imperfect and incomplete (both true). But for a definitive delineation of the 'method of physical actions,' – that is, Mikhail Kedrov's appropriation of the idea – Toporkov submits that Kedrov (now Toporkov's boss at the Art Theatre) made the process whole: 'richer, more practical.' First off, there is no evidence that the phrase 'method of physical actions,' was ever spoken or written by Stanislavsky;[48] it was most likely propagated as Stanislavsky's by the self-serving Mikhail Kedrov. His 'method of physical actions' became his instrument of power inside the Art Theatre: he proclaimed himself the heir to the co-founder's final thoughts – and, quite unlike the apolitical Stanislavsky, was a dutiful Communist Party member to boot.

Nemirovich-Danchenko's death in 1943 left the Art Theatre leaderless. After three years of intrigue and a dysfunctional Soviet 'collective leadership,' the ministry of culture entrusted the sole direction of the Art Theater to Mikhail Kedrov, who mandated his 'method of physical actions' to be the house rehearsal process. Despite some early directorial successes, Kedrov's 'method of physical action' productions became increasingly schematic, leaving out the psyche side of psychophysical. He returned to making ironclad pre-rehearsal 'directors plans,' a catalog of simple physical actions – first you open the door, then you cross to the chair – which the actors then had to carry out, with no correlative of internal life or spirit.

This was the era of 'conflict-less drama,' based on a Communist Party artistic policy that held that in a classless society there could not be conflict, only socially productive competition: Best must graciously win out over Good and Better. Études, never Kedrov's strong suit as an actor or director, were replaced by determining sequential simple physical gestures, not psychophysical actions – which the soulless Soviet realist plays at the Art Theatre had no call for. The acting company, riven by internal political and generational disputes and performing in an increasing dreary repertoire, turned to drugs, alcohol, and narcoleptic performances.[49] Kedrov's productions, once somewhat lively and interesting, were increasingly vapid and ideologic, as was his authoritarian leadership.

On the Moscow Art Theatre website, the revered house historian Inna Soloviova posted this about Mikhail Nikolaevich Kedrov:

Kedrov achieved the position of artistic director of the theater in 1946; from 1949 to 1955 he was chief director, from 1955 he was a member of the artistic council, from 1960 to 1963 he was chairman of the artistic board of the Moscow Art Theatre. The new director's devotion to his ideas dramatically turned into a disturbance of the inner harmony of the theatrical enterprise…Under Kedrov, M.O. Knebel and P.A. Markov [the longtime literary manager] were forced to leave the theater. Disputes about the creative method were now decided "at the top." Kedrov, demonstrating a rare intransigence in everything that concerned methodology, was almost indifferent to the truthfulness of the plays he had to

The Opera-Dramatic Studio 63

deal with. Alongside Chekhov, Ostrovsky, Shakespeare, Gogol...he staged an apologia for Stalin – "The Volley of the Aurora" and [plays with] early support for [Communist Party] political campaigns and trials...Kedrov, in essence, felt himself first and foremost a keeper of theatrical theory and a teacher-practitioner, no matter what the material. For a number of years, he led laboratory classes with directors, promoting the 'method of physical action.'[50]

Legacy Three: A Third Idea

Back at Leontiev Lane in 1937–1938 yet another pedagogical course was going on. This was a tutorial with a recently appointed ODS instructor just beginning a directing career at a small Moscow theatre. The young director was a mid-tier actor who had performed at the Art Theatre in small roles for a dozen years, including in several productions directed by Stanislavsky and Nemirovich-Danchenko. The novice was struggling with defining the Events in a play soon to go into rehearsal, and came to Stanislavsky, a brilliant text analyst, for directorial help. Stanislavsky knew the play well and responded:

'Very good! It's a great play for young actors. How do you define the main event? On which events are you going to do études?'
'I don't know, though I have read and thought that over extensively. I get confused in defining events, in the sequence of actions.' Stanislavsky's eyes looked at me strictly. Apparently, he decided that I was afraid of the étude method and decided to work in the 'usual' way.[51]

Stanislavsky responded in anger. The director was, after all, an instructor in the Studio that relied on Études as a central rehearsal mechanism; there was a duty to put what was being taught at the ODS into practice outside of Leontiev Lane. Finally, the shamed protégé appealed to Stanislavsky's heart, speaking of the fear of being unprepared for rehearsals. The master teacher relented: 'Bring me a list of major events of the play, I will emphasize the main one.'[52]

I did not go to bed that night. The next morning I handed Uncle Misha, the doorman at the Studio, an envelope with a list of events...A few days later Stanislavsky returned my list to me. The pen was boldly underlined: 'A shot at Ivan.'[53]

The aspiring director was shocked. The shot happens before the play starts. However, the mentee soon recognized that this offstage event shaped the actions of each character throughout the course of the drama – and the neophyte had missed its critical importance! The wannabe director realized that more training in Events was needed and sought out Stanislavsky for further tutelage. He agreed but said: "daily training is needed – we need to take a new play every day and learn to read it by events…So I dared to bring Stanislavsky long lists, and he never forgot to check them."[54]

The new director vowed to mix a rigorous structural Event analysis of the play with the passionate and the productive new technique of making Études to explore those Events, once identified. This fusion of intellectual structural analysis and physical investigation is the most widespread and enduring of the three main pathways that emerged from the Opera-Dramatic Studio. Today this approach is broadly accepted as Analysis through Action (and titular variants such as Active Analysis).

The name Analysis through Action and its practice were later first fully formulated by the novice director Maria Osipovna Knebel.

Notes

1 The story of Stanislavsky's first heart attack is digested from И Виноградская, *Жизнь И Творчество К. С. Станиславского: Летопись В Четырех Томах: 1863–1938*. 2-е изд. Москва: Московский художественный театр, 2003. V. 4. 1928–1938. 495 с. 65–66; Vinogradskaya I. N. *Life and Creative Work of K. S. Stanislavsky: Chronicle*: In 4 volumes: 1863–1938. 2nd ed. Moscow: Moscow Art Theater, 2003. V. 4. 1928–1938. 495, pp. 65–66.

2 авторы проекта Smelianskii A. M Ol'ga Egoshina. 2004. *Режиссерский Театр*. Moskva: Московский художественный театр. Т.1 67–68; Interview with Lev Dodin: project authors Smeliansky A. M and Olga Egoshina. 2004. *Theatre Directors*, Moskva: Moscow Art Theatre. V.1, 67–68 trans. Author.

3 составитель В and В Львов. 2011. *Школа Бориса Зона: Уроки Актерского Мастерства И Режиссуры*. Санкт-Петербург: Мастерская СЕАНС; Compiled by V and V Lvov. 2011. *The School of Boris Zon: Lessons of Acting and Directing*. Translation: Yulia Kleiman/Ilya Khodosh, St. Petersburg: Workshop SEANS. pp. 453, 456.

4 Zon, *Lessons* 460.

5 Zon, *Lessons*, p. 461.

6 Zon, *Lessons*, p. 462.

7 Zon, *Lessons*, p. 463.

8 *Физические действия и работа над частью* V. Прокофьев В " Театр," декабрь 1950/январь 1951; *Physical Actions and the Work on the Role*, V. Prokofiev in "Theater," December 1950/January 1951, 3.

9 Г. В Кристи, *Воспитание Актера Школы Станиславского*, 1968 Moskva: Iskusstvo; G.V. Kristi, *Education of an Actor at the Stanislavsky School*, 1968, Moscow: Art, 26.

10 Виноградская, И.Н., *Станиславский Репетирует: Записи И Стенограммы Репетиции*, Moskva: Московский Художественный театр, 2000; Vinogradskaya, I.N. *Stanislavski Rehearsing: Notes and Transcripts of Rehearsals*, Translation Ilya Khodosh, Moscow: Moscow Art Theater, 2000, 364 (Online access: https://library.mxat.ru/books/18 as of June 2023).

11 https://www.larousse.fr/dictionnaires/francais/%C3%A9tude/31591 Accessed June 29, 2023.

12 Stanislavsky, Konstantin, and William Shakespeare. *Stanislavsky Produces "Othello."* London: Bles, 1948.

13 *The Last Stanislavsky in Action: Translation and Analysis of the Experiences of the Opera and Dramatic Art Studio* (1935–1938) by Diego Fernandes Garcia Moschkovich, Brazil: Sao Paolo, 2019 unpublished PhD thesis, citing Stenogram

(KS 21162) as found in the Moscow Art Theatre Archives. Translation by Moschkovich, who has cataloged all the Stanislavsky ODS transcripts and published sixteen which had not been public. Later we will also rely on the transcripts published in Irina Vinogradskaya's *Станиславский репетирует, Stanislavsky Rehearses*.

14 Л. П. Новицкая *Уроки Вдохновени: Система К.С. Станиславского В Действии.* Moskva: Всесоюзное театральное общество, 1984; L.P. *Novitskaya Lessons of Inspiration: K.S. Stanislavsky's System in Action.* Moskva: All-Union Theatre Society. 1984, p. 143.

15 G.V. Kristi, *Education of an Actor*, p. 44.

16 G.V. Kristi, *Education of an Actor*, pp. 44–45.

17 Novitskaya *Lessons*, pp. 122–23.

18 Черкасский, Сергей *Мастерство Актера: Станиславский-Болеславский-Страсберг: История Теория Практика.* Sankt-Peterburg: Издательство Российского государственного института сценических искусств, 2016; Tcherkasski, Sergei, *Mastery of the Actor: Stanislavsky-Boleslavsky-Strasberg: History Theory Practice.* Saint Peterburg: Publishing house of the Russian State Institute of Stage Art 510.

19 Vinogradskaya *Chronicles*, V.4, p. 454.

20 Novitskaya *Lessons* p. 145.

21 Novitskaya *Lessons* pp. 155–156 [Translated, condensed and enumerated by Chambers]

22 Novitskaya *Lessons*, p. 156.

23 Novitskaya *Lessons* pp. 209–210.

24 From a memoir by Б.Л. Левинсон (B.L. Levinson), http://www.alpklubspb.ru/ass/a359.htm, accessed July 1, 2023. Also found in Vinogradskaya *Rehearsing*, p. 405.

25 Кнебель, М. *Вся Жизнь.* Moskva: Всероссииское театральное общество, 1967; Knebel, M. *A Whole Life*, Moscow: All-Russian Theatrical Society 1967. 269.

26 И Виноградская 2003. *Жизнь И Творчество К.с. Станиславского.: Летопись В Четырех Томах: 1863-1938* Moskva: "Moskovskiĭ khudozhestvennyĭ teatr" T.4, p. 386; I. Vinogradskaya 2003. *Life and Work of K.S. Stanislavsky.: Chronicle in Four Volumes: 1863–1938* "Moscow Art Theatre" V.4, p. 386.

27 Vinogradskaya *Rehearsing* p. 368.

28 Vinogradskaya *Rehearsing* pp. 379–380.

29 Vinogradskaya *Rehearsing* pp. 381–382.

30 Vinogradskaya *Rehearsing* p. 388.

31 Vinogradskaya *Rehearsing* p. 389.

32 Vinogradskaya *Rehearsing* 401.

33 B.L. Levinson in *Rehearsing* pp. 405–406.

34 Vinogradskaya *Rehearsing* pp. 401–402.

35 Excerpted from Vinogradskaya *Rehearsing* pp. 422–424.

36 Vinogradskaya *Rehearsing* p. 428.

37 Vinogradskaya *Rehearsing* p. 423.

38 Fromgold, Vladimir, *The Memoirs* (Unpublished), 8 sheets, Moscow Art Theatre Museum, #21706, 3. Found in Ignatieva, Maria. *Stanislavsky and Female Actors: Women in Stanislavsky's Life and Art.* Lanham: University Press of America, Inc., 2008, p. 122.

39 Moschkovich, Diego. "'Everything Now Is Lost': Stanislavsky's Last Class at the Opera-Dramatic Studio." *New Theatre Quarterly* 39, no. 2 (2023): 85–91. doi:10.1017/S0266464X23000039 85.

40 Галич Александр Maria R Bloshteyn and Alexander Galich, 2008. *Dress Rehearsal: A Story in Four Acts and Five Chapters.* Bloomington Ind: *Slavica* 48. Galich was the pen name of Alexander Ginzburg who had played King Claudius in the ODS *Hamlet*. He later made his name as a dissident Moscow songwriter/singer and was forced to emigrate in 1974.

41 Вениамин Фильштинский. 2014. *Открытая Педагогика* 2-E izd ed. Sankt-Peterburg: "Baltiĭskie sezony"; Veniamin Filshtinsky. 2014. Open Pedagogy 2-E ed. Saint Petersburg: "Baltic Seasons".

42 Senelick, Laurence. *Stanislavsky: A Life in Letters*. London: Routledge, 2014. p. 606.

43 Stanislavsky, Konstantin, and Jean Benedetti. *An Actor's Work on a Role*. London; New York: Routledge, 2010, pp. 47–48.

44 Benedetti *Role* p. 71.

45 Ignatieva, Maria. "Stanislavski's Best Student Directs: Maria Lilina's First and Last Production." *Stanislavski Studies* 4, no. 1 (January 2, 2016): 3.

46 Toporkov, Vasily Osipovich. *Stanislavski in Rehearsal: The Final Years*. New York: Routledge/Theatre Arts Book, 1998.

47 Toporkov *Stanislavski in Rehearsal* p. 111.

48 See Autant-Mathieu Marie-Christine. *La Ligne des actions physiques: Répétitions et exercices de Stanislavski*. Montpellier: L'Entretemps Editions, 2007, p. 19: "In 1935 when Stanislavsky is officially granted the direction of the Opera-Dramatic Studio, he will develop a new type of approach to the role by the "line of physical actions" (he does not use the term "method")." Diego Moschkovich, who has read all the original transcripts of the ODS classes and all of KS's diaries, says KS never used the phrase "method of physical actions," although others around him, Kedrov for one, did. (E-mail: Moschkovich to Chambers, July 13, 2023). Stanislavsky expert Sergei Tcherkasski concurs, saying method of physical actions is "Kedrov's wording." (E-mail: Tcherkassky to Chambers and Moschkovich, July 16, 2023).

49 Author interview with Anatoly Smeliansky, Cambridge MA, July 9, 2015.

50 Soloviova, Inna at https://mxat.ru/history/persons/kedrov/ Accessed July 13, 2023.

51 М Кнебель. 1967. *Вся Жизнь*. Moskva: Всероссииское театральное общество; M Knebel. 1967. *A Whole Life*. Moscow: All-Russian Theater Society. 310 Translation Ilya Khodosh.

52 Knebel *Whole Life* p. 311.

53 Knebel *Whole Life* p. 311.

54 Knebel *Whole Life* p. 267.

3   Maria Knebel

Toward Analysis through Action

Introduction

Maria Osipovna Knebel was a diminutive female of Jewish descent – not a good combination in Soviet Russia – and by her own evaluation 'not pretty' enough to play leading roles as an actor. Nonetheless, she played a gigantic role in the history of Russian theatre.

Through her directing, artistic direction, teaching, and extensive writing she virtually single-handedly began to extricate the Russian theatre from the hammer and sickle of Soviet realism. She tirelessly inspired her passionate apostles as they forged their (sometimes subversive) theatrical pathways. Knebel's courageous and dexterous efforts with her protégés, her writing, and her own directing gave birth to one of the most exciting and profound artistic theatre cultures in the world today.

None of Stanislavsky's first three books, *MLIA*, *AWH1*, and AWH2, which expound the principles of the System, address a fundamental question: how does the System-trained actor – one who has been drilled in the psychotechnique of Experience and the Elements of Embodiment, one who aspires to realize the goal of reaching the subconscious by conscious means – actually *do* that?

This was to be the topic of book four – for which Stanislavsky made numerous notes but never started. A simulacrum, what Hapgood called *Creating a Role (CAR)* and Benedetti titled *An Actor's Work on a Role (AWR)* and the equivalent Russian volume, all differ in some measure. But each is a disconnected series of essays and fragments from the early days of the System to the late 1930s cobbled together by Soviet scholars from Stanislavsky's archives. The few pieces included from the 1930s certainly provide some insight into KS's 'new approach,' but this pastiche volume is hardly the systematic 'actors manual' Stanislavsky dreamed of. Reading the 1930s fragments of *AWR*, one is tantalized but still left with the question: what exactly do I do to get from here to there – from the conscious to the subconscious?

There are various rehearsals strategies in the contemporary theatre, but there is still much reliance on extensive table work, then to blocking, then to runs, then to tech. But in the 1930s Stanislavsky threw out that formulaic

DOI: 10.4324/9781003475576-5

procedure – which he himself had first installed – to seek a 'new approach' to rehearsal: something vigorous, something based on physical actions, something that engendered spontaneity – with little extended table talk. But KS died before he figured it all out.

However, as observed in the previous chapter, KS's late 1930s work engendered three main disciples, each advocating a related but differing 'new approach': Boris Zon and the Étude Method, Mikhail Kedrov and The Method of Physical Actions, and Maria Knebel's Analysis through Action. Without these three disciples, most particularly evangelist Maria Knebel, it is probable that all the work of those last years of Stanislavsky's life would have gone for naught.

The quiet dynamo who was Maria Knebel – the woman who was preparing to study mathematics at university but ended up in an acting class; the woman who as a mid-tier Art Theatre actor who was not considered for leading roles and mostly played children or crones; the woman who married a different wrong man three times and once lost a child at birth; the woman whose father's venerable art publishing house was destroyed by anti-Semitic vandals; the woman who herself was under the constant Soviet threat of 'metropolitanism' (read anti-Semitism and anti-German xenophobia) – certainly one reason she was fired from the Moscow Art Theatre, her artistic home for twenty-five years – somehow this woman not only survived personal and political perilous times, but through her creative brilliance, mathematically deductive mind, warm humanity, devotion to her mentors and students, sparkling humor, and quiet persuasive determination, she persevered – persevered, and forever changed theatre history in her homeland and beyond.

It is time we in the West fully absorbed her lessons too. Other authors, particularly Professors Sharon Carnicke and James Thomas, have already contributed their volumes,[1] both with an emphasis on Knebel. Due to space limitations and a somewhat dissimilar approach to Analysis through Action (which both Carnicke and Thomas as well as others call Active Analysis), what I offer here on Maria Knebel will only be introductory and will not do full justice to this physically small but artistically towering genius.

Four Mentors

Talent is not enough. It must be discovered, then mentored by experienced talents. Maria Knebel was fortunate enough to not only have been discovered and mentored by geniuses, but in her later years her greatest talent was for exactly that: discovering and mentoring genius-level talent.

Mentor One: Osip Knebel

Of her four major mentors, Maria Osipovna's first was her father, Osip Nikolaevich Knebel. Raised as an Ashkenazi Jew in a perennially contested region of the Austro-Hungarian Empire, he spoke German and Yiddish when he arrived impecunious in Moscow. Like many Jews of Germanic descent in Russia (for instance, Meyerhold's father, Friedrich Emil Meierhold) Osip Knebel converted to Lutheranism but did not change his German surname.

By the time Maria was born – 1898, propitiously the birth year of the Moscow Art Theatre – Osip had established a distinguished publishing house specializing in elegant and expensive colorized art and travel books. Maria regularly pored over these volumes and others in the family library. Her father regularly took Maria and her two siblings to museums, asking them to describe in minute detail what they saw in a particular painting. Years later, Maria conceived 'the painting exercise,' in which a student director creates a full-scale staging, depicting before, during, and after the critical moment shown in an assigned painting. This exercise is still in the directing curriculum at GITIS and elsewhere in Russia.

The family lived in a spacious central Moscow flat located above the street-level bookshop (which was completely destroyed by anti-German vandals in 1915, shortly after Russia's entry into what we call the First World War). Maria's mother, originally of Ukrainian-Jewish heritage but now also a Moscow Lutheran, was an accomplished pianist. Like young Konstantin Alekseev, Maria and her family were regulars at concerts, ballet, and best of all for Maria, theatre. At age ten, she attended Stanislavsky's fantastical Art Theatre production of Maeterlinck's symbolist fairytale *The Blue Bird*, an experience that marked her for life. Some two decades later she played a small role in a 1927 revival.

At home, Maria made performances for the famous visiting artistic cognoscenti and wealthy mercantilists; she of course played the lead in these pageants and directed her siblings and friends in lesser roles. Without knowing it, she was replicating Stanislavsky's childhood, molding her brethren into an acting company. Maria began avidly reading and reciting poetry to prepare for her future career on the stage. But one day her revered father placed her in front of a full-length mirror, saying "Look carefully. Is it possible to dream of becoming an actress with such an appearance? I looked in the mirror and though my heart was breaking with grief, I understood that my father was right."[2]

Osip's severe assessment, with which her mother concurred, stayed with Maria for a lifetime as some traumatic moments do. Nevertheless, Maria Osipovna Knebel remained forever grateful for the deep and broad cultural capital her parents had bestowed upon her.

Mentor Two: Michael Chekhov

In 1918, while studying for an exam in the parentally validated pursuit of a mathematics degree, Maria looked out her window and spotted a companion hurrying along the street; her friend was on her way to a new acting studio led by Mikhail Chekhov, nephew of Anton. Maria, who had seen this dazzling actor perform – many said he was the best in Russia – pushed aside her dense math books and raced to join her companion.

> The first impression of Chekhov was unusually sharp. He came in awkwardly, pulling up his falling pants, unsightly. But at once I saw his eyes – directed somewhere, looking at no one and waiting for some answer. I was so struck by these light bottomless eyes, full of pain, loneliness and some silent question that I completely forgot about myself.[3]

After the class, in which shy Maria participated in some improvisatory exercises, Mikhail Chekhov urged her to join his studio. Naturally, she feared her parents' reaction but relented to the bottomless eyes of this master acting teacher. Soon, Maria was a class favorite of her second mentor. Her destiny was sealed, parents be damned.

By age 26, Mikhail Chekhov, nephew of playwright Anton, was already recognized as a true genius of the Moscow stage following his stunning portrayals at the First Studio of the Moscow Art Theatre. His charismatic performances had a mercurial, improvisatory quality, as if he were inventing his characters on the spot. Yet these widely varying characters were always intensely focused, psychologically complex, concentrated, and commanding – impossible to watch without rapt fascination and heartfelt compassion.

But in 1917, while rehearsing with Stanislavsky for a new production of Uncle Anton's play *The Seagull*, Mikhail Chekhov, even in the best of times prone to mental illness and bouts of severe alcoholism, was beset by two personal tragedies. His beloved wife left him and soon afterwards a dear cousin committed suicide, perhaps with a gun that belonged to Mikhail. It became impossible for Chekhov to play Treplev, the young artist who after his beloved leaves him terminates his life with a pistol shot. Chekhov withdrew from the stage for almost three years, rarely ventured outside, and devoted himself to teaching in his apartment. Knebel remembers: "Later he said that he recovered only because of his work with us. I think that was the case. He needed contact with young, healthy people in love with his creative personality."[4]

At that time, Chekhov was still very much in thrall to Stanislavsky and his System, and the respect was mutual. Later, to a group of students including Maria who were observing Chekhov rehearse one day, Stanislavsky turned and said: "If you want to study my system, watch the work of Misha Chekhov."

Knebel later identified teacher Chekhov as *the* consummate Stanislavsky actor:

> If you look for an example of an actor who, in practice, achieved an exhaustive completeness of *reincarnation on the basis of experience*, this is, first of all, Mikhail Chekhov…everything that happened to him on stage led him to the deepest faith in the power of the subconscious.[5]

As is well known, Stanislavsky and Mikhail Chekhov were later to come to a bitter impasse over how best to reach the subconscious – Chekhov argued adamantly against affective memory and strongly for imagination – but during Maria's time in the Chekhov Studio, her teacher was still very much an unwavering advocate of the fundamentals of the System. "Chekhov translated into his own language the complexity of Stanislavsky and Nemirovich's requirements and developed their positions based on his own individuality," wrote Maria years later.

As her Chekhov studio education progressed, Maria Knebel was able to absorb some fundamentals of the System that her mentor often taught by theatrical demonstration, or by just plain improvising on a particular Element for great lengths of time. The future teacher Maria Knebel remembers:

> We knew Chekhov in all his complex contradictions – weaknesses, failures, inspired searches, doubts, disappointments, and discoveries. There was no consistency in his lessons, probably this was necessary for our systematic growth. But through these lessons I understood forever that a creative personality of a teacher is a huge formative force...He did not teach us but gave us the opportunity to participate in his quest, and for this I am forever grateful to him.[6]

Whether by participation or more regularly through watching extended demonstrations, the novice acting student Maria Knebel took from Chekhov a visceral understanding of these essential System Elements

Imagination:

Chekhov, as already mentioned, was endowed with a completely exceptional gift of imagination. With amazing ease, he plunged into the proposed circumstances of any play, saw the role in the smallest detail, heard his future character speak...Everything was decided by the power of Chekhov's imagination – it was incredible, truly fantastic. At its behest, that restructuring of the actor took place, which amazed everyone...Chekhov was sure that this creative energy could and should be developed, maximized, and that was the whole point.[7]

Imagination was the absolute central premise of Chekhov's technique and remained so throughout his life.

Attention: "In the process of attention," Chekhov writes, "you internally perform four actions simultaneously: First, you imperceptibly focus on the object of your attention. Second, you attract it to you. Thirdly, you draw yourself to it. Fourth, you penetrate it."[8]

Attention accompanies Imagination. One can concentrate on a stage partner or an imaginary image of a character you are rehearsing using the four-step process above. Knebel made Chekhov's attention process a staple of her directing courses at GITIS.

Atmosphere:

I felt Malvolio [a famous role of Chekhov's] from the moment I mentally delineated a space around me. I tried to walk, move, listen and speak, keeping a distance between myself and the others, the distance generated by my majesty. I gradually began to believe that my appearance threw others into awe. I radiated contempt and narcissism. It was my atmosphere for Malvolio.[9]

Unlike the atmosphere of a production, Chekhov concentrated on the atmosphere of a *character*. Knebel notes that this is related to Stanislavsky's idea of the 'kernel' or 'seed' of the character.

In addition, Knebel wrote about Chekhov's interrelated characteristics of improvisations and Études, which became crucial components of Analysis through Action.

Improvisation:

But the most impressive in his playing, the miracle and magic that everyone talked about, for which they watched the same performance dozens of times, was, of course, the gift of improvisation…Konstantin Sergeevich said that in moments of inspiration, devices are born subconsciously and come out with a sparkling stream, dazzling the audience…how the given circumstances are justified, what form of communication arises, etc., should be prompted by the subconscious. Only then will there be precious impromptu.[10]

Études:

Chekhov was looking for direct ways to the subconscious, and that is why many of us had difficulty with the exercises that he gave us; the number of unsuccessful études was huge. But he taught us to 'dive head-first into cold water.' Chekhov loved études on 'self-discovery', i.e., études in which the unexpectedness of what was happening did not give time for reflection. As an actor of great spontaneity, he loved these exercises, which he learned from Stanislavsky.[11]

Through a fluke sighting of a companion on the street, Maria Knebel landed in the studio of a genius, a complicated, often tormented man who would have a profound influence not only on Maria personally, but on the core DNA of Analysis through Action. Knebel, who later was tutored by mentors Stanislavsky, Nemirovich-Danchenko, A.D. Popov, and others, was nonetheless inspired by Chekhov throughout her life and owed much of her genius to that genius.

These words she wrote honoring Mikhail Chekhov coincidentally summarize the Supertask of Analysis through Action as envisioned by Maria Knebel:

Chekhov perceived the ability to absorb the play's content in such a way that it became an area that he studied down to the smallest detail. He knew exactly what was going on in the play, who treated him how, when, and what he himself was trying to achieve in a play, for this or that purpose. With all this, he freed up his subconscious. And that dictated to him how he would accomplish this or that task in the play.[12]

Decades later, Maria Knebel co-edited a set of Chekhov's writings which had only been seen in *samizdat* (literature copied and passed around) up to that time.[13]

To the Art Theatre

In the bewildering birth and death cycles of the many Art Theatre studios – see Rebecca Gauss's *Lear's Daughters* and Maria Shevtsova's *Rediscovering Stanislavsky* for full accounts – 1922 was a pivotal year. It was then that the brilliant director Evgeny Vakhtangov died at age 40. Mikhail Chekhov, who had returned to acting with great success, was asked to head the First Studio, succeeding his deceased colleague and close friend Vakhtangov. (Vakhtangov, just to confuse matters further, had been simultaneously running the Third Studio, which had emanated from his own private classes.) Chekhov promptly closed his private home studio and invited Maria to join him in his new endeavor. Although he was not convinced that Knebel would be a great actor, he was convinced of her imagination, focus, literacy, and intelligence. She said no.

Instead, she entered the esteemed acting school of the Second Studio (yet *another* studio – there were twelve different MAT-related studios at one time or another). Here, Knebel found a very singular kind of education from the scintillating impulsivity of Mikhail Chekhov. At the Second Studio she was immersed in a demanding orderly training of Stanislavsky's psychotechnique with particular emphasis on psychological analysis of text, Communion (interaction with partners), and Affective Memory. Now surrounded by peers of high ability – including one Mikhail Kedrov, whom a recent biographer asserts had a romantic interest in Maria which she assiduously evaded[14] – Knebel thrived in her new studio. She was immediately promoted to the final-year student cohort, joining the Second Studio's professional acting company the next year, 1923.

The Second Studio soon ceased to exist; in 1924 it was absorbed into the Art Theatre itself. Here, Maria Knebel spent fourteen years in what we would call advanced intern status (known as 'second order' actors) playing cameos, including a mute in the revival of her cherished *Blue Bird*. She was not fully promoted to the main body of the troupe until 1938. But her secondary position allowed her to regularly observe and sometimes act for the two founding directors of the Art Theatre: Konstantin Sergeevich Stanislavsky and Vladimir Ivanovich Nemirovich-Danchenko.

A Doomed Initial Agreement

When Stanislavsky and Nemirovich-Danchenko were hammering out the initial terms of the Art Theatre, they made an agreement that would inevitably create ongoing contretemps, then deep-seated enmity, finally reaching the point of their refusing to speak with one another. While there remained mutual if distant respect, by the end there was no love lost between these two 'partners.'

The doomed pact in the founding agreement was that Nemirovich-Danchenko would be in charge of all literary matters – choice of plays, protecting the intent and words of the playwright, educating the acting company in the meaning and genre of each new play, and sharing in the overall selection of company actors and appropriate casting of roles.

Stanislavsky was in charge of production: design elements, the course of rehearsals, and most importantly, the work with the actor. Although he directed frequently – barring illnesses or absence he often staged several productions a year up to 1928 – Stanislavsky says little about the director's tasks. As a born performer, regularly starring in his own productions, his concentration was primarily on the process and performance of the actor. Over time, the text became a kind of pretext which offered Stanislavsky the director opportunities to explore the inner springs of acting; much to the disgruntlement of company actors, rehearsals became System lab sessions.

The acrimony between the two founders festered over the years to the point where in the end they communicated through written messages, some of them reportedly hand-delivered by courier Maria Knebel. In one of her books, she wrote: "in my own pedagogical and creative work all my life I have been 'unraveling' how the views of Stanislavsky and Nemirovich-Danchenko combine, what a mighty synthesis they form"[15] (*To Me* 137). There was a lot to unravel. She was able to synthesize wisdom from both, as she developed her own process, Analysis through Action.

Mentor Three: V.I. Nemirovich-Danchenko

In an interview with Moscow Art Theatre longtime house historian Inna Soloviova, she described Vladimir Ivanovich Nemirovich-Danchenko to me as "an average genius."[16] He was of Georgian noble birth, a literary scholar, a critic, a novelist, and a mediocre playwright. While he had taught acting in the drama division of the Moscow Philharmonic Society – Meyerhold and other future luminaries of the Art Theatre studied with him – his interest was predominantly in how the actor could best comprehend and fulfill the artistic intent and literary design of the author. But over time, Nemirovich-Danchenko adopted and adapted many acting techniques from his Art Theatre co-founder. Stanislavsky certainly did likewise; certain techniques attributed to Stanislavsky initially came from his partner.

In rehearsal Nemirovich-Danchenko rigorously protected the exact text of the author as the nucleus, the central determinant of the actor's work. To him, wandering off into speculative Études was meaningless, even destructive; instead, Nemirovich-Danchenko ordered that the actors learn their lines prior to rehearsal. Fealty to the text – in its macro structure and its micro intricacy – was the basis of all rehearsal choices. (He suspiciously tracked the lines of Mikhail Chekov's highly improvisational star performance as Khlestakov in the 1921 *The Government Inspector* and was shocked to discover that this way-above-average-genius was word perfect.)

Nemirovich-Danchenko was a champion of the 'director's plan,' a detailed prepared kind of novella, with character interiority, mood, and specific movement ideas to be implemented in rehearsal, albeit always in his gentle and accessible manner (see *Novel of Life III* in Part II of this book). The Art Theatre actors, duly impressed with Nemirovich-Danchenko's compelling intellectual acumen, his protracted preparation, and his calm demeanor, preferred working with their average genius Danchenko to enduring their rambunctious, inconsistent, irascible, experimenting genius Stanislavsky.

Below are four fundamental postulates of Nemirovich-Danchenko's (where certainly echoes of Stanislavsky can be heard). Maria Knebel later incorporated these priorities into her own directorial work and teaching of Analysis through Action.

A Definition of the Director:

Knebel quotes Nemirovich-Danchenko's postulate: the director is 'a three-faced creature':

The director as thinker, actor and pedagogue, helping the performer to create his role;
The director as a mirror that reflects the individual qualities of the actor;
The director as the organizer of the whole production.[17]

A corollary to the first two tenets is that 'the director dies in the actor,'[18] meaning that the audience sees *only* the actor, who has fully ingested and embodied what he was taught by the director. In the second postulate, "the director can become that polished mirror that reflects any slightest movement of the actor's soul, any noticeable mistake."[19]

The Second Plan:

[T]he inner spiritual 'luggage' or baggage of the character/actor which they come into the play with. It consists of all the character's life experiences, from all the circumstances of their personal fate and embraces all the shades of their feelings and perceptions, thoughts and feelings.[20]

We will develop this idea (in film jargon 'backstory') as a central component in the Reconnaissance of the Mind section of this book (see *Novel of Life II*).

Inner Monologue:

While one is silent, one [internally] discusses, argues, tries to convince oneself or someone else. Currents of thoughts flash like lightning through the mind…If we turn to literature we see that great writers, masters of the psychological portrait, lead us continually into the hero's innermost secret thoughts, which prompt him to decide, to evaluate, to act.[21]

The Word:

Knebel quotes Nemirovich-Danchenko:

The word is the summit of creativity. It must also be the source of all the work, physical and psychological…The actor's work will affect the audience only if molded into the author's magnificently written phrase…The content of a phrase is the source of all your experience; its subtle meaning is the stimulus which sends a thought to the nerves.[22]

Mentor Four: Konstantin Stanislavsky

In her book *About What I Consider Especially Important*, Maria Knebel writes:

Stanislavsky's system was formed at a time when all sorts of currents collided in the arts. Meyerhold, Tairov…New, revolutionary forms. Stanislavsky was considered obsolete. [But] I consider myself lucky – my life has been spent next to Stanislavsky…I was one of the people into whom he placed the fire of his heart: I became one of his pupils. I saw him laughing, angry, demanding, affectionate, justified, intolerant, stubborn, patient, confident, doubting, sad, cheerful, and tired.[23]

As we shall see in the second part of this chapter, Stanislavsky's impact on Knebel and Analysis through Action is immeasurable. While she generously gives due credit to her other genius mentors – her father, Mikhail Chekhov, and V.I. Nemirovich-Danchenko – Konstantin Stanislavsky is granted principal focus in her writing. All six of her books, including the two-hundred-page study of Nemirovich-Danchenko's school of directing, make innumerable references to Stanislavsky. Part of this is probably politically deliberate – certainly she was trying to keep his faith in humanity alive in dire times – but her indebtedness to Stanislavsky unquestionably makes him the central focal character of her memoirs and theories.

In the 1920s, acting in small roles for Stanislavsky or simply observing rehearsals, she felt in awe of him, even when at one point he removed her from a cameo role for pandering to the audience – and for being recruited by

Meyerhold. After a lengthy discussion, in which she vowed not to join Meyerhold's' troupe, she was reinstated in the role. This episode during years of observing his Art Theatre rehearsals brought her to a deeper understanding of Stanislavsky's process and principles.

But she recalls her confusion upon first encountering his 'new approach' at the Opera-Dramatic Studio. In a brief 1952 essay – where her first published use of the term Analysis through Action appeared – she wrote about working with Stanislavsky in the mid and late 1930s:

> When I first became acquainted with this method in 1935 it all seemed so new and unexpected that I thought Stanislavski had eliminated everything that he himself had known and established; Then, as the years passed, I came to understand. He did not eliminate, he did not reject; he summarized and synthesized, the new method absorbs everything discovered by him before, his whole life and his whole previous work.[24]

As was Boris Zon, Maria Knebel was initially bewildered by what Stanislavsky was up to in the mid-1930s. At the acting school of the Second Studio they had resolutely drilled the Elements of the System into her and marched her through Stanislavsky's demanding text analysis work. As a young 'second order' Art Theatre actor in the 1920s she had witnessed the perpetual table discussions attempting to identify and pierce the psychological 'inner life' of characters. She had admired the tremendous advance preparation of both Stanislavsky and Nemirovich-Danchenko, including the latter's meticulous directorial plans, explication of the text, and his 'pedagogy' to the actor.

But at the Opera-Dramatic Studio, Knebel struggled with Stanislavsky's 'new approach.' Where was the text? Where was the director's plan? She now observed collective inquiry rather than direct pedagogy. When asked a question by an actor, Stanislavsky would reply in effect: 'I don't know. Let's find out.' The way of finding out would be through physical action Études, not by verbal discussion at a table.

Emphatically, her time with Mikhail Chekhov had exposed Maria to the power of improvisation and Études. And while KS's 'new approach' was still being fully defined, she saw promising and exciting results of student Étude work at the ODS. But in 1938, Stanislavsky died, leaving two of his books and the work at the last studio unfinished. Knebel mourned the unfinished business of the ODS, and the loss of the students' work on plays by Shakespeare and Chekhov:

> [I]f fate had given Konstantin Sergeevich a few more years of life, we would have witnessed a grand pedagogical experiment. The young students, free of habits, were mastering Stanislavsky's most difficult ideas, and an art that was completely new in its freshness and vitality was being born, and the great classical works were taking on a completely unfamiliar, astonishingly stirring sound.[25]

But vexing problems remained unsolved.

> What conditions awaken an actor's action, stir his whole spiritual and physical being, keep his inner world from becoming stagnant and stale?…And another matter: How to avoid the dichotomy of mind and body? How to unite them immediately during the first stages of work?[26]

It was from these unfulfilled inquiries, which touch the very root of the actor's organism, that Knebel dedicated herself to formulating in Analysis through Action.

Exiled from the Art Theatre

When Vladimir Ivanovich Nemirovich-Danchenko died in 1943, Maria Knebel lost her guardian at the Art Theatre. Her status became unstable, although from 1943 to 1948, she co-directed three productions at the Art Theatre (one entitled *Kremlin Chimes*) as well as taught at the Art Theatre school. Her ideas and strategies about what became Analysis through Action, initiated in her work at small theatres in the late 1930s, had just begun to coalesce at the Art Theatre, in their school and in productions at outside theatres.

But by 1949, Michael Kedrov had accumulated numerous Communist Party awards and positions, and more importantly had attained the artistic director-ship of the Art Theatre. He declared that his Method of Physical Actions would be the house process for all productions and the exclusive training method of the school. In June of 1949, just prior to leaving for a summer va-cation, Maria Knebel was summoned to a meeting with the Committee on the Arts, where she was told by Kedrov that she was a pupil of Nemirovich-Danchenko and only Kedrov's students could now work at the Art Theatre.

On her return to the MAT in the fall no one said anything to her; she hoped that maybe the storm had passed. But she soon was officially informed that she would no longer be considered as a director in the Art Theatre and would be paid only for her infrequent appearances as an actor in the repertoire. By her own choice, she departed her longtime artistic home after a final performance as Charlotta in *The Cherry Orchard*, the role she would always be remembered for.

Of course, there are reasons beyond institutional jealousy that account for this cruel termination. Certainly, Maria Osipovna Knebel's Semitic heritage was unspoken but active in the Art Theatre's decision – meaning Kedrov's. And, if we are to trust Knebel biographer Gérard Abénsour, Maria's rejection of Kedrov's romantic advances in 1922 may well have played a role. More im-portantly, there was clearly a conflict of artistic methodologies and belief in what theatre should stand for.

Fortunately, Maria had options. A dear colleague, prominent director Alexei Popov, had engaged her as an assistant in his directing course at GITIS; she also had offers to direct in small Moscow theatres. Then in 1950, at age 52 she was given her own course at GITIS and appointed a resident director at the

Central Children's Theatre, just around the corner from the Art Theatre. She advanced to become sole artistic director there in 1955. It was these two institutions – GITIS and the Central Children's Theatre – that became *her* research laboratories as Maria Knebel refined and proselytized Analysis through Action.

A Digest of Maria Knebel's Analysis through Action

While Maria Knebel disseminated Analysis through Action in rehearsals and lesson plans, in her six books, and in several articles, there is only one publication where she comprehensively explains the process. This is a chapter entitled "About Analysis through Action of the Play and the Role" in her 1971 volume, the title of which translates as *To Me What Seems Especially Important*. What follows is a selective digest drawn from those pages. The many direct quotations – her explanations are better than my attempts to encapsulate them – are taken from pages 43–113 of the book, in my translation. The topic headings are mine as well.

The Opening Definition

Knebel begins her seventy-page chapter with the definition of Analysis through Action cited in the Introduction of this book:

> We shall talk about the rehearsal technique proposed by Stanislavsky, the so-called analysis through action of the play and the role. The essence of this technique, if you put it in a nutshell, is that at an early stage of work, the play chosen for staging is not rehearsed, as usual, at the table, but after a certain preliminary analysis is analyzed in action through études with improvised text. These études serve as steps leading the actor to the creative assimilation of the text of the play, that is, to the author's word as the main means of stage imagery.[27]

Knebel does not specifically define 'Études' here or anywhere in the chapter. But we can take the word 'action' in this case to mean onstage physical/verbal action, through Études – 'studies' – with improvised dialogue replacing the words of the author.

Stanislavsky: To the Table or Not to the Table

Knebel describes the 'table rehearsal' stratagem Stanislavsky (and Nemirovich-Danchenko) developed at the Art Theatre. Often at great length these sessions preceded "stage rehearsals of the play by painstakingly analyzing it at table rehearsals, where all internal motives, subtext, relationships, characters, throughline-action and supertask of the work, in short, the entire ideological and artistic structure were thoroughly analyzed."[28]

This arduous technique was first created by Stanislavsky to facilitate his life-long "'red thread'" dream of a conscious actor, an actor-creator who can independently comprehend a work."[29] But later in his directorial life, Stanislavsky became dismayed with "how the actor in his [Stanislavsky's] hands was becoming malleable, like clay…How inertia can arise in the actor; how easily he becomes accustomed to the thought that the director will decide everything for him."[30]

Knebel points out that the director is typically much more prepared than the actor. "He is, naturally, ahead of the team." Therefore, the director rushes ahead, "imposing his own vision on the performers, frustrating their creative independence."[31] The actor is thus confronted by "a multitude of diverse, broad, but at first unnecessary information, while he eagerly looks for his own special path that would lead him to that mysterious stranger whose words are printed in the [text]."[32]

Knebel then addresses a second concern of Stanislavsky's with his self-created table rehearsal process which leads to an: "artificial unnatural gap between the mental and physical aspects"[33] of the actor's approach to the role, leading to understanding only the psychology of the character long before departing the table to explore the 'life of the human body.'

> With the old rehearsal system, when many hours were devoted to the speculative analysis of the play and the role, talk about the acting, reasoning "what he is like", the actor got used to seeing the character as separate from himself, outside himself, unintentionally thinking about him as "he" rather than "I", thus the actual transition to merging with the role gave him great difficulty. Removing this gap, Stanislavsky clearly formulated the law of the psychophysical unity of the actor's creative process.[34]

Knebel then reviews Stanislavsky's directorial processes, at first as a self-proclaimed "dictator" staging his deferential actors from his pre-determined director's books, such as the 1898 *Seagull* director's score plus twenty-four more up to 1909; then to mutual actor/director table discussions in search of the psychology of the characters; then to the "physical behavior of the characters. Gradually, he concluded that the two sides of the formation of a role [psychology and physical behavior] must be joined not only in the process of the role, but also in the process of analysis."

Yet another concern troubled Stanislavsky. Table work inevitably involved repetitive readings of the author's text; thus

> the word, not yet supported by internal impulses, not connected with the full life of a person on the stage, is already mechanically in the memory of the actor, and falls on the 'muscle of the tongue,' as Stanislavsky loved to say…Moreover, a memorized word often functions for the actor as a sort of screen, under the cover of which one cannot think, feel, act, or exist.[35]

Stanislavsky, Knebel writes, determined that rehearsing with the actual words of the text "before the huge realm of external and internal motives that give rise to that text has been mastered,"[36] was counterproductive. Consequently, he rejected his past approaches and instituted "the new order in which the play is analyzed in action, in an étude with improvised text."[37]

Next, Knebel insists that the "legend of the so-called elimination of the table period" is erroneous. With the "etude method" she asserts that "'working at the table' is retained…but acts in a different capacity…[The play] is recurrently comprehended at the table." This means that the play is no longer analyzed psychologically, role by role; instead, the entire company participates in a preliminary analysis of the play itself, accomplished at the table.

Knebel begins her conclusion of her first section with a summary:

> The significance of the new technique is that it destroys the wall between analysis and embodiment, which is artificially erected under the old rehearsal system…Analysis through Action is organic and therefore the shortest way to embodiment – this is, from my point of view, one of the strongest aspects of the method.[38]

Knebel then analyzes the components of this binary rehearsal approach, first discussing Études. She recounts that both Stanislavsky and Nemirovich had used improvisations for years: "Études were made on the past of the role, études were made on the themes of events, about events between acts."[39] For Stanislavsky these would be useful for the 'Line of the Role,' and for Nemirovich-Danchenko's 'Second Plan.'

But in his later years, Stanislavsky introduced the idea of making Études on specific situations in the play – scenes or 'Bits' from the text – as part of the actor's process of analysis. Thus, the actor "almost immediately puts himself in the living conditions of the character…replacing the author's text with his own words for the time being, retaining loyalty to the development of the author's thought."[40]

Reconnaissance of the Mind

To learn that 'development of the author's thoughts,' the actor must first engage in what Stanislavsky called Reconnaissance of the Mind, learning the basic content of the play, that which Knebel refers to in her introductory comment as 'a certain preliminary analysis.' Reconnaissance of the Mind at this early stage is focused on the company determining the Supertask of the Play, and the actor the Supertask of their Role. But, Knebel insists, the actor must learn the *play* before learning the role; then the role's Supertask will be easier to identify. This procedure asks the actor to understand their actions through the play, step by step, in order to perceive their Throughline Action. To do that the actor must examine each Event they participate in and ask: what would

I do if such and such happened to me? Formerly this was 'what do I want'; now it is 'what would I *do.*' Knebel explains this vital distinction:

> There is an essential difference between 'I want' and 'I do'…'I want' – has an element of passivity, but 'I do' means there is activity, dynamism, a concrete element…Together with the question: 'What do I do now?' – the actor should ask the question: 'Why am I doing this?' Only then will he be able to penetrate the complicated world of the character's soul, capture the whole multifaceted character of the 'life of the human spirit' in the role.[41]

Knebel, following Stanislavsky, insists that the actor's Supertask must vibrantly excite the actor; it must feel personally intimate to the actor, something that is faithful to the play but arouses this particular actor's Action and Imagination through Emotional Memory. The plan of this early-stage Reconnaissance of the Mind is for the actor to pursue their unique Supertask by examining Events.

Events

Maria Knebel proclaims that "Event analysis is the most important concept in the system."[42] Again, she does not give a specific definition of an Event. For now, we can borrow Stanislavsky's idea of an Event being an 'action-fact' – something that *happens* in the play, a unit of action – and additionally something that happens before the play, between acts, or offstage.

Readers will recall that it was for tutelage in Events that Maria Knebel approached Stanislavsky at the Opera-Dramatic Studio. He surprised her by naming as the most important Event something that happened before the play begins: a gunshot. This we can call – per a disciple of Knebel's pedagogy Alexander Polamishev – the Initial Event. This is the Event that takes place "outside the borders of the play" – here meaning before the actual play begins – that affects everyone in the play and sets off a 'Chain of Events' that is the Throughline Action of the play. Knebel clarifies with some examples of Initial Events:

> *Hamlet*: the death of the king.
> *Twelfth Night*: the shipwreck that casts Viola into Illyria.
> *Uncle Vanya*: the arrival of Serebriakov and his lovely wife at the Voinitsky estate.[43]

The actor, Knebel notes, must be curious about key Events concerning their character that happen before the onstage action of the play, 'Second Plan' Events that deeply influenced or even formed their character. For example, in *The Cherry Orchard*, the then-adolescent serf Lopakhin, whose father had just beaten him bloody, was taken into the manor house and nursed by the divine young aristocrat Liubov; Orgon was awestruck by Tartuffe's fervent prayers in church. Knebel makes clear that these 'outside the borders of the play' Events–meaning the Initial Event that occurs prior of the play or Events between acts or offstage – are not an idle literary interest; they are crucial components of the life of the play and of a character's life.

The Chain of Events and the Two Supertasks

Knebel's workplan for the actor starts with the analysis of the Events of their role which will lead to a preliminary sense of the Supertask of The Role. "These events, or, as Konstantin Sergeevich called them, the active-facts, are the skeleton of the work, the spine on which the writer built his play."

Knebel quotes Stanislavsky on the question of evaluation (aka assessment) of Events:

> This means mining below the external facts and events, to find there, in the depths, beneath them, another, more important, deeply hidden spiritual event that may have given rise to an external fact…In a word, assessing the facts means recognizing (feeling) the internal scheme of the life of a person's soul. Assessing the facts means making some other person's facts, events, the entire life created by the author, your own. Assessing the facts means finding the key to unraveling the secrets of the personal spiritual life of the person portrayed, hidden beneath the facts and text of the play.[44]

Again, citing Stanislavsky, Knebel recommends that at the end of their reconnaissance on their character, each actor must tell the others their 'Line of the Role' – the sequence of Events and Actions from start to the finish (but perhaps more succinctly than Rozanova's ODS Hamlet recitation in Chapter 2). Doing this, the actor's attention is focused not on what the character says, but on how he acts, what he achieves, for what reason(s) he does this or that action.

> Since each of the participants does this, and all the others are present, correcting, arguing, prompting, then already in the course of Reconnaissance of the Mind the whole team will have a clear knowledge of the actual material of the play.[45]

These individual accounts of Actions and motives Found through Events lead to a shared analysis of the play – and most importantly, culminate with a collective definition of the Supertask of the Play and the Roles. This is the premise and promise of Knebel's communal Reconnaissance of the Mind procedure.

To review: the process Knebel recommends is 1. Each actor undertakes independent analysis of their role's Events and Actions; 2. One by one, the results of those analyses are shared with the group; 3. The team then collectively deduces the Supertask of the Play. In practice, analyzing the Events and Actions of each character in consort will reveal analogous Supertasks of the

Roles; analysis of that aggregation of will reveal the overall Supertask of the Play.

If this sounds like a lengthy amount of discussion spent at the table, Knebel asserts that there is no need to think that this first step of Reconnaissance of the Mind – studying Events to ultimately reveal the Supertasks of the Role and the Play – eats up rehearsal time:

> No need to think that the cognitive part of the work on the play, its anal-ysis during the period of "reconnaissance of the mind" takes a lot of re-hearsal time. From the very first meeting, the participants of the future performance receive in their hands "Ariadne's thread" – penetration into the play through events, actions, deeds – and this immediately puts the work on a concrete basis. Of course, everything depends on the degree of complexity of the play, on the wealth of its internal steps. But in all cases, the actors do not have to wander around and around the play, wasting energy and talking "in general" about the play, about the roles.[46]

In short, these discussions have one sole focus: defining Events in search of the Supertasks of the roles and the play. Staying focused exclusively on those pur-suits presumably keeps the work moving forward judiciously. The actors should do their Event analysis on their own, and not hijack the table doing their anal-ysis in front of their peers. (Also the director has previously done all this work and can curtail the prolixity of the deliberations.)

Now the actor "knows the main events of the whole play, knows the lifetime purpose and Supertask of the character."[47] This is the 'certain preliminary analysis' referred to above that leads to 'études with improvised text.'

Études

Now the company circles back to the beginning of the play. "To begin with, we take a passage – and it is with this that the actor goes to the stage to do a étude." And, Knebel points out, "the very first étude rehearsal confronts the actor with all the details of the physical life of the scene,"[48] the immediate ex-ternal Given Circumstances.

> [Is it] Summer or winter, cold or hot? What time of the day? How and what are the characters wearing? Where did they come from, what do they have in their hands, are they tired or, on the contrary, are they full of vigor and strength? How does the actor behave...?[49]

The actor, Knebel continues:

> immediately has a complex perception of what is happening, and his in-ternal psychological sensations become inseparable from the physical, material sensations...It is impossible to imagine what an invaluable

service this étude provides to the actor, how easy it is, how imperceptibly he comprehends in an étude what he tried so hard to attain at the table.[50]

Having concluded this first Étude – meaning the probe of the selected passage with improvised physical actions and dialogue – the actor now returns to the table

> heated, exhilarated with the just-rehearsed analysis experience...the text is immediately read again...The post-étude transition to the table and the reference to the text of the author enable the actor to check himself, to understand both his mistakes and his correct movements in the role...and the actor has a desire to go onstage and rehearse again.[51]

Knebel notes that during this period of Études followed by reviewing the actual text, the actors' questions now come "from the inside," expanding and penetrating deeper into the given circumstances of the play, into their relationships, and into the logic and actions of their particular character. It is with "tremendous creative joy that the actor perceives the text of the author, if he did the étude correctly" – meaning successfully conveyed the author's thoughts through their improvised words and actions.

Knebel recommends moving along to the next Event at time the "actors come close to the text and the content of the scene becomes clear in the étude...No fixation [freezing] and polishing of études is necessary." She also warns of the danger if the actor's own words become habitual, a faux 'text,' which ossifies the life of the actor and prevents further movement toward the actual words of the author.

The Étude should prepare the actor for "perceptions of the author's vocabulary forcing him into a deeper understanding of all the internal steps" of the author's text.

The Advantages of Analysis through Action

Knebel lists numerous reasons why she believes Stanislavsky worked "so hard to implement this method:"

Analysis through Action "dramatically increases the responsibility of the actor, develops the creative activity of all participants in the production;"[52]

The actor should respond to Reconnaissance of the Mind; otherwise they "will not understand all the richness of motives, all the consequences, all the turns of action;"[53]

Thus, the actor "will not be able to organically act in the étude...will not be able to improvise in the étude, will not be able to participate in the general work, will fail his comrades, will spoil the étude;[54] the actor "has no text which can hide his helplessness—he must create for himself his own text;"[55] [This presumably also refers to hiding behind a printed script, incognizant of or your partner.]

"The actor in the étude cannot help but be concentrated. The étude is full of surprises for the participants themselves: you can never predict in advance what will come from a partner, how the conversation will develop";[56] "The actor in the étude does not wait for another cue from a partner: he immediately grasps a new-born thought."[57]

Knebel then expounds on what she believes to be the unseen benefits of Études:

> Throughout analysis through action, in the subconscious of the actor a consoling thought resides: 'We are still only doing a étude!' The actor firmly knows that the étude is only a path from himself to the character. This awareness makes him bold. A mistake in an étude is not terrible. An étude is a trial, a search, a test, it is a step to creating a role; the étude is a rough draft (which exists so that there are no blank spots in the work of the actor, in the performance no empty or inexpressive places). In the étude nothing is absolutely fixed, nothing is done once and for all.
>
> This consciousness – 'we are still only doing a étude!' – removes psychological handcuffs from the actors; the actors feel liberated. The collective willingly experiments; easily relinquishes what they just discovered if a better new idea arrives; their imagination works actively, sharply; they develop an improvisational feeling not only for the period of étude rehearsals, but, most importantly, for the entire period of work on the play and the performances. It often happens that in the later stages, the actors will argue and not unite on some point, and then surely someone will say: "So, let's do a étude!" And they go on stage and check out an unclear episode, easily moving back to improvisation at a time when everyone already firmly knows the author's text.[58]

Knebel then concentrates on Analysis through Action's liberation of the individuality of the actor: "During the étude work…the actor quickly accumulates a personal, concrete experience of the role of the given circumstances, taking on the actions of the character, thinking his thoughts, plunging into the nature of his feelings."[59] The actor is continually forced to "answer the question: 'What am I doing in this episode?'"

But the Étude also necessarily makes demands on the actor to creatively examine and re-shape their own 'I.' An Étude will often reveal a gap between the life of the character and the life of the actor. The actor must then relinquish a personal pathology which does not align with the character and use their imagination and affective memory to evolve into another "I."

Knebel then moves to elucidate one aspect of character embodiment that is close to her heart: verbal expression:

> The actor needs to master the text of the play not formally, but through all the richness of the inner content that is inherent in it. Études pursue

this goal – to bring the actor to the form of expression of thought, which is given by the author. This means that this form itself needs to be studied, since it is necessary to find out why the author needed to write this way, this way and in no other way.[60]

After a lengthy discourse on the topic of the author's language, style, and genre, Knebel returns to cataloging the benefits and advantages of Analysis through Action. Along with Études providing a path to exploration of a character's Second Plan, the formative Events and hidden secrets [of the character], Études also "are impossible without internal monologues."[61] The same can be said of Stanislavsky's film of visions – the images, often based on emotional memories – that are the subjective 'documentary' of the actor/role's life.

Knebel again maintains that this technique "not only does not draw out, but, on the contrary, sharply reduces"[62] rehearsal time. This was proven to her in various professional production of hers which "showed that we would not have been able to produce performances at exactly the appointed time if I hadn't been able to bring to the collective analysis through action."

Reaching the Precise Text of the Author

This issue, crucial to many – certainly to Knebel, the ODS instructor of 'verbal action' – confounds systematic implementation. She writes: "For Stanislavsky, the question of the transition to rehearsals with the exact text continued to be experimental until the last day: he did not give us exact instructions on this matter. This question still remains experimental today."[63]

Knebel has no concrete recommendations, other than to avoid a hard-and-fast bright line, a due date, between the Étude period and total fidelity to the precise words of the author. She observes that the transition to "rehearsals with the exact text usually takes place gradually." The actor studies the play deeply during the Reconnaissance of the Mind period (Events, Supertasks); during post-étude analyses; then reads and re-reads the text on their own, searching for a deeper understanding of the given circumstances and the inner world of their character. "Thus, the actor learns the role, learns it imperceptibly, without stress, without forcing it."[64]

> When an actor comes to the author's word in such a complicated, so deep a way, through all the wealth of internal movements, [the author's text] easily fits in his memory, in his mind, because now there is a whole series of associations, sensations, emotions…he will inevitably come to the conviction that nothing expresses so well a given situation, a given thought, as the genuine text of the author.[65]

In the 'Études' section in Part II of this book, the question of attaining fidelity to the author's word (if that is what is desired) will be further addressed.

Analysis through Action versus The Method of Physical Actions

Knebel finishes her seventy-page chapter with a four-page consideration of her method versus Kedrov's – although she is careful never to mention his name or theatre.

Knebel begins by clarifying the term 'physical actions' itself, stating that what their mutual teacher Stanislavsky absolutely meant was *psycho*physical actions, signifying that concealed inside a 'correct' physical action, there had to be an "internal aspiration…an unbreakable connection between 'the life of the human body' and 'the life of the human spirit.'"[66] Physical action Études might be deployed to find that 'inner urge,' but every truthful physical action must be *psycho*physical.

She continues, clarifying that Stanislavsky used the term 'physical actions' on "two levels with two dissimilar functions, [related] to two different stages of the creative process." Knebel defines the first level as an early rehearsal device:

> When Konstantin Sergeevich speaks about the initial stage of preparing a production, about the study and analysis of the play, he uses the term "physical actions" to mean actions which are physically carried out and actually realized in the course of analyzing a work. I, the actor, physically exist in the play, in a specific episode of it. I put myself physically in the place of the person-character, "I exist" in the situation proposed by the author – this is what, from our point of view, Stanislavsky understood by the term "physical actions" for a given rehearsal period.[67]

She concludes:

> At first…actions carried out physically open the little door into the realm of the unconscious. But later, when the actor has already created the role and mastered it, when the production is ready, or the work on it is near completion, physical actions begin to serve another purpose, to become, as Stanislavsky said, 'a lure' for feelings, a kind of creative storage cell.[68]

Executing a physical action 'correctly' will trigger the psyche and thereby produce a psychophysical action.

As we have seen, Stanislavsky recommended a pathway he called a "very simple line of physical and elementary psychological tasks and actions"[69] as a road map for the actor's journey through the play. This line consisted of a sequence of simple physical actions, animated by sense and emotional memories, as milestones; these became the 'lures' that flush out *feelings* as a hunter uses lures to flush out a bird from undergrowth in the forest; these physical actions are a pathway built of creative storage cells.

Knebel concludes with her quiet but pointed censure of The Method of Physical Actions quoted here in full:

But between the actions physically performed during the initial analysis of a role, and the plan of the simplest tasks, according to which the actor enters the role already prepared, there are significant differences that cannot be forgotten. When this is forgotten, it turns out, for example, that, "according to Stanislavsky", one can go on stage and, by performing only physical actions, make a role without studying the play, without design, without subordinating the author's idea. And that through the "human life of the body" miraculously, by itself, the "life of the human spirit" of the role will appear.

But, in fact, according to Stanislavsky, physical actions can only serve as storage cells for feelings because they were once loaded with this feeling, that they were created in the closest connection with psychology, the character, the inner world of the role and they expressed all of this.

The experience of my own work has proved conclusively to me the enormous creative impulse which lies in the method of analysis through action.[70]

Given the experiences of my own work in classrooms and rehearsal halls, the author of this book enthusiastically agrees.

Notes

1 See Sharon Carnicke *Dynamic Acting through Active Analysis: Konstantin Stanislavsky, Maria Knebel, and Their Legacy*, Methuen Drama, 2023; and Thomas, James, and M. Knebel. *A Director's Guide to Stanislavsky's Active Analysis: Including the Formative Essay on Active Analysis by Maria Knebel.* London: New York: Bloomsbury Methuen Drama, 2016.
2 М Кнебель, 1967. *Вся Жизнь*. Moskva: Всероссииское театральное общество; M Knebel, 1967. *A Whole Life*. Moscow: All-Russian Theatrical Society, 36.
3 Knebel *Whole Life* 53.
4 Knebel *Whole Life* 59.
5 Кнебель, Мария в *Михаил Чехов: литературное наследие: в двух томах*, Искусство, Moskva, 1986 Т.1; Knebel, Maria in *Mikhail Chekhov: Literary Heritage: in two volumes*, Art, Moscow, 1986 v.1 27.
6 Knebel *Whole Life* 59.
7 Knebel *Heritage* v.2 8.
8 Knebel *Heritage* v.2 16.
9 Knebel *Whole Life* 75.
10 Knebel *Whole Life* 92.
11 Knebel *Whole Life* 62.
12 Knebel *Whole Life* 92.
13 Michael Chekhov and M Knebel'. 1986. *Михаил Чехов: Литературное Наследие: В Двух Томах*. Moskva: "Искусство"; Michael Chekhov and M Knebel'. 1986. *Mikhail Chekhov: Literary Heritage: In Two Volumes*. Moskva: "Art."
14 Abénsour, Gérard *Maria Knebel: Uma Vida Para O Teatro No Tempo De Stanislávski e Stálin*, Editoria Perspectiva, São Paolo, 2019; Abénsour, Gerard *Maria Knebel: A Life for the Theater in the Time of Stanislavsky and Stalin*, Editoria Perspectiva, São Paola, 2019 43.

15 Knebel' M. 1971. *О Том Что Мне Кажется Особенно Важным: Стаьи Очерки Портреты.* Moskva: "Iskusstvo" 137; *On What Seems Especially Important to Me: Articles Essays Portraits.* Moscow: Art 137.
16 Author interview, July 11, 2013.
17 Кнебель М. 1959. *О Действенном Анализе Пьесы И Роли. В Помощь Коллективам Театральной Самодеятельности.* Moskva: Искусствоь. *On the Effective Analysis of the Play and the Role.* In Assistance to the Collectives of Theatrical Amateur Activity. Moscow: Art Translation Ilya Khodosh 8.
18 Knebel *Whole Life* 369.
19 Knebel *Play and Role* 9.
20 Knebel *To Me* 192.
21 Knebel, Maria, "The Nemirovich-Danchenko School of Directing" in Moore, Sonia, ed. 1973. *Stanislavski Today: Commentaries on K.S. Stanislavski.* New York: American Center for Stanislavski Theatre Art Translation Moore 52.
22 Knebel, in Moore *Stanislavski Today* 51 from В И Vladimir I Nemirovich-Danchenko and I. N Solov'ev. 2003. *Театральное Наследие В Четырех Томах.* Moskva: "Moskovskiĭ khudozhestvennyĭ teatr" T.1; Vladimir I Nemirovich-Danchenko and I. N Solov'ev. 2003. *Theatrical Heritage in Four Volumes.* Moscow: Moscow Art Theatre v. 1 213.
23 Knebel *To Me* 19.
24 Knebel, Maria "Superior Simplicity" in Moore *Stanislavski Today* 45.
25 Knebel *To Me* 41.
26 Knebel "Superior Simplicity" in Moore *Stanislavski Today* 46.
27 Knebel *To Me* 44–45.
28 Knebel *To Me* 45.
29 Knebel *To Me* 45.
30 Knebel *To Me* 46.
31 Knebel *To Me* 46.
32 Knebel *To Me* 47.
33 Knebel *To Me* 49.
34 Knebel *To Me* 50.
35 Knebel *To Me* 51.
36 Knebel *To Me* 52.
37 Knebel *To Me* 52.
38 Knebel *To Me* 53.
39 Knebel *To Me* 53.
40 Knebel *To Me* 54.
41 Knebel *To Me* 57.
42 Knebel *To Me* 59.
43 Knebel *To Me* 59–60.
44 Knebel *To Me* 62.
45 Knebel *To Me* 63.
46 Knebel *To Me* 63.
47 Knebel *To Me* 64.
48 Knebel *To Me* 66.
49 Knebel *To Me* 66.
50 Knebel *To Me* 66–67.
51 Knebel *To Me* 70.
52 Knebel *To Me* 83.
53 Knebel *To Me* 83.
54 Knebel *To Me* 83.
55 Knebel *To Me* 83.
56 Knebel *To Me* 83.

57 Knebel *To Me* 84.
58 Knebel *To Me* 84.
59 Knebel *To Me* 84.
60 Knebel *To Me* 91.
61 Knebel *To Me* 92.
62 Knebel *To Me* 95.
63 Knebel *To Me* 105.
64 Knebel *To Me* 109.
65 Knebel *To Me* 106.
66 Knebel *To Me* 109.
67 Knebel *To Me* 110.
68 Knebel *to Me* 109.
69 Knebel *To Me* 112.
70 Knebel *To Me* 113.

4 Georgii Tovstonogov

A Voluntary Dictatorship

Introduction

> "I am inedible! Remember that: Inedible!"

Thus declaimed Georgii (geh-ORG-ee) Alexandrovich Tovstonogov to the stunned acting company on his inaugural day as chief director of Leningrad's Bolshoi Drama Theatre (BDT).[1] From his appointment in 1956 to his death in 1989, Tovstonogov directed 80 BDT productions (out of 140 lifetime), salvaging the company from public apathy and internal chaos – in the previous five years, four directors had been "eaten alive" – to acclamation as one of the best acting troupes in the world, while enjoying enormous popular and governmental favor at home. He was regularly rewarded with Soviet state prizes, including the Lenin Prize, the Stalin Prize, and the Hero of Soviet Labor prize.

On Tovstonogov's first day in February 1956, the Bolshoi Drama Theatre was on the brink of implosion. Backstabbing, duplicity, and deception were the house instruments of governance – for those who bothered to show up. Performances by the disaffected actors were anesthetic, the audience sparse; on some nights there were more people onstage than in the audience. In a local cabaret skit, court-martialed soldiers were given a choice: go to the brig or attend a performance at the Bolshoi Drama Theatre. They all chose the brig.[2]

When Georgii Tovstonogov was first approached about accepting the position of chief director at BDT, he had no reason to be interested. He was secure in his fiefdom at the Leningrad Komsomol theatre, where as chief director he staged numerous plays, many sympathetic to the Soviet cause; Lenin and Stalin were recurrently hailed and sometimes appeared as characters onstage. He had a sinecure, money, a family, his Party red star was on the rise; why walk into the mouth of hell?

But local government promises to fully support an extreme overhaul of the Bolshoi, evidenced by the city council's appointment of a pitiless managing director ordered to execute a purge, dissolved Tovstonogov's resistance. He left his fiefdom to build an empire.

DOI: 10.4324/9781003475576-6

In his first days, he fired thirty of the BDT's ninety actors; most others were told they could remain but not to imagine playing significant roles. He brought in a new literary and artistic staff, completely eradicating the old lot. In the fall of his first season, he put up four frivolous but well-produced plays, light entertainment designed to fill the 1,100 seats that had been barren for years. The strategy worked: almost immediately there were many more people in the house than on the stage.

"By the beginning of 1957, a lot had already changed at the BDT – the hall was full, playwrights and translators began to send plays to the theater, the 'flow' that is necessary for every theater was revamped."[3] Over time, as public trust developed and the entire organization conceded to the absolutist power of the new regime, the repertoire gradually deepened: Dostoevsky was mixed in with French farces, Tolstoy was followed by Russian comedies. Top-level actors were aggressively recruited. Tickets to BDT ultimately became dearer than tickets to the moribund Art Theatre in Moscow.

To carry off his imperative internal reforms, Tovstonogov made no bones about his role, both as a supreme leader and a civic personality. Anatoly Smeliansky writes:

Inside the theatre he was a dictator. He was feared and adored. He had been hardened under Stalin and he perpetuated the mentality of that era in his own theatre. He loved power and enjoyed the art of exercising it. His guttural voice, with its pleasant Georgian accent, the large ring he wore on his finger, his thick horn-rimmed glasses, his boldly sculpted face rather like a bird of prey, his deadly irony and his great diplomatic charm – all suggested he was one of the lords of life.[4]

Kama Ginkas, a Tovstonogov student-protégé, today a celebrated Moscow director, described the ethos of the Theatre under Tovstonogov:

[It was] a "voluntary dictatorship," according to the well-known definition by Tovstonogov himself. Or a kind of monarchy. They adored him like Stalin, feared him like Stalin, listened to him like Stalin, followed him like Stalin, and cried after his death in the same way. I speak harshly on purpose. This is exaggeration, but he himself was raised at a certain time. And the theater was from those times.[5]

In 1989, thirty-three years after taking over the BDT, Georgii Alexandrovich Tovstonogov died at a traffic light while at the wheel of his prized Mercedes sedan, purchased abroad. By the time of his death, just as the early days of glasnost and perestroika were arriving, the "voluntary dictator" was recognized as one of the great stage directors of the world, comparable to European peers like Peter Brook and Giorgio Strehler.

The vast pale green rococo building on Fontanka Canal is now officially titled The Tovstonogov Bolshoi Drama Theatre.

Tiflis to Moscow to Leningrad

Tovstonogov's birthplace is uncertain – either Tiflis (now Tbilisi) in Georgia or, according to his sister, Saint Petersburg. His birth year is also debatable; he falsified his age by two years to qualify for admission to GITIS.[6] Arriving in Moscow from Georgia, where his aristocratic parents had fled during (or maybe after) the Bolshevik Revolution, Tovstonogov was mentored by two master teachers who couldn't have been more different in style. The first of these was Andrey Lobanov. Tovstonogov remembers his initial impression:

> [Lobanov] said: Yes…here…They sent me to you, asked me to teach you directing…I don't know how to do it, but…I'll give it a try, maybe it'll work…We, the students, were disappointed: at that time Stanislavsky, Nemirovich-Danchenko, Meyerhold, Tairov and Popov were directing at the same time, and we were given a little-known young man.[7]

Lobanov's idea was to direct his students in productions. Once a week, the aspiring directors, now serving as actors, were permitted to ask questions.

> This work continued for a year. We all fell in love with our teacher, in love with his enthusiasm…We worked and asked questions. He answered. He knew how to do a play. He had an amazing logic for analysis of the play, the logic of a surgeon.[8]

Tovstonogov's other master at GITIS was Alexey Dmitrievich Popov, a highly respected Moscow director who had passed through various Art Theatre studios as an actor and director. When Tovstonogov arrived at GITIS in fall of 1933 A.D. Popov was the esteemed head of The Theatre of the Revolution (a former home of Meyerhold's) where he staged Shakespeare, Schiller, and Russian classics with great success. Then, in 1935 he was assigned as chief director of the new Russian Army Theatre, with the largest stage house in all of Europe at the time. Here, the artistically inclined Popov dutifully staged patriotic pageants with tanks, mounted cavalry, and giant ships. (Significantly, it was A.D. Popov who in the mid-1930s encouraged Maria Knebel to pursue directing, and later brought her to GITIS as his assistant.)

Popov had an enormous influence on the directing student from Tiflis.

> Aleksey Dmitrievich was, in my opinion, an excellent pedagogue, because he was one of the very few directors who in his pedagogical practice took an analytical approach to the laws of the art of theater…He tried in his pedagogy and his directing to pass on to us his love of analysis…Popov was, surprisingly enough, eloquent, unhurried, slow, but amazingly profound…A piercing way of thinking! All this left a vivid mark in my memory.[9]

On completion of his GITIS studies in 1939, Tovstonogov returned home, directed nonstop mostly in Tiflis, but returned to Moscow in 1947 age 32 (or so). Opportunities in the Soviet capital were scarce, so in 1949 Tovstonogov relocated to Leningrad to begin a highly successful run at the Lenin Komsomol Theatre – Komsomol being an acronym for "All-Union Leninist Young Communist League": the youth organization of the Communist Party of the Soviet Union. In his seven years as chief director at the Komsomol, Tovstonogov, the directing machine, staged twenty-seven productions, almost all at his home theatre. Then the BDT called.

Artistic Director, Director, Pedagogue

These three interrelated professions above are the job description of a successful director in Russia. The polymathic commandant – presumably an insomniac – is expected to run their own theatre; direct at that theatre and sometimes elsewhere, abroad if possible (you can get a Mercedes); and teach in the theatre's own academy or one nearby.

In 1958, two years after his upheaval at the BDT, Georgii Tovstonogov ticked the last box, beginning a teaching career at the Leningrad State Institute of Theater, Music, and Cinematography (LGITMiK, henceforth "the Institute") with Arkady Katsman as his brilliant second teacher. For thirty years, Tovstonogov and Katsman led several directing "courses" – a course being a four-year program with a master teacher, a second teacher and assistants educating the same set of students. Tovstonogov's impact on those students who survived the rigors of the course – generally about ten students entered per course, half or fewer graduated – was as potent as his impact on the actors at the BDT. Kama Ginkas spoke of his teacher in a 2005 interview.

> The training he gave me is my skeleton, it holds my personal meat; this may be my personal face, but the skeleton is his. For many years, almost all my creative life, I have been trying to overcome this skeleton. I wanted to be taller, slimmer, I wanted to be more graceful, less oily, less carnal – I can't be![10]

Former student Maria Ganeva, who in the 1980s attended the last two courses Tovstonogov taught – the second course was for her PhD[11] – remembers:

> With Tovstonogov classes were always stressful, highly difficult…It was more a military study (in spirit), than an art study…Tovstonogov did not shout, but he had an amazing way to look at you and freeze you if he didn't like your thinking or your scene presentation. But Katsman – oh, he shouted at us all the time, totally neurotically. But actually we all received more from Katsman than we did from Tovstonogov.[12]

The first year with Tovstonogov was basic actor training – mostly grueling objectless physical exercises in the style of the Opera-Dramatic Studio. The second year of the course was dedicated to Tovstonogov's version of Analysis through Action, including a page-by-page, character-by-character surgical dissection of some twenty plays. But, excepting for the first-year physical exercises, Études were neither taught nor performed – at all.[13]

Georgii Tovstonogov and Maria Knebel: A Crucial Distinction

Here it is important to individuate the Tovstonogov and Knebel forms of Analysis through Action. There is no evidence that Tovstonogov studied or consulted with Knebel or vice-versa, as is often supposed. In a chapter of *The Profession of the Director*, Tovstonogov writes:

> Although I had the good fortune to meet Stanislavsky a few times, I mainly acquired my knowledge and understanding of his method through pupils and followers of his, who were my teachers, and from my own practical work. My understanding of his method is individual and subjective, and far be it from me to suggest that it is the only valid one.[14]

Tovstonogov does not mention Knebel here, nor any of the 'pupils and followers.' Presumably one was Popov, an ardent student of Stanislavsky, and the text-forensic Lobanov another. A digital search of numerous volumes, interviews and studies by or about Tovstonogov reveals that he rarely mentioned Knebel's name; he definitely never cited her as a mentor or a close colleague. Staroselskaya's 400-page study of Tovstonogov briefly mentions Knebel as another disciple of Popov, nothing more. Certainly, Tovstonogov paid due tribute to Knebel's warm personality and her dedication to teaching in his brief introduction to her *Poetry of Pedagogy* (1971); he recognizes her as Russia's first teacher of directing. But he makes no suggestion that she was his tutor or even a close colleague.

But Tovstonogov could not have been ignorant of Knebel's theories and practices. In 1952, by which time Tovstonogov had settled in as chief director at the Leningrad Komsomol Theatre, Knebel had published her first effort, a twenty-eight-page monograph entitled *Tips for Directors*. Two years later came her first full book, *The Word and the Work of the Actor*, followed by her holy bible five years later: *On the Analysis through Action of the Play and the Role*. Presumably Georgii Alexandrovich Tovstonogov read these books, but nowhere do I find any of Knebel's titles referenced in the numerous Tovstonogov tomes, primary or secondary.

Valery Galandeev, professor of voice at the Russian State Institute of Performing Arts (RGISI) and teacher-tutor at Lev Dodin's Maly Drama Theatre, notes a general alignment of the Knebel and Tovstonogov approaches to Analysis through Action – with one big distinction:

You could say that both theories are very close sisters. Tovstonogov left us with a few more terms than Knebel did. For Knebel the paramount thing over the last twenty years of her life was teaching, using many études. For Tovstonogov directing in his theatre [BDT] was definitely paramount…But he very quickly realized that time is money in the professional theatre. So he threw études out the window.[15]

Georgii Tovstonogov and Maria Knebel: Opposing Views of Études

Here are two examples of Tovstonogov's view of Études (there are many more in the same vein):

> Many regard as an essential feature of the method the practice of working on études. I disagree…In working on études, the actors' attention is distracted from the play itself, so they find analogous given circumstances and act in those circumstances. The material is similar but not identical to that of the play.[16]
> Every étude is sinful in its approximation to the source. A preoccupation with the étude method alone impedes the transition to the author's material.[17]

Former Tovstonogov student Genrietta Yanovskaya tells a story of observing her future husband, Kama Ginkas, working on a scene at the Institute with Tovstonogov observing:

> Ginkas' rehearsal lasted about two minutes. Ginkas began by saying: "Come on, guys, let's do a étude about what happened beforehand." Tovstonogov asked: "Why?" – "Well, so they can start." – "And what if they just start like this?" Silence. It didn't occur to Ginkas (or to me) that maybe an actor's imagination was enough to go into the circumstances with. It was just that back then it was universally considered (it was fashionable!) to work the "étude way." "And how will you do an étude?" – Tovstonogov asked. – "Maybe you'll have to make a étude about what came before the étude, and then another étude to know what came before that étude? Finally, maybe do a étude about how the character was born?"[18]

In a seeming contradiction, Tovstonogov did have his BDT actors rehearse using their own words, but only after an extensive director-led study of the play, the role, and the Event at hand. Tovstonogov wrote: "I try to follow the author in the sequence of the scenes, but I don't allow my actors to say the exact text. The actors at this time don't know it yet. If the performer starts to memorize the text at once, there's a danger that he'll go the wrong way."[19]

While this may sound like an Étude approach, Maria Ganeva clarifies that Tovstonogov employed only "an improvisation within an absolutely strict scheme of circumstances and conflict, already prepared by the director."[20] Requiring the actor to use their own words was a test for Tovstonogov: does this actor fully grasp the line of logic of the scene and the character, as created by the author? Exploratory Études are, of course, the heart and soul of Knebel's approach. Surely, a "certain preliminary analysis" is fundamental to her methodology, but the goal is to promptly get the actor on stage doing Action-based Études, followed by specific analytical inquiry based on the Étude: hence Analysis through Action.

So, Knebel and Tovstonogov, while employing many of the same terms, including Analysis through Action, due to their temperaments and training they practiced and taught comparatively different methodologies. Knebel had matured during a period of relative cultural and intellectual freedom before the Bolshevik Revolution; Tovstonogov grew up in an increasingly deterministic and materialist environment. Knebel was a born teacher with the playful spur-of-the-moment spirit of Michael Chekhov in her warm and nurturing heart. Conversely, "G.A. Tovstonogov was protected by an iron armor of analysis."[21] M.O. Knebel grew up as an actor, thus when teaching directing her focus was on collaborative work with the actor. G.A. Tovstonogov, other than the Lobanov GITIS student laboratory and some roles in his hometown theatre, had barely worked as an actor; his entire professional and pedagogical focus was on the director leading the actor toward a preconceived goal.

For a time, Knebel's Étude approach was considered the "Moscow School"; Tovstonogov's analytical approach was the "Leningrad School." But those distinctions no longer make sense: director/teacher Boris Zon, as well as descendants whom we shall meet later – Zenovy Korogodsky, Lev Dodin, Veniamin Filshtinsky, Yuri Butusov – all became avid practitioners of Études in Leningrad/Petersburg, while many of Tovstonogov's text-analysis strategies are taught today at GITIS.

This book has no stake in the rivalry between these two great cities and their prodigious theatre practitioners. Instead, we aspire to blend these "sister" theories into a single dynamically interactive pathway for classroom and rehearsal action: *Reconnaissance of the Mind* and *Reconnaissance of the Body* practiced in tandem as a holistic process – mirroring the two "lungs" of Stanislavsky's System.

Tovstonogov: Strategies of Analysis – Some Basic Definitions

Anyone who has struggled with the terminology of Stanislavsky's System is aware of the challenge of trying to pith precise definitions and practical applications of his technical vocabulary. Fluctuating use of terms, even contradictions, are plentiful, unsurprising as his ideas and neologisms evolved over the years while he struggled to delineate concrete procedural matters of the System. Tovstonogov, ever the dialectician, took it as his task to compress some of the

Stanislavsky's inconsistent proposals into singular practical descriptions. He then structured those terms into a step-by-step workflow plan for the private analysis of a text by the director and for coaching actors at rehearsal.

The initial undertaking, called by Tovstonogov "the director alone with the play"[22] or "storming the play,"[23] kicks off this method of sequential analysis, and continues through several more steps. In our *Reconnaissance of the Mind* section in Part II of this book, we call these steps Text Actions (we have ten of them) which are largely derived from Tovstonogov and Katsman's lessons, explained to me by Irina Malochevskaya (Tovstonogov's longtime assistant) and PhD student Maria Ganeva. As we will cover those Text Actions in full later on, at this point we will give only a brief preparatory introduction to some of the key operative terms that we will help us unpack Part II.

Event(s)

S.I. Ozhegov's *Dictionary of the Russian Language* reads: "An event is something that happened, a significant event, a fact of public or personal life."[24] Stanislavsky neatly called Events "action-facts." Tovstonogov, like Knebel, stresses the centrality of the Event, as reported by Malochevskaya: "The 'Event' is the main structural element of stage life, it's the indivisible atom of the action process...It is very important that an event is an active conflict-fact that happens 'here, now, before my eyes.'"[25] (Again, in the US we often use the term "beats" – a Russian pronunciation of "bits" – for Events. But the latter is more specific: something that *happened*.)

At the Institute, Arkady Katsman described the process of identifying an Event in great detail. This procedure is reiterated by Irina and Igor Levin in their American volume *Working on the Play and the Role* (Irina had studied under Tovstonogov and Katsman). The Katsman definition of Events via the Levins is "logically independent units, each of which has one leading character involved in only one conflict, and one action."[26] In the *Events* section of Part II, we ground our method of partitioning and examining Events from the Levins' book.

Conflict

Tovstonogov was insistent that finding the Conflict be compulsory in every moment of every Event.

> The essence of the method is that every minute, every second of scenic action is an uninterrupted duel. The director must remember that there is no scenic life without conflict...The chain of conflicts, reaching the point of "psychological boxing," so to speak, produces the score of the production.[27]
>
> Conflict is often understood as open confrontation. However, in life and on stage, even obvious enemies rarely engage in open dispute.

A feature of all drama is that the main driving force of the action is a latent conflict, which only rarely breaks out.[28]

Tovstonogov's star student, Kama Ginkas, later devised a less pugnacious definition: "Conflict is best described as 'competing logics.'"[29]

Action

Former student Maria Ganeva's stenographic notes capture the following characterizations of Action from lectures by Tovstonogov:

Action is a unified psychophysical process, oriented towards the achievement of some final goal. It is in coordination with the existing Given Circumstances and is expressed in some manner in time and space.

Action has three components:

1. Physical Action. (*What* would I do [in this circumstance]?)
2. The goal of the Action. (*Why* would I do it?)
3. The means of the action. (*How* would I do it?)[30]

The Chain (or Sequence) of Events

Tovstonogov follows Stanislavsky's notion of first identifying the major or critical Events of the play, thereby designating minor Events as well. This is done by pursuing the consecutive Chain of Events:

As I see it, the essence of the method of active analysis consists in determining the appropriate sequence of events in the play itself. The director and the cast must try to split the play into a chain of events, [each Event being a link] proceeding from the most important to the minor ones, to find what are called the 'molecules of scenic action," [the Events] the ultimate units beyond which the action cannot be split any further.[31]

The event structure of the play is the core point of the action analysis method…Without creating such a complete system of event-actions of the play's development, a director…has no moral or professional right to a first meeting with the actors.[32]

In conclusion: an **Event** is a discrete unit of text (a 'bit') in which there must be a **Conflict**, no matter how latent or concealed between two or more characters; this conflict creates psychophysical **Action** (dynamic interaction) through the "competing logics" of the two or more characters participating in the **Event**. As the play progresses, **Events** advance one-by-one, creating a **Chain** or **Sequence of Events** which propels the **Throughline Action** of the play on stage.

Strategies of Analysis: Some Tovstonogov Innovations

From the Stanislavsky-originated terms above, we move to a set of key analytical strategies conceived by Tovstonogov, summarized briefly below. Much more to come in Part II.

The Novel of Life

Analysis through Action is basically a process of transformation: transforming a set of glyphs on the page into dramatic action on stage. At the outset of the director's "assault" on the play, Tovstonogov recommended that the text should be transferred into a different medium: a novel, called "The Novel of Life" to be written by the director.

> What does "novel of life" mean?...I try to translate the play into the language of literature, to suggest that I am faced, for example, not with Ostrovsky's play *The Tempest*, but with the novel *The Tempest*. I try to imagine the lives of the play's characters as the lives of people who really exist or have existed. It's important for me to know what happened to them before they appeared on stage, what they did between acts of the play. It's important to know what they were thinking.[33]

Maria Ganeva's class notes elaborate on this process:

> The major things are not the separate facts extracted from the play but the very FLOW OF LIFE...What we are talking about is an epic novel with details, in the way Balzac depicted the houses of his characters. It is a novel in which the director should think of the characters as actual living people.[34]

In Part II: *Reconnaissance of the Mind* the reader will see that we have divided this demanding exercise into three distinct Text Actions placed at separate points in our text analysis workflow.

The Three Circles of Given Circumstances

Given Circumstances is a much-bandied-about phrase heard in rehearsal halls, yet few could define it in specific practical terms. As Given Circumstances are the backbone of any Event, they are crucial to the implementation of Analysis through Action. Let's begin with Knebel's excerpt of Stanislavsky's summary of Given Circumstances, which includes

> the plot of the play, its facts, events, historical epoch, the time and place of the action, life conditions, the actor's and director's understanding of the play, their additions to it, the *mise-en-scènes*, the production, sets and

costumes, props, lights, noises and sounds, etc., that are given to the actors to take into consideration as they create.[35]

For a director or a leading actor a comprehensive catalog of Given
Circumstances could encompass hundreds of facts – and bring up many areas
for speculation. Tovstonogov endeavored to schematize this confusing jumble
by creating a taxonomy of Three Circles (aka "Rings") of Given Circumstances:
three concentrical spheres, each containing a specific set of Given Circumstances.
(See Figure 14.1)

In a Tovstonogov directing class a student succinctly identified the domain
of each circle:

> The large circle lies outside the boundaries of the work, it is time, envi-
> ronment, epoch, birth and death. It is man's place on earth; his purpose
> [his Supertask]. The middle circle is confined to the play itself. The mid-
> dle circle defines the system of characters' relationships and the entire
> series of event. The small circle directly affects the definition of the local
> conflict [aka a particular Event].[36]

Thus, the Large Circle is the environment or backdrop of the play, the con-
tainer often referred to as the "world of the play." This means the
socio-economic, historical, technological, moral, legal environment in which
the characters live.

The Middle Circle is the overall Throughline Action of the play as revealed through the consecutive Sequence of Events and the evolving relationships of the characters. Throughline Action emerges as the play moves
forward Event by Event, which the audience witnesses in time and space.
The play has its Throughline Action, as does each individual actor/
character.

The Small Circle is the realm of the onstage Event happening here, now,
today in front of the audience; the audience is witnessing this Event for the first
time. These are the independent living Events, the "beats," with intra-personal
immediate Conflicts which create Actions. Each character in each Event should
be somehow changed, even if minimally, by the conclusion of their Action in
the Event.

In a class, Tovstonogov put forth his description of the three circles:

> The large circle is that we live in the Soviet Union, that we are members
> of a certain social category, etc. The middle circle is that we are directors
> who have come to our lab and each day make things happen. And finally,
> the small circle of given circumstances – those real physical circumstances
> that make us act in a certain way today, now.[37]

Two important features must be noted here:

1. The circles are permeable – components may migrate as needed from one ring to another. Thus, all Small Circle Events are informed by specific Given Circumstances 'drawn down' from the Large and Middle Circles.
2. Tovstonogov encouraged what he called "the principle of exaggeration,"[38] meaning that any character's Given Circumstance should be taken to its utmost extreme, to the very edge of plausibility to find the "hottest" choice. If a character has a headache, start with a *bad* headache! This principle will test the limits of a Given Circumstance; it's always easier to pull back than push out.

The Initial Given Circumstance of the Play and Each Act

Related to the Initial Event discussed in Chapter 3, the Initial Given *Circumstance* of the Play is the "condition," the "atmosphere" which pre-exists the action of the play, prevails in the beginning of the play, and continues to the denouement of the play. While it precedes the narrative, *the Initial Given Circumstance is the one without which the story cannot take place.* It is pervasive and affects the Actions of *all* characters in the play.

The Initial Given Circumstance may be brought about by a specific Event-fact, a thing that happened: King Hamlet is dead and Elsinore is in transition; there has been a storm-tossed shipwreck off the coast of Illyria. Or it can be a more generalized fact of life, the way things are in this world – Verona has lived in civic conflict since time immemorial. While the Initial Given Circumstance may or may not be overcome during the play, it is always palpable up to the resolution of the play, where it has either been extinguished or triumphed.

Let's start with a simple example. The Initial Given Circumstance of *Romeo and Juliet* is that Verona is a world of hatred, suspicion, and violence due to the "ancient grudge" of the Montague and Capulet families. This is the pervasive Given Circumstance of the play, the civic state of things that everyone lives under; it is the overriding *fact* of the play that will prevail or be altered by the end.

But at some point, the Initial Given Circumstance will be challenged by an Event which counters this all-pervading initial fact, setting off the struggle inside the Throughline Action. Late in Act I, Romeo Montague and Juliet Capulet meet at the masked ball and share a "tender kiss" (actually at her behest, two), thereby countering the perpetual Veronian hatred and violence with their innocent love. The conflict between the Initial Given Circumstance of hatred and violence versus the transcendent love of Romeo and Juliet will drive the Throughline Action up to Juliet stabbing herself in Act V.

In a standard three- or four-act realistic drama, one should identify the Initial Given Circumstance of Each Act, as we will examine in Part II.

There is no overstating the requirement to detect the Initial Given Circumstance of the Play. To borrow from Othello in another context: "It is the cause" – it is the pervasive condition or specific Event which lays the initial foundation for the Throughline Action struggle of the play. It is the state of the world we are entering into and which must be contended with.

The Five Event Structure[39]

To identify and categorize the Given Circumstances of the Play or the Role requires examining the play through a jeweler's loupe, scrutinizing its facets for minute details. Consequently it is easy to lose sight of the full play itself as one meticulously sorts through the minute data of the text. After such meticulous scrutiny, it becomes important to dolly back and re-examine the play as a whole. This is where one of the most beneficial aspects of Tovstonogov's Reconnaissance of the Mind process comes into play. He called it the Five Event Structure.

Tovstonogov determined that one could "score" the major movements of a production through five Events which would be theatrically visible vital to the audience. These five events (in our terms; Tovstonogov used different titles) are:

1. The Initial Event
2. The Counter Event
3. The Climactic Event
4. The Resolving Event
5. The Crucial Event

The whole play, thus the whole production, is a journey from the Initial Event to the Crucial Event. But surprisingly, only three of these Events actually lie *inside* the body of the text. The first and the last – the Initial and the Crucial – are created by the director and/or the company, not the playwright.

The Initial Event

The name of this Event intentionally reverberates with The Initial Given Circumstance. This first Event is a bespoke creation of the production which contains the ruling idea of the Initial Given Circumstance. It leads the audience into the play itself, setting the tone of the production and the atmosphere of the world in which the characters currently exist. *Example*: In Baz Luhrmann's film *Romeo and Juliet*, following a televised news broadcast of the prologue, we see a modern hyper-capitalist city at war with itself: military helicopters pass by giant corporate Capulet and Montague skyscrapers, police and military battle below, there is fire, unchecked urban chaos. In Zeffirelli's film we see a pitched battle on horseback between two factions in an outdoor marketplace.

The Counter Event

This is an Event inside the text which challenges or opposes the Initial Given Circumstance and runs counter to the prevailing atmosphere. This is where the conflict of the Throughline Action begins, the central struggle that will drive the action forward. *Example*: Romeo and Juliet meet, kiss and fall in love at the masked ball, generating a Counteraction to the Initial Given Circumstance. The Throughline Action of the play – the Initial Given Circumstance versus the Counteraction – begins here with the struggle for the freedom to love.

The Climactic Event

Here is the apex of the Throughline Action, the pinnacle of the struggle between the Initial Given Circumstance and the Counteraction, the pivot point at which the outcome of the struggle hangs in the balance and begins to head toward inevitable resolution. *Example*: Romeo Montague fatally stabs Tybalt Capulet. Romeo and Juliet's chances plummet.

The Resolving Event

The struggle according to the Throughline Action comes to an end; either the Initial Given Circumstance or the Counteraction will prevail; one must be extinguished. Note, this is *not* the end of the play, this is the *denouement*; there is usually some kind of coda, but the central conflict is no longer active. *Example*: In the tomb, Juliet wakes, see that Romeo is dead, takes his dagger and kills herself.

The Crucial Event

The last Event of the Performance. Like the Initial Event, this one lies outside the boundaries of the written text and provides a subjective raison d'être for the production. It reveals the filter through which the director and/or company want the audience to consider what they have just seen. *Examples*: In Franco Zeffirelli's film, the families unite, filing out of the tomb in two parallel lines, rank by rank, indicating that the "ancient grudge" will be laid to rest. Anatoly Efros' stage production and his film ended on an opposite note: members of the two households argued over who would do more to commemorate the deaths of the young lovers. This dispute erupted into the customary Veronian violence. Nothing was learned.

Tovstonogov: Conclusion

Georgii Tovstonogov's systematic and extremely productive diagnostic devices introduced above are adapted and further explicated in Part II: *Reconnaissance of the Mind*. They are presented as ten Text Actions, each written as a kind of assignment, which is what they have been in our evolving practice over the years. While Tovstonogov was thinking and writing for student directors (as was Knebel, although she was initially an actor herself), all actors will find many of the Text Actions extremely beneficial for independent research into their character and shared company investigation of the play.

Both Knebel and Tovstonogov drew heavily from Stanislavsky, albeit at different times and through different routes. She knew him well, as a student at GITIS he observed one class at the ODS. Thus some of their ideas on Reconnaissance of the Mind have similarities if different emphases. But neither should be read as an orthodoxy. Both have boundless use in rehearsals and classrooms, as well as for the actor or director alone with the play.

The days of the Moscow School versus the Leningrad School are over and were a false dichotomy to begin with. Recently, Knebel's ideas have begun to seep into the anglophone world while today Tovstonogov is barely known, much less studied. We propose that a deep artistic synthesis of these two radical innovators will provide the strongest basis for the practice and teaching of Analysis through Action.

Notes

1 Наталья Старосельская. 2004. *Товстоногов.* Moskva: Молодая гвардия; Natalia Staroselskaya, 2004. *Tovstonogov.* Moscow: Young Guard, p. 140.
2 Staroselskaya *Tovstonogov* 140.
3 Staroselskaya *Tovstonogov* 149.
4 Smeliansky Anatoly Laurence Senelick and Patrick Miles. 1999. *The Russian Theatre After Stalin.* Cambridge: Cambridge University Press, p. 48.
5 Conversation with Kama Ginkas and Genrietta Yanovskaya interviewed by Elena Gorfunkel on BDT website, 2005. Accessed March 2018 at https://bdt.spb.ru/pamiat/man/tovstonogov_ga/kulturnaia_gazeta.html (no longer accessible).
6 Staroselskaya *Tovstonogov* 16–17.
7 Tovstonogov G. A. 1972. *Круг Мыслей; Статьи Режиссерские Комментарии Записи Репетиции.* Leningrad: Искусство; Tovstonogov G. A. 1972. Circle of Thoughts; Articles Director's Comments Records Rehearsals. Leningrad: Art 163.
8 [Послесл Ю and G. A Tovstonogov. 1972. *Круг Мыслей. Статьи. Режиссерские Коммент. Записи Репетиций.* Leningrad: "Iskusstvo "; Y and G. A Tovstonogov. 1972. Circle of Thoughts. Articles. Director's Comments. Records of Rehearsals. Leningrad: "Art" 163.
9 [составитель Е. И. Семен Лосев and Е Горфункель.] 2007. *Георгий Товстоногов Репетирует И Учит: Литературная Запись Семена Лосева.* Sankt-Peterburg: Балтийские сезоны; [compiled by E.I. Semyon Losev and E. Gorfunkel.] 2007. *Georgii Tovstonogov Rehearses and Teaches: Literary Record by Semyon Losev.* Saint Peterburg: Baltic Seasons 350.
10 составители Елена Е Горфункель and И Шимбаревич. 2015. *Георгий Товстоногов: Собирательный Портрет: Воспоминания Публикации Письма.* Sankt-Peterburg: Балтийские сезоны; Compilers Elena E. Gorfunkel and I. Shimbarevich. 2015. *Georgii Tovstonogov: Collective Portrait: Memories Publications Letters.* Saint Peterburg: Baltic Seasons 64.
11 Professor Maria Ganeva, PhD, cited in the Introduction to this book, was an invaluable guide during my research into Tovstonogov. Following several in-person discussions, she supplied me with sixty professionally translated pages of her own

Russian stenographic notes summarizing his classes. and answered my subsequent questions via detailed e-mails. It was Professor Ganeva, along with a personal interview with Irina Malochevskaya, who shaped my knowledge and the perspective of this chapter more than the primary or secondary sources.

12 Ganeva, Maria, E-mail to author, January 20, 2018.
13 Ganeva, Email; verifying author interview with Kama Ginkas, October 12, 2018.
14 Tovstonogov G. A. 1972. *The Profession of the Stage-Director*. Moscow: Progress Publishers 237; Translated by Bryan Bean from Tovstonogov, Georgii Aleksandrovich. *О Профессия Режиссера*, Moskva, 1967.
15 Author interview with Valery Galandeev, May 14, 2011, Dina Dodina simultaneously translating.
16 Tovstonogov *Profession* 241.
17 *Tovstonogov Rehearses and Teaches* 338.
18 *Collective Portrait* 69; Ginkas does not use Études to this day; in the 2018 interview with the author Ginkas cited the danger of one Étude then requiring another ad infinitum.
19 Tovstonogov, Georgii Aleksandrovich. 1984. *Зеркало Сцены* 2-Е Leningrad: "Iskusstvo"; Tovstonogov, Georgii Aleksandrovich. 1984 *Mirror of the Stage* 2 vols Leningrad: "Art". v.1 264.
20 Ganeva E-mail to Author, January 2021.
21 Смолко А.А. "Метод активного анализа: М.О. Кнебель и Г. А. Товстоногов" // Вестник Санкт-Петербургского государственного университета. Серия. 15. 2011. Выпуск; Smolko A.A. "The method of active analysis: M.O. Knebel and G.A. Tovstonogov" // Bulletin of St. Petersburg State University. Series. 15. 2011. Issue 4, p. 82.
22 И.Б Малочевская 2003. *Режиссерская Школа Товстоногова*. Sankt-Peterburg: Акад. Театрального Искусства; I.B. Malochevskaya 2003. Tovstonogov's School of Directing. Saint-Peterburg: Acad. of Theatrical Art 35 Translation Ilya Khodosh (All subsequent translations of Malochevskaya's book are by Khodosh).
23 Malochevskaya *School* 37.
24 Staroselskaya *Tovstonogov* 73.
25 Malochevskaya *School* 43.
26 Levin, Irina, and Igor Levin *Working on the Play and the Role: The Stanislavsky Method for Analyzing the Characters in a Drama*. Chicago: Ivan R. Dee, 1992. 11.
27 Tovstonogov *Profession* 240.
28 *Tovstonogov Rehearses and Teaches* 8.
29 Ginkas interview with author, October 12, 2018.
30 Ganeva "Summary".
31 Tovstonogov *Profession* 241.
32 Malochevskaya *School* 35.
33 Tovstonogov *Mirror* 162.
34 Ganeva, "Summary".
35 Found in Кнебель М. 1959. *О Действенном Анализе Пьесы И Роли. В Помощь Коллективам Театральной Самодеятельности*. Moskva: Искусствоь. Knebel, M. 1959. *On the Active Analysis of the Play and the Role*. In Assistance to the Collectives of Theatrical Amateur Activity. Moscow: Art 18 Translation Ilya Khodosh; Knebel is quoting from Volume Two of Stanislavsky's *Collected Works*, 1954 p. 62.
36 *Tovstonogov Rehearses and Teaches* 356.
37 Tovstonogov *Mirror* v. 1 256.
38 Ganeva "Summary".
39 The brief summary of the Five Event Structure here is drawn from both Malochevskaya's *School* and Ganeva's "Summary" as well as from an author interview with Malochevskaya, May 12, 2011.

5   The Legacy of Analysis through Action

Introduction

Up to this point, we have covered the advent of Analysis through Action from the foundation of Stanislavsky's System through his interviews with the young Boris Zon to his Opera-Dramatic Studio to the next generation of Maria Knebel and Georgii Tovstonogov.

Zon, Knebel, and Tovstonogov became the primary disseminators of Analysis through Action to the next generation, each in their own way: in Moscow, Knebel will teach Anatoly Efros, Anatoly Vasiliev, and briefly Lev Dodin, as well as influencing Oleg Efremov and many others. In Leningrad Zon will teach Dodin, Zinovy Korogodsky, and Veniamin Filshtinsky; Georgii Tovstonogov will teach Kama Ginkas and Genrietta Yanovskaya; and Tovstonogov's associate Irina Malochevskaya will teach Yuri Butusov. Furthermore, the three primary proponents – Zon, Knebel, and Tovstonogov – invisibly but profoundly influenced the students of their students: let's recall the recurrent question 'who was your teacher's teacher?'

Thus, Analysis through Action as a living practice in Russia has evolved generationally down to the present day. And, as Russia has transformed politically and culturally, sometimes convulsively, theatre has correspondingly reflected its changing times. Accordingly, Analysis through Action as an artistic instrument has been individually reconsidered and rejiggered by successive teachers and directors as the decades passed. Today, in some form or other, Analysis through Action, or unmistakable traces of its DNA, can be found in rehearsal halls and classrooms throughout the country, as well as in former Soviet bloc countries of Eastern Europe.

The following chapters will trace the genealogy of Analysis through Action through three generations of Russian cultural history that follow Zon, Knebel, and Tovstonogov: (1) The Thaw, a brief period of artistic liberation after Stalin's death in 1954; (2) the Glasnost era of the 1980s and 1990s before and just after the collapse of the USSR; and (3) post-Soviet up to the 2022 invasion of Ukraine (which has brought a huge crackdown on the arts and thus a tragic diaspora of noted theatre artists.)

DOI: 10.4324/9781003475576-7

In each of these three generations, we will identify one or two leading directors who robustly represent the spirit of their era and who practiced and taught
their version of Analysis through Action. Regrettably, space limitations pre-
vent consideration of numerous other extraordinary directors trained in
Analysis through Action – Efremov, Vasiliev, Ginkas, Yanovsky, and more – as
well as those who emerged from other schools of directorial process such as
Brechtian Yuri Lyubimov. But hopefully, the cultural eras that we trace and the
directors of those generations that we follow will elucidate various implemen-
tations of Analysis through Action and how those variants are related to the
director's zeitgeist.

Governing the Russian Theatre[1]

Renowned Russian theatre historian Laurence Senelick tells us: "Only in soci-
eties where art and literature are taken so seriously are they regarded as potent
and dangerous."[2]

Thus, from the reign of Peter the Great (1682–1725) to today's Russian theatre, the potent and dangerous art of theatre has been tautly interlaced with
watchful government regulation.

The first established theatres in Russia were the small court and private theatres of the eighteenth century, created in the wake of the "Petrine (Peter the
Great's) revolution." Then, in the nineteenth century lavish edifices known as
the Imperial Theatres were erected in Saint Petersburg – the Alexandrinsky
(1832), the Mikhailova (1833), and the Mariinsky (1860) – all named after no-
bles. In Moscow, equivalent Imperial Theatres had already been established:
the Maly Theatre (1824) and the Bolshoi Theatre (1825). These five state theatres were variously devoted to dramatic works, opera, and ballet. The Maly,
serving dramatic fare to the Moscow nobility and later also to the emergent
mercantile class – for example, young Kostya Alekseev's family – became the
birth site of the classic Russian plays by authors such as Griboyedov, Pushkin,
Gogol, and Ostrovsky.

The Imperial Theatres were established for a specific nationalist task: the
elevation of the Russian nobility (and later mercantilists) to European standards of literacy and cultural sophistication. Baked into the foundations of
these principal theatres was the premise that all art must fulfill a govern-
ment-authorized cultural and moral purpose, and that each theatre would be
held accountable to standards established and maintained by that government.
Those stipulations became universal throughout Russia.

Regulatory oversight of the performing arts in Russia has now been in effect
for three centuries, if in mutable manifestations. The situation has only wors-
ened since the invasion of Ukraine, which has caused many Russian avant-
garde theatre artists such as Kirill Serebrennikov, Yuri Butusov, Dmitry
Krymov, and others to emigrate. A great many of the remaining artistic directors have been removed from their theatres, replaced with appointed compliant
'managers.'

Glory Days before and Just after the Revolution

From the turn of the twentieth century up to the years immediately following the 1917 Revolution, Russian artists enjoyed a halcyon period of relative freedom from interference, and even government support for new arts. As society pulsed with new sociopolitical ideas, an explosive eruption in the arts was world concurrently discharged, relatively unfettered as various regimes were preoccupied with recurrent governmental transitions. The late nineteenth century Russian realists – Tolstoy, Chekhov, the painter Repin, and others – were surpassed in the early twentieth century by a new generation of modernist writers, directors, composers, and visual artists: Akhmatova, Blok, Chagall, Mandelstam, Malevich, Mayakovsky, Meyerhold, Scriabin, Tsvetaeva, and many more. The work of these radicals sprouted a whole new set of isms: acemeism, symbolism, primitivism, expressionism, constructivism, suprematism, futurism. Heady days, during which Meyerhold famously wrote to Anton Chekhov: 'I want to burn with the spirit of the times!'[3]

But it did not take long after the 1917 Revolution for the new Soviet apparatus to pick up the fallen reins of artistic control previously held in golden-gloved hands. Lenin immediately saw the opportunity for the arts to serve the socialist cause and appointed the liberal and highly educated Anatoly Lunacharsky as Commissar of the Enlightenment. While the new cultural mission remained the elevation of the audience, the target demographic was now the illiterate "masses" who had been denied an education, as well as the scant remaining intelligentsia, whom the Bolsheviks demanded to convert. If a theatre and its director at least nominally toed the Party line, financial support from Lunacharsky's Commissariat would arrive.

Consequently, one of the most exciting periods of modern theatre history ensued, most famously exemplified by Meyerhold (whose biomechanics, he claimed, displayed a new communal form of labor), accompanied by his collaborators Popova, Mayakovsky, Eisenstein, Shostakovich, and others; the First Studio and its astonishing young actors; the founding of Alexander Tairov's Kamerny Theatre starring the brilliant Alicia Koonen, an Art Theatre ex-pat; the birth of two Moscow Jewish theatres; the creation of agit-prop theatres such as Blue Blouse, and numerous other examples.

The stupefied Moscow Art Theater, which had somehow missed the Revolution, was financially insolvent and bewildered by its new disorderly audience comped in by the Bolsheviks. The Art Theatre leaders were forced to send the insolvent company on a tour to the nation Stanislavsky soon called the "money-pump," the United States. (Despite great popular success, the MAT's two US tours ultimately lost money.)

The 1920s: New Foundations of Censorship Are Laid

In 1921, Lenin and the Bolshevik government adopted the New Economic Policy (NEP), an improbable hybrid of Communism and regulated capitalism deemed necessary to recover from the Russian Civil War of 1917–1922. A decadent 'jazz age' soon erupted, with flagrant corruption and gangsterism. Newly wealthy 'NEP-men' gained enormous corrupt wealth while common people, in whose name the Revolution had been fought, starved in the streets. As Lenin's health declined following a series of strokes, a more militant leftist faction of the Bolshevik Party began plotting to take control.

As the leftist opposition to Lenin's policies solidified during the 1920s, surveillance on the arts gradually grew increasingly pervasive and intrusive. A complex bureaucracy was established inside the Commissariat of Enlightenment (aka Narkompros) with specific bureaus for literature, visual art, and theatre. "Compliance with established rules" was the mandate.[4] What these "established rules" actually were was not explained, except by example: if someone is arrested for doing such-and-such, don't do it. Judgment lay in the hands of the individual censors – some were lenient, some were not, but the harder the line, the better. One high Narkompros official wrote:

> The work of the censorship board is extremely difficult. We must constantly walk the razor's edge, let nothing pass which interferes with the construction of the Soviet state and party. Better to ban something questionable rather than allow a gap to form which would benefit the enemy.[5]

In short, anything a particular censor might consider to be counter-revolutionary, pornographic, homosexual, a perversion of Soviet reality, was to be condemned and usually removed from public exposure.

The Great Fracture and Socialist Realism

An incapacitated Lenin died in 1924. After four years of vicious in-fighting, including the murder of rival Leon Trotsky, Josef Stalin commandeered complete control of the Communist Party and installed himself as the perennial General Secretary, the ultimate and indisputable authority. Stalin declared 1928 as the year of "The Great Fracture," a full break with the past. The NEP was swiftly eliminated and extremely harsh measures were brought to bear in agriculture, industry, and culture, including what became two "Five-Year Plans" – 1928 to 1932; 1933 to 1937 – implemented to exponentially increase production.

Paralleling the industrial and agricultural fronts, Stalin's cultural revolution had enormous and long-lasting effects. Religion was crushed; chapels and cathedrals were destroyed; former Russian Orthodox holidays became Soviet honorific days. In a frantic attempt to deliver more engineers, understaffed schools graduated unqualified students. In the arts, individual initiative and personal expression were subjugated to the propagation of official ideology. An absolutist homogeneity concreted itself: ideological compliance was to be achieved through the "fundamental method" of "socialist realism."

In 1934 Maxim Gorky, president of the Writer's Union, ardently supported socialist realism, without ever defining it. Another speaker at the same congress did a bit better, classifying socialist realism as the opposing aesthetic of futurism and critical realism. Writers were meant to be 'engineers of the soul,' a term Stalin used regularly. Ultimately, guidelines for socialist realism were laid out. All work in all arts must be:

1. Proletarian: art relevant to the workers and understandable to them.
2. Typical: scenes of everyday life of the people.
3. Realistic: in the representational sense.
4. Partisan: supportive of the aims of the State and the Party.[6]

From this, a broader and more perilous term of censure arose: formalism. Any artist who did not faithfully adhere to the four strictures above could be charged with this nebulous offense. Once again, specific definitions were lacking, authorizing subjective accusations by the censorial apparatus. In practice, the term signaled that an artist was foregrounding the *form* of the work rather social-ist-positive realist *content* glorifying the advancements of socialist reality. Hence the joke about a recurring narrative of socialist realism: 'Boy meets tractor.'[7]

The Great Terror

In the late 1930s, the People's Commissariat for Internal Affairs – the secret police – detained those deemed criminally subversive to the Socialist cause. Precise figures are unsurprisingly elusive, but the best post-Soviet research contends that from July of 1937 to November of 1938 1,575,259 subjects were arrested,[8] and 681,692 of those were executed,[9] almost all by pistol shot or mass firing squads. Renowned academics and artists were not spared. In the arts, they came for composers and musicians; visual artists; actors and directors including several from the pre-Revolutionary days of the Moscow Art Theatre; and numerous writers.

Stanislavsky, sequestered in his home toying with his physical action experiments, would have known about much of this; he was an avid reader of newspapers, all of which were by now party organs celebrating the "show trials." Nonetheless, when Meyerhold's Theatre was closed by force, Stanislavsky boldly called out to his prodigal son, offering him work in the opera studio – a dangerous move. They soon co-directed a production of *Rigoletto*, completed by Meyerhold after Stanislavsky's death in August 1938. But on that date Meyerhold had lost his protector. He was arrested in June of 1939 and, after seven months of brutal torture, tried and executed in a Moscow prison basement. This could not have happened without Stalin's approval. Robert Leach notes that after the execution, in February of 1940:

> [Meyerhold's] body was tipped into 'Common Grave Number 1' in the cemetery of the Don Monastery. Later that same month, Stalin was pre-sented by the Moscow Art Theatre with its distinguished Order of the Seagull, named after Chekhov's play, and reserved for those who have performed especially valuable services for the theatre.[10]

The Post-War Years, 1945–1953

Russia's victory over Germany in The Great Patriotic War (what we call World War II) further solidified Stalin's iron grip of governmental and industrial officials, all of them Communist Party appointees known as *nomenklatura*. All Russian theatres now followed the course of the Moscow Art Theatre as outlined by Nemirovich-Danchenko back in 1937: "We have now come to a situation when [the Art Theatre] is already one hundred percent Soviet...We have a clear path – socialist realism...This path is the only true, correct one."[11] Stanislavsky's System, or rather a platitudinous socialist version of it, became the compulsory house style for theatres across Russia, the repertoire equally tightly controlled. For its part, the Art Theatre – described by Senelick as "Sleeping Beauty's castle, once the site of glory but now a cobweb-filled wax museum full of moribund dignitaries...to a theatrical morgue"[12] – continued producing Russian classics in tedious productions and Soviet "counterfeit" plays[13] such as *Kremlin Chimes* (which Knebel co-directed with Nemirovich-Danchenko).

From 1946 to 1955 Mikhail Kedrov served as artistic director and principal director of the Art Theatre, both being *"nomenklatura"* positions, meaning appointed by state cultural authorities, presumably as high as the omnipotent leader himself. For his compliant adherence to the Party line, Kedrov won four Stalin Prizes of the First Degree, the Order of Lenin award, and numerous other state prizes. And, as we know, he fired Maria Knebel from the Art Theatre directing staff.

The Thaw

Stalin's sudden death in March of 1953 left the Party without an obvious successor. After a byzantine power struggle (see the wonderfully droll 2017 film *The Death of Stalin*) Nikita Khrushchev, a member the inner circle, emerged as the next General Secretary of the Communist Party. In February 1956 the new leader gave an astonishing speech to the 1,500 Communist Party delegates who sat in stunned silence for four hours as the new General Secretary excoriated his predecessor's personality cult: Stalin's orders for torture and execution of party loyalists; his lethal policies in Soviet agriculture which led to the starvation of millions; and his grievous military errors in the Great Patriotic War which caused the unnecessary sacrifice of thousands of young soldiers. The unthinkable had been spoken aloud.

Thus began the period known as 'The Thaw,' named after the eponymic 1954 novel by Ilya Ehrenburg. Astonishingly, this book, which condemned The Great Terror and other aspects of Stalin's monstrous reign, had been approved for publication shortly after the man of steel's death. Things were changing. Over time, numerous surviving political prisoners were freed; other political prisoners who had died, namely, Meyerhold, were 'rehabilitated,' if sometimes tacitly. In the cultural arena, an easing of censorship permitted publication or re-publication of works by formerly banned authors, such as Bulgakov.

Previously forbidden orchestral and operatic works of Dmitri Shostakovich were performed in Moscow. Suppressed films by Eisenstein were allowed and European films by Fellini, Truffaut and Bergman were shown. Andre Tarkovsky and other young filmmakers responded with their own 'new wave,' introducing contemporary themes, breaking the mold of socialist realism.

In the theatre, major European troupes such as The Berliner Ensemble and the Comédie-Française appeared in Moscow and Leningrad, along with contemporary productions by directors such as Giorgio Strehler and Peter Brook. Eight volumes of Stanislavsky's long-secreted works – his unfinished books and essays, journals, letters, and the like – were published, albeit redacted by censors (complete versions were to come in the 1980s). Maria Knebel, having been pushed out of the Moscow Art Theatre, was appointed the chief director the Central Children's Theatre. This appointment, as we know, had a profound and lasting impact on the Russian theatre.

But, as Sovietologists caution, it would be a misapprehension to regard the Thaw as an all-encompassing emancipation from the repressions of Stalinism. Instead, the 1954 to 1968 Thaw was a brief historical moment in which "the steel fist of the regime slightly relaxed its grip on the strangled throat."[14] The press and media were strictly monitored and regularly censored. Boris Pasternak's epic novel, *Doctor Zhivago*, was prohibited from publication in his homeland. Polina Bogdanova stresses that during the Thaw there remained the "line of official art":[15] the administrative offices of artistic control and 'guidance' remained intact, if less visible. The Moscow Art Theatre toadied on with empty-headed state-theatre drivel; the acting troupe, claims Anatoly Smeliansky, reeked of alcohol.[16]

But, by the 1960s there had increasingly emerged a new citizen-artist, leaders of the 'artistic intelligentsia,' those who sought not the eradication of communism, but "socialism with a human face" in which artists "expressed themselves on all the current issues of the day"[17] for an audience hungry for new ideas and aesthetics. This nascent freedom of expression spawned an illusory sense of community and brotherhood among the intelligentsia – a new faith that the humane idealism that lay behind Marxist principles could be revitalized so that one could breathe, think, and speak as they wished. And remain socialist – forever.

But the Thaw inevitably came to an end. During this brief but vital period, generally the mid-1950s to the mid-1960s, unreformed Stalin sycophants had lurked in the corridors and alleyways of Moscow, awaiting their call. Festering internal opposition to Khrushchev never was alleviated; rebellions in the satellite states – Poland, Hungary, and later Czechoslovakia – cast further doubts on Khrushchev's ability to manage the Soviet empire. In 1964 a long-brewing coup removed Khrushchev from power. By 1968, almost all traces of the Thaw had been exterminated or gone underground.

But the theatre, which has always held a sacred place in the Russian soul – even more so after the Bolsheviks outlawed religion itself – remained, in the best cases, a sanctuary where the silenced intelligentsia could quietly gather. In these few theatrical refuges ingenious directors would produce Russian and sometimes foreign plays, artistically staged with concealed spiritual, social, and political messages for those who could decode them.

A quartet of these pioneering directors – all geniuses, all born after the Revolution, all educated during the worst of Stalin times – had drunk the elixir of the Thaw. These four, whom we can call the Titans of the Thaw, were Georgii Tovstonogov, whom we have covered; Oleg Efremov, who started out as an actor at Knebel's Central Children's Theatre and later became artistic director of the Moscow Art Theatre; Yuri Lyubimov, who founded the neo–Brechtian Taganka Theatre; and Knebel protégé Anatoly Efros, whom we shall focus on – became the next generation of theatrical leaders in Russia. They occupy an era on the generational/genealogical tree, one step down from their mentors, those who had been profoundly affected by Stanislavsky's Opera-Dramatic Studio.

A new generation of artists and audiences was born, thanks to the brief but crucial Thaw.

Notes

1 For the remainder of this chapter and in the ensuing chapters of Part I, I have relied on Senelick, Laurence, *Historical Dictionary of Russian Theatre. Historical Dictionaries of Literature and the Arts.* Second edition. ed. Lanham Maryland: Rowman and Littlefield, 2015; Ed. Senelick, Laurence, and Sergei Ostrovsky. *The Soviet Theater: A Documentary History*, New Haven, Yale University Press, 2014; and Leach, Robert and Victor Borovsky. 1999. *A History of Russian Theatre.* Cambridge: Cambridge University Press.

2 Senelick, Laurence, *Soviet Theater* 5.

3 Letter dated 18 April 1901, published in *Literaturnoe nasledstvo-Chekhov*, vol. 68, Moscow, 1960, p. 442; found in Meĭerkhol'd V. È and Edward Braun. 2016. *Meyerhold on Theatre* Fourth ed. London UK: Bloomsbury Methuen Drama, 193.

4 Гл ред and С Мокульский. 1961. *Театральная Энциклопедия: ГЛАВРЕПЕРТКОМ (Главный репертуарный комитет,Т. 1.: А - Глобус.* Moskva: Советская энциклопедия; Editor-in-chief and S Mokulsky. 1961. *Theatrical Encyclopedia:* GLAVREPERTCOM (Main Repertory Committee) *Vol. 1*: A - Globe. Moskva: Soviet Encyclopedia.

5 *Cenzura v sovetskom Sojuze 1917–1991. Dokumenty (Цензура в Советском Союзе с 1917 по 1991 годы), sost. A. Bljum, Moskva, ROSSPEN, 2004, p. 99; found* in Autant-Matthieu, Marie Christine at https://www.critical-stages.org/2/ du-moujik-au-kolkhozien-ou-comment-representer-la-campagne-sur-la-scene-sovietique/ (accessed July 31, 2023).

6 Juraga Dubravka and M. Keith Booker. 2002. *Socialist Cultures East and West: A Post–Cold War Reassessment.* Westport, CT: Praeger, 68.

7 The first use of this common phrase I find is in the show business journal "Variety," Variety, 8/1/1956, ISSN: 0042-2738, Volume 203, Issue 9, p. 7 While Variety is well known for its snappy headlines, it is unclear if they originated this phrase.

8 Certificates of the 1st Special Department of the USSR Ministry of Internal Affairs on the number of those arrested and convicted in the period 1921–1953 // Alexander N. Yakolev Fund. https://www.alexanderyakovlev.org/fond/issues-doc/1009312 (Accessed August 8, 2023).

 9 В.Н. Земсков К Вопросу О Масштабах Репрессий В Ссср, 123; V.N. Zemskov On
    the Question of the Scale of Repressions in the USSR 123; http://ecsocman.hse.ru/
    data/066/890/1216/016Zemskov.pdf (accessed August 7, 2023).
10 Leach Robert. 1989. *Vsevolod Meyerhold*. Cambridge, England: Cambridge
    University Press, p. 204.
11 Вл И Немирович-Данченко Владимир Иванович и В. Я Виленький. 1952.
    Театральное Наследие. 1 Статьи Речи Беседы Письма. Moskva: Государственное
    Издат. Искусство; Vladimir Nemirovich-Danchenko Vladimir Ivanovich and V.Ya
    Vilenky. 1952. Theatrical Heritage. V. 1 Articles Speeches Talks Letters. Moskva:
    Gosudarstvennoe Izdat. Art 51.
12 Senelick Laurence. 2014. *The Soviet Theater: A Documentary History*. New Haven:
    Yale University Press, p. xiv.
13 Smeliansky Anatoly Laurence Senelick and Patrick Miles. 1999. *The Russian
    Theatre after Stalin*. Cambridge: Cambridge University Press, 4.
14 Smeliansky *After Stalin* 9.
15 Полина Богданова. 2010. *Режиссеры-Шестидесятники*. Moskva: Новое
    литературное обозрение; Polina Bogdanova. 2010. Directors-Sixties. Moskva:
    New Literary Review, 8.
16 Interview with author, Cambridge MA, July 18, 2017.
17 Bogdanova 7–8.

6 Anatoly Efros
No Better Man

Introduction

Between 1951 and 1987 director Anatoly Efros created seventy-four stage productions, thirteen television films, four feature films, and four radio plays.[1] He was briefly an artistic director at two major Moscow theatres and a staff director at two others. Meanwhile his fellow Titans of the Thaw – Georgii Tovstonogov, Oleg Efremov, and Yuri Lyubimov – established lifelong regimes in their personality-driven theatres. Efros, the least politically adept of the quartet – by his own admission a "bad diplomat"[2] – encountered in-house rebellions and political condemnations at the last three theatres he was associated with. Wherever Efros went, the tendril he hung on was always fragile; even during the Thaw all decision-making appointments at all theatres were authorized by the cultural ministry. Nonetheless, Efros persisted in creating radical productions of plays by Anton Chekhov (whom the Soviets had co-opted as their own), as well as unorthodox productions of Shakespeare, Molière, Gogol, and the perennially suspect genius Mikhail Bulgakov.

Incapable of not overworking and often under political and journalistic attack, Efros suffered three heart attacks, at ages 40, 50, and 62. The last was fatal. Many believed his final official appointment was an attempt by the government to set him up for failure: Anatoly Smeliansky has bluntly declared: "they killed him."[3] Summarizing Efros' impact on his audiences, Anatoly Smeliansky wrote:

> In his book *A Love of Rehearsals*, Efros attempts to explain the essence of how he works with actors. He speaks of the 'zigzag filament' of the human soul, its contradictions, which have to be uncovered and expressed on the stage. He compares it with a cardiogram, in which the jagged peaks convey the workings of the pulsating heart, and only a straight line signifies death.
>
> For a quarter of a century, the art of Efros himself was a kind of stage cardiogram. The jagged peaks and troughs of his productions showed us the rhythm of our own heart.[4]

DOI: 10.4324/9781003475576-8

In that quarter century (and a bit more), Efros had primary associations with the four institutions that follow.[5]

The Central Children's Theatre, 1954–1964

After a brief period directing in the provinces, Efros was invited to this theatre by his former GITIS teacher, Maria Knebel, who was soon appointed artistic director. Here, deep in the heart of Moscow's theatre district, he directed thirteen productions, many of them enormously successful. Several featured future Titan actor/director Oleg Efremov, who later started his own highly successful company, The Sovremennik (Modern) Theatre, from which he ascended to the directorship of the Moscow Art Theatre. While CCT performances were nominally intended for children, adult theatre admirers and curious professionals flocked to see the latest Efros production; some even attended his now-famous rehearsals, replete with Études as encouraged and advised by his mentor Knebel. Smeliansky wrote: "In a theatre intended for children, Efros began to destroy the aesthetics of the Soviet stage."[6] All of Efros' productions were later banished from the CCT repertoire by the authorities.[7]

The Lenin Komsomol Theatre (Lenkom), 1964–1966

In the same year that Khrushchev was deposed and the Thaw began to refreeze into a period of cultural and economic inertia, Efros was appointed to lead this hitherto moribund theatre. Never a Party member, Efros was now in charge of a theatre founded for the edification of the Youth Division of the Communist Party. The governing bureaucrats presumably thought Efros would continue mesmerizing young audiences with plays on the theme of emerging youth, but at Lenkom his focus turned to the precarious role of the artist in a repressive society – artists such as himself. The majority of such performances were openly condemned by the government stooges and their puppet press; the most controversial of all, Chekhov's *The Seagull*, was banned shortly after opening. Despite the censure of the renascent cultural heavies (or perhaps because of them), ever-swelling intelligentsia audiences were numerous and enthralled. But at Lenkom, Efros had relied almost completely on the CCT actors who had followed him there; the superannuated house acting company and their entrenched upper management apparatchiks groused then rebelled, leading to Efros' expulsion by the authorities due to 'ideological deficiencies.'[8] "Nonetheless," writes Smeliansky, "the three years Efros spent [at Lenkom] became a watershed in his life and in that of the modern Russian stage."[9]

The Malaya Bronnaya Theatre, 1967–1984

From Lenkom, Efros departed with a few costumes and a dozen actors, including the devotees who had followed him from CCT to Lenkom. He was relocated to the well-managed Malaya Bronnaya Theatre in the secondary position of staff director. Unburdened from the anguish of running a theatre, Efros was now supported economically and politically by a sympathetic artistic director, enabling him to create "a repertory within a repertory and a company within a company."[10] But early on, his wildly unconventional *Three Sisters* was banned: so far two Chekhovs, two bans. Nonetheless, "by producing works whose classic status made them less subject to censorship than modem plays, but which were open to multiple interpretation, he succeeded in continuing to comment, though now indirectly, on contemporary concerns"[11] Thus, Efros' first decade at the Malaya Bronnaya was generally a happy one. But over time he grew restless: from 1974 to 1984, Efros was often elsewhere. He took on some thirty outside ventures, directing films, television films, radio plays, as well as plays in other Moscow theatres (including the Art Theatre) and at foreign theatres – Tokyo, Helsinki, and twice at the Guthrie Theater in Minneapolis, where he was offered the position of artistic director but was not permitted to accept it.[12] Then in 1984, two things happened almost simultaneously: his artistic director/ protector at the Malaya Bronnaya was dismissed; it was suggested that Efros take over, but he refused to join the Party.[13] Then, shockingly, Anatoli Efros was offered an artistic directorship at the most unlikely of Moscow theatres.

The Taganka Theatre, 1984–1987

Although of the same generation, Anatoly Efros and Yuri Lyubimov, the artistic director of the Taganka Theatre, were virtually artistic opposites. Efros had descended from the Stanislavsky/Knebel line, Lyubimov had trained at a school where most of the faculty had worked directly with Vakhtangov. He was later accepted as a company actor in the Vakhtangov Theatre and began his directing and teaching career there. It was with a group of his graduating students that Lyubimov mounted Brecht's *Good Person of Szechuan*, which took Moscow by storm. This led to the director and his young troupe of rebels being offered a remote theatre, which Lyubimov renamed The Theatre on Taganka so that people would know where it was. In the lobby he hung portraits of his artistic gods – Brecht, Meyerhold, and Vakhtangov. Soon he was forced by the government to post a portrait of Stanislavsky. Spencer Golub wrote that the

> Taganka was a child of the sixties. It speaks with the romantic and de-clamatory voice of youth. The voice is Lyubimov's – rebellious, but in an artistic rather than a political sense. Actors make no effort to transform into the roles that they perform, but rather play themselves. The Taganka company, like the troubadours of old, tell a story in which the characters are presented boldly but schematically in poetry and song.[14]

In 1975, before going abroad to direct, Yuri Lyubimov invited Anatoli Efros to be the first guest director at the Taganka, to the surprise of many. To the surprise of more, the play they chose was Chekhov's *The Cherry Orchard* – no

Chekhov play had ever been presented in Lyubimov's Vakhtangov/Brecht-influenced house. As many assumed would happen, the show was a muddle; only the two central actors responded to Efros, but by all accounts they were brilliant.

Then, nine years later, an even greater surprise arose: the cultural overlords exiled Lyubimov from Russia permanently after he made impolitic remarks to the foreign press. The ministers turned Efros, who was by this point absentee non grata at the Malaya Bronnaya. After some deliberation – friends and family advised him not to go near it – Efros accepted the position. Most of the acting company was openly hostile to Efros – they shredded his beloved American shearling coat, wrote anti-Semitic slurs on his office wall, and vandalized his car.[15]

In late 1986, the newly installed General Secretary, the liberal Mikhail Gorbachev, rescinded Lyubimov's exile. The Taganka company rejoiced, but their director pro tempore would now again be homeless. On January 13, 1987, Efros was called into the offices of the Ministry of Culture for a meeting at which, reportedly, he was subjected to a ferocious interrogation.[16] That night he died. Or, repeating what Smeliansky said: "they killed him."

Efros Directs

Given the scope of this book, we can touch on only a few relevant areas of interest about this beloved theatre magician. Let's start with his principal teacher, Maria Knebel. In 1947 Efros enrolled in a directing course at GITIS. But he was impatient with his elderly Meyerhold-oriented teacher and soon migrated to the course of Maria Knebel and Alexei Popov, both of whom were, as we know, strongly associated with the Stanislavsky line and the Moscow Art Theatre. There is no question that it was Knebel who shaped Efros' artistry far greater than any other influence. In *Beyond Rehearsal* he writes:

> When I studied with her at GITIS, and when all of us literally ran to her classes – what a radiant talent we saw!…It was the radiance of accuracy, the radiance of instantaneous response, instantaneous understanding of someone else's mistakes, and mainly her sparkling, and dazzling analysis! Analysis of scenes and analysis of improvisations! Analysis of nature! Her analysis was descriptive and ingenious, cultured to the highest degree, and to the same highest degree simple. And unusually infectious. That is why everyone was obsessed by the etude method that Knebel showed us.[17]

GITIS was his undergraduate academy, so to speak. But the Central Children's Theatre became his graduate-level practicum. Knebel brought him there in 1954, where she further guided him in Analysis through Action.

It was only at the Central Children's Theatre, after encountering Maria Knebel, Oleg Efremov, and others, that I properly, practically understood what this method is...The actors knew how to accurately determine the essence of a stage incident by an improvisational method: without even knowing the text, they joined in the acting. We arrived at rehearsal and took our seats, but soon we were on our feet – an actor must analyze in action.[18]

Along with Knebel's X-ray powers that exposed the internal anatomy of the text, she simultaneously guided her prize pupil toward a kinetic mode of analysis: the Étude Method. Efros became a virtuoso of this lively and joyful process to the delight and awe of his loyal actors, his enchanted students, and the admiring theatre practitioners who came to watch him work (all Efros rehearsals were open to visitors; this, he contended, kept the actors on their toes). Knebel's star apprentice, now an early professional, followed Knebel's pattern of an intensive but concise examination of action in the text at the table – absent of "literary chatter"[19] – and then up and on the feet. Efros wrote:

The etude method is a super-practical thing. After psychophysical analysis of the text, everything must be so clear that it should be possible to go on stage immediately and improvise...Make an analysis of what happens, consider everything in depth, extract the professional structure, and immediately play everything on stage.

For the preliminary discussion period, it is necessary to think effectively, psychophysically. The basis of this kind of thinking is that a person sees everything through action, through collision.[20]

He insists that:

If the text is analyzed and an etude does not follow immediately, this would be like learning a foreign word and not using it...a scene that is secured with an etude will be secure to opening night...Analysis and etude must not exist separately, one follows from the other. Analysis is part etude, and an etude is psychophysical analysis.[21]

And finally: "With the etude method, the action is the *trunk* and the words are the *foliage*."[22] As Efros' CCT career advanced, hit after hit, his rehearsal process became renowned; observers from other theatres, including some from outside Moscow, came to see the magician perform his tricks.

But over time Efros surprisingly abandoned the Étude Method. He wrote at one point: "improvisation, which provided so many unexpected and spontaneous adaptations, gradually ceased to be the limit of my dreams. A greater fever pitch of meaning and a sharper, original form were also wanted."[23]

Exactly how and when this transition in rehearsal strategy occurred is hard to pin down. Efros writes that the "Etude Method...work began at CCT and was completed at the Malaya Bronnaya"[24] But one of his devoted actors, Antonina Dmitrieva, who performed in seventeen Efros productions spanning CCT, Lenkom, and Malaya Bronnaya, recalls an earlier expiration date:

> At Lenkom, Efros was gradually abandoning the étude method. He was already staging *The Seagull* and [Bulgakov's] *Moliere* in a different way. We didn't understand why, even criticized him; I remember I said: 'Anatoly Vasilyevich, how well we used to work...' But by then he was bored with the way we used to work. He considered it an apprenticeship and strove ahead, not really looking to see if we could keep up with him. *He came to the beginning of the work with an idea already prepared, rather than inventing it while working with us* [emphasis mine]. And when I scolded him, he'd say,: 'Tonya, I was lying to you all. I was only pretending that you were composing something too.' And I told him: 'Lie to me again, Anatoly Vasilyevich!'[25]

So, it seems that Efros had forsaken the Étude Method by at least halfway through his professional career. This begs the question of what took the place of Études. Dmitrieva describes the new process:

> The most interesting thing he always did was the table period, although we never sat at the table. He always told his idea wonderfully, told it so captivatingly that I wanted to immediately rush onto the stage and repeat it, but then we could never play exactly the way he imagined his performance.[26]

Thus began a new phase of his work. Early on in his new approach, Efros would dynamically narrate and act out scenes from the play as the company observed these captivating demonstrations. Soon they too were on their feet, improvising – but with books in hand, not permissible when making Études – doing their best to capture some of their director's imaginative vitality, and staging ideas. In 1977, Efros explained his process to Maria Szezcow (later Maria Shevtsova):

MS: Do you work with actors in any particular way?
AE: Yes, by what I'd call an "improvisatory method"...We improvise, but we improvise which I keep inside me, so to speak. My internal draft of the thing is firm, but the process of working it out externally happens without fixed rules.[27]

To achieve this direct psychophysical exchange between actor and director, Efros rarely sat and observed. "It is necessary to train oneself not to conduct rehearsals in a sedentary manner. I am almost always on my feet and the actors, too. It's strange, but truth is 'in the feet.' An actor must understand everything with his body."[28] Truth is in the *feet*! Speaking to a new cast at Minneapolis's Guthrie Theatre, Efros told them: "Drama is the same as ballet only with words."[29] Elsewhere he repeated: "action is the *trunk* and the words are the *foliage*."[30]

> A good deal of this balletic composition has to do with how I rehearse a play…I'd say that by nature I am an expressive, demonstrative personality and that I express things in a sharp, definite way. I cross and recross the stage impetuously. I keep changing place and position. I'll turn around suddenly. I'm restless and can't sit still on stage for very long. My gestures tend to be expansive…Although this isn't premeditated, my movements on stage become the stylistics of the whole performance.[31]

It would appear that Efros had absorbed the Étude Method internally: his infectious rehearsal hyperactivity emanated from what might be seen as on-the-floor director's Études, transmitting the energy and rhythm of a character/scene/play to the actors kinetically. Smeliansky describes the results of this process, which seems to have retained Efros' idiosyncratic spontaneity and unpredictability, his own 'zig-zags:'

> His staging did not seem fixed, it was more like Brownian movement, and had a hypnotic effect. Efros's best productions are as difficult to describe as good jazz (which he adored). What won you over was the improvisatory lightness within the clearly marked boundaries of the plot. He taught his actors how to create a tough emotional geometry. He taught them to improvise within the established rectangle, the 'bounds of tenderness' as he sometimes called it at rehearsals. He had no special theory; to a large extent he relied on intuition and was simply expressing what engaged his soul at a given moment.[32]

Efros' "Brownian movement" – the random movement of particles suspended in a liquid or gas – was moderated in some measure by the 'established rectangle' or square, the 'bounds of tenderness' inside which each actor/character lived: full of vitality but with gentle boundaries which they must not cross. (We will see later that this notion of an actor/character 'rectangle' totally evaporates in the work of Butusov, Krymov, and others, where the 'bounds' dissolve.)

Efros and *The Cherry Orchard*

To get some idea of Anatoli Efros' late work, we will glance at his 1975 *Cherry Orchard*, the play which is the core study-text for this book. This work, like all Efros' Chekhov productions, fell under his guiding principle:

I want to tell about Chekhov's people...To convey all my pain through their pain and my joy through their joy.

I want them to be characters of today and not some other characters...[and] for the spectator to understand and love the art and the style which is being born today and which many people don't know yet.[33]

As for *Cherry Orchard* he said: "What, so to speak, is the main problem of The Cherry Orchard? That life is like a whirlwind. And people do not keep up with this whirlwind. The whirlwind knocks people down. Carries them away."[34] And it was a balletic whirlwind that landed on stage, vigorously manifested in the volatile spirit and agile body of Alla Demidova, arguably the finest actor Efros ever collaborated with, playing Liubov Andreevna Ranyevskaya. The Taganka actor recalled:

The entire space on stage is fully exploited. The characters move freely, generously. They emerge from all angles, their motion almost always in counterpoint. This dance-like motif is established from the very beginning...[Ranyevskaya] enters in a flutter, a sylph skimming space in joy: she forms patterns which constantly change mood, and which become emotionally more complex as the play develops.[35]

The brilliant Demidova had worked her way up the Taganka ladder; Lyubimov had cast her and everyone else in Efros' production, and this particular pairing proved to be serendipitous. She was smitten by Efros' theatrical demonstrations. She wrote in her journal: "I look at Efros with all eyes and copy him like a monkey. Even the intonation. I try to catch the rapid manner of his speech. It's almost a shorthand since the words are unimportant."[36]

Demidova and Efros shared a common passion, and compassion, for this most complex of Chekhov's characters. One observer wrote:

[They] hear the suffering in Chekhov's heroine. They find its expression not in Liubov Andreevna's traditional sighs and tears, but in her perpetual motion. Motion, to Demidova, is not just a matter of physical position or displacement, it is also a matter of emotional fluctuation...She laughs, grimaces, slips momentarily into silence only to jerk back into her own flow or interrupt somebody else's. She jokes or flirts with Lopaxin, feigns indignation, stops short suddenly, and just as suddenly launches back into signals that appear to say the opposite of what they mean. The meaning is, in fact, clear: Demidova's effervescence spells out distress.[37]

Demidova's volatility is described by Spencer Golub: "Slouching one moment, a cigarette dangling carelessly from her hand, she is seized in the next by a blast of neurotic energy which leaves her breathless."[38]

While psychophysically unpredictable, Demidova played much of the role quietly, moving about rapidly with a Mona Lisa smile on her face, a smile "that humanized the whole production."[39] Even in Act III, when she quietly asked who had bought her house at auction, "she smiled as though asking about something trivial. But it was the calm before the death of people who have suffered long. Her sheepish smile before being slaughtered was, probably, the most moving 'Efrosian' moment in the play."[40] But suddenly the slaughtered animal howled its death shriek:

> The news that the cherry orchard had been sold caused Ranevskaya physical, in the literal sense of the word, torment: straightening up to her full height, Demidova screamed hoarsely and convulsively doubled over several times, as if she had been hit in the stomach. This ugly blow, which shook both the role and the performance, was Demidova's climax. In her spasmodic painful struggles, everything that still connected Ranevskaya with the beauty of the cherry orchard, and with Russia was ripped away.[41]

Maria Szewcow wrote: "She demonstrates, through the eloquence of her acting, what [Meyerhold] meant when he spoke of the 'theatricality' of a performance."[42]

Whatever the weaknesses of the rest of the company – many had refused to work hard for Efros – Demidova gave what became perhaps the most memorable single performance of Efros' extraordinary career, and possibly hers. The collaboration between these two genius artists, communicating mostly through physical signs and guttural utterances, intuition, and instinct was an artistic pinnacle, perhaps *the* artistic pinnacle, of their storied careers.

Unsurprisingly Lyubimov disowned the production when he returned. Shortly thereafter Efros died of his final attack of the heart.

~

In tribute to this Titan who with his fellow Titans changed the course of Russian theatre, we close with a few remembrances of Anatoly Vasilyevich Efros:

Oleg Efremov: "He was a magician, and everything he touched became magic."[43]

His son Dmitry Krymov, whom we shall meet later, said:

> He was always experimenting; he was always very nervous whether a show is going to work out or not. Always trying something new, he couldn't do the same thing twice.
>
>   I think every actor of any kind who worked with him felt like an artist. That was his way. He addressed an actor as an artist.
>
>   They shut down everything he was working on. They shut down "Three Sisters," they shut down other shows, just because. They wouldn't let him do anything. He got kicked out from the Lenkom theatre, then they shut down two more shows, and there was nothing he could do.

I never think about imitating him, I don't think it's possible, I have no clue how he did what he did. That incredible atmosphere of his shows – I have no idea how he did it. I just don't know.[44]

And his wife, the extraordinary theatre critic and essayist Natalia Krymova, said:

There was no better man, I say this quite seriously. I have never met a man with such a gentle touch. It sounds a little strange about a man, but it's true. You see, I'm talking about the delicate, delicate mechanism of the soul, which, unfortunately, life always treats quite cruelly.[45]

Notes

1 Dixon, Ros *From Iconoclast to Traditionalist: A Study of Anatolii Efros's Productions of Chekhov, Gogol and Turgenev* PhD Thesis, University of Nottingham, 2003, 10. https://eprints.nottingham.ac.uk/11232/1/288087.pdf Accessed August 7, 2023. Dixon's thesis is the best English-language study of Anatoly Efros. Unfortunately she died in 2010 at age 43 before completing conversion of her thesis to a book.
2 Dixon *Study*, 77.
3 Spoken at a symposium with Efros' son Dmitry Krymov, Yale School of Drama, January 8, 2014.
4 Smelianskiĭ, A. M., Patrick Miles, and Laurence Senelick. *The Russian Theatre after Stalin*. Cambridge Studies in Modern Theatre. Cambridge: Cambridge University Press, 1999, 58–59.
5 For a fuller account of Efros' engagements with these four theatres, see James Thomas' Introduction to Éfros, Anatoliĭ, and James Thomas. *The Joy of Rehearsal: Reflections on Interpretation and Practice*. New York: Peter Lang, 2006, 5–15.
6 Smeliansky, *After Stalin* 61.
7 Golub, Spencer "Acting on the Run: Efros and the Contemporary Soviet Theatre" *Theatre Quarterly*, VII, no. 26, Summer 1997, 24.
8 Golub "Acting on the Run" 24.
9 Smeliansky *After Stalin* 62.
10 Golub "Acting on the Run" 21.
11 Dixon *Study* 16.
12 Éfros, Anatoliĭ, and James Thomas. *The Joy of Rehearsal: Reflections on Interpretation and Practice*. New York: Peter Lang, 2006, 12. James Thomas has expertly translated from four volumes of Efros' journals, converting them to three invaluable English-language editions: *The Joy of Rehearsal* (2006), *The Craft of Rehearsal* (2007), and *Beyond Rehearsal* (2009).
13 Dixon *Study* 60–61.
14 Golub "Acting on the Run" 19–20.
15 Efros & Thomas *Joy* 14.
16 Dixon *Study* 168.
17 Éfros, Anatoly, and James Thomas. *Beyond Rehearsal: Reflections on Interpretation and Practice, Continued*. New York: Peter Lang, 2009, 208.
18 Efros & Thomas *Joy* 85.
19 Efros & Thomas *Joy* 71.
20 Efros & Thomas *Joy* 40.
21 Efros & Thomas *Joy* 40.
22 Efros & Thomas *Joy* 40.

23 Efros & Thomas *Joy* 186.
24 Efros & Thomas *Beyond* 202.
25 Антонина Дмитриева, *Театр Анатолия Эфроса: Воспоминания, статьи /Сост.* М. Г. Зайонц. М.: Артист. Режиссер. Театр, 2000 58; Antonina Dmitrieva, *Theatre of Anatoly Efros: Memories, Articles*/Compiled by M.G. Zayonts. M.: Artist. Director. Theater, 2000, 58.
26 Dmitrieva *Memories* 59.
27 Shevstova Maria. 1978. *The Theatre Practice of Anatoly Efros: A Contemporary Soviet Director*. Devon Eng: Department of Theatre Dartington College of Arts, 48.
28 Efros & Thomas *Joy* 40.
29 Efros & Thomas *Beyond*.
30 Efros & Thomas *Joy* 40.
31 Shevstova *Practice* 42.
32 Smeliansky *After Stalin* 60.
33 Анатолий Эфрос Анатолий Эфрос and Н Скегина. 2011. *"Три Сестры"*. Sankt-Peterburg: Балтийские сезоны. Т. 1 23; Anatoly Efros Anatoly Efros and N Skegina. 2011. "Three Sisters." Saint-Peterburg: Baltic Seasons. V. 1 23.
34 Tatiana Shakh-Azizova in *Memories* 384.
35 Szewcow, Maria "Anatolij Efros Directs Chekhov's *The Cherry Orchard* and Gogol's *The Marriage" Theatre Quarterly*, VII, no. 26, Summer 1997, 38.
36 Алла Демидова and Алла Демидова. 2018. *"Всему На Этом Свете Бывает Конец …"*. Moskva: ACT. 11; Alla Demidova. 2018. "Everything in This World Comes to an End …". Moscow: AST. 11.
37 Szewcow *Efros Directs* 36.
38 Golub "Acting on the Run" 25.
39 Smeliansky *After Stalin* 121.
40 Smeliansky *After Stalin* 121.
41 К Рудницкий and К Рудницкий. 1990. *Театральные Сюжеты*. Moskva: "Искусство" 97; K Rudnitsky. 1990. Theater Plots. Moscow: "Art" 97.
42 Szewcow *Efros Directs* 39.
43 Efros & Thomas *Joy* 18.
44 From ГТРК "Культура"*Документальный фильм о жизни и творчестве Анатолия Эфроса*, 50 минут. Режиссёр Марина Миронова; GTRK "Culture" *Documentary about the life and work of Anatoly Efros*, 50 minutes. Directed by Marina Mironova. (Can be found on YouTube in 5 segments. Accessed August 8, 2023).
45 Натальи Крымовой Интервью с Фаина Раневская, Театръ, 3 января 2013; Natalia Krymova Interview with Faina Ranevskaya, Theater, January 3, 2013 https://oteatre.info/krymova_efros/ (accessed August 8, 2023).

7   The Glasnost Generation

Following the 1964 expulsion of Nikita Khrushchev, the Soviet Union soon slumped into the 'era of Stagnation' under the inept leadership of Leonid Brezhnev. During this time, generally accepted as 1966 to 1982, the Soviet economy foundered, at first gradually, then fatally. Meanwhile certain Stalin-era measures re-emerged including stricter supervision of the arts. While Titans Efros, Tovstonogov, Lyubimov, and Efremov struggled on, the ephemeral euphoria of the Thaw was over and they knew it. All four were able to continue up to the late 1980s period of Perestroika (restructuring), and Glasnost (openness). But between the end of the Thaw and those heady late 1980s and early 1990s days of reform was a dark and gloomy time. While Tovstonogov and Efremov dexterously played the double game – say one thing to the audience and another to the cultural *apparatchiki* (Party flunkies) – the guileless Efros and the brazen Lyubimov were regularly admonished for their ideological errors: Lyubimov to the point of exile, Efros to the point of accepting an insufferable job which almost certainly led to his death.

But the Thaw had opened doors that could no longer be sealed tight. Through the work of our four Titans and others, a re-birth of the Russian stage had begun. The waning influence of the Kedrovian Moscow Art Theatre and their dumbed-down version of Stanislavsky's System, now mandated throughout the USSR, had been openly challenged, if not yet defeated. Meyerhold's name could be mentioned again, if quietly; Vakhtangov was resuscitated; Brecht's ideas had entered Lyubimov's Taganka rehearsal hall; Peter Brook's *Lear* and *Hamlet* stunned Moscow and Leningrad, as did the US Arena Stage production of *Our Town*; foreign films by Fellini and Vittorio De Sica were wildly popular and influential, and set off a new wave in Russia, led by Andrei Tarkovsky. Maria Knebel's Étude Method was quietly infiltrating theatre practices in Moscow and elsewhere, and Georgii Tovstonogov's and Arkady Katsman's severe directing courses were legendary.

The Titans of the Thaw had managed to create acting companies, or companies within companies, that responded not only to their leaders' working methods but also to their liberal political perspectives: the Thaw directors selectively molded their "collectives of like-minded people." But it is important

DOI: 10.4324/9781003475576-9

to re-stress that while none of the Titans were Party members – surprisingly not even Tovstonogov, despite his numerous awards – the objective of this generation was not the renunciation of socialism, but the repudiation of Stalin and Stalinism. The Great Leader had died just as the Titans were entering their artistic maturity. As we know, "socialism with a human face" became the shared objective of the intelligentsia: the choir came to the Titan's churches not to be preached to but for affirmation. Torpid socialist realism, still dominant at the MAT and pretty much elsewhere, was the adversary. "The truth, nothing but the truth"[1] was the artistic cry of the rejuvenated theatres. But even those cries turned into covert whispers when recently quiescent government machinery lurched into high gear under the conservative bureaucracy of Brezhnev.

The generation following the Titans – what theatre critic and historian Polina Bogdanova labels "the directors of the Seventies" – were born during The Great Patriotic War (World War II), went through their adolescence during the Thaw, and graduated from their theatre schools just as the era of Stagnation set in. Bogdanova writes:

> They entered professional life on a wave of disappointment and disbelief because the thaw had ended in failure...The 1970s was a dark and depressing decade. Prohibitions, arrests, devastation, forced emigration – these are the signs of the beginning of the Brezhnev regime.[2]

The quartet, whom we meet in our next section – Genrietta Yanovskaya (student of Tovstonogov), Kama Ginkas (also Tovstonogov), Anatoly Vasiliev (student of Knebel and Efros), and most specifically Lev Dodin (student of Zon and Knebel) – having flourished under their master teachers, were nonetheless wanderers for years after graduating. The established theatres had retrenched as government support was increasingly scant. But most importantly, the new generation of directors, epitomized by this bold quartet, had daring post-Thaw ideas – ideas suspect in the languishing cultural environment of the Brezhnev era.

Skeptical about socialism, human face or no, these seventies directors were more concerned about the Russian individual than Russian politics. They had no expectation of social conditions changing – the steel fist had re-clenched during their theatre school years – and thus they believed that salvation lay only in the self and in imagination. Whereas the Thaw generation had focused on reconceiving society, this generation focused on reconceiving the individual. Bogdanova quotes Dodin on Chekhov:

> The Seventies largely revised the features of Chekhov's drama and Chekhov's characters. Dodin, for example, believes that "Dostoevsky, and then Chekhov – albeit in different psychological parameters – show us that the person himself is to blame for the misfortunes of a person. That a person is most responsible for their own destiny. The people are

responsible for the fate of the people. The city is responsible for the fate of the city. The nation is responsible for the fate of its history.[3]

Bogdanova continues:

> Directors began to address issues of the relationship between man and God, man and the highest meaning. At this stage of history, it became clear that human life is not determined only by society. Going beyond the boundaries of the social space and turning to the range of existential and metaphysical problems is an important and decisive step in the theater, which immediately advanced it several decades forward.[4]

Onstage, realization of these broader quests for existential and metaphysical meaning necessitated not just a reinterpreted dramaturgy – such as Dostoevsky, Chekhov above – but new rehearsal techniques and performance styles. As Analysis through Action permutated individually in the rehearsal halls, the arts of scenography played an increasingly prominent role, as did music, figurative language, and metaphor: all contributing to concealing truths perceptible to the cognoscenti but (hopefully) not to the censor. These innovators were defying the decades-old Soviet interdiction of 'formalism' – broadly defined as privileging form over content – by offering terms of engagement in the theatrical experience that exceeded psychological realism. Paradoxically in this age of resurrected repression, the individual artist became the new hero of the intelligentsia.

Ultimately, the best and brightest of the emergent seventies generation were able to land their own theatre homes: Yanovskaya and Ginkas at the Moscow Theatre for Young Generations; Vasiliev and company in a bespoke construction that the city built for him and from which they ousted him five years later; and Dodin at the now world-famous Maly Drama Theatre in Petersburg. As with the preceding generation and Anatoly Efros, here we shall concentrate here on one director, Lev Dodin.

Notes

1 Полина Богданова and Полина Богданова. 2014. *Режиссеры-Семидесятники: Культура И Судьбы*. Moskva: Новое литературное обозрение 3; Polina Bogdanova. 2014. *Directors of the Seventies: Culture and Destinies*. Moscow: New Literary Review, 3. t.
2 Bogdanova *Seventies* 5.
3 Bogdanova *Seventies* 9, quoting Dodin in Додин Л. *"Дядя Ваня". Перед выходом на сцену* // Додин Л. Путешествие без конца. S. 302; Dodin L. "Uncle Vanya". Before going on stage // Dodin L. Journey without end 302.
4 Bogdanova *Seventies* 7.

8   Lev Dodin

The Rabbinical Lion

Introduction

Lev Abramovich Dodin, son of a geologist and a doctor, was born in southern Siberia in 1944. His Jewish parents had been deemed necessary citizens and were evacuated from Leningrad during the relentless two-and-a-half-year Nazi bombardment of the legendary city called in Russia the Leningrad Blockade, in the West known as the Siege of Leningrad. Alongside the devastation of many of the city's magnificent promenades and Baroque palaces, an estimated 1.5 million citizens died from bomb explosions, starvation, disease, and minus-40°F temperatures.

Lev Dodin has seen the rejuvenation of his beloved city evolve from post-Siege rubble into a vibrant metropolis, today parading posh international chain stores down its neon-festooned boulevards. Dodin, in over almost four decades at the Maly Drama Theatre (MDT) – the theatre was initially established in an unprepossessing side-street outpost after the Blockade ended in 1944 – has created and maintained what Peter Brook called the "the finest ensemble theatre in Europe."[1] Along with their Petersburg seasons, the MDT has regularly toured throughout the globe, and for a period had a second home in Paris. As Dodin has declared: "A theatre, according to an ancient formula, should carry on a dialogue both with its city and with the world."[2]

The artistic paterfamilias of this world-renowned 'theatre home' is a rabbinical and avuncular soul, who like many of his peer directors after graduating drama school wandered from job to job, in his case seventeen years, before being able to begin the work of building his own "collective of like-minded people."[3] Remarkably, unlike most artistic leaders in Russia and around the world today, Dodin has managed to preserve his inspiring first principles: a superior resident acting company – some fifty actors at this point (more in the past), many of them trained by Dodin himself at the nearby theatre school (now called RGISI)[4] – performing artistic works of existential depth with profound intellectual, physical, and emotional theatricalism.

As Dodin developed from childhood to artistic directorship, he studied and apprenticed with a varied set of mentors. Consequently, theatrical eclecticism has permeated his work since he began assembling his MDT company in 1983.

DOI: 10.4324/9781003475576-10

While his artistic baseline remains Stanislavsky (cum Meyerhold), he avoids the attendant numbing System terminology – objectives, given circumstances, and the like – and mindless adherence to the so-called laws of the actor on-stage. Instead, it is the moral ethos and deep spirituality of Stanislavsky that has always motivated Dodin – ideas mostly found in the Stanislavsky journals, not in the tedious books – as well as KS's incessant inquiry into what is acting, what is theatre, what is professional behavior, and what is the role of the theatre artist in the world today.

Teachers and Mentors

Dodin's initial theatre lessons came during his adolescence from a benevolent outcast, a man surely aware of Stanislavsky but more influenced by the then-forbidden Meyerhold, with whom he had briefly worked. Dodin recalled teacher Matvey Dubrovin as "a Prophet, a teacher in the Biblical sense of the word – a rabbi"[5] He held his rambunctious lessons at The Theatre of Youth Creativity (TyuT) in the Leningrad Palace of Pioneers. In a 2012 interview Dodin spoke of Dubrovin with great affection:

> He considered Stanislavsky way too formal. He was a very talented and bright theatre fantaticist. He would come up with absolutely fantastic angles for the horrible Soviet plays we used to have to rehearse. Using one of his favorite terms from Meyerhold, Dubrovin would make the action "rear up" as high as it would go. And this would make these simple and boring plays sound heroically fascinating, astoundingly interesting…he was an absolute waterfall of ideas."[6]

Maria Shevtsova cites Dubrovin as the inspiration for

> the Meyerholdian touch in a number of Dodin's productions whose play is highly articulated, self-aware, reflexive, ironic, brazen and charged with the actors' fantasy, which they keep going at a high pitch. In other words, the play at issue exploits what Meyerhold termed *teatralnost* [theatricality][7]

But as powerful as Dubrovin's acting lessons were, Dodin experienced something else at the Palace of Pioneers: the idea of theatre as a spiritual and cultural sanctuary in dark times:

> [In the 1950s] life was quite cramped, narrow, not free…At The Theatre of Youth Creativity, life was special, completely different from the one that reigned over us. For us, these times with [Dubrovin] were times of complete creative freedom, manifestations of kindness, love and interest in each other, the feeling of theater as a kind of magnetic miracle…I think he instilled in us *the very concept of morality, a sense of honor, hope, kindness, inner freedom and, perhaps, the joy of life.*[8] [emphasis mine]

The emphasized words above would be an apt description of Lev Dodin's the-atrical mission throughout his career.

In 1961, age 17, Dodin was admitted to the course of Boris Zon, whose Leningrad Institute classes had the reputation of being the most difficult to get into – and the most difficult to graduate from. Fellow instructor Georgii Tovstonogov called Zon "the best theater teacher in the USSR."[9]

Readers will recall that the young director Boris Zon, having read a draft copy of Stanislavsky's first attempt at *An Actor's Work*, traveled from Leningrad to Leontiev Lane to meet the godfather of the System. Zon was shocked by what he saw there: not the rigors of System 'training and drill' he expected but improvisations and open free play – the early physical action experiments which over time led to Knebel's Étude Method. Five years of sporadic week-end meetings with Stanislavsky inspired Zon to renunciate his earlier aestheti-cized approach to directing and teaching; he began seeking, in Dodin's words, the "incessant vibrations of life."[10] Dodin recounted his teacher's approach:

> As for the system itself, Zon was very free, he very rarely used the termi-nology because over his last years Stanislavsky had come to despise his own terminology. Zon tried to describe stage life in the same vocabulary we use to describe everyday life; to analyze the conditions of life, he would very, very specifically ask: where have you been, where are you going, what steps do you have to take to get there? When I became a little more mature after graduating, I found out these were the objectives and given circumstances, but he would almost never have used these words.[11]

Russian scholar Nikolai Pesochinsky has written: "Zon was one of those fol-lowers of Stanislavsky who overcame the schematic consciousness of the 'sys-tem' of acting by études, fantasy, improvisation, freedom of creative well-being."[12] Shevtsova describes the effects of Zon on Dodin:

> Dodin's constant emphasis, as he works with his actors, on the 'living life' of moments and the actors' 'aliveness' to them is related to what in the later work of Stanislavsky…may be termed research into possibilities at the quick of feeling…[this] can be paraphrased as follows: something that has come alive in the actor takes root, which ensures its regeneration and growth in successive performances where it is fresh every time.[13]

The Lion without a Den

While Lev Dodin – his given name translates as "lion" – was recognized by the Institute faculty as an exceptionally promising student, upon graduation no per-manent offers from establishment theatres appeared. Over the next sixteen years he directed in various venues, including the Leningrad Maly Drama Theatre, which had a liberal artistic director, but Dodin latched on to none full-time. As most

Russian directors do at some point, he took up what became a life-long corollary profession: teaching. His first assistantship was in 1967 with Institute instructor Zinovy Korogodsky, who would later write "the best book on Études,"[14] *Nachalo*, meaning *Beginning*, from which we will draw extensively in Part II of this volume.

Korogodsky, who had earlier also studied with Zon, offered Dodin an internship on his directing team at The Leningrad Young People's Theatre (Len TYUZ). Like Knebel at the CCT, Korogodsky had brought his theatre to national recognition as a site for bold new work, appealing to older audiences as well as young. Dodin was able to direct or co-direct a few notable productions there; some were so popular that a jealous Korogodsky ushered Dodin out of his theatre.[15]

But before his expulsion, one significant event in Dodin's professional apprenticeship took place: from 1968 to 1970 he attended several workshops led by Maria Knebel. At that time, the youth theatres were far more innovative and artistically influential than the larger civic theatres; the censors ignored them because the children's theatres were, well, for children.[16] Maria Knebel, the acknowledged leader of the youth theatre field, would periodically lead Analysis through Action symposia with the directors of these allied youth theatres. Dodin recalled: "Since Korogodsky was way too grand to go down to Moscow to study under Knebel, I was designated to be his representative."[17] He continued:

> I participated in a dozen of her lessons. She would idealize action analysis and she did it with a wonderful method…She was charm personified. Very kind, very subtle. And she was one of the few people to be talented at formulating her own thoughts on paper. Sometimes she would explain things on paper that Stanislavsky wasn't as good at explaining…we remembered her lessons well.[18]

In 1979 Dodin was invited to assist in the Institute course of Arkady Katsman, who had been Tovstonogov's teaching partner for years (recall Ganeva's comment in Chapter 5 that Katsman taught Tovstonogov better than Tovstonogov did). With Katsman, Dodin was exposed to yet another interpretation of Stanislavsky, based on rigorous text analysis. It was with two productions featuring the student actors from this course that made an ineradicable mark on the Russian Theatre – and resulted in director Lev Dodin inheriting the Maly Drama Theatre as his permanent home.

Brothers and Sisters

Over a three-year period, Dodin had worked with the 1979 Katsman students adapting a 'village prose' trilogy by one of the most famous authors of this topical genre, Fyodor Abramov. Although Abramov wrote in a straightforward realistic manner about the suffering of an isolated northern village during The Great Patriotic War, Dodin and company took a Meyerholdian theatricalist path with his *House* and *Brothers and Sisters*. Pesochinsky evokes the impact of these stories, as adapted by Dodin and students:

> It was not a reflection of "objective" history that was revealed, but a collage of sensual, local, private, simple human stories and passions, each of which was individually, in detail, nervously, personally experienced by the actors on an unusual stage set. The action did not consist of elements of everyday life, but of audible and visible music, of songs, fairground booths, folklore, ritual reflections of life as nature...The action was organized in a musical way. The collage as a whole took on a non-realistic, tragic, even mysterious depth. In this performance, a bold renewal of the form of the "psychological" theater was declared, an openly theatrical and mythological artistic language was found which, as it developed through experiencing different genres and different types of material, determined Dodin's art at the MDT for a long time.[19]

It was the successful 1980 production of *House*, the first segment of the Abramov trilogy, along with his prior productions at the MDT, that elevated Dodin, age 40, to the artistic directorship of the theatre in 1983. But it was *Brothers and Sisters* two years later that put Dodin and the MDT on the international map. Heralded as "the first post-Soviet production,"[20] clearly denouncing the horrors of the communist past, *Brothers and Sisters* traveled the globe continually, earning universal recognition for the Maly company. (In 2015 the performance was revived, with several original cast members now playing older characters, their earlier characters filled by recent students.)

Dodin's Theatre Home

As of this writing, Lev Dodin has been leading the Maly Drama Theatre for four decades. He and his trusted resident team have created an enormous body of work, much of it seen on stages around the world, simultaneously winning innumerable prizes in their homeland. Unlike most American and European theatre companies (save perhaps Ariane Mnouchkine's Théâtre du Soleil and Thomas Ostermeier's Schaubuhne), Dodin has built a long-standing "theatre home" with an unbroken chain of leadership, a renowned permanent company of artists – actors, designers, and artistic specialists (particularly vocal director Valery Galandeev) – with consistent creative programming emphasizing the struggle for humanity and individuality in oppressive circumstances.

Much of the early work at Dodin's MDT continued the dramatization of fictional works – commonly termed "theatre of prose" – as seen in *House* and *Brothers and Sisters*. Dodin has stated that prose is "often richer than drama with the exception of Shakespeare and Chekhov, who can hold their own."[21]

Here are some noteworthy examples from Dodin's and the Maly's theatre of prose:

1986 – *Lord of the Flies* from Golding
1990 – *Gaudeamus* from Kaledin's *Construction Battalion*
1991 – *Demons* from Dostoevsky's *The Possessed*
1994 – *Claustrophobia* drawn from four Russian authors
1999 – *Chevengur* from Andrei Platonov's suppressed novel
2004 – *Moscow Chorus* from Lyudmila Petrushevskaya's *Chorus*
2007 – *Life and Fate* from Vasily Grossman
2020 – *The Brothers Karamazov* from Dostoevsky

Maria Shevtsova, who has followed Dodin's work for decades, summarizes:

> [W]hen Dodin's 'theatre of prose' is assembled and studied as a corpus, prose allows him to restore a cultural memory that had been damaged, lost or threatened with loss by censorship and semi-clandestinity...or by the solitary exercise of reading in a country that had stifled public debate. The theatre, the most immediate and collective of artistic practices, is the keenest means by which culture, and thus also the history that it carries, can be remembered.[22]

Here lies the central mission of Dodin and the work of his Maly Drama Theatre – as first inspired by Dubrovnik: 'theater as a kind of magnetic miracle.' The restoration of cultural memory helps provide a spiritual antidote for an individual enduring a world 'cramped, narrow, not free' and through self and cultural knowledge to aspire toward 'hope, honor, kindness, inner freedom – and perhaps the joy of life.'

Dodin's theatre of prose created a unique means of rehearsing with Études, a procedure of actor/director co-authorship which takes place over many months – even years. It begins with the full company – all actors are required to attend all rehearsals – reading the entire prose work aloud to one another, page by page. The actors, often on their own, then proceed to make investigative Études – Dodin and company use the terms "probes" or "tries," as in "let's try it."[23] The entire novel is chronologically "probed" on the floor; no Étude is preplanned or repeated. There is very little discussion at this point; no roles are cast, nor any scenes selected. These expository probes are then encouraged by Dodin to become more subjective, often deviating from the direct narrative into personal memories or impressionistic fantasies evoked by the text. Events of the prose work may be updated to modern times, apposite songs and music may be introduced, a narrative section may be danced, mimed, or vernacularly paraphrased. Literal re-creation of the text is discouraged.

Dodin's responses at this point will typically be non-evaluative but will raise questions for further inquiry – meaning more probes; by the end there will have been hundreds of them. His rehearsals are activated by asking questions, not by finding solutions: "I think all work is a continual asking of questions and finding answers that give rise to new questions...because, as they say, the devil is in the details. And each detail creates a new question."[24] Shevtsova writes that Dodin stresses that this interrogative process which makes the actor "a researcher instead of a mere interpreter, or just a wearer of masks." She continues:

> Dodin's principal task as a director is best described as catalytic: he prompts actors to 'dig' through the layers of their existence – memories and subconscious experiences included – in order to find in themselves whatever they are playing and stimulate their existential and creative potential. The actor involved in this process is not primed to...execute the director's will, but becomes what Dodin calls an 'active co-author' of a production along its entire research path or 'journey of birth.[25]

While at the Academy under Dodin's keen eyes, the actors, some of whom were subsequently invited into the MDT company, were intensely trained by masters of improvisation, dance, acrobatics, combat, musical instruments (they all must play at least one very well), singing, vocal dexterity and, oh yes, acting – the last with Dodin himself. Unlike American academies, there is no separation between 'scene study' and technique classes, everything is interrelated and put to work in ongoing rehearsals. It is a holistic unity of pedagogy, collectively dedicated to making cohort performance pieces starting with simple stories, gradually elevating to complex major productions. Again, Shevtsova:

> [The actors] defy physical-spatial limits. They crawl up the walls and sway perilously away from them or crash their way through them. They walk on ledges and dance on barres. Men dance *en pointe*. Dialogue is sung. Brass instruments are played satirically as barbed asides on socio-political realities.[26]

As the probes continue and the theatricalism expands, several provisional scripts are produced. Ultimately, Dodin edits everything down to the "final" rendition – which is never in fact final; alterations to the script, staging, or casting may be made months or even years later, well into public performances.

Laurence Senelick describes *Gaudeamus*, co-authored by Dodin and his Institute class of 1990, drawn from a bleak novel about the barbaric training of young Russian army conscripts.

> [T]he final production was put together from 40 hours of sketches prepared by a cadre of students. Song, dance, circus routines, music and parody were incorporated. In performance, the actors were put through extremes of physical and psychic endurance...However, each episode made a social point: a ballet commented on hazing, vaudeville routines

pointed up ethnic discrimination, circus balloons stood for substance abuse, a push-up competition degenerated into a farting contest. The audience watched morally deficient youths be forced into molds and then graduate into society.[27]

What emerged from this visually stunning and theatrically exuberant performance was ultimately the tragic tale of a generation crushed by a militaristic regime.

Rehearsing a Dramatic Text

At some point, every Russian director must wrestle with the Chekhov problem, as has every director mentioned in this book. Dodin began late, with *The Cherry Orchard* in 1994, followed by *The Seagull* (2001), *Uncle Vanya* (2003), *The Three Sisters (2010)*, and a very different *Cherry Orchard* in 2014. As well as the established tetralogy, he also directed *A Play without a Title* (aka *Platonov*) in 1997.

The MDT rehearsal process for dramatic texts such as Chekhov's plays resembles the process for 'theatre of prose,' although the script is already prescribed by a Dodin edit. Therefore the rehearsal probes are focused on characters and events as found in the text; the free-association techniques used in the prose works exist but are restricted. However, affective memory probes remain: enlisting fellow actors in supporting roles, an actor might improvise a personal life experience comparable to an event experienced by their character in the play. A vast array of tries – textual and personal – are interspersed with extensive seminar-style inquiries led by Dodin, the MDT actors contributing their own perspectives and questions. After a run of a scene, an act, or the whole play these colloquies generally start with Dodin asking the actors "What were your impressions?" – about their work of the day, and typically end with him sharing his own responses – often with exacting observations and questions for each actor. These colloquies can last for hours, most are recorded for future reference, and some are published.

Instead of instructive "notes," Dodin will usually ask questions of the actor, or sometimes deliver an impromptu personal performance, demonstrating a fictional event parallel to a moment in the play. But whatever means Dodin deploys – Études, affective memories including his own, demonstrations, spoken notes, or repetitive "tries" on a single moment or even a single word – the goal is always to instill in the actor the internal sense of *ya yesm* – the *I am*, but expressed with Meyerholdian theatricality, a full-body physicality even if standing still, a Meyerholdian/Dubrovian sense of rhythm and Stanislavskian spiritual communion with whomever else the actor is onstage, and the audience. To achieve this higher state of consciousness, Dodin's rehearsals can indeed be unsparing, physically, and emotionally. Shevtsova explains:

The expenditure of energy in rehearsals is immense. Dodin believes it is worthwhile especially because extreme creative effort, when the mind-body is pushed beyond its limits, releases tension, relaxes the mind-body and lifts it onto another plane of spiritual awareness. This is the point when an actor can make a breakthrough and achieve what cannot be achieved in any other mind-body state.[28]

Valery Galandeev, Dodin's right arm at both RGISI and the MDT, summarized the goal for the actor in Dodin's exhaustive training and rehearsal processes as a form of anti-naturalism:

Naturalism is the conservation, the mummification of reality, the ultimate graveyard of inanimate nature. Dodin's art consists of the opposite. His basic principle is to launch living (vital) currents and juices, pulses, breaths, tenderness and squirming of the flesh, miasmas and fragrances, a living delight in life, horror, and confusion into the mechanism of theatrical thinking and feeling.[29]

Cherry Orchard 1, 1994

Glasnost and perestroika were prematurely celebrated in the West as initial steps in a post-Soviet advance toward Western capitalism and liberal democracy – in short, in the Western view, the chance to join the community of enlightened nations. But the mood in Russia was hardly that sanguine. As the keys to the Kremlin passed from a deposed Mikhail Gorbachev to the volatile alcoholic Boris Yeltsin, the faint hope for long-term stability soon perished. Moscow and Leningrad natives were emigrating in droves, civil services were disrupted, the ruble was a yo-yo, citizens' homes and apartments, long underwritten by the Soviet government, were being scarfed up by unscrupulous speculators forcing massive evictions and homelessness.

In this precarious atmosphere the collective artistic souls of the MDT rehearsed and presented *The Cherry Orchard* – a play that originally premiered just prior to the 1905 'bloody Sunday' revolution, only two generations after the emancipation of the serfs. This *Cherry Orchard*'s onstage setting was as dark as the times. Shevtsova recalls: "seemingly invisible hands…gradually break away bits of the decor…until the spectators realize with a shock at the end that nothing, but a skeleton remains."[30] But these seem to be the invisible hands of fate, not of social history. At the end it is clear that this is the last time many of the characters will see each other. Their house is dispossessed: they disappear into unknowable futures, into a life they are unequipped for – refugees blind to the fact that the old world is vanishing around them, unable to see salvation ahead.

Two key events in the production underscored the sense of inertia and dread that permeated this dark production. The Act III dance continuously snaked out of the ballroom, through the sitting room where Ranyevskaya and others waited for the results of the foreclosure auction and back into the ballroom through a second door; the line dance and music carried on almost through the entire act. But the music stopped during Lopakhin's euphoric account of winning the auction. He commanded them to play on, and the young dancers, now ghostly lit, continued in a slow palsy of awkward gyrations. A future generation had become a grotesque skeletal apparition: Meyerhold redux.

A second memorable event was simpler, but equally powerful. As per the script, at the end of Act IV everyone departed, leaving only a barren divan onstage. Ancient valet Firs slowly tottered in, muttering indecipherably, and lay down on the divan, face up, eyes shut, immobile for a very long time. Nothing happened. More time passed. Is he asleep? Is he dead? Is somebody going to return to get him? Is the play over? Will it ever end? After an excruciating passage of time the lights slowly faded – possibly indicating destiny extracting of the soul of this ageless exemplar of a bygone Russia. Or not. Even Firs' death was uncertain.

Throughout the performance, I was reminded of Antonio Gramsci's prophetic words: "the old order is dying and the new cannot yet be born; in this interregnum a great variety of morbid symptoms appear."[31]

Cherry Orchard 2, 2014

The inevitable question was why revisit this play twenty years later. Dodin replied:

> It was a different world then; we had a premonition of something new coming, but we thought we could handle whatever it would be. But then, when we started working on the play again a year and a half ago, we realized that the new things coming our way today are far more frightening than those that came before. I don't mean only in Russia—I think the world has become ill from these terrible things.[32]

Dodin has a simple analysis of what happened between 1994 and 2014: "Yes, [today] everything is about money, we understand that a little bit more now."[33]

For his 2014 edition, Dodin made many changes to the original text. The role of Dunyasha became almost non-existent; the neighboring landowner Semyon-Pischik was removed entirely. The production opened with lines from Firs; Lopakhin slept in a chair until Ranyevskaya's arrival. A significant revision was the reinsertion of an extraordinary 'absurd theatre' scene between Firs and Charlotta that Chekhov intended to be the final scene of Act II – until Stanislavsky cut it.[34]

The front three rows of the theatre were removed and the furniture, for the most part scattered around the cleared floor, pushed up against the knees of the audience. In the center aisle sat a billiards table where Gayev periodically retreated for a round. An old film projector showed a lyrical soft-focus film of Ranyevskaya, dressed in white, walking through a cherry orchard in happier times. When Lopakhin made his pitch about turning the orchard into sites for *dachas* (cottages), he showed his edit of the same film: as he spoke, small squares with ruble signs (₽) ticked sequentially across the sheet, obliterating the orchard.

For the famous "broken string" sound in Act II, Dodin set off a siren, meant, he said, to "evoke images of the gulag prisons or concentration camps to come."[35] The production concluded with a shattering final image: while the entire company stood on the floor in front of the stage, on the sheet behind them appeared an image of these same actors dressed in white prison outfits, as if about to executed. The siren rang out for the second and last time as the lights faded.

Danila Kozlovsky's Lopakhin, the main focus of this production, was a whirlwind of entrepreneurial energy, passionate about his goal of converting a dying estate into cottages for New Russians like himself. He was also passionate about his potential future wife, the family adoptee and estate manager Varya, played by the equally stunning Elizaveta Boyarskaya. This charismatic couple (both were graduates of Dodin's 2007 course and have active movie careers) were clearly sexually drawn to one another: 'accidental' touches, two long onstage kisses, and a brief disappearance offstage, returning with what could only be described as post-coital smiles. Thus, when the serf-to-millionaire Lopakhin declined to propose to her, the agonized Varya fell to the floor, howling in agony. Lopakhin purposefully walked out of the theatre. He had what he wanted, the estate; now he was off to new conquests.

If the 1994 MDT version of *Cherry Orchard* was shrouded in the uncertainty and dispossession of the new post-Soviet era, the 2014 version was a dirge for what came next – the Putinization of Russia, as exemplified by the nouveau oligarch-wannabe, Lopakhin.

'Yes, everything is about money, we understand that a little bit more now.'

Postscript

In 2022, Lev Dodin courageously posted a passionate renunciation of Putin and his invasion of Ukraine. It can be found in the March 3 edition of *The Economist*; or as of this writing at: https://www.economist.com/culture/2022/03/03/lev-dodin-an-acclaimed-russian-theatre-director-decries-the-war

Notes

1 *Time Out* 13-20 April 1994; found in Shevtsova Maria. 2004. *Dodin and the Maly Drama Theatre: Process to Performance*. London: Routledge. 29.
2 Lev Dodin "Live theatre. Notes and considerations" https://www.mdtdodin.ru/publications/?url=/publications/237.json (Accessed August 12, 2023)=

3 Полина Богданова and Полина Богданова. 2014. *Режиссеры-Семидесятники: Культура И Судьбы*. Moskva: Новое литературное обозрение. 20 Polina Bogdanova. 2014. Directors of the Seventies: Culture and Destinies. Moscow: New Literary Review. 20.

4 Now called RGISI: The Russian State Institute of Performing Arts, formerly known as St Petersburg Theatre Arts Academy (SPGATI), formerly Leningrad State Institute of Theatre, Music, and Cinema (LGITMiK).

5 Fifth Channel Saint Petersburg: Cultural Program "Founder Of Tyut"; accessed July 10, 2021; no longer on YouTube.

6 Interview with author, May 15, 2012, Live translation by Dina Dodina.

7 Shevtsova Maria. 2004. *Dodin and the Maly Drama Theatre: Process to Performance*. London: Routledge. 29.

8 Author interview May 12, 2012.

9 Школа Бориса Зона. Уроки актерского мастерства и режиссуры / Составитель В. Львов. - Санкт-Петербург: Сессия, 2011 6.; School of Boris Zon. Acting and directing lessons / Compiled by V. Lvov. - St. Petersburg.: Session, 2011 6.

10 Author interview May 15, 2012.

11 Author interview May 15, 2012.

12 Песочинский, Николай "Дом, который построил Додин" *Театр* 07 апреля 2014; Pesochinsky, Nikolai "The House that Dodin Built" *Teatr*, April 07, 2014 https://oteatre.info/dom-kotoryj-postroil-dodin/ (Accessed August 12, 2023).

13 Shevtsova *Dodin and Maly* 38.

14 Author interview with Veniamin Filshtinsky, May 19, 2012.

15 Senelick, Laurence *Digital Theatre Plus* "A Concise Introduction to Lev Dodin," https://edu-digitaltheatreplus-com.yale.idm.oclc.org/content/guides/lev-dodin (subscription or affiliation required).

16 Author interview with Russian director Adolf Shapiro, Cambridge, Mass, July 12, 2018.

17 Author interview May 15, 2012.

18 Author interview May 15, 2012.

19 Pesochinsky "House".

20 Delgado Maria M and Dan Rebellato. 2010. *Contemporary European Theatre Directors*. London: Routledge 70.

21 Shevtsova *Dodin and Maly* 63.

22 Shevtsova *Dodin and Maly* 63.

23 Author interview May 12, 2012.

24 Лев Додин Лев Додин and Анна Огибина. 2016. *Путешествие Без Конца: Погруженуе В Миры: "Вишневый Сад"*. Sankt-Peterburg: "Балтийские сезоны" 462; Lev Dodin Lev Dodin and Anna Ogibina. 2016. *Journey without End: Immersion in Worlds: "The Cherry Orchard"*. Saint-Peterburg: "Baltic Seasons" 462.

25 Maria Shevtsova in Mitter Shomit and Maria Shevtsova. 2007. *Fifty Key Theatre Directors*. London: Routledge 202.

26 Shevtsova in *Fifty Key Directors* 204.

27 Senelick *Concise Introduction*.

28 Shevtsova *Dodin and Maly* 59.

29 Валерий Галендеев and В Галендеев. 2014. *Лев Додин: Метод Школа Творческая Философия*. Sankt-Peterburg: Издательство Санкт-Петербургской государственной академии театрального искусства 42; Valery Galandeev and V Galandeev. 2014. Lev Dodin *Method School Creative Philosophy*. Saint-Peterburg: Publishing House of the St. Petersburg State Academy of Theater Art 42.

30 Shevtsova *Dodin and Maly* 127.

31 Gramsci Antonio, Quintin Hoare and Geoffrey Nowell-Smith. 1973. *Selections from the Prison Notebooks of Antonio Gramsci* First ed. New York: International 276.

32 Dodin interviewed in "American Theatre," February 22, 2016, https://www.americantheatre.org/2016/02/22/lev-dodin-plants-chekhovs-cherry-orchard-in-the-eternal-present/
33 Lev Dodin and Anna Ogibina. 2016. "*The Cherry Orchard*" 14.
34 This remarkable Beckettian scene can be found in Chekhov, Anton Pavlovich Richard Nelson, Richard Pevear and Larissa Volokhonsky. 2015. *The Cherry Orchard: A Comedy in Four Acts* First ed. New York: Theatre Communications Group.
35 Dodin interview "*American Theatre*".

9 The 2000s

A Torrent of New Wealth

Lev Dodin's 2014 *Cherry Orchard* dramatically autopsied the dead souls of Russia who emerged after the paroxysms of the Boris Yeltsin era (1991–1999): 'Yes, everything is about money, we understand that a little bit more now,' said the old Lion about his second production of Chekhov's masterwork. Yeltsin's surprise successor, a former KGB[1] officer, Lieutenant Colonel Vladimir Putin (same mid-rank as Vershinin in *Three Sisters*), ushered in a new era. His craftily evolved despotism was fortified from any serious opposition by his new laws, new police orders, many arrests, and a few murders – and, to pacify the populace, his promotion of a new cultural narcotic: Wealth.

A typhoon of hyper-capitalism blew through the big cities of the former Soviet Union. The once tawdry grand boulevards were suddenly clogged with topline Mercedes, Hummers, and Teslas; newly glistening shops were stocked with European fashions and foods; and former dilapidated communal apartments were renovated into Euro-chic condominia equipped with the latest technology and high-end appliances. Old central Moscow increasingly looked like a giant duty-free mall in an Emirates airport.

A new class of 'citizen' emerged: the billionaire/oligarchs, with palatial urban homes around the world, vast country estates, battleship-scale yachts, and top-level sports teams confettied across Europe and New York City. Of course, millions and millions of Russians found themselves suffering in conditions worse than the Soviet state-supported era; they were ignored and left alone to suffer.

The theatre was not impervious to this torrent of lucre. The former "theatre home" ideal deteriorated toward extinction as artistic directors were replaced by executive directors whose producorial assignment was to fill the seats with whatever fare the market would bear. A repertory of broadly popular fare eclipsed the consistent bespoke artistry that had been the hallmark of earlier resident collectives of like-minded souls. Theatres ceased to aesthetically differ from one another, directors were interchangeable, and actors, most of their resident companies dissolved, began accepting whatever show with whatever director would cast them in whatever medium. A gaudy commercial music-theatre scene that would embarrass Las Vegas in the 1950s flourished. TV stars

DOI: 10.4324/9781003475576-11

began appearing in saturnine Broadway/West End–style would-be dramadies, re-treads of Soviet realism without the Soviet. Boy meets Hummer.

The 'intelligentsia,' who for decades had been the moral and intellectual epicenter of the culture – thus the core audience for serious theatre – were now shunted to the periphery. Polina Bogdanova writes:

> [B]y the beginning of the new century it was material values that came first. There was a cult of money, and people began to build their lives in accordance with the opportunity to earn it. Therefore, professions that generated high earnings began to be valued – and not those that in the 1960s were considered socially and culturally important: actor, writer, scientist, journalist.[2]

She goes on to describe the still-current situation at the Moscow Art Theatre:

> Today the Chekhov [MAT] works according to the principle of *non*-repertory; its stockpile consists of many plays by different directors who are not connected with each other by a unity of aesthetic and ideological principles. The artistic policy of the Moscow Art Theater is aimed at attracting as many spectators as possible, which the theater mostly succeeds at doing. The "artistic variety" of the productions at this theater becomes the principle of its work.[3]

Nonetheless, a few outposts clung to the ideals of the theatre home with a nucleus of house directors and actors. Dodin's MDT has hung in there, despite periodic government harassment. Genrietta Yanovskaya and Kama Ginkas, graduates of the Tovstonogov directing course, have maintained the highest artistic standards at the Moscow Theatre for Young Spectators (MTYUZ). But even before the "Special Operation" in Ukraine, the government had begun to eliminate voices it didn't approve of. In Petersburg, Andrey Magouchy was appointed to revive the limping post-Tovstonogov Bolshoi Drama Theatre; he built up the acting company with young graduates of the nearby Institute and attracted a lively cohort of company directors but was removed in 2023. For too brief a time, Yuri Butusov, whom we shall discuss shortly, was earnestly rebuilding the Petersburg Lensovet company and repertoire, but was pushed out in favor of the theatre's manager; he has since emigrated to France. Kirill Serebrennikov, who was harassed and then arrested on phantom charges, moved to Berlin upon release from prison. In Moscow, two remaining theatre homes stood out for their steadfast dedication to artistry: the Satyricon Theatre headed by renowned actor Konstantin Raikin has somehow survived, but the globally esteemed Lithuanian-born Rimas Tuminas, director of the Vakhtangov Theatre, was pushed out in 2022. Dmitry Krymov, who had already lost his home base of the Dmitry Krymov Laboratory, emigrated to the US in 2022.

The former theatres of these émigré directors (and a few others) were led by true artists, open to the best new talents of the 1990s and 2000s, some avowedly avant-garde. And for a period of time the government eased their controls and censorship, although, of course, they never relinquished them. But the culture of wealth and international exchange permitted an exciting new breed of director to emerge, if only temporarily. Then came the gruesome invasion of Ukraine. The two brilliant directors of the 2000s we feature ahead – Yuri Butusov and Dmitry Krymov – both emigrated soon after Putin's invasion, as did many other artists of all media.

Despite their distinct backgrounds, educations, careers, and aesthetics, the avant-garde geniuses Butusov and Krymov carry the DNA of Analysis through Action within their creative souls, albeit absorbed through different routes. They are the most prominent contemporary descendants of the third generation of the genealogical family tree we have been tracing. Their roots can be traced back to Stanislavsky, Zon, Knebel, and Tovstonogov.

May their brilliant careers flourish in new nations.

Notes

1 Anagram for Комитет государственной безопасности, the Committee for State Security, the Russian equivalent of the USA's CIA during the so-called Cold War, 1947 to 1991.
2 Богданова П. Б. Режиссеры-шестидесятники. Москва: Новое литературное обозрение, 2010, p. 135; Bogdanova P. B. *Directors of the Sixties.* Moscow: New Literary Review, 2010, p. 135. The 2010 and later editions include a post-script on the 1990s to 2009.
3 Bogdanova *Sixties* 137.

10 Yuri Butusov

Hooligan on the Playground

DOI: 10.4324/9781003475576-12

Introduction

Yuri Butusov: jester, theatre anarchist post-dramatic text vandal, rock star, devotee of Chekhov, Brecht, Shakespeare, Gogol, fanatic of punk music, Albinoni...and more. Much more. From the critics:

A lawless comet[1]

A grandiose inventor, an unrestrained and ironic theatrical bard...On stage he creates a world that looks like a junkyard, where a piece of an antique column is lying next to a Coke can.[2]

"Rock and roll is dead, but I'm not yet" is fiercely imagined in the director's performances, coinciding with the rhythm of the time.[3]

From Yuri Butusov:

I have a kind of a hooligan way of doing things (Laughs).[4]

The director should create a playground and be playful as well.[5]

The director's task is not to create a great performance; it is to create great rehearsals.[6]

Are you asking me why I started doing non-linear theater?! I'm tired! I want the bombs to explode![7]

And crucial sage advice for our purposes: *Analysis through Action is directly connected to your heart.*[8] [emphasis mine]

This statement has become the ruling adage of our practice of Analysis through Action. During the detailed Text Action steps ahead in Part II hang on to this phrase – all that work is finally a matter of the heart.

Training

Yuri Nikolaevich Butusov came late to the theatre, entering the Leningrad Theatre Institute at age 30. He had previously trained as an engineer at the

Leningrad Shipbuilding Institute and for a time was a serious practitioner of equestrian sports.

In 1991, he was admitted to the directing course of Irina Malochevskaya, who had assisted Tovstonogov and Katsman for years before their deaths; in her own course she religiously reinforced their ultra-rigorous process.[9] She, in the tradition of most Russian theatre teachers (Knebel excepted), was disinclined to praise but quick to find fault. Butusov recalls:

> I received terrible criticism, very strong, direct, sharp. Irina Borisovna knew how to cuttingly ironize someone. Some could not stand it…I suffered, but I held on. I was 30 and I needed it. She had her method: to educate by creating difficult conditions for the student. It came from Tovstonogov's school, where discipline was one of the main components.[10]

Malochevskaya was insistent that every student practice the arduous intricacies of Tovstonogov's textual reconnaissance. As much as Butusov resisted being in a place where "a very strong, authoritarian school of Tovstonogov lived on," he realized it was the "right place…necessary for me, including from the point of view of educating the will."[11] In addition, there were unintended collateral benefits to opposing the authoritarian nature of the training: "Many interesting things were born from resistance…the desire to break away from this structure, to move forward driven by the energy of leaving it behind…a school must be understood in order to destroy it."[12]

After he departed the Institute (graduating with honors), Butusov found himself reflecting on Malochevskaya's course more favorably:

> She taught me to listen to myself, listen to my feelings and, while analyzing them, pull out of myself what is really important today…you need to hear some sound that is in the text, and absorb this sound into yourself, understanding at the same time that you are [alive] in today's time and space, and that the play is in an entirely different time and place. It's complicated.[13]

In the same interview he calls his teacher a god. "For me, she is the god of pedagogy…she gave you the keys, a kind of master key, and now you must move out on your own."[14]

The demanding foundational lessons remain beneficial to Butusov: "Sometimes when I am completely confused, I try to remember my schooling, her teaching. In such a moment it becomes very useful to me."[15] And herein lies a lesson for theatre teachers: in effect Malochevskaya was saying: 'I have taught you what I know, but don't go out and do that. Take what you will from me, but you must do what *you* want to do, for your own personal artistic life and for your own generation.' While I have never heard this pedagogical philosophy stated directly, it seems to underlie much of Russian theatre training – as compared to American training for "the industry."

As she "passed on her faith to us,"[16] Malochevskaya also embedded a sense of the power of theatre into her students.

Exploding the Theatre

Butusov's 1997 graduation production was Beckett's tragifarce *Waiting for Godot*, a play that would not have been permitted during Soviet times. *Godot* was Butusov's response to the lassitude of Petersburg culture in the late 1990s, a period of apathy and pessimism. The production shook its audiences and became an instant legend, winning numerous accolades for the three principal actors, classmates of the director. This was the first of Butusov's many nominations for best director, including at the Golden Mask awards. It may have been a bit of a late start – Butusov was 35 years old – but his career as a flame-thrower of non-linear theatre conflagrations was underway.

His credo was apparent from the start – I'm here to shock the conscience of the audience:

In order to break the shell in which the human spectator is located, one must use some strong-willed and forceful methods, to go beyond the framework of the play, knocking the spectator off his feet. Not to show how cool and smart we are, but so that a person can enter a completely different state, enter into some kind of resonance with me. To jolt his emotional nature, I need to kick him out of his chair. He must fall out of it, and then something will begin to happen to him.[17]

But his attitude to the spectator is not hostile; it is participatory, even seductive: "I want to find other relationships with the audience…so that he stops thinking that he is being told something and starts doing something himself. 'Turning on' the viewer is a terribly interesting and important task."[18] It is also an immediate social task: "We are now in an inflamed state, the world is in this state, and the theater as a reflection of the world is also in this state…I hope that soon we will receive from the theater first of all shock, and then fun."[19]

'Shock, and then fun' is a tall order, but Butusov manages to pull it off, time and again. Invariably, he captures the zeitgeist of the day, not only that of Russia (pre-Ukraine invasion), but also in much of the West: "a motif of a tilted world, insane, rushing into the abyss, not having time to recognize itself…a very strong and accurate reflection of the current state of mind and the insane emotional mode in which contemporary humanity exists."[20]

So, where's the fun in *that?* The fun is in the shock, the game. Butusov's scrambling of texts is at first frustrating then intriguing. Which actor is playing what role may change, and then change again; several actors may play the same role at the same time. Scenes are cut and re-spliced – flash back and flash forward – and sometimes repeated with different cast members playing roles previously played by others. Personages who don't appear on the author's cast list are created, monologues may be 'jammed' like a poetry slam, ice cream may be handed to the audience, and plot, such as it is, may be disregarded:

> [*Macbeth – Kino*] is shredded and rehashed. Blown up from the inside, it is scattered across the stage in chunks that do not fit together. Those unfamiliar with Shakespeare's *Macbeth* will not be able to follow the play's coherent development. But those who know the play almost by heart are also at a loss.[21]

All this challenging postmodernism is held together by mischievous fun – and lots of music. Naughty children who happen to be very talented and highly trained actors frolic across the stage, demented spirits animating their lithe bodies. Their rhythms transform from frenetic to funereal, their voices from ear-splitting to inaudible, their body movements range slow-mo to quotidian to acrobatic. These phantoms generally suggest a simulacrum of some role found in the original text, but the spectator is equally, if not more, aware of this actor's 'take' on the role, always a very personal interpretation. This is not "I in the given circumstances" playing the role, this is "me, playing *with* the role." Underlying everything is an almost-constant musical soundscape, morphing from T-Bone Burnett riffs to Brian Eno new age space music to Duke Ellington big band jazz to Roma singers to György Ligeti. The soundtrack of the play "*Macbeth – Kino*" consists of thirty-odd compositions of every possible style, nation, and era.[22]

What is remarkable in this intentionally tumultuous but deftly orchestrated carnival of theatricalism is how emotional it can be. One sees that these actors, trained at the best academies, learned their Stanislavsky but also their Meyerhold, their Michael Chekhov, their commedia, their Grotowski, their Brecht, their circus, their combat, their singing, and their incredible voice work – as they learned about *themselves* as complex and creative human beings – personal development being a major focus of Russian actor training. Watching a Butusov production, one gradually accepts his kaleidoscopic composition-ship and stops trying to make linear narrative sense of it. In the end (assuming you make it to the end, they're long), one perceives how this actor-driven collage has been tautly and imaginatively scored by Butusov. And how always what we can call the play's poetic heart, its deep inner meaning, glows through the phantasmagoric debris and skilled choreographed chaos onstage.

Rehearsing the Apocalypse

"During rehearsals sometimes we hated him, and we would say 'Fuck, what do you want!' In the end, of course, we all loved him with all our hearts."[23] Thus spoke Maryana Spivak, the wonderful actor who plays Masha (and occasionally other roles) in Butusov's *Seagull*, which we shall look at soon.

Butusov's idiosyncratic methods of preparation and rehearsal started with *Godot* and has evolved since, but there are certain constants. Referring to his education with Malochevskaya, Butusov said "It was a kind of absolute rule of the school that the director could invent everything on the stage, but the foundation is the actor."[24] That tenet has remained operative throughout. While never pandering, Butusov is an actor's director; those who will choose to go that hard way with him will, like Spivak, rejoice – in the end.

The director's task, as Butusov sees it, is to help the actor to go to places that they are not used to going to. He is not concerned with the role or the 'character'; he is concerned with the actor, *this* actor, the specific personality in front of him, always seeking the moment when

> the human being goes beyond their borders. Then the moment of change is a burst, an explosion of humanity, the release of a new human being. This is the point of interest for me, when this explosion happens, when the human being is opened up from another side, from a new angle.[25]

To achieve this, a principal rule of rehearsal is 'confession,' rather than discussion.

> We try to avoid words because the essential theatrical foundation cannot be discovered through the voice, through words; you can realize it only through relationships, you can achieve it only when some specific atmosphere is created: when there is an atmosphere of confession during the rehearsal; when everything is open.[26]

Discussion is permitted only after an étude, but that discussion must be (*a*) honest, (*b*) brief, and (*c*) in pursuit of another Étude that will go further or in a different direction than the last one – until, ideally, the actor 'confesses': that is, vaults "beyond their conventional barriers to reveal something previously concealed."[27]

Butusov talked about his preparation process before he meets with the actors:

> I read everything around the play; I'm learning the material, the question of the play. There are also circumstances that influence me because I already have some relationship with the play through studying it. I also have some inner feeling. I'm not sure if it is the right one, probably it's a completely wrong one. But then I must destroy the play. I must forget that this is Chekhov or Shakespeare. So it happens literally: *I take the play and cut it to pieces with scissors, throw it in the air, then I mix it all up and read it in some new order.* Because the director is the person who must create the composition, I have to see something new, compose something new.[28] [emphasis mine]

Not surprisingly, once rehearsals begin, there is very little discussion about the author and the text:

> I don't do sit-down readings where actors sit and read the play at the table. Never. I tried it one time and it was one of the most painful days of my life. I didn't know what to tell them, I felt shy. When we are playing with each other, when we trust each other, I am not afraid of anything, I can do everything…Discussion can only be after an étude or a probe, and it must be short.[29]

At the table

> the actor simply begins to think a lot, talk a lot, and lose energy…A certain manipulation of analysis begins, manipulation of the intellect. Nobody is canceling the intellect, but it seems to me that the theater has a more complex structure than intellectual conversations.[30]

Instead of a table read, Butusov jokes – or is it a joke? – that on his first rehearsal day, "I always try to skip it, or tell them I am sick." More probably:

> We go to a cafe and just talk and discuss the future performance in between other things. I remember one actor somehow could not stand it and said: "Well, when will we get down to business? When will the rehearsal start?" and I said: "Well, we have been rehearsing – for an hour and a half!"[31]

This collegial and oblique approach to rehearsal is all part of Butusov's plan to create the 'atmosphere of confession…when everything is open.' He happily shares his own affective memories as the work becomes increasingly personal.

Again, perhaps with a tad of tongue-in-cheek, Butusov encapsulates his process:

> We sit in the same room for hours, drink tea, keep quiet, talk, don't talk, listen to music. Then I scold them. Then we go to drink champagne. Then we return. We do some things. Then we split up. We meet again the next morning. And so on, without end.[32]

It seems that the specific language of the author's text is not discussed over tea or champagne or anywhere; scenes are fodder for creative mischief.

> We begin to explode the word, or move away from it, or crush it like clay, thereby expanding the field of the play and of the text. Because the text is just the surface. Beneath the word lies everything else. Ninety percent

of meanings, feelings, emotions. And the word – it is a result of a huge number of circumstances, accumulations. But if we go just from the word, begin to explain the word, then we find ourselves in a pseudo-psychological theater, in an explanatory theater, in the theater of socialist realism. And we must somehow get inside this word. This word must become pulp, our flesh, our blood. And this is the path to the text. And then things happen that are very pleasing.[33]

Sometimes we might talk about nonsense, to work with the text as if we don't take it seriously, make it ridiculous. And sometimes, they assume that this is just junk, a parody, and then I say yes, but let's do it this way, and they don't believe it. I have a kind of a hooligan way of doing things (Laughs).[34]

Rehearsals, of course, consist of innumerable Études, or what Butusov calls "trials." He urges the actors to come up with their own, sometimes going to the theatre buffet for hours while they create their own improvisations. "I am convinced that the actors should be co-authors of the performance. I give them great freedom, the ability to search for intonations, improvisations, and openness."[35] Sometimes the Études lead to "paradoxical solutions which are contrary to the text, [but] the text is not the law."[36] Maryana Spivak declares that Butusov "never tells the actor what to do, except maybe with music. But he may say: no, not like that. Then how? I don't know. You're the actor – not me."[37]

"But you know," says Butusov of his rehearsals:

It's all in a positive mood, it's a joke, a kind of playing around. So this playful game has the quality of the playground: anything can happen. The director should create this playground and be playful as well. Even if you suggest a direction, nobody should take it as an order: do this this way. Without joy, if I don't laugh, it won't be interesting to me and I should go kill myself (Laughs).[38]

But all this playfulness, this joyful transmogrification of the text, this reverence for irreverence has serious intent, deep motives, and personal meaning for the director and his actors:

BUTUSOV: The purpose is to tell through the author about myself and about the creators of the performance. You know, this position is quite criticized because people insist that we should discover the world of the author, but I believe that these authors are so great that they can help us to live.

DC: So the author exists to help us discover ourselves.

BUTUSOV: Yes. To help us to exist. I believe theater exists to help us to live.[39]

And, he adds:

> I think that the director, who claims to be faithful to the author, is not
> exactly deceitful, but is mistaken, or something…he hides behind an au-
> thoritative surname. The one who says that with the help of the author
> he is looking for his own meanings and attitude toward life, I think, is
> more honest. The desire to get into the head of another person, to appro-
> priate his thoughts and, as they say, to reveal the author, is impossible by
> definition.[40]

I Am the Seagull

Butusov's production of Chekhov's *The Seagull*, considered by many to be one
of his masterworks, opened in April 2010 at the Satyricon Theatre in Moscow
(and is viewable with English subtitles thanks to Stage Russia.)[41] Butusov had
directed at this theatre before – *Richard III* in 2004 and *King Lear* in 2006 –
both noted in the program as "based on" – and had worked happily with the
resident actors. Butusov spoke about his sense of the play's core:

> This play is dedicated to creativity, to the nature of creativity. Of course
> that is naturally mixed up with love, so it makes for a kind of frightful,
> wonderful theater. We all put into it our recollections, our reflections, and
> feelings – as people in the theater, and as people who fall in love.[42]

The Satyricon company actors' first shock came before *Seagull* casting was
fully determined. During a series of private conversations with the actors, asking only infrequent readings from the text, if that, Butusov announced that
Agrippina Steklov – 37 years old, a mite hefty, and popularly recognized as a
zesty comedienne with a mop of unruly red hair – would play the ingenue
Nina. Butusov recalled:

> When I told Agrippina that she was Nina, she said 'you are a crazy man.'
> But I was sure that it was the right decision because I don't categorize
> actors by age in the theater…I have stopped thinking about a character
> as a summary of characteristics.[43]

The same held true for Timothy Tribuntsev, also 37, slightly balding, who
would play the young aspiring writer, Konstantin. The role of his mother,
Arkadina, in the play the aging drama queen of mediocrity, was 22-year-old
Polina Raikina.

But the biggest surprise was Butusov casting himself – during rehearsals.
Throughout the public performances, the director periodically raced onstage,
a kind of Konstantin doppelgänger dancing frenetically to loud brass band
music as the cast dashes through labyrinthine scene changes. Always

madly dancing, never speaking, he sometimes grabs a partner – Steklov/Nina at one point – then wanders off as the transition completes. (His equestrian training seems to have built up particularly powerful leg muscles; he's quite a dancer.)

As evidenced by the cast executing the complex set changes – they repeatedly handle a *lot* of stuff, sometimes with their head-setted crew racing alongside – the entire production has a DIY quality. What 'scenery' there is ranges from flimsy flats and rehearsal room door frames to a wretched excess heap of plastic fruit. The women's costumes extend from Nina's baggy brown *schmata* to slinky black dresses with thigh-high slits; the men are clothed in commonplace street wear such as one might wear to rehearsal or elegant tuxedos. Arkadina's lover, the middlebrow author Trigorin, wears a white dinner jacket over his otherwise bare torso. Butusov wears old jeans and a loose black T-shirt. The set pieces, hand props, and costumes look like plunder from a boozy night's raid of the theatre's storage rooms – except in fact Butusov and his designers choose or fabricate everything with great care.

As the audience enters they observe on- and offstage the kind of idle rituals one might see backstage prior to a performance: actors come and go chatting quietly with one another, Nina applies make-up at a downstage dressing table, Butusov jokes with castmates, and Konstantin paints two interlaced body silhouettes on paper-covered flats, labeled Nina and Konstantin. The lights remain on, while Nina and Konstantin watch an erotic pas de deux by what one assumes to be Masha and Medvedenko. It seems the performance has begun, although exactly when is hard to say.

Nina's famous Act I symbolist monologue is first whispered into a rock-show stand mic, then increasingly bellowed as the actor's copious red hair is blown asunder by an actor fanning it with a large sheet of cardboard. Konstantin stops the performance, yells at his carping mother, and ignites the paper set with a mock blowtorch and accompanying SFX. Blue jean–clad Butusov races through the seats, jumps onstage and systematically rips the paper off the shaky flats; the sound of a firestorm and pulsing music rises as he ascends the rickety framework – visibly braced by a crew member behind the structure) – and destroys the set.

When asked how this shocking action came about, Butusov laughed once again:

> It was in one of the rehearsals. I didn't know how to finish the fire scene. I started to become so angry that I ran onto the [rehearsal room] stage and just began throwing everything. It was from me feeling powerless, from my fury that I couldn't find a choice. But when I did it, I started to feel that it should be done that way. That was the decision. It is one of the principles of Malochevskaya's classes: you should put yourself in a position where there is no exit, no way out, where you cannot find an option. If you are in such a condition where there is no way out, your body, your nature, will give you the key.[44]

When someone in the cast questioned this decision, Butusov replied "It's my show, I want to do it."[45] The Satyricon artistic director Konstantin Raikin loved it and that was that. Thus, while Butusov was the head of the Petersburg Lensovet Theatre from 2011 to 2018, he would periodically travel to Moscow to perform in his *Seagull* and never missed a show.

The second act setting is wonderfully described by critic Natalia Kaminskaya as: "a gluttonous feast…The table with its snow-white tablecloth is piled high with mountains of the brightest fruit and armfuls of white flowers, the kind you put on a coffin."[46]

The table is later upended, dumping the mountainous plastic feast with some naked baby dolls all over the floor, leaving Nina and Trigorin alone for their crucial private Act II conversation/flirtation. Their initial tryst is interrupted by Arkadina – Trigorin's sugar mommy – rolling in on a wheelchair, wearing a large dog mask of and brandishing an oversized axe. Nina swoons and faints. Arkadina takes the axe, aims it at fallen Nina, but then suddenly chops off her own leg, a plastic prosthetic. Trigorin watches with "there she goes again" indifference and revives Nina once Arkadina wheels off. Cheesy horror-movie music accompanies the entire ridiculous sequence.

The third act is notable for its rendition of the famous "bandage scene" – a staple of acting classes across the globe. Trigorin – not present in the scene according to Chekhov's text – stands motionless facing upstage for the duration: Konstantin's ubiquitous nightmare is everywhere. Konstantin asks 'Mama' to change his bandage – which is in fact a very long thick rope bulbously wrapped around his head; it takes a full 40 seconds for Arkadina to unwrap the dressing (done with a creepy eroticism); Konstantin's revealed face is caked with blood – obviously cheap red make-up – his shirt is also splattered with fake blood. As the scene proceeds, Arkadina, again with an inappropriate sensuality, washes the blood away from her son's face. Kneeling over a copper tub of water, Konstantin suddenly pushes her head underwater, then she does the same to him. She crawls back to him, now in high-octane carnal mode, and caresses him slowly as she coquettishly asks for forgiveness.

Act IV contains Butusov's longest and most crucial appearance. As the cluttered stage is readied for the famous Nina-Konstantin reunion, Butusov rushes onstage and dances to blasting music with Nina/Steklov, then solos akimbo as the stage continues to be reset. On the near-empty stage he sits on a bare iron bed. He smashes his face with a full blood pack as a gunshot goes off. The director, the surrogate Konstantin, has shot himself – as Konstantin himself does offstage at the end of the play. Butusov's corpse is dragged off by one of the actors.

Immediately comes a sequence of three hyper-charged bad drama school takes of the famous Nina-Konstantin farewell scene, each about three minutes long, each with a pairing appropriate to the couples in the play: Masha and Medvedenko, Trigorin and Nina, Dorn and Polina – played by the actors who are the principals in those roles. All the variants are played at a frenzied eleven, extreme parodies of an out-of-control acting class, yet somehow very moving. Each concludes with a gunshot.

Then, for the first time, the oft-overcrammed stage is stripped completely bare, leaving only the dilapidated iron bed and soft music. The 'real' Konstantin – Tribuntsev – sits quietly on the bed and soon the 'real' Nina – Steklov, with smudged lipstick, hair in shambles, and black raccoon circles around her eyes – sits beside him. The play the entire scene sitting on the edge of the bed, mostly facing forward, speaking quietly, smiling tenderly, laughing warmly, tenderly touching hands briefly, with random slow tears from Steklov/Nina, streaking her make-up down her face. At the end they rise exultantly crying out the opening lines of Konstantin's play that Nina had performed in Act I: "Human beings, lions, eagles, quail…" He falls to the floor, she covers him with a sheet, and lifts one end of the bed and drags it behind her offstage – a clear visual quote from Helene Weigel's Mother Courage – continuing crying out the Act I speech as she disappears offstage.

After a long silence, Konstantin arises, climbs into overhead ropes, and hangs above the stage as the lights fade.

Throughout all four feverish acts, the Satyricon *Seagull* actors – who had rehearsed with endless Études, very little discussion, and a lot of personal confessions – 'earned' the precise words of Chekhov. In the final edition of the production, a large quantity of the original text is spoken exactly as written – although no one has ever heard it this way before.

Conclusion

In 2018 Butusov left his post as artistic director of Petersburg's Lensovet Theatre, due to internal administrative resistance and civic objections to his programming. He was soon taken in as the principal house director at Moscow's liberal Vakhtangov Theatre, where he had previously directed with great success. In November 2022, the director of the Vakhtangov Theatre announced that Butusov had decided to quit due to the fact that "he is in Paris and cannot come to work [here] in the near future."[47]

What follows are selected passages from Butusov on his reasons for leaving Russia, published in August of 2023 in Moscow and online:

> With the beginning of [the invasion of Ukraine] there slowly began to develop restrictions. Censorship began to enter my life. They began to ask me to remove some texts from performances that sounded anti-war.
>
> [The Audience] began to change. During the performance of *Cabaret Brecht* there were reactions from the audience, whistling at some anti-war texts…[An] actor spoke that he would rather be a refugee than go to war. His position: 'I do not accept the war.' And from the audience there was a cry: 'You must be shot!' It was scary.
>
> I cannot agree with cruelty, with injustice. For me, this is an impossible thing. For me, my Motherland is kindness, mercy, forgiveness. And when I understand that something is undoubtedly changing, that there are some replacements for these concepts, I cannot agree with this.

Our world is destroyed, I feel the devastation. I can't accept it. I can't forgive it.

I don't understand how they can make so many people unhappy and deprive us of the future. Because it seems to me that a person is created in order to bring joy to other people.

The purpose of life is joy.

Notes

1 *Ольга Егошина*,«И воздух пахнет смертью» Театр, *30 апреля 2015*; Olga Egoshina, "And the Air Smells of Death" *Theater*, April 30, 2015; http://www.smotr. ru/2014/2014_vah_beg.htm#niz (accessed August 16, 2023).

2 Наталия Каминская and Н Каминская. 2014. *Вот Тебе И Театр: Московская Сцена: 2000-Е Годы До И После*. Moskva: "Артист. Режиссер. Театр" 277; Natalia Kaminskaya and N Kaminskaya. 2014: Moscow Stage: 2000's Before and After. Moscow: "Artist. Director. Theater" 277.

3 Александра Шестопалова "Режиссерский портрет Юрия Бутусова" *Театр 21 октября 2012*; Alexandra Shestopalova "Director's Portrait of Yuri Butusov" *Theater* October 21, 2012; https://oteatre.info/rezhissersky-portret-yurija-butusova/ (accessed August 16, 2023).

4 Interview with Author: June 6, 2014; Live translation by Yulia Kleiman.

5 Interview with Author: June 6, 2014.

6 Stage Russia Theater Talks: Yuri Butusov w/Anatoly Smeliansky https://www. youtube.com/watch?v=yDwO8s1DFBU (accessed August 16, 2023).

7 Нина Мочалова, "Для меня есть только один путь – бороться" Театралб 5 ноября 2015; Nina Mochalova, "There Is Only One Way for Me – To Fight" *Театралб* November 5, 2015.
https://teatral-online.ru/news/14605/ (accessed August 16, 2023).

8 Interview with Author: June 6, 2014.

9 Having stood beside the inedible one for years, Malochevskaya later wrote a book titled *Tovstonogov's School of Directing*, from which this book draws extensively and was the basis of her course.

10 Дмитрий Трубочкин "Юрий Бутусов: "Я страдал, но держался" "https://teatral-online.ru/news/30556/ 27 НОЯБРЯ 2021; Dmitry Trubochkin "Yuri Butusov: 'I Suffered, But I Held On'" https://teatral-online.ru/news/30556/ (accessed November 27, 2021).

11 Trubochkin "Yuri Butusov"

12 Trubochkin "Yuri Butusov"

13 Trubochkin "Yuri Butusov"

14 Trubochkin "Yuri Butusov"

15 Interview with author June 6, 2014.

16 Interview with author June 6, 2014.

17 Людмила Громыко "Юрий Бутусов: Выбить зрителя из кресла" https:// gromykotheatre.org/2016/10/20/юрий-бутусов-вышибить-зрителя-из-кре/ (accessed October 20, 2016); Ludmila Gromyko, "Yuri Butusov: 'Knock the viewer out of their chair'"; https://gromykotheatre.org/2016/10/20/юрий-бутусов-вышибить-зрителя-из-кре/ October 20, 2016 (accessed August 16, 2023).

18 Mochalova, November 5, 2015.

19 Роман Должанский Юрий БУТУСОВ: «Меня больше всего на сцене пугает и расстраивает глупость»; Roman Dolzhanskii "Yuri Butusov: "What Scares and Upsets Me Most on Stage Is Stupidity" December 18, 2020, https://screenstage. ru/?author=345 (accessed August 16, 2023).

20 Kaminskaya *2000's* 277.
21 Kaminskaya *2000's* 305.
22 Kaminskaya *2000's* 305.
23 Spivak, Stage Russia interview: https://www.youtube.com/watch?v=8Tp5flP2Pzc (accessed August 16, 2023).
24 Interview with Author: June 6, 2014.
25 Interview with Author: June 6, 2014.
26 Interview with Author: June 6, 2014.
27 Interview with Author: June 6, 2014.
28 Interview with Author: June 6, 2014.
29 Interview with Author: June 6, 2014.
30 Gromyko "Chair"
31 Mochalova "Fight"
32 Михаил Тихонов "Юрий Бутусов: "Театр – единственное место, где можно всю жизнь оставаться ребенком" 20 декабря 2019 https://teatral-online.ru/news/25888/; Mikhail Tikhonov "Yuri Butusov: 'Theater is the only place where you can remain a child all your life'" December 20, 2019, https://teatral-online.ru/news/25888/
33 Gromyko "Chair."
34 Interview with Author: June 6, 2014.
35 Алексей Коленский, Режиссер Юрий Бутусов: Идея постановки формируется не в начале работы, а во время ее встречи со зрителем" Газета Культура от 20 января 2021 года; Alexei Kolensky, Director Yuri Butusov: "The idea of a production is formed not at the beginning of the work, but during its meeting with the audience" *Culture Gazette* of January 20, 2021, https://vakhtangov.ru/press/rezhisser-yurij-butusov-zamysel-postanovki-formiruetsya-ne-v-nachale-raboty-a-vo-vremya-ee-vstrechi-so-zritelem/
36 Radosavljević, Duška. *The Contemporary Ensemble: Interviews with Theatre-Makers*. London, New York Routledge, 2013, p. 57.
37 Spivak, Stage Russia interview.
38 Interview with Author: June 6, 2014.
39 Interview with Author: June 6, 2014.
40 Даниил Поляков «Не надо загонять авторский театр в подвалы и лифты» Известия, 28 ноября 2019; Danila Polyakov, Yuri Butusov "It is not necessary to drive the author's theater into basements and elevators" *Izvestia*, November 28, 2019, https://iz.ru/943622/daniil-poliakov/ne-nado-zagoniat-avtorskii-teatr-v-podvaly-i-lifty (accessed August 17, 2023).
41 https://vimeo.com/ondemand/theseagull
42 Interview with Author: June 6, 2014.
43 Interview with Author: June 6, 2014.
44 Interview with Author: June 6, 2014.
45 Spivak Stage Russia interview.
46 Kaminskaya *2000's* 292.
47 This and the subsequent quotations can be found at: Антон Желнов Юрия Бутусова интервью режиссера Юрия Бутусова «Мой переезд — это попытка остаться живым» ForbesLife, 12 августа 2023; Anton Zhelnov, Yuri Butusov interview with director Yuri Butusov "My move is an attempt to stay alive" *ForbesLife*, August 12, 2023, https://www.forbes.ru/rubriki-kanaly/video/494452-moj-pereezd-eto-popytka-ostat-sa-zivym-interv-u-rezissera-uria-butusova (accessed November 3, 2023).

11 Dmitry Krymov

The Accidental Auteur

Introduction

Unlike every other practitioner cited in this book, Dmitry Anatolievich Krymov studied neither directing nor acting. Instead, he accidently backed into directing at age 48 on a dare, taking on the Everest of theatre: *Hamlet*. It did not go well, or so the critics said. Twenty years and thirty-four productions later, Dmitry Krymov is now globally recognized as one of the foremost stage directors anywhere, a brilliant auteur – meaning a director whose unique directorial authority and audacious altering of the source texts makes the director the 'author' of the event – viz. Vsevolod Meyerhold, Tadeusz Kantor, Robert Wilson, Thomas Ostermeier, and others.

But however belatedly and accidentally it happened, Dmitry Krymov did not come into directing blindly: he was the only child of Russian theatre royalty, director Anatoly Efros and renowned theatre critic, editor, and author Natalia Krymova, as discussed in Chapter 6 of this book. It was from his mother that his surname was given, his parents deciding that a Jewish-Ukrainian last name would be a burden to place on a Russian-born child – especially the son of a famous father often afoul of the cultural authorities.

As one can imagine, Dima (as he is still known) grew up in a household alive with eclectic art, music, and literature, often visited by celebrated artistic personae of the Thaw such as Maria Knebel and composer Dmitry Shostakovich. Amid this febrile ongoing salon, Krymov found his own path; he was uncommonly skilled in visual arts and spent hours alone sketching and painting. This led to acceptance into the scenic design department of the Moscow Art Theatre School, from which he graduated in 1976, age 22. He immediately began an in-demand professional career as a scenographer, fashioning some eighty productions in Moscow, Leningrad, and elsewhere – a dozen of those for his father at the Malaya Bronnaya and Taganka theatres.

Two years after his father died in 1987, Krymov, feeling an "internal lack of freedom,"[1] decided to abandon designing theatre settings and pursue painting full-time, thereby escaping a designer's dependence on directors, fellow designers, and production schedules. "I had always been drawn to painting," he later

DOI: 10.4324/9781003475576-13

said. "But it always seemed that it was not for me. This is done by special people…It all seemed like some kind of celestial occupation."[2]

It was not long before Krymov met with great success as painter, both critically and financially. International exhibitions led to commissions and foreign travel. He was ascending the ladder of global contemporary visual artists. His works, many of them featuring sleeping people, had an ephemeral quality, reminiscent of Chagall and Matisse. One critic later noted: "His pictorial subjects seemed theatricalized. Even framed and static, they were perceived as matter in motion."[3]

Then, after twelve years of artistic success a creative restlessness set in. "Painting ended just like everything in life ends. Relationships end, love ends. I was once in love with painting. And now I didn't feel like doing it anymore."[4]

A Backdoor Return to the Theatre: *Hamlet*

In 2002, his passion for painting foundering, Krymov was unexpectedly enticed by two experiments: directing *Hamlet* at an established Moscow theatre and teaching scenography in one of the world's leading theatre schools.

Hamlet came about through what Krymov has described as a "dare."[5] In a casual conversation, Krymov entranced an actor friend with his imagining of Prince Hamlet meeting his father's ghost on the ramparts. The friend then approached the directorate of the Stanislavsky Theatre, who approved a production of *Hamlet* with Krymov as designer/director (the friend playing Hamlet, of course). Krymov recalled: "My return to the theatre was completely accidental. And for a year after it happened, I didn't even really tell anyone, not my wife, not even myself, that I'd come back to the theatre."[6]

Alongside resident company actors, Krymov brought in a few outsiders who had worked with his father. He chose a jarring contemporary translation, from which speeches and scenes were often spoken simultaneously: it was "semantic porridge" as Krymov put it.[7] "The whole father-and-son theme is exactly what I centered my direction on."[8] The critics were not pleased: "What to do with Dmitry Krymov…[this] enthusiastic amateur…Poor, poor Dmitry Anatolievich!"[9] read a typical response. Krymov acknowledged mistakes but vowed to continue directing.

GITIS

The fall of 2002 found the amateur director accepting another challenge, this one to impact him far beyond the naive lark of prematurely directing a monumental play. At the invitation of the chair of the GITIS scenography department, internationally renowned Sergei Barkhin, Krymov began his teaching career. Remembers Krymov: "He asked me to do it because my father was a teacher at GITIS, my mother was a teacher at GITIS, and therefore I should do this as well."[10] Announcing the appointment Barkhin said: "Because there are genes, a prince must become a king."[11] Krymov recalled:

"The first thing I said to my students was, 'I do not know how to teach you. Let's learn how together.'"[12] Thus began his twenty-year teaching – and directing – career at GITIS.

Barkhin, believing that design pupils should get as close to the making of theatre as possible, had introduced the idea of inviting accomplished directors to stage pieces created by the GITIS student designers. Krymov, after watching his first-year students in a show "composed by them, made by them, invented and felt by them"[13] with the support of an invited director, realized that he had stumbled onto an approach to teaching design – not through laborious hours of sketching, drafting, and model-making, but through his pupils creating stage performances utilizing design as the central component.

Krymov's student performances were prepared outside the department's daily curriculum. The young designers rehearsed and fabricated late at night, on weekends, and during vacations. The shows were performed outside the school as well. To implement all this, Krymov established his own producing entity – once more evading interdependence and oversight.

The Dmitry Krymov Laboratory

It is via the Dmitry Krymov Laboratory that Krymov has directed to date thirty-two singular productions in nineteen years, 2004–2023; there will be more in years to come. While almost all premiered in various Moscow theatres (two were created in the US), the Laboratory goes wherever Krymov goes; he *is* the laboratory – now based in New York. A survey of these nineteen years reveals a prodigious and personal artistic odyssey. Starting in small rooms with discarded garments, cardboard, and paints, to creating large-scale masterworks in prestigious mainstream theatres, he has rendered some of the most sophisticated mise-en-scènes anywhere in the world today.

Krymov's choices of literary sources are always radically reinterpreted, defiantly truncated, whimsically renamed, and mischievously pilfered from revered Russian authors – Chekhov, Tolstoy, Pushkin, Lermontov, and so forth, to Shakespeare. At the core of his productivity lie three things arguably osmosed from his father: improvisation, joy, and a brilliantly distinctive theatricalism. But Krymov's theatre works look and feel like no one else's.

A Brief and Incomplete Chronology of Krymov Lab Productions

2004–2008

Krymov's work resists verbal description; no words can capture the fantastical visual and aural theatricalism and the deep nuances of his works. The best we can do here is to leap chronologically from mountain top to mountain top, sketching thumbnail accounts of what I, with Krymov's agreement, consider to be key productions (unfortunately his Russian website has been shut down, so photos and videos must be found elsewhere).

2004 *Not Yet Finished Fairy Tales*: The students painted their own bodies and faces and created custom-built outsized colorful costumes with huge masks from scraps, cardboard, and thrift store clothes. After months of silent 'character' Études, the theme of fairy tales was suggested by a student with the title indicating that they, like their fairy tales, were also not yet finished - with school. This initial performance of the Lab was a great success, earning the newly formed experimental troupe the first of numerous Golden Mask nominations.

2005 *Sir Vantes or Donkey Hot*: a collage of loose riffs on fragments from the classic Cervantes story *Don Quixote*. For this production, three GITIS graduating actors joined the designers causing intramural tension that was soon overcome as the two camps began to admire each other's skills and talents. Once again, the stage settings and costumes – giants and tiny people – were self-created by the performers out of sparse resources; the final 'settings' were fabricated onstage during the production – this became a custom up to this day. Once again, not a word was spoken.

These and other early productions were publicly presented courtesy of radical director Anatoly Vasiliev in his School of Dramatic Arts (SDA) hundred-seat theatre. The city then built Vasiliev an impressive idiosyncratic complex which he designed, containing four stages with support areas and offices to which Krymov moved the Lab. When Vasiliev departed Russia in 2006 the Krymov Lab became the anchor tenant of the SDA from 2006 to 2017.

2006 *Demon. A View from Above*: The main hall of the SDA is informally called "the Globe" due to the three steep U-shaped seating tiers rising high above a thrust stage. Here, the Lab put on their largest and most complex show to date, again wordlessly, creating live various exotic images and objects suggested by Mikhail Lermontov's poem *The Demon*. A winged Demon-bird was made by the actors and hoisted to the rafters as the entire Globe stage floor descended fourteen feet, giving the audience a birds-eye view as well. On white paper flooring sheets the artists sculpted and painted eleven episodes directly or loosely prompted by the poem, from Adam and Eve to the launching of a Soviet satellite.

Excited by the possibilities of the Globe, the Lab immediately began work on their next production. This one generated international attention and wide-spread touring, including London and New York.

2008 *Opus No. 7*: This milestone production comprised two parts, *Genealogy* and *Shostakovich*, which were connected only inferentially. Their unspoken linkage was that both examined oppression and violence forced upon the outsider: the religious, ethnic, or artistic 'other.'

In Part I, *Genealogy*, the 'other' was Jewish populations from the Old Testament to the Holocaust (the latter encapsulated by a horrifying coup de théâtre which blasted hundreds of sheets of paper eulogies throughout the theatre, reverberant of the ashes of Nazi gas chambers). In *Shostakovich* the 'other' was the eponymous Soviet-era composer, haunted and co-opted by Mother Russia, embodied by a twelve-foot-high busty fat-assed puppet, operated by students. The first piece was shocking, apocalyptic, elegiac; the second was tragicomic theatre of the absurd.

Opus No. 7 – the seventh work of the Dmitry Krymov Laboratory – was a vital turning point in the Lab's history, introducing two artistic advancements: Lab performers spoke onstage for the first time (in *Genealogy* reading eulogies of Holocaust victims from the scattered papers) and in the mute *Shostakovich* an actual ongoing narrative between two principal 'characters' in conflict: the long-suffering composer versus almighty Mother Russia, who births and then suffocates her progeny. The brilliant former GITIS actress Anna Sinyakina in the title role of *Shostakovich* was acrobatic, Chaplinesque, and heartbreaking. She was to be the principal actor of the Lab for several years.

2010–2017

Significantly, *Opus No. 7* was the last Krymov Lab performance created entirely through company Études and improvisations – an archive 'script' for touring was assembled only after the Moscow run of a show ended. But after *Opus*, Krymov embarked on a new approach which he follows to this day:

> I write a text, it's not a play but something that I call "the proceedings" which is *a recording of the future performance from the beginning to the end*. With music, sounds, pauses, mise-en-scenes, and places for improvisations. I bring this figment of my imagination to the company of designers and performers, and we bring it to life, that is to say rehearsals…As a result of the rehearsals, some things are changed, added, or omitted, and many passages remain improvised until the end.[14] [emphasis mine]

This is reminiscent of his father moving from all-Étude rehearsals to his own embodied demonstrations.

2010 *Tararabumbia*: Created for a Moscow Chekhov anniversary celebration, this pageant with music was more akin to Eisenstein's "montage of attractions" than to Aristotle's elements of tragedy. On a long airport-style ambulator with spectators seated on either side Krymov mounted a continual 'parade' of images suggested by Chekhov characters and scenes. Led by a military band per the end of *Three Sisters* came twenty Chekhov characters on stilts; Tusenbach's post-duel corpse on a stretcher; a gaggle of Chekhov's servants; a game of Bingo shattered by a gunshot inside a glass cube that exploded with blood covering the glass, and Kostya Trofimov. Tributes to Chekhov were paid by Soviet cosmonauts and the Soviet Women's Synchronized Swimming Team. Finally came a ten-foot-tall lady in a white dress walking somnambulantly, waving farewell: 'Mama' from *The Cherry Orchard.*

2012 *A Midsummer Night's Dream (As You Like It)*: After the ill-fated but pivotal *Hamlet*, Krymov had stayed with original pieces or deconstructed Russian texts for a decade. Then in 2012, he accepted the invitation of The Royal Shakespeare Company's World Shakespeare Festival to be the Russian entry.

Krymov took up King Theseus' command and ordered up the 'a tedious brief scene...of young Pyramus and his love Thisbe' – and nothing else from the play. The ill-fated lovers here were two stunning fifteen-feet-high puppets, assembled onstage by a group of 'mechanicals'; the puppets fell apart and were hastily re-assembled, as wealthy 'patrons' in box seats hissed scorn at 'avant-garde nonsense.' This *MSND (AYLI)* was a testimony to the agonies and joys of composing theatre which aspires to simultaneously entertain and enlighten. Wrote Krymov: "We tried to make a performance about how all this [theatre making] is not effortless...It's not easy and it's shaky. But, if it occurs, then it is very beautiful and even durable."[15]

2015 *Russian Blues*: Here Krymov premiered his first – and to date only – piece not drawn from a pre-existent text but written in full by him. The complex story began with three separate small groups each preparing for a quasi-religious pursuit in Russia: hunting mushrooms. A couple is delayed by their toilet overflowing, spilling out a large white human turd; shiny-suited plumbers arrive and dance with it. Undersea, from a submarine, floated cardboard effigies of drowned sailors evoking a notorious Russian submarine disaster in which 118 seamen perished – a catastrophe Putin infamously ignored. The mushroom hunters returned home and slowly counted out their meager gatherings. A man in a shiny white suit closed off their meager rooms and tossed a lit cigarette over the wall, setting the stage 'ablaze.' Above the smoky conflagration, as the song *Russian Blues* played, an aerial gymnast did circus tricks with РОССИЯ (Russia) prominently emblazoned on his Olympic shirt.

When I said to Krymov, "You're literally playing with fire," he replied, "I have to."

2018–2022 Nomadic Years

In 2017, presumably acting on directives from above, the manager of the SDA refused to allow the Dmitry Krymov Laboratory to present any new productions in the complex. Krymov decamped from the SDA to find various producing partners elsewhere in Moscow, unleashing a fury of personal creative energy. The Lab generated six masterworks in four years, all sourced from well-known texts by illustrious authors. All six received luminous reviews from the notoriously stringent Moscow critics; all became 'must-see' sold-out events. The man without a theatre, now eerily echoing his father's nomadic career, was reborn.

Space limitations prohibit descriptions of each production – and their complex artistry would be demeaned by doing so. But by briefly surveying these six productions we can identify certain shared ideas, common themes, and some thrilling theatricalist legerdemain. These leitmotifs will be noted in hopes of illuminating certain preoccupations of this preeminent now-matured artist, working at peak creative capacity.

First off, while Krymov had always appropriated material from known authors, typically Russian, his aim here is higher. He re-authored known chefs-d'oeuvre by Turgenev (*Mu-Mu* from *Muma*), Tolstoy (*Seryozha* from *Anna Karenina*), Pushkin (*Boris* from *Boris Godunov*), Wilder (*Everyone Is Here* from *Our Town*), Mozart (*Mozart Don Giovanni Dress Rehearsal* from *Don Giovanni*), and Chekhov (*Kostik* from *The Seagull*).

Krymov was invited to make five of these six pieces at well-known Moscow theatres. All but one of the houses – an underground garage where KGB vehicles were once serviced – were the scale of Broadway or West End stages, several with their own resident acting companies. These highly subsidized institutions were technologically far more sophisticated than the SDA and had larger budgets and support staff. Presumably, due to his earlier years of designing for theatres of this scale, Krymov thrived inside these state-of-the-art houses.

To these venues Krymov invited Moscow stars to play leading roles, almost invariably opposite Maria (Masha) Smolnikova, who had replaced Anna Sinyakina, and whose tragicomic genius was now heralded throughout Moscow; she was featured in five of the six productions.

Prior to rehearsal, Krymov again prepared his 'in my own words' scenarios. Larger in scale and cast size, more elaborate in technical conception, these new pieces also further advanced his reliance on spoken language and the centrality of the actor. Nonetheless, the liberal cutting, deconstructing, and superseding of master texts for his own subjective interests remained the modus operandi, as did Études in the rehearsal process. One critic noted:

> Krymov is an all-consuming director. He is the author, he is the Demiurge, and Tolstoy is rather a pretext, a decoration, a hint. This is neither good nor bad, just that *Seryozha* [the name of Anna Karenina's lonely eight-year-old son] is not *Anna Karenina*, just like cinema is not painting and theatre is not literature.[16]

As gloom, fear, and social despair increasingly permeated Putin's Russia during these years, Krymov penetrated ever further into the dark cavities of the national soul: "*Mu-Mu* managed to push the boundaries of the bare stage…and break into the expanses of the Russian soul, the fragility and defenselessness of

any living life."[17] While Krymov's ingenious theatrics and vaudevillian absurd-
ities remained, one critic wrote that these recent scripts were

> much harsher and more sarcastic: the director in *Don Giovanni* kills the
> bad singers without thinking twice, Shamrayev in *Kostya* mutters the
> current Ministry of Culture's 'Fundamentals of State Cultural Policy'
> and the play by the crippled Kostya Treplev is not "people, lions, eagles,
> and partridges" but the last words of Yegor Zhukov [a student opposi-
> tion leader who had recently been viciously beaten and jailed].[18]

The critics recognized Krymov's underlying personal anguish: "There is as
much fun and charm throughout [*Mu-Mu*] as there is deaf despair in the finale."[19] Or, from *Kostik*:

> Scene after scene is hilarious and at the same time hopelessly dark. Life
> around Kostya [Konstantin in *The Seagull*] has neither meaning nor per-
> spective. It is precisely that tragedy of emptiness and everyday life, un-
> bearable in its infinity, which constitutes the essence of the drama of
> Chekhov's plays. The deceptively simple, outwardly buffoonish perfor-
> mance reveals the despair of miserable people who, with their waning
> strength, convince themselves of success in life and fit into the vulgarity
> of common mores. Vanity hides total insensitivity.[20]

Further intensifying his theme of the innocent and unloved child as social vic-
tim, first seen in *Opus No. 7*, Krymov now created his own: Seryozha, Kostya
Treplev, Nina Zarechnaya (Smolnikova in *Kostik*); Mu-Mu (in Turgenev's
story *Muma*, here a farcically overeager acting student played by Smolnikova
in a dog suit); and the sniveling False Dmitri in *Boris* (again Smolnikova).
Cruel fates abounded: Krymov's Kostya had no arms and spent most of the
first act face down in a puddle where his mother Arkadina had pushed him.
Nina's aspiring dreams of becoming an actress were reduced to drunkenly performing stripteases on rural trains; her final speech was about Russian alcoholism, domestic violence, and suicide – hardly the satiric symbolist poetry of
Chekhov's Act I speech. Anna Karenina's young son, Seryozha, was a quite
convincing wooden mannequin, totally reliant on his nursery-room manipula-
tors; but in a shocking reveal the marionette was replaced in his bed by a *live*
six-year-old boy who vanished the moment his long-yearned-for mother finally
attempted to hug him. Mu-Mu, the annoying wannabe actor, was swept under
the stage by a giant wooden hand; False Dmitri, not too tightly wrapped to
begin with, disintegrated into a blithering monster.

But the gloaming darkness was often offset by sudden bursts of vaudevillian
stage effects; sometimes schtick, but often *good* schtick (a colleague of mine
once said "He's never seen a gag he didn't like.").[21] Defying the theatre dictum
'never act with animals or children,' both nemeses regularly popped up: two
real German Shepherds preceded young acting student Mu-Mu's arrival, she

in her dog outfit; in *Kostik*, a huge black Newfoundland sat patiently by the suffering young writer as he lay helpless in his puddle through most of the first act; a black cat made a pre-show stage entrance in *Everyone Is Here*, coolly glanced at the audience, then in full feline indifference wandered offstage; in *Boris*, a live black raven shockingly swooped through the former KGB garage, stunning and disrupting the alarmed audience – which then burst into applause.

Larger-scale Krymovian technical mischief also often softened the darker undercurrents. When Smolnikova's Anna and her future lover, Vronsky, first sighted each other, her many portmanteaus shockingly blasted open, exploding a colorful flock of airborne bras across the stage. In an unforgettable coup de théâtre at the end of the first act of *Mozart Don Giovanni*, the elderly hack director slashed a nearby rope which caused a giant overhead chandelier to fall and demolish the onstage set; in the upstage rubble, where the second act took place amid smoke and snow, a Soviet factory appeared, as did a cemetery, and a pair of giant zebra legs which become an entryway for the singers. Inexplicable – but right.

A recurrent obsession of these six shows is what we can call making-theatre-about-theatre-making, specifically the exhilaration and fragility of creating theatre that is at once effervescent and meaningful. *Mu-Mu* centered on a hyperactive untalented acting student and a professional actor with a huge wooden mechanical hand whom she persistently annoyed. *Seryozha*, with its numerous references to the Moscow Art Theatre (where the show played) continually reminded the audience of the glory – and the devolution – of Russian arts that had transpired in this sacred hall. *Mozart Don Giovanni Dress Rehearsal* was an autopsy of a bedraggled opera director, "a worn-out master, an 'extinct volcano', a hostage of his aging and the 19 tricks that follow him from one stage to another."[22] *Kostik*, based on *The Seagull*, remained a story about unexceptional writers and actors. But in Krymov's rendition the older actress Arkadina was a foulmouthed pop singer in gaudy fur coats and tight pink pants, the writer Trigorin was a slovenly shaggy-haired songwriter in a red Coca-Cola jacket cum Harley Davidson T-shirt, and Nina (Smolnikova of course) arrived overly made up, pantyhose drooping and dress unbuttoned – this was a world populated with parodic simulacrums of contemporary crass entertainers posing as artists.

From 2018 to 2021 Dmitry Krymov was in his mid-60s, no doubt imaginatively creating from memories and fantasies of his own life in the theatre. But one performance, his extraordinary reading and kneading of Thornton Wilder's *Our Town*, called *Everyone Is Here*, moved from artistic imagination to autobiography. The inciting event for this play was the 1973 performance *Our Town* as presented in Moscow by Washington DC's famed Arena Stage acting company. This performance opens traditionally enough but soon the Stage Manager is interrupted by an actor, called The Host in the program, but clearly a Krymov surrogate – baggy sweater, cargo pants, and all. He tells that while still a student at theatre school he attended the first Arena Stage performance and ecstatically rushed home to urge his illustrious parents to join him at the next performance. They do: Mama in her red beret, Papa in his classiest hat. The family wept together at the show (the actors visibly sprayed water into their eyes from squirt bottles). It was an extraordinary moment of profound mutual affection for the Krymov family.

While following the three-act structure of Wilder's play – *Act I: Daily Life; Act II: Love and Marriage; Act III: Death and Eternity* – The Host interrupted Wilder's Stage Manager and blithely rewrote Wilder's text as passages from the original play triggered his own memories of daily life, love and marriage, death, and eternity.

Early on in *Everyone Is Here*, his father 'died' and walked out of the theatre; his mother started to follow, but the Krymov surrogate, The Host, said to her "No, no, Mama you stay a while," as did Natalia Krymova for several years. Efros' dramaturg and lifelong associate Nonna Skegina (Smolnikova) appeared in a cheap Vegas sequined jacket, hoarse and swearing, clamoring on loudly about Efros, that he had had his own theatre for only four years and how he had been persecuted. Later, The Host showed a picture of 'himself:' young Dmitry Krymov with his beloved grandmother.

The title *Everyone Is Here* becomes clear in the last act – the cemetery is the gathering place for those who have departed: here are Papa, Mama, Nonna Skegina, Grandma – and Emily Webb from *Our Town*. But this cemetery did not visually reiterate Wilder's stark black chairs and umbrellas on a bare stage. Krymov's cemetery of memories was an elevated trestle set parallel to the fore-stage on which his now-departed memories stood. Periodically, this contraption shook and chattered violently, throwing its unstable occupants off-balance, even threatening to make them fall. 'Here' is the cemetery, 'Here' is death and eternity. But even 'Here' there is no rest, only troubled souls and troubling memories. Everyone is here – or will be.

Krymov in Rehearsal

Krymov did not have any formal education in directing; it was all on-the-job training:

> When I started directing plays, I really wanted to see how other directors did it. I had never learned how. All my timid attempts were unsuccessful: To all my 'may I's' I was told: "Yeah, sure, but let's do it a little later, okay?" I agreed, but that 'later' never came.[23]

Young Dima rarely visited his father's rehearsals, and when he did "it was just childish curiosity. I didn't follow the process, how he did it…was outside my interests then."[24] He did attend many of his father's finished productions; the results of his father's work he remembers vividly – but not how it got there.

As Krymov was finishing scenography studies at The Moscow Art Theatre School, his father casually said to him: "Think about *Othello*. I'm going to stage it."[25] Thus began a long struggle of a son trying not only to please his exacting father, but also trying to figure out what that father wanted, which naturally changed as the director delved deeper into the play. As it turned out, *Othello* was the first of twelve productions that Krymov designed for his father. From those productions, and growing up next to Efros – silent or not – Krymov now acknowledges what he inherited:

> [T]here's a huge amount from him in me. Generally, there's a foundation of the idea of what's good and what's bad…It's such an unshifting plateau in me. But, of course, it's him. And the main memory of his performances is some kind of "smoke" that enters you and becomes your feelings.[26]

But Krymov is not one for self-reflection. "It's so hard for me to understand myself, and I don't want to."[27] But whether recognized or not, Krymov's rehearsals bear a resemblance to those of his father in many ways, especially during Efros' later years, which is when Krymov was working with his father.

Readers may recall that after abandoning Études, Efros shifted to writing out very elaborate directorial plans for each production and each rehearsal. Krymov's *My Own Words* 'scenarios' are even more elaborate and precise – they are a written blueprint for the entire piece, beginning to end, with text cuts, stage actions, new characters or characterizations, design and technical ideas. Both father and son continued the use of rehearsal Études within their premeditated structures, but their directorial hands became more and more authorial as their careers progressed.

As did his father, Krymov is quick to leap to his feet and demonstrate something – a gesture, a stage action, a tone or a mood, the use of a prop, a stupid gag; often he will break out laughing at his own gag. But as playful as it is, the process is equally rigorous: he can repeat a particular moment like a conductor repetitiously drilling a short musical passage. Being the 'author,' he can change his text in the moment. His musical knowledge is far-reaching; often he spontaneously calls out to his sound designer for a particular genre or piece to play under a scene or a transition. After running a scene, he will silently ponder for a few moments, then spring into action. Into *action* – not into "notes" or discussion but into suggesting or demonstrating physical actions that will enhance the scene.

A personal anecdote: After watching the first student Étude in one class he and I co-taught, Dima got up and said: "That was charming – which in Russia means it was terrible." The shocked students laughed aloud – and the work began.

Krymov and Stanislavsky

As we know, Efros was an ardent devotee of reading Stanislavsky and later studied with Knebel. Conversely, I recall Krymov years ago at a director's colloquium at a Moscow Art Theatre conference on Stanislavsky. As one panel progressed, several famous Russian directors sequentially extolled their Stanislavsky pedigree – at length. Seated at the end of the panel, Krymov was finally called on; he quietly replied: "I'm sorry, none of this means anything to me; I don't know anything about this subject; it is not my interest."[28] It was years later, after Krymov became a co-teacher of a collaborative actor-director class at GITIS and encountered American-trained actors at The New School for Drama and the Yale School of Drama that he ultimately and meticulously read Stanislavsky's works. He now regularly cites Stanislavsky in classes. However, he says that when he is in rehearsal, "I don't think about Stanislavsky at all. But it's like swimming in the ocean – it's good to know you can reach for the boat if you need to."[29]

There is a hallmark of Krymov's directing process which descended – through osmosis or not – from his father's rehearsal rooms: joy. Krymov's rehearsals are lively, funny, playful, sometimes whimsical, high-energy experiences. But whether gags or deeply disturbing matters are being explored or exacting finishing touches are being painstakingly fine-tuned, there is always forward motion – no rehearsal time is wasted and levity keeps the motors spinning. Despite the written scenarios, the demonstrations, the sometimes-perilous stage settings, the actors know that they are the foci, they are ultimately the masters of the revels, they are finally, for all his theatricalism, the raison d'être of Krymov's theatre.

While Efros was famous for his radical interpretations, particularly of Chekhov's plays, Krymov has taken at least one step, if not more, away from the tree he fell from. Unlike 'Papa,' Dmitry Krymov authors his own texts, designs (sometimes with current or former students), improvises alongside the actors, and directs his bespoke works – all this unconsciously culled from his brilliant affective and artistic memory. His father was a genius radical director. Dmitry Krymov is a genius auteur – the author of the text and the director of the production.

In 1954 (coincidentally the year of Krymov's birth) the French film critic and future film director François Truffaut first advocated that the director of the future must become an auteur. Here we appropriate Truffaut's vision of the film director of tomorrow, shifting his word '*cinéma*' to 'theatre':

> The theatre of tomorrow thus seems to me to be even more personal than a novel, individual and autobiographical like a confession or an intimate diary. Young directors will express themselves in the first person and will tell us what has happened to them…The theatre of tomorrow won't be made by functionaries but by artists for whom rehearsals will constitute a formidable and exalted adventure…The theatre of tomorrow will be an act of love.[30]

2022–2023 Epilogue

On February 24, 2022, Russia invaded neighboring Ukraine. On February 25, Dmitry Krymov and his wife, Inna, departed Moscow on what proved to be the last Moscow–New York flight to date. Krymov immediately went to

Philadelphia to direct his English-language rendition of *The Cherry Orchard* at the remarkable Wilma Theatre; this jubilant production, unique as always, opened on April 12. The director had planned to return directly to Moscow for the Golden Mask awards ceremony, in which the supreme prizes for the best theatre and opera productions of the prior year from all Russia are announced. Krymov's performances had a total of sixteen nominations, including two – *Mozart Don Giovanni Dress Rehearsal* and *Kostik* – for best direction, the highest possible honor in director-centric Russia.

Dima did not return to Moscow. Instead, given his vocal opposition to Putin's overall policies and specifically the Ukrainian invasion, he made the agonizing choice to forgo his native country. He left behind nine performances running in major Moscow theatres – imagine having nine shows running simultaneously on Broadway – seven of which were quickly closed, his name taken off the posters of the other two; three years of new productions lined up in Moscow and Saint Petersburg theatres; an almost completed first film; his parents' graves; and perhaps most painfully his beloved students at GITIS.

The highly confidential Golden Mask jury deliberations were held one day after Krymov had again publicly repudiated the Kremlin cultural policies and specifically Putin's invasion. As the jury met, the chair of the panel received numerous text messages from Golden Mask officials with instructions not to grant any award to Krymov. The jury leader intentionally didn't reply to these messages, nor tell the panel of their existence. The vote for Krymov as best director for *Mozart* was unanimous.

The panel leader then informed the full jury of the admonishing messages she had received. The jury voluntarily stayed in the room while the chair texted the higher officials saying it was too late, the vote had been taken, and everyone had left.[31]

Krymov requested that his Golden Mask – they are an actual object in the manner of an Oscar or a Tony (albeit more artistically designed) – be given to the Russian Nobel Prize–winning journalist Dmitry Muratov. This anti-Putin dissident had recently been attacked in a Russian train compartment, his face, body, eyes, and belongings covered in toxic red paint. Krymov asked a friend to "give my Mask to Dmitry Muratov, the editor of Novaya Gazeta. If suddenly someone wants to throw something terrible in his face again, this mask can cover and save him."[32]

In 2022, Krymov established The Dmitry Krymov Laboratory/New York with American actors. The transplanted Lab gave its first showings at the LaMama Theatre in December of that year, and again in October 2023. While directing and teaching in the US and abroad (Israel, Lithuania), the New York Lab remains his passion and his home.

Dmitry Anatolievich Krymov doubts that he will ever be able to return to his homeland.

Notes

1 Виктор Березкин, Russia (Federation). Ministerstvo kul′tury and Gosudarstvennyĭ teatral′nyĭ muzeĭ im A.A. Bakhrushina. 2012. *Дмитрий Крымов: Книга О Лаборатории. Театр Художника.* Moskva: Московский культурный центр АРТ МИФ; Victor Berezkin Victor Berezkin Russia (Federation). Ministry of Culture and Government of Russia and Museum of A.A. Bakhrushina. 2012. Dmitry Krymov: Book About the Laboratory. Theatre of the Artist. Moscow: Moscow Cultural Center ART MYTH. 26, fn21.
2 Berezkin *Krymov* 26.
3 Наталья Казьмина. 2019. Другие: Режиссеры и их спектакли. Москва: Прогресс – Традиция; Natalia Kazmina. 2019. Others: *Directors and their performances. Moskva*: Progress-Tradition, p. 96.
4 Berenzin *Krymov* 34.
5 Interview with author: June 25, 2020.
6 Krymov "Conversation with Tom Sellar and Dmitry Krymov" TMU 1985–2015, Trust for Mutual Understanding, New York, p. 21 (Available as pdf through Trust for Mutual Understanding).
7 Berenzin *Krymov* 43.
8 Sellar *TMU 1985-2015* 21.
9 Александр Соколянский. Еще один Гамлет. Путешествие дилетантов не имеет конца // Время новостей. 2002, 28 октября. Alexander Sokoliansky. Another Hamlet. The journey of amateurs has no end // New Times. 2002, October 28; Found in Berenzin *Krymov* p. 41.
10 Thomas, James. "My Manner of Telling the Story: An Interview with Dmitry Krymov." *Contemporary Theatre Review* 24, no. 1 (2014), 84.
11 S. Бархин. "Все относительно, кроме счастья." Беседу вел Александром Смоляковым, ГИТИС. М., 2004. S. 461; S. Barkhin. "Everything is relative, except happiness", GITIS. M., 2004. S. 461; found in Berenzin, 46.
12 Thomas *My Manner* 85.
13 Berenzin *Krymov* 49.
14 Дмитрий Крымов И Соловьева Д Годер and Новое литературное обозрение. 2021. *Своими Словами: Режиссерские Экземпляры 9 Спектаклей Записанные До Того Как Они Были Поставлены.* Moskva: Новое литературное обозрение; Dmitry Krymov I Solovyova D Goder and New Literary Review. 2021. *In My Own Words: Director's Copies of 9 Plays Recorded Before They Were Staged.* Moskva: New Literary Review, 6.
15 Formerly on the now-closed website: Krymovlab.org
16 Юлия Зу, Musecube, 01/12/2019 "Сережа в МХАТе: Крымов, Каренина, Смольникова" https://musecube.org/otchet/otchet-theatre/serezha-v-mht-krymov-karenina-smolnikovaJulia Zu, Musecube, December 1, 2019 "*Seryozha* at the Moscow Art Theater: Krymov, Karenina, Smolnikova" https://musecube.org/otchet/otchet-theatre/serezha-v-mht-krymov-karenina-smolnikova (accessed August 19, 2023).
17 Нина Агишева "Му-музыка и небо в алмазах" СНОБ 17 апреля 2018; Nina Agisheva "Mu-music and the diamond skies" SNOB, April 17, 2018, https://kiozk.ru/article/mu-muzyka-i-nebo-v-almazah (accessed August 19, 2023).
18 Dina Goder in Krymov *In My Own Words* 213.
19 Наталья ШАИНЯН, Газета о театре и кино, "Несладкая «Му-му»" Май 25, 2018; Natalia Shainyan, Gazette of Theater and Film, "Unsweetened 'Mu-Mu'" May 25, 2018, https://screenstage.ru/?p=8669 (accessed August 19, 2023).
20 Николай Песочинский, bezformata "Комедия о трагедии «Костика» Дмитрия Крымова" November 27, 2022; Nicholas Pesochinsky, bezformata "A Comedy about tragedy: 'Kostik' by Dmitry Krymov" November 27, 2022, https://

sanktpeterburg.bezformata.com/listnews/nominant-na-zolotuyu-masku-kostika/111855585/ (accessed August 19, 2023).

21 Professor Liz Diamond of The Yale School of Drama.

22 Татьяна Власова "Бывших Дон Жуанов Не Бывает" 10 июня 2021; Tatiana Vlasova "Former Don Juans Don't Exist" June 10, 2021 https://teatral-online.ru/news/29568/ (accessed August 19, 2023).

23 Krymov *My Own Words* 6.

24 Мария Михайлова, Дмитрий Крымов: «Понять, Набравшись Опыта И Боли» Театральная, 3 июля 2020; Maria Mikhailova, Dmitry Krymov: "To Understand, Having Had Experience and Pain" Theatrical, July 3, 2020, https://teatral-online.ru/news/27455/ (accessed August 19, 2023).

25 Mikhailova *Experience and Pain.*

26 Mikhailova *Experience and Pain.*

27 Mikhailova *Experience and Pain.*

28 Panel discussion at Moscow Art Theatre, October 15, 2012.

29 Discussion with author: October 10, 2022.

30 François Truffaut, "Le cinéma français crève sous les fausses légendes", *Arts*, n° 619, 15 May1957; François Truffaut, "French cinema is dying under false legends", Arts, n° 619, May 15, 1957. English quotation from Richard Brody, "The Truffaut Essays That Clear Up Misguided Notions of Auteurism," *The New Yorker* June 7, 2019.

31 This account was relayed to the author by RGISI scholar and critic (and my friend) Nikolai Pesochinsky in an e-mail, October 1, 2022. Pesochinsky was member of this jury.

32 Told to author by Krymov.

Part II
The Practice of Analysis through Action

The Practice of Analysis through Action

Introduction

Introduction

The chart on the facing page (Figure II.1) depicts the two indissoluble processes of Analysis through Action: Reconnaissance of the Mind and Reconnaissance of the Body. According to Maria Knebel, these terms were coined by Stanislavsky during the Opera-Dramatic Studio period, using the Russian word разведка (RAZ vied kah), translated as exploration, reconnaissance, or intelligence – as in strategic intelligence. Derived from French, the English word Reconnaissance is related to cognition, recognition, and reconnoiter, all of which pertain to knowledge acquired through investigation or surveillance. Accepting its common martial implications Reconnaissance connotes a dedicated campaign to survey the play intellectually – Reconnaissance of the Mind – and physically – Reconnaissance of the Body – for discoveries that lead to theatrical Action.

These interdependent processes of Mind and Body discoveries are "essential in the search for stimuli of artistic fascination, and fascination is essential for the birth of intuition, and intuition is essential for the excitation of the creative process."[1] In short, psychosomatic and somatopsychic forays into the play inspire fascination, which inspires intuition, which inspires psycho-physical energy for creative action in the rehearsal hall and on stage. *Reconnaissance of the Mind* and *Reconnaissance of the Body* are the invigorating bilateral agents that activate imagination and the expressive release of physical action. The following pages will describe how to put these dovetailed tools into play.

A few things are important to keep in mind as we move forward. First, what is proposed here is but one rendering of Analysis through Action. Following Knebel's own admission, Analysis through Action has no singular concrete rendition; it is multivalent, depending on who is using it and on what material. Second, while there is typically an interaction between the two Reconnaissances, we know that for Knebel, Reconnaissance of the Mind was a direct runway to Reconnaissance of the Body through Études. Georgii Tovstonogov, the hard-nosed forensic researcher, microscopically inspected the play for knowledge to be passed on to the actor in rehearsal; Études played an ancillary role, if any.

DOI: 10.4324/9781003475576-15

ANALYSIS THROUGH ACTION

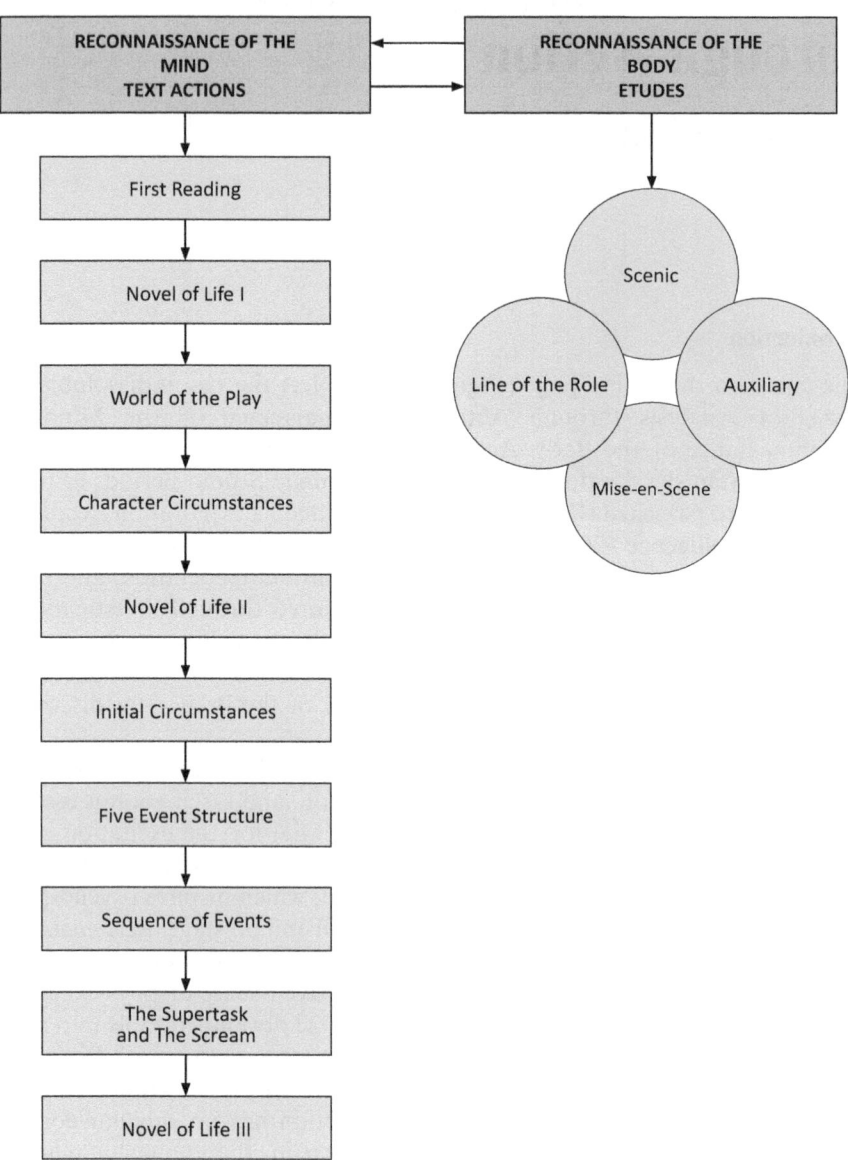

Figure II.1 An Analysis through Action Flowchart.

What follows is a hybrid of these two schools – Tovstonogov (Leningrad) and Knebel (Moscow). The first section, *Reconnaissance of the Mind*, is mainly adapted from Tovstonogov, drawing from his own books and his longtime assistant Irina Malochevskaya's volume *The Tovstonogov School of Directing*. In addition, I cite personal interviews with Malochevskaya and detailed class notes from former Tovstonogov student Maria Ganeva, a director and teacher in Romania (who voluntarily took Tovstonogov's grueling course twice, the second time for her PhD). We have adapted Tovstonogov's exhaustive text analysis process into ten "Text Actions" (our term). In the Text Action called "Events," we have adapted Igor and Irina Levin's essential *Working on the Play and the Role*; she was a student of Tovstonogov and his associate Arkady Katsman.

As Tovstonogov was a master teacher of directors, his methodology addressed what he called "the director *tête-à-tête* with the play," meaning an extensive monastic study of the play prior to rehearsals. But there is every reason that highly motivated actors will be intrigued by at least the first five of these Text Actions (see chart) which will prove very beneficial to their role quest. And there is no reason why a dedicated actor should not undertake the last five Text Actions.

Maria Knebel will appear in the Reconnaissance of the Mind section as well, albeit more regularly in the Reconnaissance of the Body. She was a believer in the director privately deciphering the Events of the play prior to rehearsal and leading the same process with actors participating at the table – before initiating Études (her student directors acted in her classroom projects). Knebel felt two or three days of isolating Events at the table was sufficient. Then it was up and onto the floor, activating the Reconnaissance of the Body method of analysis through physical Actions.

In the Reconnaissance of the Body section, which is exclusively concerned with Études, we will hear from Knebel as well as from the detailed writings of Zinovy Korogodsky, a Leningrad director and teacher who was strongly linked with Knebel, Boris Zon, and Tovstonogov. We will also hear from Veniamin Filshtinsky, a current master teacher of Études in Saint Petersburg, a compatriot of Dodin and a disciple of Korogodsky, Knebel, and Zon.

In recent years, I have had the good fortune to teach Analysis through Action to classes comprising ten to twelve advanced actors and three or four directors. In these classes everyone, actors and directors alike, goes through the same drill at the same time. The "First Reading of the Play" and "Novel of Life I" are prepared prior to class or rehearsal. Études start on day one and continue to the end. Meanwhile, over time and at home everyone is completing the remaining eight Text Actions, one per week, discussing them as we progress. Following Knebel's lead, the directors participate as actors only. Specific roles are not assigned until three weeks into the semester; larger roles are usually double-cast. Thus, from the outset everyone's focus is on the whole play, not their individual role. This has proven to be greatly beneficial for the actors, who, instead of sitting at a table highlighting their lines, are learning the *play* as intensely as a director. The result is that everyone goes further, faster, deeper as the Études proceed.

Over time, my sequence of Reconnaissance of the Mind steps – here called Text Actions – has varied; the progression enumerated here might continue to evolve or be re-ordered by a user. Surprisingly, the autocrat of the Soviet directing classroom endorses such trial-and-error tinkering:

> Under no circumstances should you follow any given regulations, theories, or methods blindly, it's important to reveal their spirit in your own way…The objective of the method is…making the creative process to be animated and joyful…I think that everyone must discover Stanislavsky's method and do it in their own way…It will become your own and personal property. Only then will you master the method.[2]

Reconnaissance of the Mind

With Tovstonogov's above counsel in mind, let us look at a few guidelines which should help the process of working through the suite of ten Text Actions. First, we cannot get around the fact that this is a labor-intensive process. A Harvard student's anonymous course evaluation said, "The workload is ridiculous but worth every second of it." Several of these investigations require extended time, isolation, and uninterrupted concentration. Some Text Actions may initially feel tedious, others redundant, others bursting with insight.

Several of the initial Text Actions resolutely prohibit premature interpretation, opinion, or creative flights of imagination (although you should keep a notebook nearby to capture your brilliant flares of genius). Just the cold text, the verifiable facts, that's all you are after at the start. The goal is to forestall leaping to premature conclusions and facile solutions. Persistently, seek "knowledge before opinion" – you will see that phrase a lot. The effort is to *know* the play first, *know* it in your heart and soul, which will lead to *knowing* it in an intuitive sense. All these intensive efforts will seep into your subconscious as you begin to divine the poetic heart of the play, aka the Supertask. You could call this process "Zen and the Art of Text Analysis."

Six arguments undergird following the Reconnaissance of the Mind text analysis model:

1. You will not be randomly reading the play over and over without purpose – each Text Action has a specific purpose and contributes a specific result; these accumulate and intersect.
2. Each Text Action will expand your knowledge base and therefore your imaginative and emotional universe.
3. Through a process of osmosis, you will begin to dream the play while awake and in your sleep (it happens); you will begin to live *inside* the play, it will live in you.

4. The at first seemingly prosaic fact-gathering will inevitably infuse the Études you do, producing joy, shock, and unpredictable creative possibilities.
5. You will get better at this each time you do it, it will move faster, it will become second nature.
6. If you are a director, you will not be subject to the ultimate nightmare in rehearsal: being unable to answer an actor's simple text question. (On the other hand, keep your comments brief. At the ODS Stanislavsky often used to answer questions with "I don't know. Let's find out.")

The sequence of ten Text Actions as laid out here (Figure II.1) intentionally delays the two most critical components – Events and The Supertask – to the end of the process. Notably, Knebel advocated digging into Events with the actors right away. But I have found that the more basic knowledge amassed before attempting to pith these critical and concealed constituents, the better. Identifying both Events and the Supertask requires time and a ripening intuition about the play and the roles. Stanislavsky admitted that the Supertask might not even reveal itself until after several public performances; Events may be discovered, or at least clarified in rehearsal, as we shall see.

Nonetheless, as you arrive there in the Text Actions sequence you will find it valuable to take your best shot at identifying Events and the Supertask. By then Études should be hopping in the rehearsal hall, assisting in your identification of Events and a Supertask. Even if your first suppositions are only provisional, better to have some proposition than no proposition.

As you absorb the components and procedures of *Reconnaissance of the Mind*, you will very likely determine a different order with greater or lesser emphasis on certain steps: you will make it your own, as Tovstonogov recommends. Tovstonogov's protégé, Irina Malochevskaya, heartily endorses personal ownership of what at first feels like an inflexible catechism:

> Tovstonogov compared the parameters of the action analysis method, as outlined by him, with parallels and meridians which, by crossing on a map, make it possible to locate the geographical point one needs. If you know only some of them and you are not aware of another, this will not lead you to success…As we can see, there is not any term in the method that can be separated from its unity, no term that doesn't have multiple strong connections with other parameters.
>
> Which of these parameters should be guessed at first of all? It doesn't really matter. You can start from any of them, from one that seems most clear to you. It's important only to "ascend," as Tovstonogov said to the play's super objective.[3]

Coupled with the six benefits listed above, this procedural flexibility, the fact that this methodology can be seen as a map or even a globe ('parallels and meridians" – longitudes and latitudes) rather than a tedious catalog of terms, and the idea that each Text Action has a specific process and concrete result make this the deepest yet liveliest text examination process I know of. One can think of this practice as Études of the mind – a playful set of text games that will not only reward you with tremendous knowledge, but that will also become "a matter of the heart" as the play moves toward your own subconsciousness, emotional world, and onstage co-authorship.

Notes

1 М Кнебель and М Кнебель. 1976. *Поэзия Педагогики.* Moskva: Всероссийское театральное общество; M Knebel and M Knebel. 1976. *Poetry of Pedagogy.* Moskva: All-Russian Theatrical Society. 309.

2 [составитель Е.И Семен Лосев and Е Горфункель. 2007. *Георгий Товстоногов Репетирует И Учит: Литературная Запись Семена Лосева.* Sankt-Peterburg: Балтийские сезоны; [Compiled by E.I. Semyon Losev and E. Gorfunkel. 2007. *Georgii Tovstonogov Rehearsing and Teaching: Literary Record by Semyon Losev.* Sankt-Peterburg: Baltic Seasons 168–169.

3 И.Б Малочевская and Malochevskaia I. B. 2003. *Режиссерская Школа Товстоногова.* Sankt-Peterburg: Санкт-Петербургская гос. академия театрального искусства; I. B. Malochevskaya and Malochevskaia, 2003. *The Directing School of Tovstonogov.* Sankt-Peterburg: St. Petersburg State Academy of Theatrical Art. Translation Ilya Khodosh 35

Section A

Text Actions

12 Text Action 1

The First Reading

The first reading of a play can be a difficult, even a maddening, experience. Remembering who is related to whom; keeping track of the secondary characters; stumbling over unfamiliar names – Liubov Andreevna Ranyevskaya – and places – Kharkov, Yaroslavl – all the while just trying to hang on to the narrative flow.

All of these vexations and more can make a first reading a restless and confusing experience. The very form of a play text:

CHARACTER NAME: Words, words, words. (*Stage direction*)

can be numbing due to a frustrating oxymoron: too much information and too little.

Given these impediments, distractions beckon at every turn of a page: your phone, a good book or a movie, a nap, or a nice cup of tea are all so close by, so tempting: "I'll get back to the play later" you tell yourself. Well, maybe.

Indeed, starting out on *Reconnaissance of the Mind* can initially seem like a forced march. This rigorous scrutiny of the text, unabashedly labor-intensive, necessitates close reading, hard study, and a deeply personal emotional and imaginative response to the play. But the extensive time you expend drilling into the core of the play can yield a hidden mine of emotional energy, set off imaginary voyages deep into the interior of the play, and ultimately result in a thrilling artistic confederacy of directors, actors, and all others who participate in the venture.

The investment is indeed large. But the return on investment – the ROI to use an MBA phrase – is huge.

So, here at your first reading, the crucial cautionary words are: *go slowly*. Knowledge before opinion. *You don't need to know much at this point*. If the play affects you at all during the first reading, you'll come out sensing a vague *something*; ideally, you'll *feel* something; and inevitably you'll have a lot of questions. That's all you need from a good first reading: a *something* or two, some kind of feeling or two, and a lot of questions. Right now, you need no decisions, no genius ideas for your brilliant performance. The game is just beginning.

DOI: 10.4324/9781003475576-17

A Protocol for a First Reading

1. Find a large chunk – three or four hours – of uninterruptible quiet time; no looming meetings, rehearsals, personal obligations, or screen time.
2. Don't read the play on your computer or phone; use a paper copy.
3. Silence your phone and put it under the mattress.
4. On a single sheet of paper, write out (not photocopy) the cast list page, and any character information the author provides:

> RANYEVSKAYA, LIUBOV ANDREEVNA, *a landowner*
> ANYA, her daughter, 17
> Etc.

Check this sheet as you read, rather than having to flip through text pages to find it.

5. Don't worry about pronunciations, geography, and history – for now.
6. Make your cup of tea before you start reading.
7. Set your tea, your cast list, your journal, and a pen nearby. (But, N.B., the first reading is *not* about note-taking; that comes afterward.)
8. Settle into your reading *chair* – not your couch or bed, for obvious reasons.
9. Now: line by line, speech by speech slowly read the play *straight through*, no outside distractions, no pauses.

The last is the most significant rule of the game right now: **read the play straight through, no outside distractions**.

As you read, be equally wary of *interior* distractions of the imaginative kind. Out of nowhere a fitting piece of music plays in your mind; or you envision the perfect actor for the lead, maybe you; or a rush of excitement runs through you as a brilliant event/monologue/argument/plot-twist unfolds; you admire the complex humanity of the characters. You laugh out loud at one character, pity another. One or all of these things might entrance you, as might the poetic elegance of the language, or the moral and political power of the play.

Naturally, it is tempting to pursue these evanescent sirens, drift off the page to explore imagistic dreamscapes or savor your brilliant insights and ideas. "This matters!" you tell yourself, and you reach for your journal and pen.

Please don't! Not now! These distracting flashes can enchant you away from your real project: finishing the play in one *straight-through* reading.

Straight through: why is that compulsory? Well, nothing in *Analysis through Action* is compulsory. But it's a really good idea to read straight through, for two reasons.

First, a straight-through first reading is as close to the audience's experience as you will get now. If you read slowly but directly, your elapsed reading time, and comprehension of the play, will be roughly equivalent to their viewing time. Today, you, like your future audience, will be meeting the play for the first time. Your questions probably will resemble their questions. Your initial emotional responses may be similar. Like you, they will experience some *somethings*, but not everything. It is likely that most audience members, if not all, will witness this particular play once in their lifetime; you will live with it for quite a while. So, first take it in as an audience member would – all new, and don't leave your seat.

The second reason to read straight through is more substantive. If indeed you are inspired by the play, seduced by it, then open your journal immediately after finishing your first reading. The practical purpose of the slow but direct straight-through reading is to get to the journal.

Best case: after reading the play through, you now have a fully charged if chaotic collage of information, images, emotional reactions, questions, and a couple of brilliant ideas. Go to your journal. Free associate – draw pictures; play that music that the play suggested to you; get up and move or speak like a certain role; make an *unorganized* list of questions about the characters, the epoch, the morality of the play – but don't try to answer them now; where is Yaroslavl anyway? (Resist the urge to look it up just now.)

This flood of first impressions, images, and questions, as naive and scattered as it may feel now, is the first random probe toward piercing the epicenter of the play.

Don't be hyper-rational, go all OCD or judgmental here – capture whatever flashes come to mind in whatever farrago they come to you. Don't make sense of all this. This is not the time for spreadsheets, taxonomy, or depth analysis (that's all coming). This is the time for random scribbling, drawing stick figures of key moments, playing music, dancing, and most of all noting what and how the play made you *feel*.

This is a time to *play with the play*, for an hour or more. (Actors: if you're already cast, don't zero in on your role yet! Read the *play*, not the role.)

Then, in a more sober vein, ask if there is reason to do the play or the role *today* – will it "shock the conscience of the audience"[1] in a manner you consider significant? Is it worth expending the enormous quantity of hours, compulsive energy, and creative spirit it will take to transform this thick text, step by step, into an artistically fulfilling stage event?

Theatre is usually more fun to do than watch. Can you contribute to making this play/role into something that is truly worth a viewer's attention *now*; something that has *value* to you and to today's world? If not, find another play or role.

An Important Digression about First Impressions and The Supertask

Now, let's assume the play holds your interest. The play at this point is a shiny object that attracts your eye and your soul, although you can't coherently say what it is made of, or exactly what to do with it. But you want it – like a new lover – next to you. You want to break through the surface of the play into its submerged interior, find your way to the underground rivers, then navigate all the way to its headwaters, its source. At this point, you can feel the play, it stirs you, but you cannot yet embrace it fully. But you have an intuition, "a profound formless hunch which is like a smell, like a color, like a shadow."[2] That intuitive hunch can be a first step in Analysis through Action. Director and educator Mar Sulimov describes the process:

> What is intuition? It is our pain responding to the play, our "pressure point." The response is not through contemplation but through sponta- neous feeling...A pressure point is a heightened emotional responsive- ness, accelerated by our life experience, our position, our human and artistic main objective...In intuition, there is the kernel of the *Supertask* [emphasis added] of the future production.[3]

The process of identifying and connecting all to the Supertask that Sulimov refers to here – also known as the "suffering of the author"[4] – is, as we shall see, the holy grail of *Analysis through Action*.

The Supertask of the play is the unifying core idea around which all charac- ters and all events circulate. It is the highly charged nucleus of the play's molec- ular structure. It is the reason the author put pen to paper, even if the author did not recognize it at the time.

But, at this point, we are a long way from precisely naming that Supertask or stating what comprises the author's suffering. We have many steps to take before that can be done with exactitude. However, Sulimov contends, "the ge- netic connection between intuition and the main objective is doubtless."[5]

He then proposes that one take the next steps of Analysis through Action with that nucleus as a kind of advance scout, akin to a hypothesis in the scien- tific method. It is to be tested by and altered by further encounters and exper- iments with the material of the play.

Conversely, Georgii Tovstonogov is adamant that the initial glow, that intu- itive *something* after a first reading, is to be disregarded out of hand:

> [T]his elementary vision of the director...is his dangerous and terrible enemy. In addition to the fact that this first vision is often trivial...[it] always lies on the surface. And the more the director develops this sur- face vision, the more vigorously he saws off the branch on which he sits. He remains stalled at the most banal performance level, readily imagina- ble to any person who can read the play.[6]

So, Sulimov holds up that first intuition as a lantern to be sent into the caverns of the play to see if it stays alight; the canary in the coal mine. For Tovstonogov, this first vision is a "dangerous and terrible enemy...trivial" and "banal." What to do?

Analysis through Action is not a dogma. It is not a rule book. To again quote director Yuri Butusov, "Analysis through Action is a matter of the heart." Sulimov and Tovstonogov were very different directors, with very dif- ferent temperaments, personalities, and artistic processes. Like them, each di- rector and actor today must proceed with each new play in the way their particular life and this particular play dictate – here, now, today. After your first reading, you may propose an intuitive initial Supertask or dismiss the thought altogether – both are viable options.

That said, *if* your first intuition has been striking, *if* something resembling a budding Supertask feels *hot*, it is certainly worth jotting down in your journal. But this scribbled notation is only a provisional step. A long-term reward of Analysis through Action is to succinctly and accurately define the Supertask. We have several steps to go before we get there.

So Now What?

Now, close your journal, presumably filled with random thoughts, sketches, quandaries, maybe a few genius ideas, maybe a premature pass at a Supertask, all based on a simple first reading.

Let the play marinate in your soul for a while – a few hours, or days if you have the time. Maybe jot some things down in your journal now and again. What images leave retina burns? For whom does your heart ache? What role might be your gateway drug into the play? What questions do you keep pondering?

Then, read the play a few times more with no particular purpose, just getting to know it better. Keep the random scrawls going in your journal. Actors: again, don't zero in on your role yet! Read the *play*, not the role. Directors: don't think about your brilliant production yet. You don't know enough. But do think about the play. A wise person once said: "All filings are drawn to the magnet of our preoccupations."[7]

After some time passes, say, three or four readings, move on to the next Action: Novel of Life I. Some of your mounting number of questions will get addressed there – many more, and deeper, questions will arise. More questions are a good thing. Up to the closing night of public performances, you are *re-searching* the play and the role (or roles), not locking them down.

A great play "hath no bottom," says Shakespeare's Bottom, and thus can never be fully known. But it can be known *better*.

Notes

1 Kama Ginkas, author interview, June 12, 2018.
2 Labeille, Daniel. "'The Formless Hunch': An Interview with Peter Brook." *Modern Drama* 23 no. 3, 1980, 221–226.
3 М.В Сулимов 2004. *Посвящение В Режиссуру*. Sankt-Peterburg: Спбгу; M. V Sulimov. 2004. *Dedication to Directing*. Saint-Peterburg: Spbgu, 339–341.
4 Irina Malochevskaya, interview with author May 12, 2011, Saint Petersburg, live translation Nikolai Pesochinsky.
5 Sulimov *Directing* 341.
6 Г Товстоногов. 1984. *Зеркало Сцены* 2-E izd. Leningrad: "Iskusstvo" T.1; G Tovstonogov. 1984. *Mirror of the Stage*, 2 volumes. Leningrad: "Art" T.1. pp. 150–151.
7 Spoken by Zelda Fichandler, founder and Artistic Director of Washington. DC's Arena Stage. Knowing her, I find it quite possible she made this up. I find no other source.

13 Text Action 2
Novel of Life I

Introduction

The next Actions in this process, *Novel of Life I* and the ensuing *Three Rings of Given Circumstances*, are among the most time-consuming of the series. Hours of concentrated work lie ahead. But, if you skip or rush through these two steps, you will accrue only a superficial understanding of the play. Consequently, a superficial performance will be the result. The American theatre is too often beleaguered by banal productions, basically plot recitals with the staging simply illustrating the text, not illuminating it. All of this only saves the audience the reading of the play.

When American theatre is predictable, shallow, and boring, its inadequacy is typically rationalized, with some good reason: a paucity of rehearsal time due to economic constraints. Some propose that the easiest way to accommodate this brevity of rehearsal time is to instruct the cast to learn their lines before rehearsals start, a tactic increasingly employed. But then why rehearse? Like much short-form daily television or regional opera, just memorize the words (and music), get some quick staging and: done deal, we're on. Of course, that's not rehearsing, that's just blocking; that's not acting, that's just reciting a cavalcade of words presumably soaked in false emotions.

A more productive approach is for everyone to learn the *play* before rehearsal: not learn the lines, learn the *play!* Learn the play so as to *inhabit* it, to create action from inside the play, not just illustrate the obvious. Ideally, everyone would get to the first day meet-and-greet buzzing with a personal and visceral connection to the stored energy of the play.

Next, lose the time-wasting table talks, as did Stanislavsky – a master of the table. Instead, after a brief introduction, immediately get on the floor for Études. This is how to best use the limited rehearsal time allotted. In the end, advance preparation and Étude rehearsing will be deeper, more creative – and more expedient. *Novel of Life I* and the related *Three Rings of Given Circumstances* are designed to activate dynamic pre-rehearsal preparation for actors and directors.

We begin with what Tovstonogov named the Novel of Life. In readings by and about Tovstonogov, the definitions of the Novel of Life vary. At one point,

DOI: 10.4324/9781003475576-18

there seems to be a call for absolute objectivity, while another proposes imaginative and emotional work on characters and events. Consequently, the process recommended in this book entails three separate but related novels, distributed at appropriate points in the *Reconnaissance of the Mind* ten-step progression. The three Novels replicate a fiction or screenwriter who first maps out a complex and detailed plot, then complexifies and enriches the characters who inhabit that plot, and finally composes the full opus.

1. *Novel of Life I (NOL I)*: A totally objective and meticulously detailed written account of the detailed *plot* of the entire play, done individually by the director(s) and the actors. It is an act of conversion from one medium to another: transforming a dramatic text to a fictive objective account of the whole play. In *NOL I* there is no interiority, no atmosphere, no speculation, simply a rigorous recording of what is happening on each page, in each line, in each moment, of the play. (Take a pause here to preview the example found toward the end of this chapter.)
2. *Novel of Life II (NOL II)*: For the actor, a deep study of their character, for the director, a deep study of *every* character in the play. Both must incorporate most or all of the known facts about the character(s) and imaginatively address crucial offstage character event-facts that are alluded to in the play but are not conclusively explained – why did Ranyevskaya flee to Paris? Who are Varya's parents? Where has Petya been? – and more. This highly subjective backstory can take many forms – diary, letters, deathbed dictation, psychiatrist sessions, and the like – and is written in the first person of the character under study. This is further explicated in an upcoming chapter.
3. *Novel of Life III (NOL III)*: The final novel, resembling full subjective fiction, including events past and present, interiority, hidden motives, environments, mood, tone, color, and so forth. For the actor, this is a full and intimate expansion of *Novel of Life II*, including your character's relationships with all other characters in the play, self-perception, behavior, and covering all events, both fully realized, or only alluded to, in the play, as well as settings, mood, and so forth. It is your autobiography, covering the events and world of the play. For the director, *Novel of Life III* is a subjective and imaginative epic novel covering the whole play and everyone in it; including the mysteries of their past; private thoughts; all the events prior to the play and during the play; and possibly speculating on events following the play (what becomes of Ranyevskaya after her return to Paris?). It is not your production, but helps you find your production. Again, *NOL III* is further explicated ahead in the grand finale of Reconnaissance of the Mind: Step 10.

Novel of Life I: What It Is – What It Isn't

Intended for both actors and directors, *Novel of Life I* is a scrupulously objective account replete with all the details of the entire play – and *nothing* else. This Text Action is about notating line-by-line the *facts* of the play, not your interpretation, explanation, questions, or emotional-imaginative response to those facts. You *do not add anything*: no coloration, no atmosphere, no internal life, no interpretation, no explanations; nothing that is not right there on the surface of the script but rephrased by you.

Again: knowledge before opinion. You'll hear that again.

Is this simply a very detailed plot mapping, and nothing else? Yes, it is. You are gathering the hard facts, transcribing the given textual *data* of the play, chronologically cataloging the 'where-we-are,' the 'who-says-what,' and the 'who-does-what' of the bit-by-bit plot of the play. You are a magnet, picking up the filings of the play – in consecutive order. You are micro-photographing and transcribing the play, moment by moment. In the end, you will have a documentary record of the facts of the play, like a meticulously detailed police report, albeit in the present tense.

All this work! For what reason?

First, this is a major step toward "taking up residence" *inside* the play; learning its environments and the characters you will ultimately cohabit with. As you proceed, you will begin to see them, hear them, be surprised by them; they will teach you the play they are in. You may be disappointed by them, perhaps yearn to love them, or to scream at them. But first you have to get to know them, what they say and what they do.

Second, you will begin to sense the action plan of the play: what changes, when and how and by whom. And, again, if you work straight through each act – admittedly hard to do as each act takes a long time to transcribe – you will begin to feel the *flow* of the play, get a preliminary sense of the musical score embedded in the piece. The plot of the play resembles the notes and staves on a sheet of music; *how* to play that music requires further study and deeper emotional connection. But first study the printed score as a violinist or conductor would, note by note – in our case the precise elements of the plot of the play.

About the early process of learning the play Knebel wrote "that Stanislavsky said 'to skeleton' [the play], i.e. to be able to determine its structure, tissues, nerves. It is difficult, laborious, and requires a lot of concentration of thought."[1] Plot is the 'skeleton' of the play: plot has no heart, no soul, no breath. Plot is only plot. *Story* is something else again, something that emerges as the interior life of the characters – the heart, the soul, the breath – stirs and grows. We will get to story, absolutely – but not now. First, we need to know the hard, cold facts, we need to 'skeleton' the play.

When you are done notating *Novel of Life I*, you will know this play far better than if you had read it twenty-five times. You will begin to *own* this play by the time you are done.

Novel of Life I: A Protocol

1. *Write in longhand*: more energy will pass through your body and your mind. Yes, it is slower – slow is a good thing. Longhand is a full-body physical event, far more engaging than thoughtless typing. Fill up your journal or buy a separate notebook just for this.

2. As in a novel, write full sentences, and paragraphs (direct quotes can be used, but sparingly). No bullet points. This is a creative act of conversion, not stenography; you are ultimately looking for the *flow* of the dramatic action

3. Beware "performance decisions" creeping in by adding adjectives and adverbs that are yours and not the author's: "he speaks in his *charming* voice" or "she says *loudly.*" You don't know these things yet. Just record what the author has given you. If the author writes "charming" or "loudly," grab it; if not, don't embellish the author's text – just record what is there.

4. Be especially cautious with verbs; keep them simple and neutral. You will *repeatedly* use "says," "speaks," "tells," or "replies," and so forth, rather than "demands," "cries," "shouts," or "attacks," and the like. Those last four are prematurely determinant.

5. Inevitably, your mind will stray off the page. Questions will arise: Why are we in the nursery? Why is the sun coming up at 2 a.m.? Images will appear: "Ooh, dogs barking! Great SFX!" Questions arise: what happened the day Grisha drowned? Affective memories arise: maybe a bedraggled but sexy old boyfriend appears in your mind: my God, it's Petya! These reactions are inevitable, critical, and wonderful. But don't linger on them now. Make brief notes in your journal but then move on, move on, move on – slowly, carefully. Magnet and filings.

6. With any of the four major plays of Chekhov, converting each act of the script will probably consume six to nine hours. Your final copy of an act will likely consist of somewhere between 5,500 and 7,000 words depending on the length and complexity of the act. For your own sanity, it's advisable to do at the very most one act per day; maybe two days. Let each act marinate before you move to the next.

7. Don't despair as you start out on Act I. It gets easier and more fun as you go along. No, really, it does. And the ROI is mammoth. So is your pride when you have finished.

8. This can be a killer exercise; it can take hours. If time is at a premium, at minimum do Act I. That should be mandatory.

Novel of Life I: An Example

From the first act of *The Cherry Orchard*, Paul Schmidt translation:

Chekhov/Schmidt	*Novel of Life I*
ACT ONE	ACT ONE
A room they still call the nursery. A side door leads to Anya's room. Almost dawn; the sun is about to rise. It's May; the cherry orchard is already in bloom, but there's a chill in the air. The windows are shut. Enter Dunyasha with a lamp, and Lopakhin with a book in his hand.	First light is appearing through the closed windows of a room they still call the nursery. Off to one side of the room is a door that leads to Anya's room. There's a chill in the May air, but the cherry orchard is in bloom. A maid [Dunyasha] and a man [Lopakhin] enter the room. She has a lamp, he a book.

(Continued)

Chekhov/Schmidt	*Novel of Life I*
LOPAKHIN: The train's finally in, thank God. What time is it? DUNYASHA: Almost two. (She blows out the lamp.) It's getting light. LOPAKHIN: How late is the train this time? Must be at least two hours. (He yawns and stretches.) That was dumb. I came over on purpose just to meet them at the station, and then I fell asleep. Sat right here and fell asleep. Too bad. You should have woke me up. DUNYASHA: I thought you already left. (She listens) Listen, that must be them. LOPAKHIN: (He listens) No, they still have the luggage to get, and all that. (Pause) She's been away five years now; no telling how she's changed. She was always a good person. Very gentle, never caused a fuss. I remember one time when I was a kid, fifteen or so, they had my old man working in the store down by the village, and he hit me, hard, right in the face; my nose started to bleed. And we had to come up here to make a delivery or something; he was still drunk. And Liubov Andreyevna – she wasn't much older than I was, kind of thin – she brought me inside the house, right into the nursery here, and washed the blood off my face for me. "Don't cry," she told me. "Don't cry, poor boy; you'll live long enough to get married." (Pause) Poor boy…Well, my father was poor, but take a look at me now, all dressed up, brand new suit and tan shoes. Silk purse out of a sow's ear, I guess…I'm rich now, got lots of money, but when you think about it, I guess I'm still a poor boy from the country. (He flips the pages of the book.) I tried reading this book, couldn't figure out a word it said. Put me to sleep. (Pause)	Lopakhin comments that the train has finally arrived and asks what time it is. Dunyasha replies that it is almost two, and blows out her lamp; light is dawning, she says. Lopakhin wonders how late the train is this time; must be two hours or more. I was dumb, he says: I came here to meet them at the station and then I sat right here and fell asleep. "You should have woke me up," he says to the maid. Dunyasha replies "I thought you had already left." She thinks she hears a noise – they are arriving. He listens but rebuts that it is too early; they have luggage to get. After a moment, Lopakhin speaks about a woman [Ranyevskaya]. She has been away for five years; who knows what she is like now. She was always good, easygoing. He recalls an act of great kindness on her part when he was young, maybe 15 years old. They had his father working at the store near the village and one day he hit his son right in the face so hard that his nose was bleeding. They came up to make a delivery or some such – father still drunk – and Liubov Andreyevna – roughly his age, thin, took him inside, right here into the nursery, and washed the blood off his face. "Don't cry, poor boy," she said. "You'll live long enough to get married." Lopakhin pauses and then comments on the fact that his father was indeed poor but now he, Lopakhin, is all dressed up: new suit, tan shoes" – "silk purse out of a sow's ear." He's rich, has lots of money, but if you think about it, he's still a poor peasant boy: the book – it made no sense to him. Put him to sleep. No response from Dunyasha. (Pause)

(*Continued*)

Chekhov/Schmidt	*Novel of Life I*
DUNYASHA: The dogs were barking all night long; they know their mistress is coming home.	Then Dunyasha notes that the dogs have been barking tonight. Their mistress is coming home. Lopakhin dismisses
LOPAKHIN: Don't be silly.	Dunyasha: don't be silly. Dunyasha says
DUNYASHA: I'm so excited I'm shaking. I may faint.	that she is so excited that she is shaking and worried she might faint. Lopakhin
LOPAKHIN: You're getting too full of yourself, Dunyasha. Look at you, all dressed up like that, and that hairdo. You watch out for that. You got to remember who you are.	chastises Dunyasha for being too full of herself. Here she is all dressed up, fancy hairdo. He warns her to beware, remember your status.
Enter Yepikhodov with a bunch of flowers. He wears a jacket and tie and brightly polished boots, which squeak loudly. As he comes in, he drops the flowers he is bearing.	A young man [Yepikhodov] wearing a jacket and tie, and highly polished, if quite squeaky, new boots enters the nursery, bearing flowers. He drops the flowers on the floor.

Novel of Life I: Closing Thoughts

After you are done converting the entire play to objective fiction, you must take the time to read your work in one sitting. Be proud: it's all there, the whole play, it's your work coming to life. But don't try to answer your increasingly numerous questions just yet. A lot of that will be addressed in the next step: *Three Rings of Given Circumstances*. But do note discoveries in *Novel of Life I* which seem especially important – or especially perplexing. In life, it's important to celebrate the victories, and a completion of *Novel of Life I* is certainly a victory – so celebrate. Your detailed knowledge of the play is now galaxies beyond where it was after your first reading. You may be amazed by how much you now know.

Soon you will be amazed at how much more there is to know. (Dare we say "knowledge before opinion" again?)

Note

1 М Кнебель and М Кнебель. 1976. *Поэзия Педагогики*. Moskva: Всероссийское театральное общество; M Knebel and M Knebel. 1976. *Poetry of Pedagogy*. Moskva: All-Russian Theatrical Society Translation Ilya Khodosh, 296.

14 Text Action 3
Three Rings of Given Circumstances

Introduction: The Problem of Objectives and Actions

Maria Knebel presciently described where we are now in our Text Action process: "So far, we have only the play before us, and we must now penetrate into the world of its reality."[1] The question is how do we do that?

In traditional American rehearsal halls and acting classrooms, the search typically begins with a collective expedition, everyone hunting for their dynamic 'active verb' for each 'beat,' that electric verb that the actor will deploy as an Action to achieve an Objective on their partner(s). Identify the Objective, Play an Action to achieve it; that is the governing axiom. Hamlet's simple Objective with the Players is that he wants them to act well (his hidden larger Objective: to catch the conscience of the king). So, the Hamlet actor's *Action* on the Players to achieve his "play well" Objective is to (insert active verb here)...*Instruct them? Command them? Shame them? Humor them? Frighten them? Impress them with his theatre knowledge?*

This reliance on the Objective/Action precept, derived from an early phase of Stanislavsky's research on the System, makes the identification of Objectives – "I want X from my partner" – and Actions – "I will get X by activating active verb Y toward my partner" – the foundation of most actor training in the United States. But all too often, the Objective/Action dyad, with its borderline solipsistic "I want" and the ensuing cerebral naming of things at home, rather than *experiencing* things in Études, leads to generic performances: yes, the actor has an Objective; yes, the actor plays an Action – but the results are all too often impersonal, simplistic, intellectual, predictable, and physically static.

No wonder that in his ever-evolving quest for theatrical truth, Stanislavsky abandoned the predetermination of Objectives and Actions debated at the table as the path to subjectively "experiencing the role" (*perezhivanie*). Later in his life he sought out deeper, more physical, and experiential strategies for activating a character and an Event, the backbone is which is experiencing *Given Circumstances*, not naming Objectives and Actions.

DOI: 10.4324/9781003475576-19

Introducing Given Circumstances

Stanislavsky's new method called for a two-fold shift in an actor's relationship to the text of the play. First, it requires not the mere naming of things, but the visceral *experiencing* of things – these things called *Given Circumstances*. Second, this method requires a shift in perception: it is not about what your character *wants* or *needs*, it is about what *you* would *do*, given the Circumstances of an event. Phrasing the question in the first person, ask yourself: *What would I do if I found myself in this specific Circumstance?* This is the famous "I in the Given Circumstances."

Let's consider three key words in the basic question: *If*, *I*, and *do*.

Central to our investigation is the word "if." Stanislavsky called this concept the "Magic If" – the imaginative step that transforms you from a rational analyzer of text into a living experiencer of Given Circumstances. He invites you to ask *What if* I were faced with the specific Circumstances that appear in this Event?

After the powerful "if," we have the word "I" – the engine behind the shift in perception. It is now not what would *my character* want or need, but what would *I* do in those exact Given Circumstances? The difference from the earlier borderline solipsism, I want, is here you are actively trying *do* something to your partner, you are trying to affect them, to change them. Your partner is the focus of your energy expended, not you. Accordingly, this proposition is called "*I in the Given Circumstances.*" It is a fundamental principle of the Études of *Analysis through Action*. It ignites numerous Elements of the System: Imagination, the Magic "If," Concentration, Communion, Emotional Memory, and, of course, Action itself.

This brings us to the word "do." What would I *do*? Not what would do I *want* or *need*. *Do* connotes Action, the behavioral psychophysical tactic that the actor will deploy. I will *do* X to change my partner's behavior.

By activating your own affective memory and imagination of the Given Circumstances you will transcend *to* the role, elevate to some point beyond just yourself. With that achieved, the character does not belong to the play; the character is sourced in *you* but transcends to a *you* who has risen to a plane beyond yourself, an imaginative plane, a transformative plane, a spiritually creative plane. You are transporting yourself *to* the character, not reducing the character to you. Your character may well have some traits similar to yours, but there will be facets of the character that will require you to transform your customary self into being someone else.

In this methodology called *Analysis through Action*, Action is the energy expended toward a specific goal. Action is not intellectually determined by plotting out our objectives and active verbs beforehand, at home or at the communal table, but through the empirical experience of living inside the Given Circumstances of the play and the role. The animating energy is found through the "I" experiencing the Given Circumstances via Études, thereby simultaneously arousing physical action, imagination, and unanticipated affective memory – here, today, now.

Given Circumstances are not just backstory facts; they are creative and visceral amphetamines, the *active chemical agents of energy*, essential to generating your Actions inside the Events of the play. Given Circumstances are not only the springs that make the lives of the characters happen; they are also the bridge between our textual research of the play and our imaginative and emotional journey into the poetic heart of the play – onstage. The deeper your intellectual and visceral knowledge of the Given Circumstances, the deeper your explorations in Études will be.

Given Circumstances – Basic Definitions

As noted earlier in this book, in 1830 the renowned Russian poet and dramatist Alexander Pushkin responded to a lesser author's play, one with the unpromising title *Martha, the Governor's Wife*. In his criticism, Pushkin wrote: "The truth concerning the passions, a verisimilitude in the feelings experienced in given situations – that is what our intelligence demands of a dramatist."[2] Clearly the author of *Martha* missed that class.

Stanislavsky appropriated Pushkin's dictum for dramatists into a basic theorem for actors: truthful passions will emerge from "feelings experienced in given situations."

In the late 1930s, based on what he called "Pushkin's aphorism," Stanislavsky renounced extensive table talk and predetermining objectives as the path to "passions" and "verisimilitude." Instead, he prioritized activating Given Circumstances through physical experiencing, which in turn incites affective memory and imagination.

Knebel quotes Stanislavsky on what he considered to be a catechism of Given Circumstances for the actor:

> the plot of the play, its facts, events, historical epoch, the time and place of the action, life conditions, the actor's and director's understanding of the play, their additions to it, *mise-en-scènes*, the production, sets and costumes, props, lights, noises, and sounds, etc., that are given to the actors to take into consideration as they create.

On the same page Knebel summarized matters more succinctly, if dauntingly: "Primary among the given circumstances I imagine to be *everything associated with learning the play*"[emphasis added].[3]

Elsewhere she wrote:

> I explain [Given Circumstances] this way: all the details about the life of the characters, their past, the environment in which they live or lived, everything that makes up their inner world, their behavior, their thoughts and feelings, everything that gradually formed their individuality, all this – these are the given circumstances of the life of the character.[4]

And she added elsewhere:

> Here lies inexhaustible work for the imagination of the actor and direc-
> tor. One must imagine not only the epoch, everyday life, and the relation-
> ship between all the characters, but also understand that the characters,
> in addition to their present, also had a past and will have a future.[5]

Given Circumstances work is indeed inexhaustible – and there is no more
bountiful and exciting work for the actor and the director. But a process is
necessary to begin that work.

Given Circumstances: An Overview of a Process

It becomes clear that gathering and evaluating Given Circumstances is the
most important task in the preparation and rehearsal period for the director
and the actor.

As you harvest the text-evident hard facts, you also will find enticing mysteries, tantalizing clues about subterranean circumstances and enigmatic events
not resolved in the text: Why did Ranyevskaya flee to Paris? What is Varya's
parentage? Why didn't Gayev inherit the estate? These will be opportunities for
creative speculation later, but at this point these unresolved teasers should simply be noted in your journal as "For Speculation." Many of these will become
inspirations for imagination in *Novel of Life II*, and material for rehearsal Études.

But first, a body of essential and verifiable hard data that is revealed in the
plot needs to be compiled and inventoried. Only then can you begin "assessing
the facts" – Knebel's phrase from Stanislavsky – which will initiate our passage
from plot to story, from gathering and sorting data to the "inexhaustible work
for the imagination of the actor and director."

Given Circumstances: Three Circles (or Rings)

Irina Malochevskaya spoke the following in an interview:

> To Stanislavsky to play the role meant to play the whole area, the entire
> area of the given circumstances. But Tovstonogov asked what does it
> mean to play the whole area? How many given circumstances exist?
> 100,000? 200,000? As many as possible, of course. But the actor, the poor
> actor, cannot do everything at one time. So Tovstonogov suggested to
> divide all circumstances into three Circles or Rings. The Large Circle; the
> Middle Circle; and the Small Circle.[6]

Per Malochevskaya, 'Rings' and 'Circles' are interchangeable terms. Here is a
graphic illustrating the Three Rings/Circles and what resides inside their cir-
cumferences (Figure 14.1):

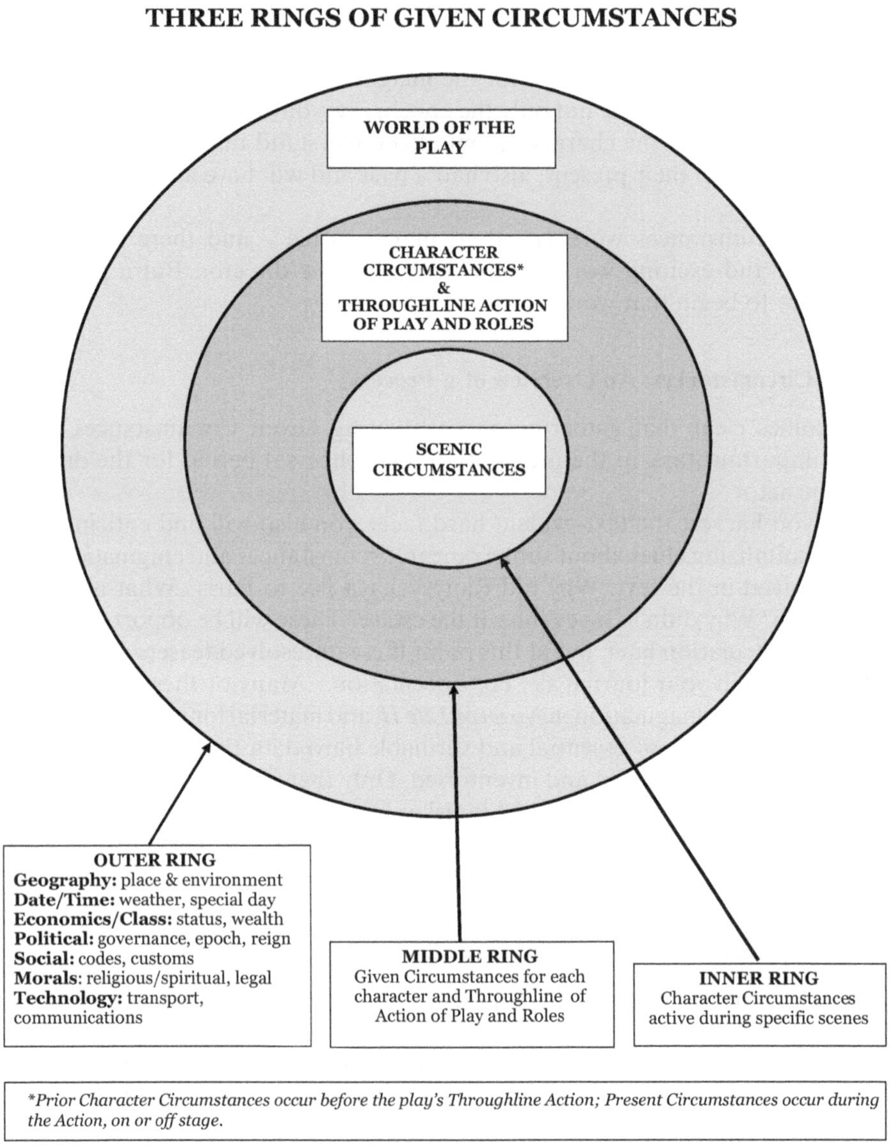

THREE RINGS OF GIVEN CIRCUMSTANCES

WORLD OF THE
PLAY

CHARACTER
CIRCUMSTANCES*
&
THROUGHLINE ACTION
OF PLAY AND ROLES

SCENIC
CIRCUMSTANCES

OUTER RING
Geography: place & environment
Date/Time: weather, special day
Economics/Class: status, wealth
Political: governance, epoch, reign
Social: codes, customs
Morals: religious/spiritual, legal
Technology: transport,
communications

MIDDLE RING
Given Circumstances for each
character and Throughline of
Action of Play and Roles

INNER RING
Character Circumstances
active during specific scenes

**Prior Character Circumstances occur before the play's Throughline Action; Present Circumstances occur during
the Action, on or off stage.*

Figure 14.1 Three Rings of Given Circumstances.

Each Ring or Circle is a domain. At any given moment, a Given Circumstance
– a "fact" of the play or of a character – will reside in one of the three domains.
However, a Given Circumstance can migrate from one sphere to another, as
needed for the action of the play. Indeed, the conflict for an Event (a so-called
beat) in the Inner Ring (Scenic) is impossible to activate without the characters
accessing their particular character's Given Circumstances from the Middle

Ring. Conversely, a Circumstance crucial to an Event may lose its value when that Event concludes and the Given Circumstance migrates out of the Inner Ring to the Middle Ring (Throughline Action).

Let's dolly in and look at these three Rings and further determine what belongs where:

Three Rings of Given Circumstances: The Outer Ring

The Outer (or Large) Ring is concerned with context: geography, time and place, and social-historical aspects of the epoch; often called "the World of the Play." All Given Circumstances of the Outer Ring lie *outside* the boundaries of the play itself, but to be of value must somehow influence the codes and behaviors of the characters inside. N.B.: this research has limits. A chronology of Tsars will not help in Chekhov, but an understanding of a nation in transformation after the 1861 emancipation of the serfs will help – indeed, it is at the crux of *The Cherry Orchard*.

In the Outer Ring, the categories listed constitute the social, environmental, and cultural world in which the characters live and struggle. However some of these categories – Politics or Social Codes, for instance – may be viewed differently character to character. Each actor should understand both the general Outer Ring Circle they inhabit and their individual relationship to these contextual realms. The director must know both the universal World of the Play and each character's relationship to that world.

Three Rings of Given Circumstances: The Middle Ring

The Middle Ring comprises two interrelated constituents:

1. Particular and personal Character Given Circumstances for each role.
2. The accruing step-by-step Events that emerge on the Throughline Action as the play transpires from the beginning to the end of the play.

The first of these – Given Circumstances for each Character – we will examine in the next exercise: Text Action 4: Character Given Circumstances.

The second constituent of the Middle Ring is the "Throughline Action." So, what is that? It is the bit-by-bit advancement of the text and the performance as the audience witnesses it. As you translated the play into your own words during Novel of Life I, you were concurrently laying out the textual Throughline Action in very minute terms. If indeed your Novel of Life I covered the entire play, you have already created a Throughline Action of the full text, which you can draw on as you isolate and harvest particular Character Given Circumstances in Text Action 4.

A technical note here: major Events often happen offstage and can have a substantial impact on the Throughline Action. But the Throughline Action is *only* what we see and hear onstage as the play unfolds. Offstage Events (sometimes called Interstitial Events) even if they are later narrated by a character, are not procedurally part of the Throughline Action. Lopakhin winning the auction is an example of this: we do not actually witness the auction itself but later he narrates his story of it. Only his narration is part of the Throughline Action. Such offstage Events are ripe fruit for Études and are related to Character Given Circumstances in Chapter 15.

Three Rings of Given Circumstances: The Inner Ring

The Inner Ring, or the Small Circle, pertains only to Events, also known as units, segments, or colloquially 'beats.' This we will examine in Text Action 8, the Chain of Events.

For now, we can define an Event as a specific unit of action containing a conflict between two or more opposing characters, which happens before the eyes of the spectator. A play, and a production, is made up of a succession of consecutive Events, sometimes called the Chain or Sequence of Events.

The Inner Ring is about the conflicts between specific characters as they happen in front of the audience: Character A versus Character B (and their backers if present). The characters' Given Circumstances from the Middle Ring – the characters' life till now including backstory, their mutual history, and what has happened to them so far on the Throughline Action – will be sources from which characters might draw during Scenic Events.

Given Circumstances: The Process of Selection and Distribution

Before we begin our harvest, let's look at some Given Circumstances guidelines:

1. Ask if the fact you are noting is *reliable*. Who says it, and is that person a reliable witness? Or is someone stating their opinion about someone, which may say more about the speaker than the target? If you gauge a "fact" not to be reliable, it is not a true Given Circumstance about the target character, but an opinion of the unreliable speaker.
2. You will find many tantalizing clues to mysteries not resolved in the text; those should be noted as requiring speculation. Many of these can become inspirations for rehearsal Études. But don't speculate now; just store those vexing enigmas under "For Speculation" in your notebook.
3. Actor, you are building evidence about the world of the play and about your character, the director about each character. Compiling all that information will necessitate some kind of orderly process. Your Novel of Life I will come in quite handy as a source text. You may be able to copy a great many items you have already noted.
4. Directors must peruse every Event and gather comprehensive data on every character. Actors may want to concentrate only on the World of the Play and their character – but it's fine to go further.

5. Once these are gathered, you will distribute the Given Circumstances into their domains:

> The Outer Ring: the World of the Play
> The Middle Ring:
>
>> Character Circumstances (see Text Action 4).
>> Actions from the Throughline Action (summarized from Novel of Life I.
>
> The Inner Ring will become operational as we pursue activating Events in Text Action 8.

So, what we need to do first is concentrate on the Outer Ring, and specifically the first seven items listed on the diagram above. To be of use, an Outer Ring Given Circumstance must in some manner influence the life of at least one character in the play; many will have some influence on all.

> Geography, locale, and built environments
> Date, time, weather, special occasion days
> Economics, wealth, class, status
> Politics/History
> Social and legal codes
> Moral and spiritual attitudes
> Technology, transportation, communication

Here is a brief sample of harvesting the Given Circumstances of the Outer Ring from the first pages from *The Cherry Orchard.*

OUTER RING: WORLD OF THE PLAY Act I Scene "titles" are optional, character notations in caps, character names abbreviated; comments and speculation in parentheses				
Geography/ Environment	*Date/Time/ Weather*	*Economics/ Class/Status*	*Social/Moral Religious/ Political*	*Technology/ Transport*
WAITING FOR TRAIN A room still called the nursery; a side door to Anya's room; windows shut Train station within hearing distance	**WAITING FOR TRAIN** Dawn, May, chill in the air. Cherry orchard in bloom Time: 2 a.m.; getting light (Where are we that dawn comes at 2 a.m.?)	**CHARACTER LIST** RAN is a landowner LOP is a businessman TRO is a university student CHA is a governess PIS is a landowner	**DUN PROPOSED TO** DUN tells LOP that YEP has proposed to her (Reliable?)	**WAITING FOR TRAIN** Train finally in Train is two hours late **DUN PROPOSED TO** Two carriages arrive (Do they belong to estate, or hired?)

(Continued)

OUTER RING: WORLD OF THE PLAY Act I Scene "titles" are optional, character notations in caps, character names abbreviated; comments and speculation in parentheses				
Geography/ Environment	*Date/Time/ Weather*	*Economics/ Class/Status*	*Social/Moral Religious/ Political*	*Technology/ Transport*
Dawn, May, chill in the air. Cherry orchard in bloom DUN: dogs were barking all night **SQUEAKY BOOTS** There is a garden There is a dining room	LOP says RAN has been away 5 years **SQUEAKY BOOTS** YEP: freezing thismorning, must be in 30s; cherry blossoms are out (new info to audience) LOP worried RAN won't recognize him; it's been five years since she left	YEP is a bookkeeper DUN is a parlor maid FIR is a valet YAS is a valet **WAITING FOR TRAIN** LOP: RAN comforted him: Don't cry "poor boy" (in Russian "peasant boy") LOP: father was poor LOP: now has "brand new suit and tan shoes"	**DUN PROPOSED TO** DUN tells LOP that YEP has proposed to her (Reliable?)	**WAITING FOR TRAIN** Train finally in Train is two hours late **DUN PROPOSED TO** Two carriages arrive (Do they belong to estate, or hired?)

When fully accomplished, this task – harvesting and distributing the Outer Circle facts – completes Part I of Given Circumstances, the objective study of the play itself. Now we move on to the next inquiry: Text Action 4: Character Given Circumstances.

Notes

1 M Кнебель 1976. *Поэзия Педагогики*. Moskva: Всероссийское театральное общество; M Knebel 1976. *The Poetry of Pedagogy*. Moskva: All-Russian Theatrical Society Translation Ilya Khodosh 304.
2 *Tatiana Wolff (tr. and ed.), Pushkin on Literature (*London: Methuen, *1971), p. 265; cited in* Whyman Rose. 2008. *The Stanislavsky System of Acting: Legacy and Influence in Modern Performance*. Cambridge UK: Cambridge University Press, p. 44.

3 Кнебель М. О. *О действенном анализе пьесы и роли.* 3-е изд. М.: Искусство, 1982. Knebel M. O. *On Analysis through Action of the Play and the Role.* 3rd ed. M.: Art, 1982 Translation Ilya Khodosh p. 10.
4 Knebel *Poetry of Pedagogy* 324.
5 Knebel *Analysis of the Play and the Role* 11.
6 Malochevskaya, Irina Author interview May 11, 2013, live translation: Professor Nikolai Pesochinsky.

15 Text Action 4
Character Given Circumstances

Step 1: The Line of the Role

In her book *The Poetry of Pedagogy*, Maria Knebel recollects a conversation she has with Sasha, an impatient student grappling with the role of Lopakhin. She gently prods Sasha to talk through the role, scene by scene, what she calls "the Line of the Role," a term taken from her mentor Stanislavsky. Sasha's ideas are jumbled. Finally, Maria Knebel interrupts:

> "Let's not rush," I say to Sasha. – Try to prepare the exact list of facts and actions for the next lesson. Do not seek at once a single, accurate justification for all of Chekhov's moves. We have études ahead of us. We will analyze in detail each piece of the play, but for now try to remember, or write down *the sequence of actions* [emphasis added]…In the next lesson, Sasha read aloud Lopakhin's line of action.[1]

Before moving on to Character Given Circumstances, do as Knebel instructed Sasha: write down the sequence of actions – the Line of the Role. This is the chronological succession of character Events, including Prior Events (aka Prelife Events) which include all offstage Events before and during the action of the play, and Scenic Events from inside the textual action of the play. This Action, The Line of the Role, is gleaned from the exercises of the three prior Actions – Reading the Play, Novel of Life I, and Given Circumstances, Part 1.

As you will see, good portions of this exercise can be lifted and condensed from your Novel of Life I, concentrating on the character under examination. Perhaps here you can be a little more liberal with quotations. However, once again, avoid "coloring" your depictions with loaded adverbs and adjectives. We are still in objective fact-gathering mode.

Let's look at a partial Line of the Role for Anya in *The Cherry Orchard*, from her birth up to her good-nights partway through Act I. We will assume the play begins in 1903, the year the play began rehearsal.

DOI: 10.4324/9781003475576-20

The Line of the Role: Anya Ranyevskaya

Year of Play, 1903; Anya is age 17 in the Character List

Prior (aka Pre-life) Events

1886

Anya Ranyevskaya (patronymic unknown) born, presumably on Gayev estate; mother Liubov Andreevna Ranyevskaya, née Gayeva; Anya's father was a lawyer, surname Ranyevsky, said to be a heavy drinker. At some point, Charlotta is taken on as Anya's governess. Anya has a sister, Varya, who is seven years older and was adopted at an unknown point. Anya's uncle is Leonid Andreyevich Gayev, who is likely older than her mother.

1890

Brother Grisha (Grigori) born; at some later unspecified point, Pyotr Trofimov (Petya) becomes the boy's tutor.

1897

Father dies. Anya is 11 or 12.

1897

Grisha, age 7, drowns in the river one month after the father's death. Anya lost her father and little brother within thirty days.

1897–98

Mother leaves for Paris; Anya is 11 or 12.

Early spring, 1903

(probably April: "Easter" per Schmidt, "Holy Week" per Senelick; there was snow on the ground)
    Anya, age 17, travels to Paris with governess, Charlotta, to bring mother back to the home estate; Anya finds mother in abject circumstances in a crowded walk-up apartment.

May (?) 1903

Departs Paris with mother, Charlotta, and mother's valet, Yasha; four sleepless nights later arrives at local train station and returns home.

Present Circumstances: Act I: May 1903

Anya arrives home with others; she is the first one to speak upon entrance: asks mother if she recalls this room (the nursery); shortly, all depart except Anya and Dunyasha.

Anya: No sleep, cold. Dunyasha calls her "sweetie" and "sweetheart" and reveals that Yepikhodov has proposed to her. Anya, who has lost her hairpins, is not interested in Dunyasha's news. She wants to get some sleep; she was worried the whole trip. However, she responds "joyfully" when Dunyasha tells her Petya is here, in the barn (*banya* in Russian = bathhouse); Varya enters and sends Dunyasha out.

Varya embraces Anya, calls her "angel...my beautiful darling." Anya tells Varya about her trip:

- Recalls she left just before Easter; it was cold.
- Charlotta never shut up and kept doing her "silly tricks;" Anya questions Varya sticking her with Charlotta.
- Paris was cold and snowy; Anya says her French is "just awful."
- Mama was living in a fifth-floor apartment, they had to walk up.
- Apartment was "crowded" with French people, "some old priest reading some book," and everybody was smoking awful cigarettes.
- She felt so sorry for Mama, hugged her, and couldn't let go; Mama was so glad to see me, she cried.
- Mama had sold the villa in Menton, the money is completely gone; all the money Varya gave Anya for the trip is gone.
- At the train station, Mama orders the most expensive thing, tips the waiters a ruble each! So does Charlotta! And Mama brings that "flunky" of hers, Yasha, along with her.
- Anya asks if the interest got paid. Varya says no, "the place goes up for sale in August." Anya: "Oh, my God, my God."

At this point, Lopakhin sticks his head in the door, makes a mooing sound, and leaves.

- Anya asks Varya if he has proposed; you know he loves you. Just sit down and discuss it honestly. What are you waiting for? "He just isn't interested," says Varya. Varya notices a new pin on Anya, a little bee. Anya sighs and says Mama bought it for her.
- Anya goes into her room and giggles like a little girl, telling Varya that in Paris, she went for a ride in a balloon.

And so forth to Act IV, her final line and departure.

Step 2: Compiling Character Given Circumstances

This second exercise, Compiling Character Given Circumstances and The Line of the Role are certainly interrelated and at times may feel redundant. But first off, redundancy is not necessarily a futile time-sucker; passing through something more than once is instructive and can kindle further inquiry. Secondly, while there is a porosity between a character's Given Circumstances and their Line of the Role, the point of the second exercise is to glean facts from the Line of the Role – and elsewhere – to compile a complete precis of the individual character(s). These summaries, extracted from the play, are often called Character Profiles.

Character Given Circumstances are text-evident and reliable verifiable *facts* about the character, the datapoints the author gives us about their background, interests, occupations, preoccupations, dreams, actions taken, and the like. A general rule: if a potential "fact" is open to speculation, then it is not a Character Given Circumstance – but might be material for an Étude. N.B.: Character Given Circumstances will evolve or alter during the play; they are not fixed in stone. Events or time-passage of the play may alter the character's profile and should be noted as a change.

Character Given Circumstances versus Line of the Role

Let's look at Anya for the distinction between her Character Given Circumstances and her Line of the Role. It is a Character Given Circumstance of Anya that she was sent to Paris with Charlotta as chaperone to find her mother and bring her back to the estate. That is an indisputable basic *fact* of this character's life; it is part of her profile as the play begins. So, as you build your profile on Anya, you would note: "Anya, age 17, travels to Paris with governess, Charlotta, to bring mother back to the home estate; Anya finds mother in abject circumstances in a crowded walk-up apartment."

We glean these presumed facts from Anya's Line of the Role, in her scene with Varya in Act I where Anya chronicles her travails: how she departed just before Easter, how Charlotta never shut up and kept doing her silly tricks, and the like. Relaying this account to Varya is something Anya *does*. Thus, these details she divulges lie on Anya's Line of the Role, the bullet-point tracking of the character's textual actions, event by event. But the specifics are *not* necessarily basic Given Circumstances, they are from an unreliable personal narrative. Anya is now physically and mentally fatigued: the entire journey was certainly deeply traumatic given the situation she found her revered mother in. Anya, in her unstable state, may be exaggerating, misremembering, or suppressing unhappy recollections. Possibly her opiated mother didn't recognize her?

So, is everything Anya says to Varya subject to speculation? Certainly, the departure just before Easter is sound; we have no good reason to doubt it. As well, it becomes clear that retrieving Mama was the intent of the trip. Moreover, it does seem factual – and crucial to the plot – that Mama sold the villa in Menton. But most everything else Anya says to Varya is questionable to some degree, given Anya's condition. Many things she says are not verifiable or concrete – Charlotta might tell a very different story – and thus *not* formal Given Circumstances; they are an area for speculation.

This is one of the things Études exist for: clarifying uncertain or speculative moments through on-the-floor probes – not through discussion but through action. The visit to the fifth-floor apartment is an essential Étude that will impact many characters in the play, certainly those who were there: Liubov, Anya, and Charlotta. The visceral results of a powerful Étude on this Event will live deeply inside those actors.

Études: don't talk about it, do it!

Identifying Character Given Circumstances – Option 1

How do we begin identifying specific and verifiable Character Given Circumstances other than extracting material from the Lines of the Roles?

Much can be learned about a character through what others say about that person when that person is not present. For example, at the very top of the play, we learn a lot about Liubov Ranyevskaya from Lopakhin: she's been gone five years, she consoled him as a young man, and so forth. Even though she has not yet entered the play, on page 1 Lopakhin is imparting essential Character Given Circumstances about her. In this case we have no reason to doubt him, so those facts fall into the Liubov profile, the fact that she has been gone for five years is important to everyone, the fact that she once consoled him is crucial to Lopakhin. But the facts are about Liubov.

Thus, one process of gleaning Character Given Circumstances is much the same as you did parsing the World of the Play in the previous exercise. As you now read the play from the top – yes, redundancy is a good thing – you are again passing a magnet over the filings of the play, step by step. But this time you are trolling for: what the author says about each character; what each character says about themselves; and what others say about another character.

Again, a big yellow flag here: you must verify what a character says about themselves and what is said about them by others. Proceed with caution, especially concerning the opinions of other characters: what Character A says about Character B may reveal more about Character A than Character B.

Once again, the place to start is the author's character list page. Here we find that Liubov owns the estate, Anya is her 17-year-old daughter, Varya is her 24-year-old adopted daughter, Gayev is her brother, Lopakhin is a businessman, and so forth. Note these simple facts, and then move through the play – and/or your *Novel of Life I* – and extract what you think might be fundamental information about each character – not recounting the step-by-step things the characters *do but* isolating what you think are key aspects about their personal life and individuality. Use your judgment – and condense as you go.

Option 1 – A Dry Run

From the very beginning of the play, take notes about information that seems particularly relevant to the individual characters. For instance:

ANYA

Has a room that adjoins the nursery

LOPAKHIN

Has a book

RANYEVSKAYA

(Via LOPAKHIN):
Been away five years now
She was always a good person, very gentle, never fussed
Not much older than Lopakhin was (15), thin,
Brought Lopakhin into nursery, washed the blood off him, consoled him

LOPAKHIN

Father a drunk; beat him bloody
They came up with a delivery to the house, Lopakhin still bloody
Liubov brought Lopakhin into the nursery; washed and consoled him
His father was poor, he is now rich, "lots of money"
Wears fancy clothes

DUNYASHA

Excited about arrivals; may faint
(Via LOPAKHIN): All dressed up and fancy hairdo (i.e., not maid's livery)

YEPIKHODOV

(Via CHEKHOV) Flowers; jacket and tie; polished boots which
  squeak loudly
Confuses big words: ("endear" vs. "endure.")
"Every day something awful happens but I just keep smiling"
On departure, knocks over chair accidently (Via CHEKHOV: "He seems
  proud of it")

DUNYASHA

YEP has proposed; she is uncertain; he is crazy about her

YEPIKHODOV

(Via DUNYASHA)

Nice, quiet, but one can't understand what he is talking about
Every day something awful happens to him
Called Double Trouble

As with the Outer Ring of Given Circumstances – The World of the Play – you can now place this data into specific character silos. What we just noted can be distributed like this:

ANYA	*LOPAKHIN*	*RANYEVSKAYA*	*DUNYASHA*	*YEPIKHODOV*
Has a room that adjoins the nursery	Has a book (presumably he can read, or try to) Father a drunk; beat him bloody Came up with a delivery to the house, still bloody Liubov brought him into nursery; washed and consoled him Father was poor, he is now rich, "lots of money" Fancy clothes	(Via LOPAKHIN): Been away five years now. Always a good person, very gentle Not much older that LOP was (age 15 or so), thin Brought LOP into nursery, washed the blood off, consoled him	Excited about arrivals; may faint (Via LOPAKHIN): All dressed up and fancy hairdo (i.e., not maid's livery) YEP has proposed; she is uncertain; she says he is crazy about her	(Via CHEKHOV) Flowers; jacket and tie; polished boots that squeak loudly Confuses big words: ("endear" vs. "endure.") "Every day something awful happens but I just keep smiling" On departure, knocks over chair accidently (Via CHEKHOV: "He seems proud of it") (Via DUNYASHA) nice, quiet, but one can't understand what he is talking about Every day something awful happens to him Called Double Trouble

Naturally, many of these columns will get lengthy as you go along. (Hint: if you are doing numerous characters, converting to landscape mode will yield more columns).

After you have gathered all the information about the characters, the next step is to read through each character for patterns, observing descriptions that are repeated or similar. Then, column by column, distill the Character Given

Circumstances you have garnered into condensed notations in your own words about each character.

Identifying Character Given Circumstances – Option 2

Another route, perhaps preferred by the actor, is making a dedicated search for an individual character. This requires perusing the entire play, seeking any allusions to that character (a scanned copy of the play that can be searched would be a big help). The danger here is obvious: if you skim too lightly, you are likely to miss important references, concealed in scenes in which your character is not present. Therefore, be watchful for any mention of the name or variant designations of the character. Liubov, for instance, is also cited as Liuba, Mama, or Andreevna.

Directors must cover every major character, as they did in the Line of the Role.

The Final Draft

Whichever path you take, you will want to do a final draft of your work, transforming your distilled notes into simple declarative sentences using your own words, blending in observations and deductions. This process will aid in fleshing out all the datapoints you have uncovered, humanizing the character, and being accessible when you review the Character Given Circumstances during preparation and rehearsal.

Here is an example from *The Three Sisters* (with thanks to director, critic, and former student Sara Holdren).

ANDREY PROZOROV
- He is the son of General Sergey Prozorov. (We know his father's name from his patronymic: Sergeyevich.)
- He has three sisters: Olga, Masha, and Irina.
- His age is unspecified, though Masha – the middle sister – refers to him as "our little brother," implying that he is younger than she and Olga. If this is the case, then he is still very young at the start of the play, only 21.
- His sisters call him "the family intellectual" and "our genius." He went to university in Moscow and studied to become a scientist. His father encouraged an academic career for his son.
- He plays the violin.
- He does woodworking as a hobby and has made several picture frames for Irina.
- His father trained him, along with his sisters, to get up at 7 o'clock every morning. General Prozorov also made sure all his children were educated in English, French, and German. In Act I, Andrey is planning to translate a book from English into Russian.

- He has gained weight since the death of his father.
- In Act I, his sisters tease him for being in love with Natasha, "a local girl." At the end of the act, he tells Natasha that he loves her and proposes to her.
- At the start of Act II, he is married to Natasha, and they have a baby son named Bobik. It is unclear how much time has passed and how old Bobik is.
- By this time, he has become the secretary of the County Council. He says that the most he can aspire to is to become a full member.
- His doctor has put him on a yogurt diet to lose weight.
- He spends time rereading his old lectures from his university days.
- He says he doesn't drink.
- He says he's afraid of his sisters.
- He leaves the house by the back door to avoid his wife.
- He gambles and has lost a significant amount of money.
- By Act III, he and Natasha have another child, a baby daughter named Sophie. Something that Irina says makes clear that almost four years have passed since Act I (see Irina's Profile).
- He now owes 35,000 rubles. He has mortgaged the family home to cover his gambling debts. He is frantic for money because his sisters get a military pension, and he does not.
- He has become a full member of the County Council.
- He considers dueling immoral.
- In Act IV, he tells Chebutykin that, though he loves his wife, she disgusts him.
- He dreams of being a professor at the University of Moscow, a famous scientist, the pride of Russia.

Looking ahead

Up to now, each Text Action has demanded objectivity and deep close reading: knowledge before opinion. The next section, Novel of Life II, is a reward for all this labor. For an actor, this is creating an idiosyncratic first-person novella of your character; for a director this is doing the same for all the characters. Novel of Life II is a subjective, imaginative, creative act. Free at last!

Note

1 Knebel *Poetry of Pedagogy* 343.

16   Text Action 5
Novel of Life II

Introduction

Now the fun begins.

In Novel of Life II, both imaginative ideas and personal affective memories are released from confinement and encouraged to seize the foreground. Free at last, here you will write a creative and detailed autobiographical novella about your character – or, if you are a director, for *all* the major characters – a deeply imagined and personally lived-through first-person psychoautobiography, drawn from the numerous objective facts and unanswered questions you have already gathered – and from comparable experiences in your own life.

As you were collecting and collating facts from Given Circumstances I and II and the Line of the Role, you were intentionally restricted to the *plot* and the hard data from which that plot is forged. Here, in Novel of Life II, you will move from objective plot to subjective *story* – your story of your character or characters. *Story*, at least in Chekhov's or any good play of any genre, comprises far more than plot. Story features external *and* internal character action, contradictions, illicit entanglements, lies, secrets, confessions, hopes, losses, joy, suffering; in short, the absurd instability of human existence – all the things that make life worth living.

In the end, you will not be performing the plot; again, that would only save the audience the reading of the play. Instead, your performance will be founded on your own personal deep *story* of the character. Your story may be secreted in subtext; life hidden beneath the surface facts; concealed in the intimate beliefs and private motivations; and driven by the mysterious motions of *your* soul – which will determine the alogical logic of your character's behavior. To achieve *story*, you will use subjective free association, personal affective memory, and imaginative invention. With these tools, you will now alchemize your spreadsheets of dispassionate plot bytes into the living, breathing character who will activate your story.

Each role now has a basic factual endoskeleton but is not yet a fully formed *character*. To flesh out this skeleton and, more importantly, to inspirit a complex live being, you will write a comprehensive fictional autobiography, sourced in textual evidence, but expanded, elaborated, and compellingly felt by *you*.

DOI: 10.4324/9781003475576-21

The goal is not for you to walk in the character's shoes. The goal is to let the character fill *your* shoes; to fill *you*. The goal is for *you* to *embody* and *experience* the character you call to life, to feel them viscerally. You are the medium who channels the character. Then, you *become* the character: "I in the Given Circumstances" starts here. It is that twinned organism – your soul and the character's plot – that authors the psycho-autobiography called Novel of Life II.

Appraising the Facts

To date, you have gathered lots of character-based facts, and organized them into an objective Line of the Role and a fundamental set of Character Circumstances. We now move to what Stanislavsky and Knebel called "appraising the facts" (variously translated as "assessing" or "evaluating" the facts). Maria Osipovna Knebel quoted Stanislavsky on this matter:

> What does it mean to evaluate the facts and events of the play? – Stanislavsky wrote. – "It means: to find in them their hidden inner meaning, their spiritual essence, the degree of their importance and impact. It means: to dig below the external facts and events and to find in the depths those other, deeply hidden events, which often drive the external facts…In a word, [it means]: to know the internal schema, which defines the relationship between people. Assess the facts – and thereby find the key to crack open the many mysteries of the life of the human spirit [in Russian *dusha* or soul] in a role, hidden below the facts of the play."[1]

Knebel follows her mentor's theme of personalized "ownership" of the facts, writing:

> Stanislavsky said that in order to appraise facts through personal feeling, on the basis of private, personally relevant relationships, the actor internally asks himself this question and solves this problem: "What among my personal, living human thoughts, desires, determination, habits, inherent qualities and shortcomings would force me, the person-artist, to relate to the people and events of the play in the way that my character relates to them?"[2]

From these and other statements, we see two interrelated projects here: (1) evaluating the impact of various life events on the character and (2) tapping a correlative set of your own private affective personal circumstances and events that would manifest the feelings and behavior of your character. From these two intertwined creative tasks, your personal novella is generated. The fun of Novel of Life II is to be both the subject and the object: to *be* the central character and to serve as the author of their story. Your affective memories, now fictionalized into your Novel of Life II, should be disguised well enough so that an outside reader cannot identify them – but they are there, for you.

Here is director Anatoly Efros, by all accounts a warm and generous soul, wrestling with becoming the vain and malevolent Solyony as he prepared to direct a production of *Three Sisters*:

> What about Solyony from *The Three Sisters*! From what material can his portrait be molded? For example, I am sure that I have nothing in common with this show-off…I know nothing about him. I never killed anyone in a duel, have not cracked stupid jokes about children, and do not look like the poet Lermontov.

Efros continues:

> So, who is this Solyony, and what is the issue here?
>   How can I draw him closer to myself?
>   Indeed, as a normal person, I like Tuzenbach more than Solyony. How can I make myself want to get involved in a duel, how can I make myself want to shoot Tuzenbach like a bird?[3]

The brilliant Russian director is not talking about trying to convince an actor playing Solyony to 'want to shoot Tusenbach like a bird.' He is struggling with how *he*, director Anatoly Efros, can make himself 'want to shoot Tusenbach like a bird.'

As Efros attempts to write out the events of the play through Solyony's eyes, he gradually draws closer to his antagonist. He then surprisingly slips into first-person singular – he *becomes* Solyony:

> But before the fourth act, I am forced to challenge Tuzenbach to a duel because he insulted me. I knew it would happen sometime, and it did.
>   So, why are you trying to turn your back on me now, old man? Why are you growling? You yourself are guilty, indeed, they themselves are all guilty. I warned you, I asked you, I predicted it, but all of you nevertheless made a killer of me. So now, you share the fault with me, but do not shake your heads in reproach. This time there is no way out – I will shoot him like a bird.[4]

As Efros shows us, mere facts about a character can be deeply appraised only by an individual struggling to give birth to their own progeny, in their own unique way. Initially, there is only you and the selected glyphs on a page we call a character. How would *you* come to want 'to shoot Tuzenbach like a bird'? Your process will only manifest itself through the kind of deeply personal struggle Efros records for us.

Contents of Novel of Life II

As Novel of Life II is a subjective and creative endeavor, its medium is open. It can be first-person autobiography with the character and you as co-authors, remembering your life. It can be a private diary, a hidden archive of letters, an interview, an epic poem, stenographic deathbed remembrances, a photo album with annotations, or a creative mixture of artifacts and specimen – a scrap-book. One actor recalled what they had said to a fictional psychiatrist. It can be chronological or illogical, documentary or poetic. But it must be *compre-hensive*. It should be enhanced by a few "portrait gallery" visual images – inter-net pics will do or draw things if you can – of the character, other characters, sites, and perhaps some of the character's meaningful possessions. Consider adding their favorite music, if appropriate.

Most importantly, it must creatively cover all the major known or suggested events of the character's life before, during, and perhaps even after the play. It must fill in the blanks, particularly Pre-life Events, and between-the-acts (aka Interstitial) Events. It must create a backstory for every major relationship the character has in the play, as well as internal thoughts and feelings that occur during the Line of the Role. In short, all the details, internal and external, that might go into a novella by Proust, Wharton, or Baldwin – or a poem by Anne Sexton, or a private diary found in an attic decades later. Or think of it as a detailed treatment for a confessional docudrama.

For *The Story of Anya* this would mean, among other things, filling out the details of her childhood. Was she close to her father or was he an alcoholic apparition whom she rarely saw? How about Mama? Anya says to Varya in Act I that she understands Mama so well; is that true? Or was Mama an absentee parent, whom Anya missed terribly but never really knew? What about Uncle Leonid Gayev: what's up with him, Anya might wonder. And Petya; why does Anya "joyfully" react to Dunyasha's news that he is here? Where was 12-year-old Anya the day Grisha drowned? Was she off playing games with 23-year-old Petya? Dunyasha calls Anya "sweetie" – was her chambermaid Anya's only friend on this isolated estate? What about Varya, her adopted older sister, who also calls her "darling" and "beauty" and who likely cooked up the plan to send Anya to Paris? What has her schooling been? (She admits her French is "awful" – has governess Charlotta failed here?) Does she have any idea who Lopakhin is, other than a fickle tormentor of Varya? Does she care?

These are inter-relationship questions, many based on Prior Circumstances. All the Throughline Action events raise more and more questions, but the Pre-life questions from before the play starts are the baseline of the character, thus a good place to start.

Novel of Life II: A Protocol, with Examples

Every Novel of Life II should incorporate the following:

The Principle of Exaggeration

Every tiny factoid and every huge Given Circumstance should be creatively pushed to the *furthest limit of credibility*. How much potential stored energy lies inside a particular Given Circumstance? The Principle of Exaggeration, Tovstonogov contends, is "not a law of life, but the most important law of theatre, of being on stage: without it, action will lose its activeness, its most essential quality, and the struggle will become passive."[5]

Let us look again at a part of Anya's description of her trip to Paris, as told to Varya:

> ANYA: We got to Paris, it was cold and snowy, and my French is just awful! Mama was living in this fifth-floor apartment, we had to walk up, we get there and there's all these French people, some old priest reading some book, and it was crowded, and everybody was smoking these awful cigarettes – and I felt so sorry for Mama, I just threw my arms around her and couldn't let go. And she was so glad to see me, she cried.

How extreme, and therefore how potent, can we legitimately make Anya's brief account of this huge event? Let's intentionally push each known fact to the edge of authenticity, the borderline of credibility – yet all too possible.

Anya probably never has traveled before, certainly not to a sooty industrial megalopolis like Paris; she is disoriented and, given the dreadful weather and fetid air, probably more than a little bilious the whole time. Mama's address turns out to be in some *la vie Bohème* ghetto where the livery drivers refuse to go. She and ever-chattering Charlotta must trudge their way through snowy slush puddles, horse manure, overflowing sewage, and fog. In the dark streets they pass frightening people – beggars, drunks, speeding carriages flinging mud spatter, gropers. Their best clothes, specially chosen to go meet Mama, are by now a sodden wreck; Anya's lovely new French doeskin boots are water-logged, cold, and limp.

They finally get to the address. Surely this can't be the place! Inside there is no elevator, no heat, no light. A shivering Anya, shoved ahead by Charlotta, who is lighting sulfurous matches as they go, must trudge up five flights inside the dank circular stairwell, redolent with odors of foreign foods and fresh urine. Nauseous, Anya finally gets to the top floor. A door is ajar, it's noisy inside, dense with smoke; Anya can barely see anything in the gloom.

As she stumbles through the dank room, Anya can make out a dark-skinned singer plucking a one-string instrument; two men sucking each other's tongues; an obese woman coughing dark spittle into a bottle, and a someone in a tattered cassock keening and muttering into a book, occasionally sprinkling liquids onto someone lying motionless on the floor – is she dead? The other figures are shapeless shadows, some mumbling cryptic languages, some snoring, at least one coughing sputum. The air is hazed from funny-smelling hand-rolled cigarettes, tobacco – or something else? – and two people are inhaling wisps of smoke from crystals in a spoon being heated by a candle.

Anya feels faint and starts weeping. No one notices her except Charlotta, who cries out at the top of her lungs in Russian, Мадам Раневская, вы здесь? – "Madame Ranyevskaya, are you here?" A weak voice from somewhere cries something inaudible, possibly in Russian. Charlotta, again calling out, supports Anya and guides her toward the wispy voice. There, on a messy bed, bedraggled in stained undergarments, ghostly pale, her clumpy hair askew, is…*Mama*?? Next to this woman are two barely clothed men sleeping scissored, one drooling. The woman looks up with glazed eyes and sees 17-year-old Anya.

"My God," the woman whispers in Russian, "who are you?" She cackles a laugh and whispers: "You look like me when I was your age."

Anya's voice cracks: "I am…Anya…Mama."

Liubov Ranyevskaya is dead silent, feels the girl's face and falls apart sobbing. Anya crawls onto the bed, wraps her arms around her mother, and weeps with her. The drooling man stirs and fumbles toward the two females sobbing next to him. Charlotta watches, smokes, and whacks the drooling man away.

From this account and the exasperating trip home, we can imagine Anya's condition when she arrives at the manor. She is not simply exhausted and cold; this we already know from the text, the plot. Hidden underneath that text is the fact that Anya has suffered a severe life trauma. Young Anya has realized that she must be an adult now, a caretaker of both her mother and hapless uncle. She also needs to seek out some way to escape the dreadful pain and confusion which has snapped her life into two parts: before Paris/after Paris. This trauma will affect Anya's behavior for the rest of the play, and the rest of her life, starting with her first scene with Dunyasha.

Imagine finding your own beloved mother in those circumstances: an emotional scar that would never heal. To let Anya's terse Act I account to Varya pass inertly as an expositional plot point is to waste an opportunity. Given Circumstances are meant to be plundered, expanded, and heightened to *their most extreme credible degree* to infuse the actor with the deepest possible inner energy source that the circumstance can provide. The audience may never guess this backstory, nor do they have to, but it is rocket fuel for the actor.

Don't be cautious – exaggerate to the breaking point (but not beyond)! Be fearless and honest. Take your imagination and your emotions to the greatest plausible extremes. Taking a circumstance to its outer limit of veracity can reveal whether the circumstance will bear the weight of such extreme amplification. If not, you can always dial it back to a lesser degree, as needed.

Source Spiritual Trauma

Leningrad director and educator Mar Sulimov wrote brilliantly about many aspects of Analysis through Action. His analysis of *The Cherry Orchard*[6] has had a major influence on this book, and certainly this chapter. One of his most compelling ideas is that every character contains within themselves a "Source Spiritual Trauma," which Sulimov describes as:

> some devastation, some powerful suffering, called upon by a particular event, which for the character's whole life, for the duration of life depicted in the play, exerts a powerful, decisive influence. It creates its own

"pressure points" for the character, the uniqueness of their logic, all systems by which they appraise occurrences, their individuality, and the peculiarity of their relationships with the surrounding people. That particular wavelength of their soul, which often forms personality in a decisive way.[7]

We can easily assign the idea of Source Spiritual Trauma to Anya's Paris experience; it influences, even determines, her life for the duration of the play – and beyond. Likewise, we can contend that Lopakhin's experience as an adolescent male – being beaten senseless by his father, and then lovingly cared for at the manor house by an enchanting young angel named "Love" (Любовь = Liubov = Love) – as the most powerful determining event of his life. (Not all traumas end in misery.)

For other characters, we may have to bore deeper in the realm of speculation. Why didn't older brother Leonid Gayev inherit the Gayev estate? When and where does Varya come from? Where was tutor Petya on the day Grisha drowned? Why does the mysterious Charlotta have no papers? If so, how did she travel to Paris with Anya? Who was Liubov's husband, the lawyer Ranyevsky?

Ferreting out a Source Spiritual Trauma by asking the unanswered questions can lead to enormously potent and imaginative resources for a character's actions, internal dysphoria, and unspoken desires. In the case of Liubov Ranyevskaya, Sulimov contends:

> For Ranevskaya, it is the tragic death of her son, perceived as punishment for an emotional indulgence, which became her "source spiritual trauma," which completely poisoned and marred her life, turned happiness into suffering, her whole life into a sense of unredeemed guilt and impending punishment.[8]

Sulimov's imagination then leads to a chilling account – Novel of Life II–style – about what happened that fateful day: "Ranevskaya overstepped her own emotional norms, either while her husband was alive or very shortly after his death, getting together with another man. And immediately after that followed her terrible retribution – the death of her son."

He goes on to imagine that her young son Grisha came to ask her to take him down to the river. But she did not go with her son; she wanted to be alone with her new lover, who waited in her bedroom.

> Quickly drawn curtains, door locked, clothes shed…And it was precisely then, in HIS [sic] embrace, in the crumpled bedding, she heard the noise, the incomprehensible hysteria, screams…And then – in the barely thrown-on dress, she ran to the river, and her legs gave way…people on the shore, crowded together…saw her…let her through…and then she saw! From this collision of circumstances, you can go insane.[9]

This certainly explains in graphic terms why Ranyevskaya departed for Paris, and the gruesome hold that "HE, that man" has on her for the rest of her life; "And along with all that," say Sulimov, "the recognition of all her suffering as due punishment."

But why does she return to her ancestral home several years later? Because, Sulimov imagines, by then, things had turned for the worse for "HIM," and therefore for her. She begins to think of the life she left behind:

> And when Anya appears in her terrible, sinful, crumbling life in France, with her purity, innocence, rare Russian spirituality – this becomes a powerful impulse for returning home. That is why she will say, during her remarkable rendezvous with the Orchard, these words, full of hope and suffering: "It's all white! Oh, my Orchard! After a dark, terrible autumn and cold winter, you are young again, full of joy, heavenly angels did not forsake you...If only I could take the heavy stone off my shoulders, if only I could forget my past!"

But as we find out, reminded of Grisha by Petya's presence, the river, and more, Ranyevskaya cannot shake the burden of the past. She ultimately returns to a more recent past: life with the possessive, diseased lover who awaits her in Paris.

Sulimov's Novel of Life II about Ranyevskaya, sampled above, is an exemplary model that realizes the potential of reaching deep into the barest of known Given Circumstances – her husband dies, her son drowns, she departs the estate followed by her lover. The result: a compelling and motivational psychogram for the actor and director, spurred by The Principle of Exaggeration and The Spiritual Source Trauma.

Embedded Affective Memory

The best versions of these novellas are written in the first person. They are personal, intimate, and *felt*, not observed. The self-aware author of a Novel of Life II will likely notice events or influences from their own life experiences seeping into their character story. This is to be strongly encouraged! Inevitably the actor/author or director/author will find parallels between the character and themselves. Go there! Keep these correlatives in the tongue of the character; if someone else – a teacher, for instance – should read your piece, what is personal to you should not jump out. But you will have begun to make meaningful connections with the character through an act of fiction, not through a public confession.

Supertask

At the end of each Novel of Life, you must try to state what you currently consider to be the *Supertask* of the character at hand. Here we can define Supertask as the main life goal of the character, as revealed by their actions and inner longings. What is it they strive for, want, need, dream of to make their life full? If all obstacles were magically removed, what and who could this person be? What is their own image of their "best self"?

In Chekhov, it is almost a given that the characters will fail to achieve their Supertask (apart from Natasha in *Three Sisters*, who gets the Prozorov house, a lover on the town council, and a babysitter husband). But his characters have a Supertask nonetheless, and each strives to achieve it; striving keeps the character pushing forward to the end.

In short, what would their idea of happiness be?

The Supertask you assign now is provisional; it may change as you come to understand the character through further investigatory experience, and numerous Études. But attempt a *one-sentence* Supertask statement that you can assign to the character, as you see them now.

Beware of soapy generalities like "to be happy," "to find love," or "to be a better person." Who doesn't crave those things? Be specific to yourself as the character. Stanislavsky constantly emphasized that the Supertask must *excite* the actor.

For the director who must complete several of these character studies, you will likely find that the main characters are seeking related goals, even if they pursue their commensurate Supertasks through different means and for different reasons. These parallel Supertasks will be helpful later as we define the Supertask of the Play.

Conclusions

To summarize: each Novel of Life II should include material based on:

1. the known Given Circumstances of the play and the character;
2. the Principle of Exaggeration;
3. personal Affective Memories;
4. a Source Spiritual Trauma (text-based or speculative).
5. and it must conclude with a provisional Supertask of the character.

A typical Novel of Life II for a major character will comprise 3,000–4,000 words, plus three or four embedded "portrait gallery" images of the character, photographic, painted, or even abstract – and maybe some music. If it can be written out longhand, all the better – more personal and even more labor-intensive (a good thing).

Creative versions have included poems, drawings, confessions to a priest, or stories to grandchildren. One imaginative Lopakhin annually left a note at his mother's pauper grave explaining how much he loved Ranyevskaya and how all the money he was making didn't fill the ache.

By creating their Novels of Life II *before* rehearsal if possible, the actors and director will avoid time-sucking discussions. Your Novel will change, it will mutate, it will demand revision – but it is a starting point that will launch you into the work. And it need not be shared with anyone (unless you agree).

For an actor faced with an unprepared or uninterested director – yes, they exist; one director I knew hated what he called "psychological gossip" – Novel of Life II will be a lifeline for creating a fully explored, idiosyncratic, and highly personalized performance by an actor. Conversely, the director, faced with an unprepared actor – yes, they too exist – might make suggestions from their own Novel of Life II for this character to stimulate the actor. At best, the actors and the director have all done their homework and can get up on their feet to do the real work faster and more productively. You may encounter dueling ideas between the actor's and director's Novels. Good! Étude, Étude, Étude till the *hottest* theatrical truth comes out.

It doesn't matter whose idea it was! What matters is finding the most dynamic source of dramatic energy for the specific characters living in the specific events on stage, in this particular production of this particular play.

Notes

1 Knebel' M. 1971. *О Том Что Мне Кажется Особенно Важным: Стаьи Очерки Портреты*. Moskva: "Iskusstvo" 137; *On What Seems Especially Important to Me: Articles Essays Portraits*. Moscow: Art 62.
2 Кнебель М. О. О действенном анализе пьесы и роли. 3-е изд. М.: Искусство, 1982; Knebel M. O. *On the Effective Analysis of the Play and Role*. 3rd ed. M.: Art, 1982, 28. Translation Ilya Khodosh.
3 Эфрос Анатолий and James Thomas. 2006. Anatoly Efros and James Thomas. 2006. *The Joy of Rehearsal: Reflections on Interpretation and Practice*. New York: Peter Lang, 44.
4 Efros and Thomas, *Joy*, 46.
5 И.Б Малочевская, 2003. *Режиссерская Школа Товстоногова*. Sankt-Peterburg: Акад. Театрального Искусства; I.V. Malochevskaya, 2003. *Directing School of Tovstonogov*. Saint-Peterburg: Acad. of Theatrical Art 22. Translation by Ilya Khodosh.
6 Сулимов, Мар Владимирович, Режиссер наедине с пьесой; Санкт-Петербургская Государственная Академия Театрального Искусства, Санкт-Петербург, 1992; Sulimov, Mar Vladimirovich, "The Director Alone with the Play;" St. Petersburg State Academy of Theatrical Art, St. Petersburg, 1992. Translation Ilya Khodosh.
7 Sulimov, "Director Alone" 41.
8 Sulimov, "Director Alone" 41.
9 Sulimov "Director Alone" 36.

17 Text Action 6

The Initial Given Circumstances

Introduction

To date you have carefully read the play, handwritten out the plot, gathered and collated Given Circumstances for the world of the play and for character circumstances. You then zoomed in for creative confessional autobiographies of the characters in Novel of Life II. With each step you have probed deeper into the heart of the play. Now is a good time to dolly back and look at some key structural elements of the play, the architectural framework inside which the characters exist. Determining these girders and beams of the full play is the topic of our next three interrelated Actions:

Text Action 6: The Initial Given Circumstance of the Play and each Act.
Text Action 7: The Five-Event Structure of the performance
Text Action 8: Episodes, Events, and Tasks – what some consider to be the fundamental structural basis of Analysis through Action

As these components are interdependent – a study of one intersects with the others – some rudimentary descriptions are in order before we move on; these proxy definitions will be expanded in detail as we progress through these chapters.

The Initial Given Circumstance of the Play is the root cause of the dramatic action of the play, something that happened before the play begins and sets off the storyline the spectators will experience witnessing the play. To be considered later are: The Five-Event Structure which designates five key Events that become the five pillars of the production, from the Initial Event to the Crucial (or Concluding) Event; Episodes, Events, and Tasks provide a plan for breaking down the play into specific constituents – first, the larger Episodes (usually four or five per act), then the procession of Events that reside inside those Episodes. Events, sometimes called units, segments, or "beats," denote specific units of conflict between two or more onstage characters. Tasks – often insufficiently translated as objectives, more correctly as tasks, goals, or a problem to solve – are what belong to the independent actors within an Event.

DOI: 10.4324/9781003475576-22

The Initial Given Circumstance of the Play

Again, this is the root cause of the play. Without this essential *prior source circumstance*, which came into existence *before* the beginning of the play, there is, well, no play. The Initial Given Circumstance must be there, it must affect all the characters, and it does not go away – it exists until the very end of the play, even if challenged or triumphed over by Events. In short, the Initial Given Circumstance is the large and pervasive *fact* of the play, beginning to end – even if totally eradicated by the final curtain.

All the characters in the beginning of the play exist inside this condition, although the audience, or even some of the minor characters, may not recognize or acknowledge its presence immediately. But ultimately, everyone in the play is impacted by the Initial Given Circumstance of the Play, in one manner or another.

Here are some examples of Initial Given Circumstances from well-known classical plays. (The first two are drawn from Russian director and scholar of *Analysis through Action*, Alexander Polamishev[1]):

Hamlet: King Hamlet is dead.
Othello: Desdemona has eloped with Othello the Moor.
Twelfth Night: Since the death of Countess Olivia's brother, Illyria has become a loveless, narcissistic world.
Tartuffe: Orgon, the wealthy patriarch of a bourgeois family, has invited the religious zealot Tartuffe to take residence in his household.

Or these from Chekhov:

The Seagull: Konstantin has prepared his new play for his family, starring Nina.
Uncle Vanya: Retired Professor Serebriakov has arrived at the manor house of his deceased spouse with his new 27-year-old wife.
The Three Sisters: General Prozorov was buried a year ago, leaving a large house that provides his four children with security and a comfortable if unfulfilled life.

And finally, let's look at a well-known Shakespearean example that we will reprise in later discussions.

Romeo and Juliet: Due to the ancient blood feud between the Capulets and Montagues, Verona is a world of hatred and violence.

Glossing these specimens, we can conclude the following about The Initial Given Circumstance of the Play: (1) Whatever occurred that caused the Initial

Given Circumstance of the Play did so before the play begins and is operative when the action starts. (2) All the characters of the beginning of the play live inside this environment or situation, at least until a major new circumstance appears. (3) It endures, if invisibly, throughout the rest of the play. (4) The argument of the play is founded on the survival or eradication of the effects of this circumstance. Finally, (5) it is not a mystery; it can be directly deduced from information in the author's text.

The Initial Given Circumstance of the Play serves as the status quo of the play. But at some point, something, or someone else of major import, comes along to challenge this prevailing circumstance. This new element released into the crucible is called:

The Counter (or Challenging) Event

Some specific action, or possibly the arrival of someone new to the scene, challenges the so-far-uncontested omnipotence of the Initial Given Circumstance of the Play. The Counter Event initiates a conflict between the Initial Circumstance and challenges its dominance. Unlike the Initial Given Circumstance, the Counter Event must occur *inside* the action of the play and be legible to the audience. In summary, the Counter Event is a strong counterforce to the prevailing condition that has affected everyone up to this point, and is born inside the onstage action of the play. This struggle will continue to the play's dénouement.

So now we have:

Initial Given Circumstance $<$ — $>$ Counter Event = The Fundamental
Conflict of the Play.

The clash between the Initial Given Circumstance and the Counter Event will generate and suffuse all the remaining events of the play. It is this struggle – Initial Given Circumstance versus Counter Event – that will give birth to, and drive, the Throughline Action of the Play – the story the audience witnesses – to its end point. Without the Initial Given Circumstance, no play. Without the Counter Event, no conflict, lame play.

Let's propose some Counter Events for the three Chekhov plays cited above:

The Seagull:	Arkadina openly ridicules Konstantin's play, causing him to abruptly terminate Nina's performance.
Uncle Vanya:	Serebriakov proposes to sell the family farm, even though it was willed to his daughter Sonya by the Professor's first wife.
The Three Sisters:	Natasha breaks up the Carnival Night party; the security of the Prozorov offspring is challenged.
Romeo and Juliet:	Romeo Montague and Juliet Capulet meet and kiss at the masked ball, challenging the Veronese ancient quarrel of hatred and violence with innocent young love.

Each of the above Counter Events is surprising in its own way as it challenges what we have come to know as the status quo of the play. That status quo and the new dramatic energy injected into the play by the Counter Event will remain in struggle until the very end of the play: for example, the ancient Veronese quarrel versus innocent love. One or the other may end up victorious, or the two contending forces may end in an ambiguous stalemate. But the contention between the Initial Given Circumstance and the Counter Event forms the struggle of the play – a conflict that continues throughout the piece to some resolution, or an intentionally ambiguous irresolution.

To Summarize the Counter Event:

1. It is live and must happen onstage.
2. Like Arkadina's interruption in *The Seagull*, it might occur relatively early in the play – though after the Initial Given Circumstance has been established. Or it might take place later in the development of the action: Serebriakov's plan to sell the farm occurs late in the third act of *Uncle Vanya*.
3. While perhaps introduced subtly (or not), it unalterably changes the course of action; it is the major pivot point in the play. It is the fundamental hinge of the play: there is before the Counter Event, and after it.
4. The clash between the Initial Given Circumstance and the Counter Event will play a role in all Events that follow and constitutes the underlying basis of the Throughline Action (see Text Action 3).

The Initial Given Circumstance for Each Act

Once you have determined the Initial Given Circumstance of the Play and its adversary, the Counter Event, now is the time to establish the Initial Given Circumstance for Each Act. Like the Initial Given Circumstance of the Play, these circumstances should be proposed in a single descriptive phrase.

The Initial Given Circumstance of the Act pervades the action of the act (or, in classical plays, a particular subdivision of the text, regardless of the numerical acts). Even if the reigning circumstance of the specific act is subliminal or barely mentioned, an astute director or actor can deduce it from the author's text.

While determining the Initial Given Circumstance for the Act may sometimes feel like stating the obvious, it can serve as a welcome pathway as one passes through the stations of that act's itinerary. Simply put, each act has its own core situation, an activating circumstance for all who participate in that act.

The Initial Given Circumstance of the first act may resemble the Initial Given Circumstance of the play, as the initial act is, of course, where the Initial Given Circumstance of the Play first appears. Later acts will take on more particular topics.

So, for our three Chekhov plays, we propose the following Initial Given Circumstances for Each Act:

The Seagull
Act I: Konstantin will present his play tonight.
Act II: Nina has returned, free for three days.
Act III: Arkadina and Trigorin are departing today.
Act IV: Sorin is dying, and all have assembled.

Uncle Vanya
Act I: Serebriakov and Yelena have arrived and plan to stay.
Act II: Serebriakov's illnesses precipitate a long dark night for all.
Act III: Serebriakov summons all to a meeting.
Act IV: Serebriakov and Yelena are departing.

The Three Sisters
Act I: The year of mourning General Prozorov's death concludes today, Irina's birthday.
Act II: It's carnival night and the mummers are coming.
Act III: The town is burning down.
Act IV: The brigade is leaving.

These guideposts, each with their own active verbs, seem simple enough. But their very simplicity might require considerable reflection to discern – they may be hidden in plain sight. Like the Initial Given Circumstance of the Play, these underlying premises for each act should interlink a chain of dramatic events and generate specific behaviors of the characters for the duration of the act.

Consider Act II of *Uncle Vanya* and *The Three Sisters*. Both happen in dark night. In both, some characters consume an appreciable amount of alcohol, leading to confessions of love and lust, despair, and potential violence. The fire in Act III of *The Three Sisters* is a powerful disruptive circumstance that ignites Olga's firm advice to Irina – "marry the baron" – and Masha's confession that she loves Vershinin. The sisters have deliberately avoided these topics; without the circumstance of the town being ablaze, these may never have been addressed.

Finding an Initial Given Circumstance for Each Act is not merely an exercise of convenience. Like rooting out the Initial Given Circumstance of the Play, the task is to discover the most essential driving force that propels the actions and behaviors of the participating characters. It provides a demonstrable basis for the action of the act and keeps one on course through Étude rehearsals.

The Case of *The Cherry Orchard*

Many theatre artists, critics, and scholars consider *The Cherry Orchard* to be the most sophisticated and elusive of Chekhov's plays (though some award the blue ribbon to *Uncle Vanya*). Certainly Liubov Ranyevskaya, the flighty central character of *The Cherry Orchard*, is hard to nail down. Interpretations of her vary widely, actress to actress, production to production, scholar to scholar.

Additionally, numerous unanswered questions arise in the play: Is Lopakhin in love with Ranyevskaya? Is Trofimov? Is Gayev suffering from dementia? Who failed to care for Grisha the day the boy drowned? Where did Varya come from? How about Charlotta? Is Firs dead at the end? These and many more mysteries are all questions an ensemble will address. The company – director and actors – must examine these enigmas through Études and come to some conclusions that permit them to proceed in the strongest possible manner.

But here we are trying build some basic structural components which underlie the lives and mysteries of the characters – before we address those and many other questions. Let's look at a workbook list of Initial Given Circumstances questions.

What is *The Initial Given Circumstance of the Play*: In the longest view one could argue that the Initial Given Circumstance of *The Cherry Orchard* is the freeing of the serfs in 1861, disrupting the social and economic order of Russia. More immediate to the play's action would be the drowning of Grisha, prompting the departure of Liubov to Paris. Or, to bring it even closer to the timeline of the play, sending Anya to retrieve Liubov and bring her home.

All of those are dramatic and specific actions. But, most compelling, it seems to me, is the fact that the Gayev estate is in foreclosure and will be up for auction if no one can pay the accrued interest much less the principle. This embraces the four candidates suggested in the previous paragraph. From there we can move to an extraordinarily compelling set of Initial Given Circumstances proposed by Jean-Louis Barrault, the extraordinary French actor and director:

Act I: The cherry orchard is in danger of being sold.
Act II: The cherry orchard is about to be sold.
Act III: The cherry orchard is sold.
Act IV: The cherry orchard has been sold.

The rest is life.[2]

This remarkable summation of each act's *Initial Given Circumstance* incorporates all the possibilities raised above: from the freeing of the serfs to Liubov's initial departure from the estate to her return, and then to her second departure. And finally to Firs being left alone – he, who must die as the old order has died. The pressure of the estate being sold is relentless on everyone throughout the play. While the internal conflict between Liubov and Lopakhin – the old order versus the new order – is nominally resolved, there is no sense of closure in the final moments. In the end the play is about the helplessness of human actions to repel the inexorable force of time and fate.

The mysteries and enigmas of *The Cherry Orchard*, and many other great plays, are not puzzles to be solved for the audience's edification (even if the *actors* need to find through exploratory Études certain things unspecified by the author). Human ambiguities and contradictions are at the very core of

Chekhov's project, increasingly so as his dramatic worked matured. *The Cherry Orchard* is *meant* to be mysterious, enigmatic, and ambiguous. That is the nature of Chekhov's poetic heart.

"If only we could know," cries Olga in *The Three Sisters*. Her lament echoes through all the major Chekhov plays. Trying to identify the Initial Given Circumstances of the Play and Each Act should lead us not into a concantenation of linear plot points, but into the breadth and depth of the dramatist's work. Into the unknowable. As will the next two steps of our Text Actions.

Notes

1 Александр Поламишев. 1977. *Событие - Основа Спектакля*. Moskva: Советская Россия; Alexander Polamishev. 1977. *The Event – The Basis of the Production*. Moscow: Soviet Russia. 40.
2 First found in Polamishev, *Basis* 15 from Jean Louis Barrault, "*Pourquoi La Cerisaie?" Cahiers de la Compagne Barrault Renaud* 6 (July 1954): 87–97; Similarly cited in Chekhov Anton Pavlovich and Laurence Senelick. 2010. *The Cherry Orchard*. 1st ed. New York: W.W. Norton, 58.

18 Text Action 7

The Five Event Structure

Introduction

Event. It has become necessary for us to further expand our definition of this word which we have been using in colloquially up to now. In Russian the word for Event is событие (sobitiye), which literally translated means "co-existence." This makes sense when we understand that an Event requires *two opposing entities that co-exist at the same time in the same space*; their opposing forces generate a specific action. In physics a glass falling and breaking on the floor is an Event. Glass vs. Floor → Event. Onstage, two parties who occupy the same time and space and conflict with one another create an Event. Character A versus Character B → Event.

Alternate translations of событие are "occurrence, happening, development." All three are useful for our purposes: an Event is something that occurs or happens and a specific happening develops the story of the play. Finally, an Event is a self-contained unit of action, a happening in the same space-time, in which a conflict occurs, which in turn develops the Throughline Action of the play. Events can be as short as two lines of dialogue or cover several pages of dialogue and action. *The Cherry Orchard* is composed of dozens of Events, some forty in the first act alone.[1] Again, what we call here Events are more loosely known as "beats" or, in Hapgood's terms "Units of Action." Events seems more fully descriptive and active than the other choices.

Aristotle wrote about Events in his *Poetics*, advancing that a play is composed of a "*sequence* of Events"; it is a sequence of Events which the actors participate in and which the spectators observe. Everything you painstakingly wrote out in Novel of Life I contains the sequence of Events that aggregate into your full play. Parsing the successive sequence of Events – where their borders lie, who does what inside those borders, and proposing the central conflict of the Event – is an essential task of *Analysis through Action*, discerned through both *Reconnaissance of the Mind* and *Reconnaissance of the Body*.

Along with determining the participants and the borders of an Event (the beginning and end), one must also determine the *significance* of that Event. Simply put, some Events are more impactive than others, some Events are incidents of lesser significance. And there are a very few crucial Events that are

DOI: 10.4324/9781003475576-23

the *pivotal* moments in the play: they determine the actions and behaviors of all the significant characters from that point forward. It is these few that we focus on as we determine the pillars of the Five Event Structure of the play.

We are obligated to start with Aristotle, who, while today frequently dismissed as archaic, still hovers over us, like it or not. While much contemporary dramatic writing is deliberately anti-Aristotelian, much is not. Regardless, it was Aristotle who first outlined a comprehensive theory of dramatic action which reigned supreme for centuries in the West (Figure 18.1). He itemized *six* progressive stages of developing action:

The Incentive moment (the promise of the central character)
Peripeteia (a reversal of fortune)
Climax (a change from happiness to unhappiness)
Anagnorisis (recognition; a change from ignorance to knowledge)
Catastrophe (nonetheless the protagonist suffers terribly)
Resolution (through catastrophic suffering the protagonist achieves redemption and moral responsibility).

Some twenty-one centuries later, the German novelist and playwright Gustav Freytag (1816–1895), given the intervening changes in Western culture and dramaturgy – particularly the post-Enlightenment advancement of free will and the plays of Shakespeare – decided it was time to amend Aristotle's six-stage proposal, taking it down to five.[2] What became known as Freytag's Pyramid (Figure 18.2), often erroneously attributed to Aristotle and commonly taught in film-writing courses, at its simplest looks like this:

Exposition
Rising Action
Climax
Falling Action
Denouement

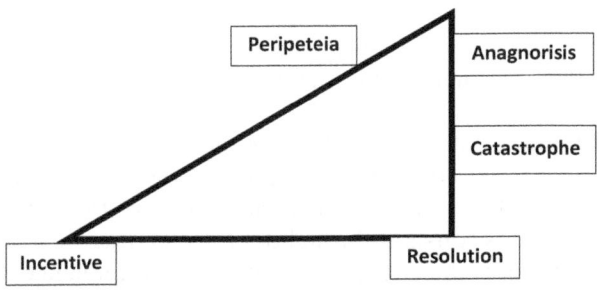

Figure 18.1 Aristotle's Triangle of Dramatic Action.

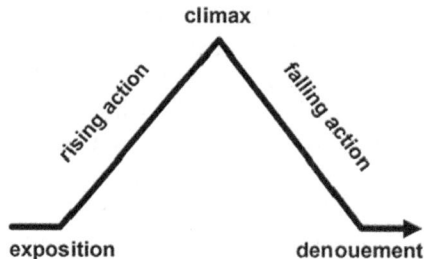

Figure 18.2 Freytag's Pyramid.

There is no evidence that Tovstonogov was influenced by Freytag's plan or even knew about it, but it was well known in his time. Intentionally or not, the Inedible One (see Chapter 4) propagated a five-event structure which affiliates with Freytag's conception.

Tovstonogov's Five Events

Tovstonogov, certainly influenced by Stanislavsky's attention to major Events, developed a systematic approach to establishing key action points of the play and the production. Without referencing Freytag's quintet, Tovstonogov proposed a related set of Event benchmarks, also five in number. These he classified as[3]:

1. The Initial Event (E-1)
2. The Counter Event (E-2)
3. The Climactic Event (E-3)
4. The Denouement Event (E-4)
5. The Crucial Event (E-5)

Surprisingly only three of these Events – E-2 Counter, E-3 Climactic, and E-4 Denouement – occur *inside* the body of the text. E-1, the Initial Event, and E-5, the Crucial Event, are created by the director and/or the ensemble and fall on either side of the boundaries of the author's text. The Initial Event takes place before the first textual moment, the Crucial Event follows the final textual moment.

Each of the five Events has a very specific and coherent purpose in the development of the performance. In brief, they are:

1. The **Initial Event**, created by the director and/or company, is performed before the author's text comes into play. This Event points the audience towards the Initial Given Circumstance of the Play, the underlying circumstance that is constant throughout the play. (See Text Action 6.)
2. The **Counter Event** is the Event which introduces a challenge to the prevailing Initial Given Circumstance which has been established. This challenge

to the status quo, that is, the Initial Given Circumstance of the Play, begins the dramatic Throughline Action of the play – defined as the struggle between the Initial Given Circumstance and the Counter Event.

3. The **Climactic Event** is the apex of the play's action, the point at which the contending forces of the play – Initial and Counter – reach a peak in their struggle and erupt. It is from here that the play begins its downward descent toward its conclusion.
4. The **Denouement Event** is the conclusion of the dramatic struggle, the final action which ends the dynamic clash between the Initial Given Circumstance and the Counterforce. (There may be a coda or even a full scene that follows, but the Initial Given Circumstance/Counteraction struggle of the play is over.)
5. The **Crucial Event** is the creation of the director and the company of actors. It:

   A. reveals whether the Initial Given Circumstance of the Play has triumphed, been altered, or fully eradicated by the Counterforce; and
   B. is the subjective raison d'être or Supertask for this sui generis production – a staged Event that reveals why we did this play the way we did it. (This is sometimes known as the "Scream of the Director" or the "Scream of the Ensemble") (see Text Action 9.)

Example: *Romeo and Juliet*

Shakespeare's *Romeo and Juliet* perfectly fits into this five-stage template:

1. INITIAL EVENT: Based on the Initial Given Circumstance that Verona is a city at war, a world of hatred and violence, Franco Zeffirelli began his stage production with children dueling with wooden swords; his film version begins with a gigantic battle on horseback, Capulets versus Montagues, destroying the town's marketplace.
2. COUNTER EVENT: At the masked ball, Romeo and Juliet meet and fall in love.
3. CLIMACTIC EVENT: Romeo fatally stabs Tybalt.
4. DENOUEMENT EVENT: Juliet wakes in the tomb, weeps over Romeo's dead body, and stabs herself. The Throughline Action of the play is now complete.
5. CRUCIAL EVENT: In Zeffirelli's productions the rival Montague and Capulet families exited the tomb in matching pairs, harmonious in grief, replacing their former hatred with sworn unity. Or, in Anatoli Efros' more cynical production, the families stood stone-faced against each other silently, lengthily, and warily, finally forced by the Prince to indifferently take hands, thus rendering the deaths of the two star-crossed children futile.

Further Explication and Examples of The Five Events

As Events are critical elements in Analysis through Action, starting a catalog with the three critical Events inside the text – Counter, Climactic, and Denouement – and imagining two others – Initial and Crucial – gives us an entry point into the myriad of other Events of which any play is composed. It's obviously simpler to start with five Events, as compared to ferreting out dozens.

Then, as we continue to anatomize the main arteries of the play, these five Events will become the vital organs through which the lifeblood of the play passes. Other Events, significant or incidental, will fall in place between these five markers. Furthermore, establishing these Five Events will abet the search for the Supertask of the Play, the Supertask of the Production, and the Throughline Action. Note: it may be useful for the director to call for Études on E-2, E-3, E-4 early in rehearsal, and return to them as the production develops.

Finally, each of the three interior Events affects *all* the main characters of the play, and radically alters the course of the Throughline Action. That is what distinguishes them from all other Events, even those of great significance.

So, let's specify each of these Five Events in greater detail.

THE INITIAL EVENT (aka Initiating, Preliminary, Original, Impelling, Source)

Is directly related to the Initial Given Circumstance, the prevailing condition of the play's world that will be altered, or unchanged, during the play.

It starts before the playtext itself is commenced and happens in front of the audience's eyes and ears.

It sets the tone, or mood of the basic atmosphere at the outset of the play.

It is the emotional "tuning fork"[4] of the production, revealing the visceral world the audience is entering.

"It is a single drop that reflects an entire ocean."

It is "pregnant" with the problem of the play.

It may not be evident again until the Crucial Event, when the fate of the Initial Given Circumstance has been determined.

It may be drawn from the Outer Circle of Given Circumstances ("World of the Play") or Pre-life Events.

Potential Examples (created by the author):

• *Hamlet*: A long wait as Francisco cautiously and edgily paces the barricades; periodic distant rumbling sounds, strange globules of viscous light appear faintly and disappear, sometimes odd bits of Fellini-esque circus music arise from the castle below. A situation of tension and danger in Denmark.

• *Tartuffe*: Offstage sounds of a violent family screaming match. Objects are being thrown and broken, a young woman sobs, a young boy screams obscene insults, an older woman who repeatedly slams her cane on a table and denounces everyone, thunder and lightning. The maid Dorine enters, smiles at the audience, sits on the forestage munching a banana, and invites the spectators to enjoy the fiasco which soon bursts through the doors into the room as Molière's text begins.

• *The Seagull*: As the audience enters, Konstantin, Yakov, and others are busy building Konstantin's stage with power tools; much rapid hammering, sawing, laughing, and friendly cursing one another in faux nutty Russian. From the distance we periodically hear a raucous, drunken, dinner party. Laughter and music join in with the excited construction noise. Masha and Medvedenko enter and watch the end of the construction. Workers depart, with beer. Masha rushes onto the stage and poses dramatically.

THE COUNTER EVENT (aka Conflicting, Basic, Primary, Main, Foundational, Fundamental)

Must happen inside the body of the text but is separated from the earliest Events of the play, sometimes by a great distance, sometimes not.

It is a challenge to, a collision with, the Initial Given Circumstance, in direct conflict with the dominant tone of the play so far.

Its appearance incites the major struggle of the play; in *Romeo and Juliet* it is the struggle to love in a world of hatred and violence.

It is drawn from the Middle Circle of Given Circumstances.

Examples might include:

• *The Seagull*: After several caustic interruptions from his mother, Arkadina, an enraged Konstantin jumps onstage, stops his play, and runs off.
• *Hamlet*: Hamlet meets the ghost of his father on the ramparts.
• *The Glass Menagerie*: Tom agrees with his mother, Amanda, to bring home a gentleman caller for his painfully shy sister, Laura, who struggles with a physical challenge.
• *Uncle Vanya*: At a family meeting he has called, Serebriakov outlines his plan to sell the estate.

THE CLIMACTIC EVENT (aka Central)

The two forces above – Initial and Counter – reach critical tension and burst here: the apex of the action.

It is the second "sudden" (unanticipated) Event in the play.

It is here that "the limit, at which unhappiness becomes happiness or happiness becomes unhappiness." (cf. Aristotle)

This change, called a reversal, leads to a 180-degree turning point in the action; Romeo stabs Tybalt, Romeo is banished, and so forth; Romeo and Juliet's love is doomed.

Everyone is affected by this Event; ultimately, their lives will change because of it.

It is the transitional event when the play passes from what it was to what it will be.

Examples might include:

- *Tartuffe*: Orgon, hiding under a tablecloth, learns that Tartuffe is a hypocritical fraud who is trying to seduce his wife.
- *Hamlet*: Hamlet stabs Polonius. (III-iv)
- *The Seagull*: Nina tells Konstantin that she still loves Trigorin. (Act IV)
- *Uncle Vanya*: Vanya attempts to shoot Serebriakov.

THE DENOUEMENT EVENT (aka Principal, Main, Concluding, Final)

The struggle of the play comes to its conclusion.

The Counterforce ends its conflict with the Initial Given Circumstance, either satisfied or vanquished; one or the other must now prevail, its opponent is extinct.

So, the Throughline Action is finally resolved, one way or the other.

Some short Events may be left in the play, but they are a coda based on the Denouement Event. Romeo and Juliet are both dead, so there is no one left to struggle for love – unless their deaths have value and can transform Verona from hatred and violence to a community based on love (à la Zeffirelli).

Additional examples:

- *Hamlet*: Hamlet dies: "The rest is silence."
- *The Seagull*: Konstantin kills himself (offstage).
- *Tartuffe*: Tartuffe is arrested by the King's men.
- *Uncle Vanya*: Astrov departs, after Serebriakov and Yelena have already left, leaving Vanya and Sonja alone.

THE CRUCIAL EVENT (aka Main, Principle)

The most creative and subjective of the Five Events

An artistic revelation about why you did this play, in this manner, today – the Scream of the production, the Supertask of the performance

The contemporary moral, social, and aesthetic rationale for this production, artistically presented

The coup de grâce of the performance, shocking the conscience of the audience

Created by the director and company (although it may be suggested in the text, e.g., Feste's song at the end of *Twelfth Night*)

No two Crucial Events should be alike, even with the same play.

Five Events: *The Cherry Orchard*

Here is a set of five major Events which occur during *The Cherry Orchard*. The Initial Event and the Crucial Event were proposed by a student.[5]

> **Initial Event**: Dunyasha walks into a room filled with dead cherry blossoms and broken furniture. She walks offstage, returns with a leaf-blower and blows the dead blossoms into the audience. Then she totes in a cart filled with ancient ancestor portraits and hangs them on walls. After a few moments Lopakhin enters and the scene begins. Dunyasha continues hanging portraits until the dogs bark maniacally, which scares the hell out of her.
>
> **Counter Event**: Lopakhin puts forth his plan to convert the cherry orchard property into plots for vacation homes. (Act I)
>
> **Climactic Event**: Lopakhin tells Liubov and others that it was he who won the auction for the estate. (Act III)
>
> **Denouement Event**: Despite indicating that he would do so, Lopakhin fails to propose to Varya; thus ends the last hope to keep the estate in the family (Act IV).
>
> **Crucial Event**: Firs takes down all the portraits and throws them in the fire, then crosses to a couch with one of them, the young Ranyevskaya. He lies down on the floor with her portrait. Dead cherry blossoms fall all over him. Wind, sound of axes.

Notes

1 Levin Irina and Igor Levin. 1992. *Working on the Play and the Role: The Stanislavsky Method for Analyzing the Characters in a Drama*. Chicago: Ivan R. Dee. 46–86.
2 Freytag Gustav. 1968. *Technique of the Drama; an Exposition of Dramatic Composition and Art*. New York: B. Blom. (17th Edition).
3 There are numerous variations on these terms; these are chosen by the author. Found in И.Б, Малочевская, *Режиссерская Школа Товстоногова*. Sankt-Peterburg: Акад. Театрального Искусства Sankt-Peterburg, 2003; I. B. Malochevskaya, *The Directing School of Tovstonogov*. Saint-Peterburg: Acad. of Theatrical Art, Saint-Peterburg, 2003, Translation Ilya Khodosh 34.
4 This and the following two quotations are from an author interview with Irina Malochevskaya, Saint Petersburg, May 12, 2011, Nikolai Pesochinsky live translating.
5 Jonathan Creed (now Claudia Creed), Harvard University, 2016.

19 Text Action 8

The Sequence of Events

Introduction

Our principal progenitors of Analysis through Action, Maria Knebel and Georgii Tovstonogov, were very different artists, educators, and personalities. The generous and humorous Knebel had great faith in her methodology: creating Études that would inspire the actor's subconscious, yielding intuitive physical and vocal expressions and unpredictable theatrical Actions. The iron-clad Tovstonogov, whose text analysis sequence – the one we have loosely adapted for this section of this book – is a hierarchical system originally developed exclusively for director preparation; here it is revised for actor use as well. As we have seen, the Inedible One habitually eschewed Études as a rehearsal method, although when rehearsing at The Bolshoi Drama Theatre he might reluctantly dredge up an Étude as a last resort for a failing actor.

While disagreeing about the efficacy of Études (among other things), the distinguished directors and educators heartily agreed on one point: the absolute primacy of Events:

Knebel: The event is the most important concept in the method of play analysis…Without events, without a sequence of events, there is no drama, no matter what genre it is created in…Events burst into life-like vortices, sweeping away everything in their path, spiraling the normal course of life, bringing confusion into human hearts.[1]…Events are the foundation on which the building of the play stands.[2]

Tovstonogov: As I see it, the essence of the method of active analysis consists in determining the appropriate sequence of events in the play itself. The director and the cast must try to split the play unto a chain of events, proceeding from the most important to the minor ones, to find what is called the 'atom' of scenic action, the ultimate unit beyond which the action cannot be split any further.[3]

(Note the poetic predilection of Knebel and the scientism of Tovstonogov.)

DOI: 10.4324/9781003475576-24

As recorded earlier in this book, in 1936 Maria Knebel, preparing for her first directing opportunity, approached Stanislavsky to help her identify the Events in the play she was soon to stage. After making her swear that she would employ Études in her rehearsals, Stanislavsky began tutoring his protégé by proxy. Regularly, she would drop off her list of Events for a particular play at his home and the next day his doorman would hand her Stanislavsky's edits, usually with a great number of Events scratched out from her original list and new ones created. To instruct her in the process, Knebel's master teacher advised his student to "get used to every day of the year taking one play after another, defining the events in it…this will require from you patience, will, and diligence."[4]

So, if 'Events are the foundation on which the building of the play stands,' why is it appearing so late in this book's taxonomy of Text Actions? Indeed, both Knebel and Tovstonogov started their rehearsals marking and decoding the play's Events with their actors. Of course, they each had done this exhaustive director's homework beforehand, but collaboratively walking through the play Event by Event with the cast was their means of cracking the play open after an initial reading. Knebel claimed that this process took the cast only two or three days before heading onto the floor to make Études from their analysis. Presumably, Tovstonogov's table work took longer as he was in no rush to get to Études.

But the question remains: if both Knebel and Tovstonogov defined Events as a means of immersing the cast into the inner world of the play, why should they not come first, or at least earlier, in this section of this book – a book intended for both actors and directors?

Well, to my mind Events can be elusive little creatures, and the more textual knowledge one has before stepping onto this slippery slope the better. However, as one becomes skilled at the progressive steps of *Reconnaissance of Mind*, it might be practical to shift Events higher up on your personal to-do list, actor or director. As Knebel did, you may even want to start your Reconnaissance of the Mind research process with Events.

Whatever your preparation you will likely find yourself – actor or director – parsing and re-parsing Events in the rehearsal hall. Indeed, one Russian author and director claims that Events are what you *discover* doing Études; just start doing Études and the Event sequence will appear; Stanislavsky said as much to Boris Zon. But even granting that option, let's get on with further defining Events, then move into the process of identifying them, and finally how to crack them open to release Action.

Toward an Even Further Definition of an Event

To momentarily reiterate what we learned in Chapter 18, the Russian word for Event is событие and this word carries other meanings, the most relevant to us being "occurrence" or "happening." If we divide this compound noun into its two components, co and бытие, we see another crucial meaning: со-бытие = co-existence. Indeed, in Analysis through Action terms, a dramatic Event requires coexistence, meaning "two, three, or ten partners"[5] onstage at the same time and place.

Next comes the critical point: it is the special demand of dramatic action that those onstage partners must be engaged in a specific *Conflict*, a single struggle that lasts until it resolves itself, stalemates, or is interrupted. Without at least two characters onstage together at the same time, involved in a specific time/space Conflict, there cannot be an Event. (Soliloquies are a different matter, although the actor might well imagine a partner or an adversary, or the audience as such.)

One of the two participants has been called the Leading Character or Protagonist, the initiator and driver of the Conflict; the other is the challenger, called the Led character or Antagonist.[6] It is the Conflict between these two (and their supporters, if present) that creates Action, and it is Action that propels the story forward. Over the course of the performance, the audience is watching and hearing Event after Event; this sequence is known as the Sequence (or Chain) of Events. The chain stretches from the very first Event of the play to the very last.

Now, let's walk through the codicils and questions that emerge from this basic definition. First, let's review some variant terms. In common rehearsal or training parlance, Events might be cited as units (Hapgood), segments (Senelick), or, in the US, Beats (derived from the Russian бит, meaning bit or piece, pronounced as *beat*). Here we will mainly stick with Event though the other terms may come into play. The same precepts apply, whatever term is used.

Additionally, let's remember that there are several viable translations for *zadacha*, including objective (Hapgood), task (Benedetti), problem (to solve), and goal. (I lean toward Task or Problem to solve, both of which are something you *do*; an objective is something you *have*.) Each of those has a slightly different shade of meaning, and therefore can be used selectively. But, as we shall see, *zadachi* – tasks, problems, goals – are the key underpinnings of an Event. Every character onstage during an Event has a *zadacha* – no one onstage is ever exempt from the issue being struggled over – and in an Event there must be opposing or conflicting *zadachi*, Tasks, which generate the Action of the Event. (We will mostly use Task, meaning something that must be done which requires dedicated energy.)

Second, let's scrutinize the term Action as it pertains to an Event. Again, recall a definition we considered before: Action is energy expended toward the achievement of a particular goal. So, Character A, targeting their opponent Character B, expends energy toward a specific goal or purpose. Concurrently, Character B expends energy to counteract Character A. Each is trying to *change* the other, alter the partner to be and to act as they would like them to. This is a basic axiom of an Event: each character is trying to *convert* their opposing character.

This oppositional struggle, this clash, is termed the *Conflict*. The word derives from the Latin *confligere*, translated as "to strike together." If, as an Action, one strikes two stones together a spark or flash is ignited – a burst of energy. This is the function of the Conflict in an Event: to ignite energy that drives the story forward. Tovstonogov, in typically combative vernacular, emphasized the necessity of Conflict inside an Event:

> Every minute, every second of stage action is an uninterrupted duel. There is no stage life at all without conflict…A chain of uninterrupted conflicts, duels, reaching, so to speak, up to "psychological boxing" creates the performance's score…[there must be] an uncompromising and fully executed struggle for the realization of the conflict in every grain of stage action.[7]

Conflict is a highly charged word, as we see above. It conjures images of physical altercation (boxing), the neighbors yelling and screaming into the night, or a bad night with a partner. But in a contemporary play the Conflict is often camouflaged, even veiled to a point of imperceptibility. Superficially, an Event may appear to be without discord, even harmonious – but in a well-written play – say, Chekhov or post-Chekhov – the Conflict generally lies below the veneer of the interaction. Indeed, Chekhov was a master of concealed Conflicts, with subtextual "duels" secreted behind seemingly quotidian behavior. The director or actor drilling into the inner springs of an Event in Chekhov (and many other modern writers) will inevitably uncover a Conflict, no matter how subtle.

Prominent director Kama Ginkas, perhaps resisting the stridency of his teacher Tovstonogov, proposed a more specific and less inflammatory perspective than "uninterrupted duel": "Conflict," said Ginkas in an interview, "can be defined as *competing logics*." Personally, I find this an illuminating interpretation, especially when one considers logic as a competing point of view in an argument or dispute. But whatever you call it, it should be there. Conflict, struggle, competing logics, duel, or whatever, patience, will, diligence, and Études will help you find it.

Now we can further define an Event:

> An Event is a demarcated container that encases a single Conflict between two competing points of view (logics), expressed by two or more opponents in a single time and space.
> The expenditures of energy toward their adversary (adversaries) ignite their own Actions, and adversarial Conflict creates the Action of the Event, which is the propellant of the play.
> Everyone onstage in the Event is involved somehow, even if they are silent; they are on one side or the other of the Conflict.
> A series of these Events is called the Sequence or Chain of Events.

NB: Remember that Action is not an Event. Action is the heat and light generated by the *Conflict* inside an Event.

The Process and Pitfalls of Marking Events

An Event is marked by its borders – where it begins, where it ends. The ending – the cessation of the Event – is often the easiest to discover. An Event ends for one of two reasons: (1) when the action, that is, the energy expended, of the Protagonist character ends for whatever reason or (2) a new circumstance emerges which interrupts the Event. The latter can occur (1) when an onstage or a recently arrived character assumes the leading position or (2) through an unexpected interruption – the frequent Russian example being "the chandelier falls" – or something less dramatic, like the dinner bell rings.

In summary, if the leading character concludes or changes their goal, or is cut off by an intrusion, the Event ends. In whatever manner the Event expires, there will then be a period of Transition and Evaluation. This shift can be near instantaneous, rapid, or gradual as a new Event begins to appear. The new Event, if not caused by the falling chandelier or another abrupt intrusion, will generally carry an echo, some trace DNA, of the preceding Event. In such a case there is a kind of subterranean flow between Events. Not everyone will necessarily enter the new Event at the same time; someone may remain stuck in the former Event or the Transition, at least internally, for some period of time. Think of an Event as a dynamic process, which gives way to another dynamic process. Recognize that an Event-change usually introduces a tempo-rhythm unlike the preceding Event.

So now we can preliminarily imagine the Sequence of Events:

Event A → Transition → Event B → Transition → Event C, etc.

But we must consider a couple of trapdoors before we move on.

Transitions/Evaluations

The first trap involves the way a playtext is laid out – it is easy to assume that one Event follows immediately upon another. In other words, you may be tempted to just delete these annoying "Transitions" and hurdle wham-bang from A to B to C. But these transitions – the Russians call them "evaluations" – have great dramatic and actor potential; they require the same psychic and physical adjustments that we make in similar circumstances of our own lives. Tip: sometimes, but not always, a Transition is marked by (Pause) or (Silence) or some similar stage direction; those are potentially electric moments.

Tovstonogov and his associate Arkady Katsman charted the three stages of a character during a Transition/Evaluation period:

1. The Transition/Evaluation begins with the emergence of a new object of attention, a shift of attention from one entity to another. (Here, "entity" could mean another character or a new circumstance.)
2. Then, the gathering of new signs is brought on by this shift of attention.

3. The final stage is determining the highest point of the new signs, the most significant. A new goal for the Protagonist, and thus the Antagonist. A new rhythm emerges as the partners enter a new Event.[8]

The evaluative process, which can be achieved in the blink of an eye or over a sustained period of time, is crucial to the actor re-orienting themselves as one Event concludes and another begins. But, again, to avoid just an illustrative reading of the play, these Transition moments are potentially loaded with sub-text, inner Action, and character opportunities.

Topics

A second trap in envisioning the Chain of Events involves the actor or director potentially confusing a *change of topic* for a change of Event. A character may pass through many topics as they pursue their singular goal, with no Event shift. As they do so, they may never reveal their goal explicitly, but their variegated topics are meant to convey their goal to the other person. The simple rule: a shift in topics does not automatically begin a new Event.

An example: the former peasant Lopakhin in his 282-word opening near-monolgue of *The Cherry Orchard* (excluding stage directions and two brief retorts by maidservant Dunyasha) speaks of the train being late; oversleeping; accusing Dunyasha of not waking him up; remembering young Liubov taking care of him years ago; his fine new clothes; his wealth as compared to his father's poverty; and falling asleep while trying to read a book. All these topics are in service of his one immediate goal: to make the maidservant Dunyasha, who didn't wake him up, understand his superior status and new wealth – which the servant girl should honor. Despite the several topics, all 282 of Lopakhin's words are deployed within one Event, which ends only when Lopakhin chooses to say no more.

Then Chekhov writes "*Pause,*" after which a new Event emerges: Dunyasha, who has barely responded to Lopakhin, possibly purposefully ignoring him, shifts the attention to herself (new entity, new topic): "The dogs were barking all night long; they know their mistress is coming home." She has now assumed the role of Protagonist and following after a Transition (the "*Pause*"), a new Event has been activated.

Structures of Events and Characters

So far, we have mostly referred to two-character scenes with no others onstage, which can be visualized very simply:

1. <u>Conflict between Two Characters:</u> Protagonist ---→ ←--- Antagonist. The Lopakhin/Dunyasha opening scene is an example of this common structure, two characters in Conflict.

But of course many scenes involve multiple characters – "two, three or ten partners,"[9] as Tovstonogov wrote. There are two kinds of multiple-character scenes. The first of these involves one or more characters who support the goal of the Protagonist. This assembly is called a Protagonist Group.

2a.   Conflict between a Protagonist Group and One Antagonist

Protagonist---→ ←---Antagonist
↑
Protagonist 2
↑
Protagonist 3
(Etc.)

All members of the Protagonist Group must have identical tasks or goals; see Anya's goal supported by Varya as Anya urges Gayev not to talk so much at end of Act 1.

2b.   Conflict between Protagonist and an Antagonist Group
Conversely, members of an Antagonist Group will have related approaches to counteract the Protagonist.

Protagonist---→ ←---Antagonist 1
↑
Antagonist 2
↑
Antagonist 3
(Etc.)

N.B. The Antagonist Group may use various counter-task tactics. In Act I when Lopakhin explains his plan to 'save' the estate, he is countered in differing ways by Liubov, Gayev, Firs, and Pischik.

3.   Conflict Interrupted by Other Event(s), Then Resumed

This is rare, but it does happen. In Act I, Ranyevskaya expresses her joy at returning home and Gayev reminds her of how much things have changed since she left, suggesting that their difficulties are grave. This back-and-forth pattern is repeated three times over two pages, interrupted by other brief Events.[10]

(For those who wish to further consider the structures of Events – two characters, multiple characters, interrupted Events, and more – I heartily recommend Irina and Igor Levin's Introduction to *Working on the Play and the Role*, cited above, pp. 15–39.)

A Workflow for Identifying Events

There's a lot to ponder here, and you may struggle to isolate some Events, depending on the play. Oddly enough, Shakespeare is relatively easy as the topics and the Events tend to align and there is little subtext; for the most part characters say what they mean and mean what they say. But as psychological realism, magical realism, surrealism, and post-dramatic texts appear, the simplicity of marking Events wanes. The text is increasingly a pretext where the real action of the play is submerged below the surface text. Nevertheless, almost any good play has some kind of form or shape to it, a structural integrity determined by the author to be decoded by actors and directors.

If you have already gleaned the Outer Ring Given Circumstances, the Lines of the Roles and the Character Given Circumstances, you are ahead of the game. The next big step is identifying the specific interactions between characters – the Events. Here, your prior knowledge of their character profiles will be the place to start.

Here is a way to begin:

1. Home in on what you conjecture could be an Event. Review the characters' *Prior* and *Present* Given Circumstances to this point in the play; select the most immediate and relevant circumstances for this Event.
2. Provisionally identify a Protagonist, then select the Antagonist. Who is driving the Event forward, who is the Counterforce? I usually identify the Protagonist as the one with the bone in their mouth who is not going to let it go, who keeps driving their argument forward.
3. If the Event has multiple characters, determine the supporting or opposing characters of your presumed Protagonist.
4. Mark the boundaries of the Event. Where does the conflict *start*, where does it *conclude*? Remember, the Event expires when the Protagonist cannot or does not continue the pursuit of their goal because they have exhausted their Action or they've been interrupted.
5. Generally, state the Conflict of the scene – insert a semicolon between the two simple Actions of the opposing characters or Groups. Protagonist is trying to do X; Antagonist is trying to do Y. Remember, they are *both* trying to alter the behavior of their partner/adversary. Use what they are *doing* to their opponent(s), not what they want or need.
6. Does the next Event occur immediately, or is there a period of Transition and Evaluation? Is there a shift in focus and rhythm? Again, these are good theatrical opportunities.

When you have made your first pass at whatever section of the play you are working on, review the cheat sheet below and make necessary adjustments:

Review: The Event Cheat Sheet

1. A dramatic text is composed of an unfolding Sequence or Chain of Events, one Event – (aka Unit, Segment, Beat) – following another.
2. An Event contains a single Conflict in which two sides are opposed: Protagonist versus Antagonist (Lead versus Led to the Levins), sometimes including groups. An Event Conflict necessitates two parties – coexistence in a struggle – *not* an individual's internal conflict.

3. The Protagonist is the leading or driving character of the conflict; the one who is relentlessly pursuing their task, the dog with a bone in their mouth who – in their persistence – won't be stopped until they achieve their Task and resolve their problem.

4. The Antagonist – aka Adversary or Opponent – is the equal and opposite Counterforce, countering with their own task against the Protagonist. (Often the Antagonist begins to feel that *they* are the Protagonist. Fine, let them think that.)

5. Each is trying to *change* the other, to alter the opposite character, to make them behave how they want them to behave; to compel the other to do what they want them to do, be what they want them to be – *here, today, now*.

6. An Event begins when the Protagonist initiates pursuit of their task. This is not necessarily the first spoken line of the Event; it can be a response to the other character, who in turn would become the Antagonist. Sometimes there can be a short "bridge" transition from one Event to another, a seeming neutral zone which inevitably leads toward Conflict.

7. In Events with multiple characters onstage, the Protagonist may have one or more characters reinforcing their pursuit of their task, sharing their side of the problem. The Protagonist and their supporter(s) are a singular collective force, a unified team, called the Protagonist Group.

8. Conversely, multiple Antagonists, each pursuing a different line of resistance to the Protagonist, can emerge. (Example: several characters oppose Protagonist Lopakhin's Act I proposal to eliminate the cherry orchard and build dachas; each Antagonist character pursues a different line of resistance.)

9. An Event ends when:

    a. The Protagonist exhausts their Task. Actually achieving it is rare, but the Protagonist is either thwarted, tactically retreats, or interrupted.

    b. A sudden change sets everyone off on a new tack. The example given is "the chandelier falls," but the unexpected change need not be that drastic. (Trofimov's Act I entrance is an example, as is Anya's appearance from her bedroom at the end of Act I.)

    c. A new character enters, but the Protagonist does not end their pursuit immediately. (Example: Yepihodov's Act I entrance with the flowers does not start a new Event until Dunyasha departs the stage.)

    d. In Chekhov and others, the stage direction "Pause" is sometimes – but not always – a marker for an Event change. (Example: Pause between the end of Lopakhin's first speech and Dunyasha's "The dogs were barking…" Here Dunyasha becomes the Protagonist and Lopakhin the Antagonist.)

    e. A change in topic does not necessarily indicate an Event change. (Example: in the first Event of the play, Lopakhin speaks on several topics – the train being late, his falling asleep, why he came to the house, chastising Dunyasha for not waking him, recalling Ranyevskaya and her compassionate act, his father's poverty, his wealth, his book – all these topics are in service to his Protagonist Task.)

Conclusion

The essence of an Event is Conflict. That does not necessarily mean loud, combative, or physical argument; it can be subtle, seductive, or charming. But there must *always* be Conflict! If a scene is dull that is likely because the conflict has not been found, intensified internally, or sustained. Character Tasks may be camouflaged by one or both parties, but every moment onstage must contain a steadfast Conflict between two characters or parties.

In short, the actors must agree to disagree.

Notes

1 M Кнебель. 1976. *Поэзия Педагогики*. Moskva: Всероссийское театральное общество; M Knebel. 1976. *Poetry of Pedagogy*. Moskva: All-Russian Theatrical Society, 299.
2 Knebel *Poetry of Pedagogy* 302.
3 Tovstonogov G. A. 1972. *The Profession of the Stage-Director*. Moscow: Progress, 241.
4 Knebel *Poetry of Pedagogy* 317.
5 Tovstonogov *Profession* 242.
6 Lead and Led are the terms used in Irina and Igor Levin. 1992. *Working on the Play and the Role: The Stanislavsky Method for Analyzing the Characters in a Drama*. Chicago: Ivan R. Dee. Irina was a student of Tovstonogov and Katsman at the Leningrad Theatre Institute, 1970–1974. This essential book, particularly Part One: "Analyzing a Play" (15–39), is the primary source used by the author throughout this chapter. I have chosen Protagonist/Antagonist rather than Lead/Led to equalize and dramatize the opponents. "Lead" also has a hierarchical implication, "Led" feels like a follower, not an equal opponent.
7 Г Товстоногов. 1984. *Зеркало Сцены*. Leningrad: "Iskusstvo "; G Tovstonogov. 1984. *Mirror of the Stage*. Leningrad: "Art" 241, 242, 244.
8 Author interview with Irina Malochevskaya at the St. Petersburg Academy of Theatre Arts, May 12, 2011, Professor Nikolai Pesochinsky live translating. Verified in detailed class notes of Professor Maria Ganeva, who took the Tovstonogov course twice, the second time for her PhD.
9 Г Товстоногов and G. A Tovstonogov. 1984. *Зеркало Сцены* 2-E izd. dop. i ispr ed. Leningrad: "Iskusstvo "Leningradskoe otd-nie.; G. Tovstonogov and G. A Tovstonogov. 1984. *Mirror of the Stage* 2-E Leningrad: "Iskusstvo (Art)" v1 p. 243.
10 Chekhov Anton Pavlovich and Paul Schmidt, 1998. *The Plays of Anton Chekhov*, Harper Perennial ed. New York: HarperCollins, 339–340.

20 Text Action 9
The Supertask and the Scream

Introduction: Gogol's Nail

Now we come to the great white whale of our voyage: the Supertask. You may recall from Chapter 1 that Stanislavsky, while preparing for a production of Nikolai Gogol's *The Inspector General* during the early days of the System, reviewed Gogol's directives for acting in his play – instructions written following the author's deep dissatisfaction with the play's 1836 premiere. The aggrieved Gogol insisted that henceforth the actor must "observe the main, the chief concern of each character, on which his life is supported, which is the constant subject of his thoughts, *the eternal nail sitting in his head*" [emphasis mine].[1]

Stanislavsky appropriated this idea, and soon was urging his actors to find the character's "nail." In a notebook, Stanislavsky wrote his own instructions on "How to Prepare for a Performance:"

> The creative process of experiencing gets its development when the artist feels the nerve of the role, which, like a leitmotif, accompanies the character in all situations. Gogol calls this main concern a nail, which the artist must drive into his head before entering the stage…Until such a nail, or emotional chord, is found, the created character is devoid of wholeness and essence. Without it, the individually experienced pieces of the role do not bind into one common, viable organism…A nail, or soul chord, of a role is that key with the aid of which you can penetrate the recesses of the soul of the created character. The actor should deeply cherish and be inextricably related to this nail, the spiritual chord of the role.[2]

Here, the nail is the 'soul chord'! In later System-speak, the "nail" evolved into the Supertask (Superobjective in Hapgood), and its scope expanded. The term Supertask now can be applied to three interwoven facets:

DOI: 10.4324/9781003475576-25

1. The Supertask of the Play (aka the Supertask of the Author);
2. the Supertask of the Role (aka the Supertask of the Actor); and
3. the Supertask of the Production, described by one Russian directing pedagogue as "your director's scream, a burning thought, your passion, which you cannot help but shout to the viewer."[3]

The Supertask of the Play has many corresponding terms: the "main idea," the "kernel," "the idea for which the author picked up their pen," "the suffering of the author," "what the play is *about*," "the main goal," "the north star of the play," and my personal favorite, "the poetic heart" of the play.[4]

The Supertask of the Play is best defined in one concise sentence, sometimes with a transitive verb, as you would in the Supertask of a character. It was critical to Stanislavsky that whatever else goes on, the Supertask of the Play, the author's main idea must be – or become in rehearsal – the core principle in the process of making the production.

As we did in Text Action 1, again we ask at what point do you define this core principle? Stanislavsky warns that the Supertask of the Play might not be precisely articulated until after several public showings. Be it voiced by the director on Day One or discovered through Études or as late as public performances, the Supertask of the Play is ultimately that which bonds everyone in the creation of the production. Like the aorta, the Supertask of the Play pumps lifeblood into the actors' hearts and souls, as well as to the director, the creative team, the artisans, and finally the audience. The Supertask is sometimes referred to as the lifeline of the play, or the role, or the production.

As to the Supertask of the Role, it is incumbent upon the actor to discover their own Supertask, which must ultimately nourish the Supertask of the Play. As an actor explores the Given Circumstances, Conflicts, and Actions in Event after Event, they must search for their own bespoke Supertask, one that animates their personal imagination, unconscious creativity, charged psyche, and expressive body – *and* supplies theatrical life to the Supertask of the Play. Lydia Novitskaya, the teacher in Stanislavsky's Opera-Dramatic Studio, wrote about the actor's Supertask of the Role:

> In other words, the main task must be sought not only in the role, but also in the soul of the actor themself…It is necessary to search for responses in the actor's soul, so that both the supertask and the role become alive, trembling, shining with all the colors of genuine human life. It is important that the attitude toward the role by the actor does not evade their sensual individuality and, at the same time, does not disagree with the writer's intentions.[5]

The same would hold true for the director as well.

As to the "Scream of the Director," we'll hold that until the final pages of this Text Action.

The Throughline Action and the Supertask

Lying inside the Middle Ring of the Three Rings of Given Circumstances (Chapter 14) is something called the Throughline Action – also translated as Transversal Action, Crosscutting Action, or End-to-End Action. This last rendering is the most descriptive: the Throughline Action is the end-to-end Sequence of Events, the life onstage that the audience witnesses from the first spark of the production to the closing moment. The Throughline Action and the Supertask are intimately interlaced: the End-to-End Action of the play or the role flows out of the Supertasks of each – the play and the roles – and ideally brings the audience to perceive these two Supertask in some way, shape, or form. A summary of the Throughline Action can be stated in one sentence that identifies the conflict of the play, such as "*Romeo and Juliet* shows the struggle between ancient hatred and young, innocent love."

The Throughline Action will incorporate the Leading Given Circumstance of the Play – Verona is a world of hatred and violence – and this does not disappear or triumph until the end of the action. It is the Counteraction – Romeo and Juliet fall in love at the masked ball – that challenges the Leading Given Circumstance, and that friction creates the Conflict of the play. So, we can identify the Throughline Action of the play succinctly: can two young lovers from warring clans alter the ancient hatred of the world they were born into? All this will be experienced by the audience as the Throughline Action advances through numerous Events and progresses to the Final (Crucial) Event.

Now, we have four strands that must be interwoven to create a tensile production:

1. The Supertask of the Play
2. The Supertask(s) of the Role(s)
3. The Throughline Action
4. The Supertask of the Production (aka the Scream)

In an ideal production, these four are magnetically fused – separable but capable of plaiting into one electrically charged nerve center. In the pre-production process of textual discovery at the desk or by Études in the rehearsal hall, insight may come by analyzing any one of these strands at any time. Each feeds and needs the others; none dominate, all integrate.

So where to begin?

Disentangling the Strands: The Supertask of the Play

If you have dutifully come this distance in the *Reconnaissance of the Mind* process, you cannot be far away from identifying each of the four components above, or at least proposing a hypothesis about them. Recall that early on, specifically in Text Action 1: The First Reading of the Play, you were cautioned not to declare a conclusive Supertask for the Play – yet. So now is the time to declare, even if what you are declaring is just "a formless hunch."[6] Trust your intuition. At this point, after all your dogged work, nothing you intuit is meaningless. Make a proposal, then test it.

The Supertask of the Play is ultimately a kind of wellspring of energy for the director and a galvanizing gift for the company. It may begin to tauntingly appear in Études, which are a method of searching for the Supertasks. Even a vague preliminary notion of the Supertask of the Play will provide some guardrails as your rehearsal Études veer all over the road (which they must: going over the rails is part of how we learn what belongs in our production and what doesn't). Meanwhile, Études may well provoke further defining your proposed Supertask or completely redefining it. Even though you have done a ridiculous amount of Reconnaissance homework, your rough, tentative Supertask will become a kind of compass to orient the work.

You can test your hunch using specific means. Knebel, citing Stanislavsky, recommended testing the *key Events* of each act via Études to see if they support or negate the proposed Supertask. Thus, for the first act of *The Cherry Orchard*, one might make Études on: Liubov's arrival; the Anya/Varya scene; Lopakhin's pitch; Liubov seeing her mother in the orchard, flowing into Trofimov's arrival. Then continue to the other acts and their crucial Events. This illumination of key Events exercise, done early on, will provide: a basic outline of the play, engaging most or all the roles, and some sense of thematic commonality among the Events. These probes might endorse or refine the early proposed Supertask or suggest a different corridor to follow.

Another means of decrypting the Supertask of the Play is by studying the Supertask of each of the main characters. While their Supertasks must be individuated and personally inspiring to the actor, in aggregate they are likely to have some shared goals, some aspirations in common. Thus, one path to the Supertask of the Play is to follow the Novel of Life II journeys of all the major characters (Chapter 15), attempting to propose a Supertask for each role at the end of their autobiography. These related individual Supertasks can then be amalgamated into an overall Supertask of the Play.

For example, three of the four major plays of Chekhov involve a house – who should own it, who should live in it, who will stay or leave. Each of the characters in these three plays has a distinct point of view about these issues, but collectively they are all seeking where and how to live. Or, in *The Seagull*, the characters are all gobsmacked by performative art. Starting with this common thread will speed the process of developing a Supertask of the Play.

Scholar and director James Thomas argues that the Supertask of the Play is inseparable from the Supertask of the main character. Identifying the central character's Supertask reveals the Supertasks of the all the other characters – all must fit into the grand Supertask which is the "nail" of the central character. Thomas likens this interrelatedness to Russian nesting dolls, where several progressively smaller dolls nest inside a large outer doll.[7] Thus, identifying the Supertask of the character named Hamlet – not so easy, to be sure – aids in revealing the Supertask of *Hamlet* the play, and the other characters. Thomas cites Edward Gordon Craig, who in his (in)famous 1924 Moscow Art Theatre production, defined Hamlet's Supertask as being "to reawaken everyone's conscience." The play, and all the other roles will attach relationally to that Supertask.[8]

In *The Cherry Orchard*, we can plausibly identify Ranyevskaya's Supertask to be: "In a period of personal and social turbulence, Liubov must find where and with whom she belongs." In the end, her answer is Paris and her dissolute lover. Following suit, Gayev goes to his bank friends in town, Lopakhin to Kharkov (presumably his business center), Varya to the Ragulins, Anya and Petya wander to "all Russia," Firs to his reward, and so forth.

In summary, the Supertask of the Play must sheathe the sum of all Actions in the Throughline of the Play and incorporate the Supertask of each character. Furthermore, the Supertask of the Play cannot be a dry analytical statement; it must pulsate bioelectric energy into the lifeline of the production at every given moment on the Throughline Action.

The Supertask of the Role

Each role has its own Supertask, which contributes to the attainment of the Supertask of the Play; conversely, the Supertask of the Play must contribute to the attainment of the Supertask of the Role. This seeming chicken-and-egg enigma may seem inscrutable – which comes first? Answer: neither. Instead, we propose an ongoing Étude dialogue between director and actor.

It is absolutely the actor's responsibility to identify their character's Supertask that is at once alert to the author's poetic heart and deliciously satisfying to play. It is absolutely the director's responsibility to have their own strong sense of each character's Supertask and how it attaches to the Supertask of the Play. Differing actor-director interpretations are inevitable. After all, the actor is experiencing what they are experiencing, and the director is trying to guide the flotilla into a single collective port. What to do?

Études, Études, Études. Get away from that table – or coffee machine, or broken rehearsal hall couch, or wherever those circular verbal debates are happening – and get on your feet. First, we do your idea, then we do mine. This why it is called *Analysis through Action*: don't talk about it, do it, analyze it through in Actions with your body heart, and soul, not through your debate skills. Often as not, some unforeseen tack will appear from these comparative investigations – first yours, then mine – crafting a new bright-line to follow, maybe even leading to a collaborative reimagining of the entire role.

Typically, the Supertask of the Role is defined as what the character is trying to attain, their life goal, their idea of happiness, and therefore is the influencing agent in each of their smaller topical Events, awakened in their Inner Ring Tasks and Actions. The Supertask of the Role should be the large goals of a life: Stanislavsky concluded that Hamlet's life goal, his Supertask, was to "save humanity." Quite a large Task. But not all roles are of Hamlet's magnitude. Stanislavsky also speaks of playing Argan in Molière's *The Imaginary Invalid*, changing his Supertask from "I want to be sick" to I "want to be *considered* sick." This turned the production from a maudlin mumbling tragedy into a buoyant comedy about philistinism.

The point is specifying the language of the Supertask is critical. "I want to be loved," isn't good enough – who doesn't? Such a generic pronouncement is dramatically feckless and could apply to an enormous number of characters, often erroneously. (I once heard an actor whine "Iago just wants to be loved." Well, yes, but…). Instead of platitudes, ask what does this particular character in this particular play with these particular Given Circumstances dream of, hope for, struggle for? What are they dedicated to attaining in life, even if they don't achieve it (which most don't)? If they could wave a magic wand, who would they *be*, what would they do, and with whom would they do it?

While identifying a specific and personal Supertask, the actor must be aware that blatantly pressing their case forward in every moment onstage will likely result in a dull, redundant performance, plain vanilla and loudly so. You will recall that Anatoli Efros was devoted to finding the "zigzags" of a character: first they zig this way, then they zag that way. Contradictions, confusions, mishaps, and reversals do not undermine the implementation of a Supertask; they *complicate* matters, adding human unpredictability and audience interest to the character's Throughline Action.

Bella Merlin – an accomplished actor, superb teacher of acting, and Stanislavsky expert – has written about her former resistance to the actor's Supertask. Her judgments began to alter as she thought about Gogol's nail "banging away inside one's head, an ongoing obsession, a nagging concern," which she finds "very imaginatively juicy." More importantly, Merlin began to ally "the character's supertask with their *self-image* or *world view.*"[9] What is your character's best self-image that they are trying to present to the world?

Citing a second book by Irina and Igor Levin – co-authors of the book *Working on the Play and the Role*, the source text for much of our Chapter 19 – Merlin writes that each Conflict "contributes to the character's self-image, which they are building throughout the whole play…this self-image is what Stanislavsky called the 'Superobjective.'"[10]

The Supertask as projecting a self-image seems a very useful instrument. As Merlin points out, one gains both internal satisfaction – I am being who I want to be, acting how I want to act – and external action – I am transmitting my worldview so that others will see what it is and come to my side of the argument. Merlin extolls this interpretation of Supertask as "heartfelt, grounded, non-analytic: 'How do I want the world to see me, so what do I have to do to infect other people with my view of the world?'"[11]

In short, who do I want to *be*, what do I want to *do*, and how do I want to *act* in my time on this planet? For the actor, this idea of self-image proposes a theatrical, imaginative, and experiential pathway to the Supertask of the Role.

The Scream of the Production

In the case of a play, the "Scream" of the production typically emerges from the Supertask of the Play, even if still in a formless hunch stage. But it could be reverse engineered. A play could be chosen because the director or the ensemble has something they need to scream about, some urgent issue that drove them to produce this play as they did. In the case of devised theatre – specifically a collective creation – the need to scream about something may have preceded rehearsals – talk in the dressing room, at the bar after a show, or watching televised news in the green room.

Of course, like Conflict, Scream is a loaded word. Nobody likes screaming, except maybe the person doing it. But Screams, as we know from Helene Weigel's famous "silent scream" in Brecht's *Mother Courage*, can be, well, silent – or sly, or seductive, or funny, or horrifying, or tragic, or fast, or slow, or barely audible.

Unleashing the Scream of your production is a personal, passionate, imaginative public Action. It comes from personal anguish about something and a need to alleviate it through the production. It inspires the artists at hand and ideally impacts the people who come to absorb the Scream, and witness those doing the screaming. The Scream is indeed the Supertask of the Production. What effect do we want our production to have not only on us, but in the world we live in? Will it really have that effect? History says no, it won't, but that's no reason not to try! All the more reason to scream even louder – or softer.

If you never ask for the impossible, you never get it.

Notes

1 Nikolai Gogol, *Polnoe Sobrante Sochinenii*, vol. 4 (Leningrad: AN SSR, 1951), pp. 112–13; found in Whyman Rose. 2008. *The Stanislavsky System of Acting: Legacy and Influence in Modern Performance*. Cambridge, UK: Cambridge University Press, 100.

2 Станиславский К.С. Собрание сочинений: В 9 т. М.: Искусство, 1993. Т. 5. Книга. 1. Статьи. Речь. Воспоминания. Художественные записи 630 *Stanislavsky K.S. Collected Works: V 9 t. M.: Art*, 1993. V. 5. Book. 1. Articles. Speech. Memories. Artistic Records, 630.

3 *"The Director Alone with the Play: a director's analysis of "The Cherry Orchard"* in the book by M.V. Sulimov; found at http://www.theatre.spb.ru/newdrama/bibl/sulimov/sulimov0.htm Translation Ilya Khodosh.

4 "Poetic heart," my favorite of the bunch, was spoken by the eminent scholar/translator Paul Schmidt about The Wooster Group's *Brace Up*, their rendition of *The Three Sisters*. He said he felt their version captured the "poetic heart" of the play and of Chekhov better than any he had seen outside of Russia. The Wooster Group used Schmidt's translation and he played Chebutykin.

5 Л.П Новицкая. 1984. *Уроки Вдохновения: Система К.С. Станиславского В Действии*. Moskva Москва: VTO Всероссийское театральное общество; L.P. Novitskaya. 1984. *Lessons of Inspiration: Stanislavsky's System in Action*. Moscow: VTO All-Russian Theatrical Society, 166.

6 Daniel Labeille *"The Formless Hunch": An Interview with Peter Brook* Modern Drama, 23, no. 3, Fall 1980, 221–226.

7 Thomas James Michael. 2005. *Script Analysis for Actors Directors and Designers*. 3rd ed. Boston: Focal Press, 195.
8 Thomas *Script Analysis* 196.
9 Merlin, Bella "'Where's the spirit gone?' The complexities of translation and the nuance of terminology in An Actor's Work and an actor's work," *Stanislavski Studies*, 11/1/2012, 1, no. 1, 48.
10 Levin and Levin (2002), *The Stanislavsky Secret*, Colorado Springs: Meriwether Publishing, pp. 64–65; found in Merlin "Spirit" 48.
11 Merlin "Spirit" 48.

21 Text Action 10
Novel of Life III

Introduction

Novel of Life III is a creative Text Action designed to help reveal what you feel about the play and how you might convert those premonitions into images and Actions. The other two novels you made, Novel of Life I and Novel of Life II, were preparations for this one: a full-fledged novelization of the play as *you* envision it. Here, the formless hunches and awesome discoveries begin to mold into form.

You will recall that your Novel of Life I – that handwritten monster that made you want to renounce Analysis through Action forever. It necessitated a particle-by-particle recounting of the plot of the play – just the plot, just the one-by-one facts – not the flesh and blood story. Then, Novel of Life II tore off the yoke of objectivity, releasing speculation, idiosyncrasy, affective memory, imagination, and viscera as you portrayed specific characters in your own manner. From then on, you were absorbing the play through a set of Text Actions that required clear-eyed but creative forensic investigation of structural elements: the Five Events, the Sequence of Events, and finally the Supertasks and the Scream.

One reward for all that work is significant practical knowledge; this will serve you well in Étude rehearsals. But in Text 10 Action your deep, ineffable "feeling" for the play will rise to the surface. As a collateral benefit of all the previous steps you have taken, the play has gradually grown alive inside you, and you are alive inside it. If that sounds like "oh-wow" mysticism, so be it. The inexplicable, the intuitive, the felt, and the formless hunch are now more important to your rehearsal actions than all your concrete textual knowledge. By now you have dreamt the play deeply due to all the labor (and fun) you have invested in the preceding nine Text Actions.

The time has come to capture your hunches, your what-ifs, and your daydreams by telling *your* story of the play in a full-bore fictive mode: events, interiority of characters, atmospheres, colors, environments, sounds, smells, and the procession of life from the beginning of the play to the end. This is a joyous creative deliverance.

DOI: 10.4324/9781003475576-26

What form this novel takes is up to you. To Georgii Tovstonogov – who coined the term Novel of Life – and also Maria Knebel, the text was a sacred object (more so than to Stanislavsky). All their work on Analysis through Action was intended to produce the deepest psychological and realistic rendering of the playwright's words. In their models the author is the supreme authority, and it is the task of stage artists to serve the author: the author is the author, the director is the midwife of the author's ideas, and the actors are the embodied conveyers of the author's words and actions. Thus, if one approaches Novel of Life III from that traditional perspective – à la Tovstonogov and Knebel and many others – your fictional piece will resemble the character-driven novels and stories by Tolstoy, Edith Wharton, Alice Walker, or Haruki Murakami. Environmental and social detail will surround real people living in real time. This certainly can be said for an enormous number of plays from the late 1800s to today: Ibsen, Chekhov, O'Neill, Wilson, and so forth, and so on.

But directors subsequent to Knebel and Tovstonogov approached this process in various modes, some re-arranging, cutting, and/or adding material and theatrical elements not called for by the author. How you choose to write your novel is as important as what you write in it. By doing this, you will discover *your* style, *your* genre, *your* flare, *your* Scream – all of which will inform your production or your performance. This does not mean surgically extricate the poetic heart of the play (almost impossible with a good play) but let your own heart pulse inside it with your own lifeblood.

Here are three examples of Novels of Life III.

Example 1 Anatoly Efros on *The Three Sisters*

Here is a specimen from Anatoly Efros as he envisions the opening scene of *The Three Sisters*, interpolating his thoughts and questions as he summarizes the action.

"When father died it rained and my sisters were in mourning. Now it is spring and everyone is cheerful. Irina is wearing a white dress and she is shining. Today the windows can be opened up, although the trees haven't budded yet. Eleven years ago, it was like this in Moscow. Irina is beautiful today, and Masha is beautiful too, Andrei would be handsome if he hadn't grown so stout." So says Olga.

She speaks for a long time, the others interrupt her, and then she speaks again about the weather and about her marriage that did not take place. And about the fact that she would love her husband.

Ever since school, I have known that it is necessary to search for the action. Is this so easy to do?

I think: why does Olga suddenly remember her father now; why does she indicate that the clock struck then in the same manner?

She indicates that only a few people walked behind their father's coffin, and that since then she has grown old and plain.

She walks around the room checking her notebooks and speaking about everything.

I think the entire play speaks about exiles.

The characters probably feel themselves to be in exile. Torn away from Moscow, from the theatre, Chekhov knew this feeling of provincial Russian intellectuals very well.

"A golden chain hangs around that oak," Masha says, as though speaking about shackles.

A gathering of sad intellectuals.

A gathering of intellectuals in exile.

Everyone inspires cheerfulness in the others. We cannot lose heart, we have to live and work!

"Father died exactly a year ago...Now a year has passed...Your face is shining..." Possibly this is also a bit of cheerfulness.

In the course of the play, Masha will be in love. Irina too has loads and loads of things going on. But for Olga only the search for happiness remains.

"You are shining today, you look especially beautiful, and Masha is beautiful too, Andrei would be handsome if he hadn't grown so stout..."

Everything is seemingly arranged to support a good mood in each other. It is necessary to live, it is necessary to work, in spite of everything. Today is even Irina's name day. Olga is the oldest sister, but there is no father or mother. The need to sustain everyone's cheerfulness rests mainly on her shoulders.[1]

Efros is simultaneously observing the characters in Action, homing in on one (Olga who is the central character of the scene), and immediately proposing core ideas about the play itself: "A gathering of sad intellectuals...A gathering of intellectuals in exile."

Being a protégé of Knebel's, Efros did not use the term Novel of Life. But he scrupulously wrote out what might be called diaries or journals as he read and thought out the play at hand.

Example 2   Chambers on *The Cherry Orchard*

These are the first two pages from the author's Novel of Life III notebook on *The Cherry Orchard*:

In a dank nineteenth-century nursery room, cluttered with children's toys and old furniture, a gloomy daybreak is just beginning to appear in the 12-foot arched windows; fading moonlight vaguely lights a corner portion of the room as do the fading embers of a fire. A clock ticks. Nothing happens. Dull leaden light.

A large lump is asleep in a bulky armchair, head to toe covered by a tattered blanket made of dark animal fur; only one hand shows, holding a book. The intermittent snorts and grunts tell us this is probably a man. The sleeping giant scratches himself under the blanket causing the book to drop unnoticed to the carpeted floor. The clock ticks, the dying fire occasionally crackles a bit, the wind blows a bit. Nothing happens. He stirs and farts.

Then a girl-woman, maybe seventeen, a bit stocky, opens the door to an adjoining room; warm orangish light from an oil lantern spills out into the gloom. The girl flounces into the nursery, dressed in the special-day finery of an aristocratic ingenue, her hair akimbo like a fright wig. She sashays around the room uncomfortably, awkwardly practices curtsying. Stooping by a short mirror made for children, she tries to primp and pose. Dissatisfied, she disappears back into the side room; the cuff of the fancy dress rips off on the door handle as she impatiently tries to close the door. She mutters "shit." The door closes, the nursery darkens. Small sounds continue: fire crackle, wind, light snoring, maybe some nose picking. The clock, the clock. Nothing happens.

Suddenly, several dogs bark outside the house. This prompts the now half-undressed girl – in working class underwear, one fancy shoe on – to blunder out of the adjoining room as hastily as she can. The warm light falls through the open door. She wipes the frost from one of the tall windows to peer out. The man underneath the bear blanket remains immobile, but snorts loudly, startling her. Realizing she is not fully dressed, the girl hobbles back into the room she came from, closing the door, darkening the nursery again. Nothing happens. Dawn is struggling to appear but not doing well. The clock.

In the distance, a muted train whistle. Suddenly the man rustles, wakes fitfully, opens his gold pocket watch, stares, shakes it twice, slaps it hard on his palm, and then calls out loudly to the empty dim room: "What time is it?" This man is Lopakhin. His right leg asleep, he confusedly stumbles around the room yelling repeatedly "What time is it?" Tonight is maybe the biggest night of Lopakhin's life; knowing what the time is urgent. The barely audible voice of the girl finally replies through the door: "Almost two." Aha, he thinks, that insolent twit Dunyasha is in there.

He mutters "I came here to meet them at the station and fell asleep. Dumb!" He struggles out of the heavy animal skin. He is expensively dressed, if gauche, mismatched, and disheveled; one yellow silken legging is falling to his ankles, a garter has failed. He goes to the low mirror, achingly drops on his knees to the floor, combs his hair with his silver comb, scrapes his finger deep in his mouth, smells it for halitosis, painfully rises, and then storms toward the adjacent room. He pounds the on the door, shakes it. It is locked; he finally yells: "You should have woken me up!" She shouts back: "Fuck you!" He goes back to the little mirror, stoops to adjust his cravat, cleans his nose with a silk handkerchief, and works on the loose legging.

The girl appears at the door, putting her hair up with antique ivory hairpins, looks at her face an ebony hand mirror, and says spitefully: "I thought you had left." She has re-dressed herself in new finery. She cannot button up the back – she's too large for this dress – so she has draped herself with a floral Pashmina shawl and a mismatched sapphire broach. She leaves the door open; the light fully spills in as she walks smartly to the mirror. She cuts in front of Lopakhin, who has now dropped his pants to pull up the errant legging. She curtseys, stoops, and admires herself in the short mirror. She has found the right look for the right moment.

Dunyasha has a Big Important Thing to tell someone. So does Lopakhin.

In writing this moment-to-moment sample with no forethought I realized several things:

1. There is immediate conflict between Dunyasha and Lopakhin.
2. Both have attempted to dress themselves as grandly as possible, though we will learn that they are not aristocrats (we will later deduce that Dunyasha's fancy clothes and hairpins belong to Anya).
3. Light, sound, and costume are crucial elements in the scene. The atmosphere is leaden, with sudden splashes of warm light; continual near-silence is interrupted by two key sounds – the dogs and the train – each creates intense physical action. Both characters are anxious to look their very best.
4. Tonight is a huge moment for both characters; whoever is on that train matters to them.

5. The play so far seems to live in Beckett-land: existential disorientation and cheap farce.

All of these discoveries were revealed to me as I started this Text Action without much thought. As Bella Merlin says about Études: "It's impossible to know too little."[2] Novel of Life III is a kind of lengthy written Étude; it is a creative novelization, not a precise recitation of the text (as was Novel of Life I).

In your novelization of the play, you might follow yet another route. Instead of feeling beholden to the Event-by-Event score of the play, you might grab certain elements of the text, and play a game with them: twisting the words and the characters like a Rubik's Cube, arcing off on tangents, allowing the Études and the actors to make a text, inspired by the text. This "riffing" on the text is the working method of many directors today, as seen in our profiles of Yuri Butusov and Dmitry Krymov. Both, in their own ways, were exposed to Analysis through Action and have developed it into a personal aesthetic process.

Example 3   Dmitry Krymov on *The Cherry Orchard*

Krymov writes in a Preface:

> In the sixteen years since I started staging performances, not immediately, but rather quickly, a way was born, a method, a system, no, probably a way – a way to start work.
>
> I'm writing a script, it's not a play, but something that I call "the progress of the situation" which is a record of the future performance from beginning to end. With music, sounds, pauses, *mise-en-scènes*, and spaces for improvisation. I bring this figment of my imagination to the company of actors and artists, and we begin to revive it, that is, rehearse it. This "course" is a plan, a scheme for revitalization.[3]

Here is an opening scene of Dmitry Krymov's scenario/text that was the basis for his 2022 production of *The Cherry Orchard* at the Wilma Theatre in Philadelphia. Krymov created this "novel" following two prior periods of making Études with the Wilma 'Hothouse' company of resident actors.

Waiting for the train.
A huge train board at the train station. The lights in the auditorium go out and the board begins to frantically flicker letters and numbers, like a slot machine.

The numbers of the tracks and the arriving trains appear. However, the cities are strange for this Russian play – they are American:

NY to Philadelphia, Grand Central to New Haven, NY to Boston.

There are a lot of them, it's like the train board at NY Grand Central gone crazy.

The lines change places, some of the lines get written next to each other...they disappear, reappear, blink. All of this is accompanied by the characteristic sound of signs turning over in a train station, that peculiar clacking of thin metal plates.

Gradually, tragic Mozart music emerges and begins to gain momentum. After a while an inscription forms on the board:

Moscow-Kharkov train arriving on Track 1.

All the other lines disappear, leaving only that.

At that moment, LOPAKHIN runs onto the stage. He is in an untied coat and untied boots, his shoelaces are following him in a long train, he is holding a coat rack with his jacket and shirt. Behind him, a woman runs in, who, just stepping onto the stage, falls and scatters a vase of fruit – cherries, small and, as it turns out later, tasteless – all over the floor. She begins to pick them up, but many berries remain on the floor and will be crushed by her feet throughout the scene, leaving red and purple stains on the floor.

After making sure the train is here, and before he can catch his breath, the man walks to the front of the stage and addresses the audience. He almost screams as the Mozart is now very loud. Quickly he changes his clothes.

LOPAKHIN. How late is the train?...An hour or two...(Checks his watch for a long time). Well...it arrived, thank God...(He tries to untie the knot in his shoelace with his teeth to tie his shoes.) Liubov Andreyevna lived abroad for five years; I don't know what she has become now...She is a good person. An easy, simple person. I remember when I was 15 years old, my late father – he worked in a shop in the village at the time – he hit me in the face with his fist, my nose bled...We came up to the big house for some reason, and he was drunk. Liubov Andreyevna, as I remember it now, was still young and so thin, she led me to the washstand in this very room, in the children's room. "Don't cry, little man," she said, "it will heal before your wedding..."

Pause

The board begins to turn rapidly. LOPAKHIN freezes with his shoe in his hand.

An inscription appears on the screen:

Baggage claim is at the baggage carriage.

LOPAKHIN. Well, ok...Baggage claim, now this, then that...(Standing on one leg, the other in some ridiculous sock, continues to speak confusedly). A man...My father was a man, but here I am in a white vest and yellow shoes. With a pig's snout, but rich...just rich, lots of money, but if you think about it, a man's a man ...

Inscription on the screen:

Baggage delivery will take place by the last carriage...

LOPAKHIN. Oh, shit! What a chore!

EPIKHODOV comes out carrying a bouquet of cherry blossoms in a vase and a huge portrait of a boy in an old mourning frame: it's Ranevskaya's son Grisha who drowned five years ago.

EPIKHODOV. Here, the gardener sent this...

LOPAKHIN. (Continuing to dress) Put it there.

EPIKHODOV puts the portrait on the stand and places the vase of cherry twigs under the portrait. He tries to place it so that when Liubov Andreyevna Ranevskaya enters, the portrait will be immediately visible.

DUNYASHA. (Rises from the floor and looks at the portrait) What's happening with me...I'm so cold ...(Looking at her hands). My hands are shaking...I'm going to faint...

The train board starts spinning frantically. ALL are watching. An inscription appears:

Baggage received.

After a pause, a second message appears:

Now this, then that...

LOPAKHIN. (understandingly) Well, yes, of course, out of the way...

DUNYASHA. I'm going to fall...

LOPAKHIN. You're very simple, Dunyasha. And you dress like a young lady, and your hair, too...You can't do that. You must remember yourself.

There's a line for the ladies' room.

Mama is third.

While LOPAKHIN and DUNYASHA are picking cherries from the floor, through pauses and railroad clanking, inscriptions appear on the board:

MAMA is second.

MAMA is next.

MAMA went in.

MAMA is out.

The shrill whistle of a locomotive.

A large blast of smoke covers the stage.

> Mozart stops abruptly.
> An inscription on the board:
> MAMA
> When the smoke clears, six people stand on the stage in overcoats and with suitcases: RANEVSKAKYA, ANYA, CHARLOTTA, GAYEV, VARYA and YASHA. CHARLOTTA has a small dog in her arms. LOPAKHIN AND EPIKHODOV stand on either side of the of the portrait, like a guard of honor. DUNYASHA is holding a vase with her collected cherries.[4]

In an interview, Krymov explained the process of making this scenario/novel. "I read the play, I make some impressions, then we play with the play [through Études], and then I put the play away. Sometime later, I write and draw pictures in my notebook of what I remember and what I think is interesting – in no order. And I make the story from that. What I don't remember or is boring doesn't get in."[5]

Much changed as the Wilma rehearsals unfolded. One example: instead of those arriving from the train station appearing in a cloud of smoke, the seven characters descended the steep house-right aisle stairs bundled in coats and thick scarves, carrying a huge amount of luggage. They then squeezed their way through a fully seated center row, disrupting the patrons who necessarily stood up to let them pass, then continued down the house-left stairs to the stage.

Krymov's *The Cherry Orchard* took place during the opening weeks of the Russian invasion of Ukraine; images of refugees were ubiquitous in his production. This startling entrance – and similar gestures like the train board increasingly determining the actions of the characters – exposed Krymov's very personal Scream. His Scream – expulsion from a homeland – became pertinent without any direct reference to the war. We are all refugees, the production seemed to say; nonetheless, we must do theatre to preserve some sense of community, gathering to pay witness in a sanctuary.

Novel of Life III – Recommendations

1. Novel of Life III is a process of creative self-discovery: start from what you sense about the play, what you feel about it, how you see and hear it.
2. Review your Novel of Life I and other Text Actions before you start.
3. Do not plan; you will find your voice as you proceed. Just start doing it.
4. Like writing a novel, you can cut or re-write anything you want, at any time.
5. There are no guidelines about length; it will be as long as it needs to be.

6. But do write it out in full – start of play to finish, handwritten or computer. Don't outline or bullet point; you are looking for the flow of characters and Events.
7. Take your time and take breaks. At the very most, do one act a day (which is a lot). The novel will grow on you as you do it. Sleep on it.
8. Directors: ***do not go into rehearsal to stage your Novel of Life***. That is not its purpose. Like Butusov, maybe cut it up with scissors, maybe throw it away, and see what happens when actors are on stage with you.

Novel of Life III is a director's written Étude, and the culmination of *Reconnaissance of the Mind*. Therefore, *Reconnaissance of the Body* – meaning Études, what they are and how to do them creatively and productively – is where we go from here.

Notes

1 Эфрос Анатолий (Anatoly Efros) and James Thomas. 2006. *The Joy of Rehearsal: Reflections on Interpretation and Practice*. New York: Peter Lang, 30.
2 Merlin, Bella "Here, Today, Now" in White R. Andrew. 2014. *The Routledge Companion to Stanislavsky*. London: Routledge, 333.
3 Дмитрий Крымов Дмитрий Крымов И Соловьева Д Годер and Новое литературное обозрение. 2021. *Своими Словами: Режиссерские Экземпляры 9 Спектаклей Записанные До Того Как Они Были Поставлены*. Moskva: Новое литературное обозрение. Dmitry Krymov Dmitry Krymov I Soloviova D Goder and New Literary Review. 2021. *In Their Own Words: Director's Copies of 9 Plays Recorded before They Were Staged*. Moskva: New Literary Review, 6.
4 This pre-rehearsal script was given to the author by Krymov. Eight other similar scenarios can be found in the book cited in note 3 above.
5 Author interview June 3, 2023.

Section B
Études

AN ÉTUDE PROTOCOL

In rehearsal, the psychophysical *body* is the starting and the finishing point (not the mind).

So, spend more time on *physical Étude analysis (85-90%)*: discoveries made through on-the-floor Action-based improvisations.

Anything you might talk about at the table, do *here, today, now* on the floor.

No scripts onstage ever: "It is impossible to know too little." Focus on your partner, not some pages.

The author's exact language is *last,* not first; it is the culminating physical action. In rehearsal the text is a *resource,* not *the* source.

So, *no need to memorize text!* In Études, first use no language, then add expressive sounds, then chosen key words from the text, then your own personal paraphrase of the text - until the precise words of the author organically appear.

Focus on the "I" **in the** '*I in the given circumstances:*' what would I do if I found myself in this situation? *Here, today, now!*

So: there is not a character; *there is only you,* in increasingly specific given circumstances, determined by the author, the director, and you.

Creating vigorous physical Actions inside the Given Circumstances is far more important than naming things; it is not about what you want, it is about what you *do.* Re- examine, re-calibrate, and heighten given circumstances with every **Étude** pass. If some sense of a Task or a Goal appears, acknowledge it - but be open to letting go of it as you learn more.

Rehearsal is a series of *'probes' or 'tries'* - a purposeful set of joyous trial-and-error **physical explorations. Nothing is incorrect; a failed Étude is a gift.(The only bad Étude is one in which** someone is physically lazy, mentally sloppy, or unfocused on their partner.)

Download with your partner and director what you found out after each Étude.

The goal is fully activated physical/emotional life onstage inside a wide corridor of truth; not **"fixed"** but always *experiencing* from your own life and body.

Figure II.2 An Étude Protocol.

22 Études

An Overview

An Introduction to Études

All roads so far taken in this book have led us here. Now we are at the culmination of the work, capping a methodology that has proven durable yet flexible, artistically fruitful, and exciting over four generations in Russia and Eastern Europe, and just getting known in the West. At first glance, Études seem a relatively simple matter: abandon the table asap and, with nothing memorized and no scripts in hand, make exciting improvisations about the scene under scrutiny. But describing how to do that in a productive yet creatively unpredictable – sometimes even anarchic way – evades easy explanation.

While the ten Text Actions enumerated in the Reconnaissance of the Mind section are potentially variable in sequence – the order can be altered – not everyone will do all of them (even if directors should) – they are nonetheless concrete, describable, specific tasks, interwoven in a holistic sphere. Adapted from Malochevskaya's *The Directing School of Georgii Tovstonogov* and many other sources including Maria Knebel, our Text Actions are a suite of tête-a-tête homework endeavors, rooted in Stanislavsky's efforts and classified by Tovstonogov and Katsman for directing students. Only Knebel, while a teacher of directing, was an actor herself and fully embraces the actor and their role in her pedagogy.

Some Russian directors contend that Reconnaissance of the Mind *is* the Method of Analysis through Action, and Reconnaissance of the Body is a separate but related process that should be known as the Étude Method. Certainly a director could successfully work through the Text Actions and confidently lead a conventional rehearsal process disregarding Études, as could an actor benefit from the first several Text Actions without rehearsing via Études.

But unlike Reconnaissance of the Mind, Reconnaissance of the Body is nowhere categorically delineated as is Tovstonogov and Katsman's text analysis progression; there is no definitive ten-step how-to manual for deploying Études in the classroom or the rehearsal hall. Russian directors and teachers – and their teacher's teacher – employ Études for idiosyncratic reasons, in various ways for various purposes. Hence, while many major masters of

DOI: 10.4324/9781003475576-28

Études – Efros, Dodin, Butusov, Krymov, and others – regularly utilize Études and improvisation, none of them pull off the road to methodically explain *how* they do what they do. We are left to glean their processes by reading between the lines in books, articles, and interviews.

Here we will cite five advocates of Études who in some measure discuss their process, albeit in disparate and sometimes contrasting ways. In chronological order they are Russians Boris Zon, Maria Knebel, Zinovy Korogodsky, and Veniamin Filshtinsky, and British-American Bella Merlin, who trained in Russia.[1]

Zon, readers will remember, was the young Leningrad youth theatre director who first recorded Stanislavsky's 1930s experiments with Études and interviewed KS up to his final year. In turn, Zon trained Korogodsky, and Korogodsky later hired Filshtinsky and Dodin into the Leningrad Youth Theatre. Knebel we have already discussed at some length and will do so more here – after all, she is the mother of us all. Merlin, who has written extensively about Stanislavsky, has contributed the single most practical Étude article there is, entitled "Here, Today, Now" found in *The Routledge Companion to Stanislavsky*.[2] Naturally our Étude advisory quintet differ on certain points. Each has its own perspective, but it is these artists whom we shall hear from the most on the following pages.

Ahead, drawing from our five originators, we will track three variant methodologies. In shorthand, the three lines we will explore are:

1. The canonical Moscow Knebel method, additionally illuminated by Merlin.
2. The Leningrad/Petersburg Line: Zon, Korogodsky, and Filshtinsky.
3. The Fusion Line: Tovstonogov and Katsman's Text Actions (done off-site) while in rehearsal mostly following Korogodsky and Filshtinsky's Etude Method.

In more detail:

1. The Knebel methodology begins with a determination of Events led by the director at the table prior to Études, and in the end emphasizes strict allegiance to the author's text. This method is excitingly and concisely delineated in contemporary terms by Merlin and digested in Chapter 3 of this book.
2. The Zon-Korogodsky-Filshtinsky Line, which harkens back to Stanislavsky's experiments as notated by Zon and work on *The Cherry Orchard* at the Opera-Dramatic Studio. In these experiments (and some of KS's writing at the time), the text is meant to be *discovered* through Études led by the director after one or two readings, discussion kept to a minimum.
3. A Fusion methodology developed and advocated by this author with invaluable input from the teaching associates noted in the Introduction. This line primarily echoes Zon, Korogodsky, and particularly Veniamin Filshtinsky, whom I have interviewed at length, observed in classes, and whose writings

I have read with excitement. The notable variance in our Fusion approach is that unlike any of the other methodologies, we require that the actors individually complete the first six Tovstonogov-based Text Actions (Chapters 12–17), ideally finishing at least the first three (12–14) *before rehearsals or classes begin*. This allows the company to hit the ground running and almost immediately go into Études. But even if time forbids such advance preparation, these Text Actions can be done off-site, parallel to first rehearsals.

So, What Is an Étude?

An Étude is a purposeful improvisatory investigation of a selected segment of a text (or other source) executed by two or more actors on the floor without scripts in hand, relying on spontaneous physical actions and speaking their own impromptu words paraphrased from the text. There are also various 'auxiliary Etudes' meant to investigate characters and situations paratextual or subtextual; more on this later. The common goal is to generate visceral knowledge of the play and the roles *experientially*, not through deductive reasoning. As Stanislavsky presciently wrote: "This process is nothing like the cold, cerebral study of a role which actors usually take at the beginning stages of work."[3]

Zinovy Korogodsky specifies that an Étude is applied to "a section of a play…which necessarily contains an incident, an event."[4] He quotes Stanislavsky: "Through an étude we remember life."[5] This statement suggests a major collateral benefit of Études: through direct physical and intuitive action, an actor will often arouse a compelling affective memory without having to rummage in their tattered psychic baggage to find it. Involuntary affective memories, alongside other rewards of Études, become a key resource as the actor strives for *perezhivanie*.

Our blunt axioms: Through table work we remember some data. Through Études we experience life. Or, as Professor Sergei Tcherkasski of RGISI once said to me: "Whatever you talk about at the table, we do on the floor."

The Étude rehearsal strategy immediately brings the actor to the center of the discovery process. Sharon Carnicke summarizes the actor-centric features of theatrical Études:

> Everything in Stanislavsky's last experiments throws greater and greater responsibility for the interpretation of the play onto the shoulders of actors. Physical actions make them aware of how their bodies create characters. Improvisations ensure that they encounter the play experientially…Paraphrasing takes away the usual crutch (recitation of the playwright's words), forcing them to think as the character.[6]

The root word of Étude in French is *Étudier*, meaning to study. As touched on in Chapter 2 of this book there are twelve definitions of Étude in the online *Larousse French-English Dictionary*; here we look further at eight definitions that apply to us. All hold true when converted from an intellectual study to a psycho-physicalized theatrical Étude [brackets mine]:

1. Work of the mind [body and soul] which applies itself to knowing, to deepening something.
2. Intellectual [Psychophysical] effort directed toward acquiring knowledge, learning something.
3. Intellectual [Psychophysical] effort directed toward observing and understanding beings, things, events, etc.:
4. Preparatory work or research: Study of a project.
5. In-depth examination of something; analysis: the detailed study of a text.
6. A Study.
7. Drawing, painting or modeling executed from life, in order to capture reality on the spot. The study may be executed for its own sake, or as preparation for a more elaborate work.
8. A piece of music composed for teaching purposes.[7]

In theatrical usage, Études are a dedicated means of embodied research or 'study' to ascertain and develop actions and visceral knowledge. This specificity of focus explains why Stanislavsky, Knebel, and others (including me) have used the word 'Étude' and not 'Improvisation.' The latter typically refers to something more general and open-ended, especially now in the US where improvisations in improv groups or comedy classes indicate a means of *creating* an event or a story rather than *investigating* an event or story already created by an author. Yes, in an Étude the actor and director certainly employ certain improvisational *techniques*, but with the specific purpose of analyzing a specific component of a body of work. Says Filshtinsky: "The étude is a pathway, not a result."[8]

Synonyms for theatrical Études include investigation, study, sketch, probe, text, embodied research, or embodied analysis. Korogodsky suggests a "touchstone, a feeler…an unreliable draft…a laboratory, a research method."[9] Dodin uses "work-play,"[10] and theoretician director Mikhail Butkevich puts it bluntly: "*an étude is an experience* (italics his)".[11] Whatever the definition, toward the end of rehearsal, the fruits of the numerous and varied Études will be harvested and blended into a production, and that production will inevitably be notable for its collective 'improvisatory feel' throughout.

Unlike typical rehearsal or classroom work which rely on objectives (intentions, tasks), Études rely on the actor and the Given Circumstances of the play and the role: 'I in the Given Circumstances' is a fundamental tenet of Étude work. Knebel endorses this principle and underlines one of its benefits:

> The actor must do an étude going from his own individuality. This means analyzing oneself – the human actor in the given circumstances of the play. But precisely because these circumstances are not at all the ones that shaped the personality of the actor in their own life, an étude immediately reveals a gap, the distance between the two; it becomes clear what

the actor needs to give up, what to overcome in himself, and which elements of his own life are the 'building blocks' for creating a character.[12]

Actors who have previously depended on pre-designating Tasks may find that during or after an Étude some Action verb will spontaneously arise. Fine. Jot it in your notebook then let it be; nothing can kill an Étude faster than an actor attempting to prove a pre-ordained Task. In each Étude pass, deeper and more personal Given Circumstances will be explored and activated, and in those moments new Tasks or goals will likely arise. Therefore, hastening to 'freeze' life by prematurely naming a Task is contrary to the entire premise of Études. As the "Given Circumstances" deepen, so will the "I" of "I in the Given Circumstances – and vice-versa. Ever forward, embrace the unknown. Name it later if you must. Or don't name it.

A maestro of Études, Zinovy Korogodsky goes back to the fundamental question of Tasks. He reminds us that the three elements of a Task are (bold-face his, examples mine):

1. What I do is an **action** [I open the door]
2. How I do it is an **adaptation** [very quietly]
3. What I do it for is **the task**[13] [to surprise you]

Notice the word "do" in each step. This simple construct underscores Stanislavsky's late-life mandate, paraphrased as 'it is not about what you want, it is about what you *do*.' Études are designed for the actor to find *what* they do, *how* they do it, and *why* they do it. Their actions and their adaptations (aka adjustments or means) will lead to discovering their goal – kinetically, not intellectually, in the live moment, not offstage but on. *Doing* unplanned and unexpected things generates the electricity of Études.

Along with "I in the Given Circumstances," the other by-law of Études is "here, today, now" from Stanislavsky. Bella Merlin addresses one's knowledge of the play/scene/event/character: "Whatever you have 'here, today, now' is enough to kick start the creative process."[14] This goes alongside her brilliant "it's impossible to know too little."[15]

As a codicil to "here, today, now," whatever you are feeling here, today, now – fear of failure, elation, a bad stomach – use it, activate it, here and now; it would be lying to deny it. A further "here, today, now" assumption holds that what you did yesterday – that was then, this is *now*. When today's Étude suddenly veers off in another direction from yesterday's, go with it. That brilliant Étude the other day, or just a moment ago? That was then; whatever this is, it is here, today, now. Follow it, see where it wants to go.

The Director and the Étude

The centrality of the actor in the Étude method in no way abrogates the importance of the director; indeed the director is the other half of the co-authorship of the production. But the director working with Études will find that sharing the creation of the production requires a mindset different from ordinary approaches. Nonetheless, in the end, after reams and reams of Études, it is the director who will blend and cohere the work as the production's mise-en-scène is established (see *From 'Étude to Mise-en-Scène'* ahead).

However, it is not simply at the end of the rehearsal process that the director emerges. On Day One with the actors the director is the initial leader of the collaboration, eager to distribute authority of the work process in order to facilitate what Knebel calls "the necessary creative atmosphere." Instead of the typical 'meet and greet' demo in which the director holds forth on 'why this play now' and designs are displayed, the Étude-oriented director might start with various theatre games and physical exercises; not only warm-up routines (which can usually also be led by actors who volunteer) but also ensemble activities. (See *Getting Started*, ahead.)

These games should flow into introducing the Étude concept to the ensemble. Some actors may have had some Viola Spolin or Keith Johnstone improvisational exercises in their training, maybe a sketch comedy class somewhere, but next to no one in the English-speaking world has been trained in the Étude process of theatrical rehearsal. The director should (briefly) explain what the Étude Method is, how it works, and why they have chosen to rehearse this way, on this play. (A handout of the "Étude Protocol' at the beginning of this section, or something like it, could be useful here.)

Thus from jump, the director initiates two of their primary rehearsal missions that will recur throughout the rehearsal period: ensemble-creation exercises and preliminary training in Études. The former is crucial to the success of the latter: early Études may be duds or tepid, but establishing a true culture of collective creation will soon produce Knebel's 'necessary creative atmosphere,' which will support the actors' efforts as the Études progress.

Again, in contrast to the typical first day, the director would be wise not to inundate the acting company with excessive background information and production plans. Maria Knebel wrote:

Konstantin Sergeevich warned directors against detailed explication at the very beginning of the work. Details of life, epoch, style, literary-critical studies – all this will be essential for an actor in due time, when he plunges into the elements of the dramatic material. At first, when the actor still knows nothing about the person he is supposed to play, and the director immediately overloads his imagination with all sorts of generalized information, the actor usually accepts it coldly, rationally. He is confronted by a multitude of diverse, broad, but initially unnecessary information, while he eagerly searches for his own special path that would lead him to that mysterious stranger whose words are printed in the script.[16]

This does not mean that the director doesn't have all that information ready when the time comes. 'Ripeness is all,' in this case meaning when the actor is 'ripe' – ready for or needs the details of 'life, epoch, style, literary-critical stud-ies' – the director is fully prepared and eager to share this knowledge, and that of their designers and dramaturgs, with their collective of co-authors, the actors.

In terms of running a lively and focused rehearsal room, and completing the mise-en-scène, we will have more to say in the upcoming section. But in ad-vance I submit these strategies, which will apply to everything in that section:

1. Prior to rehearsal period (or a semester-long class) it is imperative that the director study the play employing all the Text Actions listed in the previous section. If prep time is inopportunely short, the director must at least strive to complete the first six Text Actions (maybe limiting Novel of Life I to the first act), do an Event breakdown, and take a crack at Novel of Life III (at least the first act) to see how the play 'feels' at this point. Then make a stab at a Supertask. Any less and you will be bluffing.

2. DIRECTING IS A PHYSICAL ACTION! Ditch the table or music stand. Get up and move along with the actors, even spontaneously join them in an Étude sometimes, as did Efros and certainly does Butusov. Sitting and ob-serving is passive and implies a privilege that a true co-authorship will not tolerate. Get up and MOVE. You are a worker too!

3. Side coach – a lot. Make sounds: grunts, whimpers, aahs, whoo-hoos to show you are there with them emotionally. Encourage the actors verbally, keep them moving forward with phrases like "Follow that impulse…follow it, follow it;" or "Keep moving, keep moving…Feet! Feet! Move your feet! Yes, go for it, go, go, go!" Or "it's ok to cry." These are not the magisterial imperatives of an autocratic director; they are compassionate encourage-ments to keep the creative psychophysical energy of the actors free and alive.

4. Chairs are the death of theatre. So are couches, benches, stools, and window seats. If for some reason you must have those chattels which seduce lazy bodies and induce lazy thinking, train the actors to avoid them – or use them kinetically, even gymnastically. If your king must sit on a throne, how can that throne be a Pilates chair? Better yet, how fast can the king get out of it? Sittable objects lead the actor directly to people-talking-plays passiv-ity, physically and emotionally inert.

5. If an actor is lost in a scene, throw out a *paraphrased* cue from whatever section of the Event they are in or should advance to. No one else, including a very supportive stage manager, should do this. Conversely, no stuck actor should ever call out "Line!" If they do, the director should respond with "make something up" or "fake it."

The rewards of the Étude process for the director are innumerable. With proper guidance, physical presence, side coaching, and a vital creative atmosphere in the room, the actors will spontaneously come up with kinetic actions, strategic adaptations, perspectives on the role, and revelations about the scene or even the play that no director could possibly cook up at their lonely little desk. The actor, left alone naked onstage with nothing but a partner and maybe some mock-up props, must turn to that partner – not to a highlighted handheld script, not to a director 'blocking' the scene, not to a stage manager calling out their lines – but to their onstage partner, for energy and action – for *life*. With proper directorial encouragement and caring support, with an affirmation of 'I am here with you, and for you,' the partners will often as not generate actions, emotions, and ideas that are the stuff of a director's dreams.

Types of Études

On the "flowchart" that prefaces Part II of this book, four types of Études are shown: Scenic, Line of the Role, Auxiliary, and Mise-en-Scène.

Scenic Études

The basic and most common form of rehearsal Études is what are called Scene or Scenic Études or Event Études. Korogodsky coined a useful hyphenated term describing this type of Étude: 'Étude-scout,' in which the Étude itself serves as an advance scout, a pathfinder reconnoitering a specific tract of textual terrain to find the most productive path.

These synonymous terms – Scenic (or Scene) Étude, Event Étude, or Étude-scout – all rely on improvisatory exploration of a specific scene or Event containing two or more roles, each actor creating spontaneous physical actions and language in search of conflict, adaptation, goals. You will recall schematic diagrams in Text Action 19: The Sequence of Events, which chart various Protagonist/Antagonist structures of Conflict. In establishing a Scenic Étude, it will be important for the director to have foreknowledge of who are the Protagonists and who are the Antagonists of the Event. (Actors often think that whatever role they are playing that they are the Protagonist and thus shun the label Antagonist. Fine, if it makes both parties more active.)

Études on the Line of the Role

At any time in the rehearsals process, but especially prior to run-throughs or dress rehearsals, it can benefit a principal actor to do a scene-by-scene suite of Scenic Études for every appearance they make onstage – a kind of kinetic yellow highlighting of their role, but live and on the floor. Based on their Line of the Role, this Étude "run" of the role will invariably prove to be crucial, not only for the actor and their onstage partners, but to the company as they observe the life of each major character. Important pre-life and inter-life Events can be woven into in these character probes. These invaluable Line of the Role Étude runs can illuminate, reinforce, and specify the Supertask of the role and actor. It is the character's Throughline Action brought to life through Études.

Auxiliary Études

Korogodsky endorses the predominance of Scenic Études and calls other modes *"Auxiliary Études."* Among these he foregrounds *Pre-life Études*, which are dedicated to exploring the life of the play and its roles prior to the beginning of the play, or between acts (Filshtinsky calls the latter *Inter-life Études*). In contemporary parlance, taken from screenwriting, we also call pre-life and inter-life 'backstory Études.'

Stanislavsky, during his Opera-Dramatic Studio years, wrote out these possible Pre-life Études for *The Cherry Orchard*:

ETUDE #...
   (for physical actions)
   "The Cherry Orchard" (spontaneous actions, spontaneous words)

I. Etudes on the past:

   a. A trip to Paris (Anya and Charlotte).
   b. Meeting with mother in Paris.
   c. Traveling to Moscow.
   d. Approaching the estate.
   e. Meeting at the railway station.
   f. Arrival, inspection of the rooms.[17]

Other ensemble Pre-life Études for *Cherry Orchard* might include Grisha's funeral, done quite brilliantly in a recent class of mine (Ranyevskaya fell to her knees choking with grief, Trofimov threw himself on top of the coffin – believably). So too was an Étude about Varya and Gayev informing a resistant Anya that she must travel with exasperating Charlotta to Paris to retrieve her mother. The actors playing Varya and Gayev in this Étude deduced that Lopakhin must have been the mastermind of this scheme, an unexpected bonus for the actor playing that role.

The actor who has completed writing their Line of the Role and Novel of Life II will find abundant resources for Pre-life Études. For Anya, the role whose line we tracked in Text Action 4, several important opportunities arise, all unspecified in the playtext. In the Pre-life realm Anya will certainly want to explore her childhood relationships with her mother, Liubov, her deceased alcoholic father, her drowned brother, Grisha, her annoying governess, Charlotta, and especially Grisha's tutor, Petya Trofimov.

Most crucially for Anya, as noted by KS above, would be "b) Meeting with mother in Paris." In our teaching practice, we have used this Étude as a first-day example with the full class participating: the apartment can be populated by all kinds of interesting, improvised characters, foreign and probably threatening to cosseted Anya, maybe fascinating to Charlotta. And did Anya's mother *really* hug her and weep – or is that how Anya emotionally camouflages this soul-crushing moment when speaking to Varya? An important inter-life Étude for Anya would be her plea for money from her wealthy Yaroslavl aunt, which occurs between Act I and Act II. Études on Anya's unpleasant and futile encounter with this relative likely becomes influential in Anya's later agreement to flee the estate with Petya.

Filshtinsky describes a set of pre-life Études for the actor playing Hamlet: his loving relationships with his mother and father; courting Ophelia; life at Wittenberg; his pre-life relationship with Claudius.[18] Correspondingly, these Études benefit the actors inhabiting the opposite roles. For Inter-life Études, Filshtinsky suggests exploring Hamlet's time between Acts 4 and 5 – which includes being attacked by a pirate ship which Hamlet jumps onto;[19] is he that brave, that good at swordplay? Surely, it's a fun Étude to do.

Conversely, the poles can be reversed from Pre-life Études to *Études of the future*. What do each of the three sisters dream life will be when they get to Moscow? What does Tom in *The Glass Menagerie* imagine life will be when he leaves Saint Louis? What do George and Martha hope for in *Who's Afraid of Virginia Woolf* – a sober life? More and better liquor? A real child? What is Juliet's vision of her future with Romeo – and vice-versa. Études of the future can profoundly contribute to determining and securing a character's Supertask.

Crucial to Pre-life Études would be a creative enactment of what is determined to be the Initial Given Circumstance of the Play. This might become a basis for Event One of the Five Event Structure or Event Five, the Crucial Event.

A further set of auxiliary Études can explore the idiosyncratic *characteristics* of a role. Why is Varya always weeping – is it demonstrate her suffering to God? What about Charlotta and her magic tricks? In a Czech production I saw, the prestidigitations the actor pulled off from her Act I entrance onward were thrilling, as was she. Or are Charlotta's tricks just ordinary coin-behind-the ear stunts? Tics, stutters, awkward gaits, miens, and habitual gestures – for example, Gayev's imaginary pool game – would fall into this category.

Auxiliary Études would also include those on *environment* and unusual conditions. Korogodsky writes: "The truth of behavior depends on environmental conditions, different physical circumstances, such as rain, heat, coldness, illness."[20] Filshtinsky suggests an environmental Étude for the opening scene of *Hamlet:* "It's night, it's cold, there's a harsh wind. You need the étude to feel the weather, the chills. (However, the guards shiver not only from the cold, but also from the fear that the appearance of a ghost has instilled in them.)"[21]

Filshtinsky proposes what he calls "*associative Études*," which might also be termed "*affective memory*" Études. He writes (as if the actor):

> I start doing études from my own life, which relate to Hamlet's life. Hamlet was in love with Ophelia, so I do études about love. Hamlet had a fondness for his father – I do études of love for my own father. Hamlet was attached to his mother – I do études of love for my mother…Hamlet has a fight with Laertes – I do études of a fight with a friend.[22]

As noted earlier, Dodin as well has used this type of personal Étude in his classes and professional rehearsals.

An inspired company can surely kindle more Étude modes than those we have touched on here. Indeed, even if not doing specific Études but "rehearsing in a Étude manner" (as Lev Dodin once said)[23] – meaning a free and open rehearsal but without improvisations – will produce an artistic benefit to any rehearsal process. Training and practicing a variety of Étude approaches should be fundamental work for actors and directors, whether they end up in Étude rehearsals or not.

For a discussion of Mise-en-Scène Etudes, see *From Études to Mise-en-Scène* in Chapter 23.

Études and the Text

The text is an anxious object during Étude rehearsals. Ask any hard-laboring playwright how much they want to hear their words paraphrased, riffed on, maybe even butchered in rehearsal. Likewise, a so-called classic text knows that it will be tough going for a while, if not permanently (ok, imagine that it is sentient). What would Chekhov have to say to Yuri Butusov and his *Seagull?* Dmitry Krymov and his *Cherry Orchard?* (Maybe he would like them?)

This is where we come to a fork on Étude Road: Is the author's text sacrosanct as Maria Knebel would have it, or is the text a *pretext* for directorial/ensemble imagination and creative plunder? Citing Stanislavsky (as she regularly did), Knebel stipulated her opinion in no uncertain terms:

> For Stanislavsky and his students, the faithful defenders of Analysis through Action, the question of whether the actor needs to know the author's text exactly does not exist. It is *indisputable gospel*. It is necessary for all actors. The question lies in how to arrive at the author's text – not through mechanical memorization, but organically, so that the author's text becomes *the only possible expression* of the internal condition of the incarnation created by the actor.[24] [emphasis mine]

Herein lies Knebel's entire philosophy, the orthodoxy of her Method of Analysis through Action: The ultimate goal is a precise psychophysical and vocal rendering of the author's verbal text reached through discoveries made in Études; this leads to the actor's holistic incarnation of the role, expressing the author's exact language. The precise words of the author are the starting and finishing points of the process.

In the Étude rehearsal period the text serves as a resource, consulted only before and after Études. Once on the floor, the actor is to paraphrase the 'thoughts' of the text by creating their own words. In each repeated Scenic Étude, the actor must increasingly capture the sequential ideas of the playwright. Some of the original language will seep into the actor through osmosis during pre- and post-Étude discussions and while the actor privately researches their role at home. But 'mechanical memorization' is forbidden. As Stanislavsky reasoned, the Étude process emulates the evolving thoughts of the playwright as they authored an Event – in time the exact words will become as crucial to the actor as they did the author.

Knebel recognizes the inevitable disparity between the actor's spontaneous language and that of an esteemed playwright: "Their words may be primitive and vulgar compared to Chekhov's. But [when] we have understood the sequence of the character's thoughts and mastered those, having then…come into Chekhov's text, we will again delight in its precision and poetic power."[25]

In summary – recalling that Knebel's pedagogical specialty was vocal expression – the actor arrives at the author's specific words only when Études cultivate an authentic internal *need* to release those particular words. But writes Knebel: "For Stanislavsky, the question of the transition to rehearsals with the exact text continued to be an experimental until the last day: he did not give us exact instructions on this matter. This question remains experimental still today."[26] We shall address the transition to the exact text problem ahead in *From Étude to Mise-en-Scène* – although there are no hard and fast rules.

But there are those who are less text severe than Maria Osipovna, those for whom the text is a pretext, an object to be played with in a game. For centuries, dramatic texts have been adapted, condensed, deconstructed, re-purposed, or cheerfully abused by directors and/or a company of actors. Radical revisions of Shakespeare date back to the seventeenth century and are ubiquitous today. In European countries it is common, even compulsory, for directors to have their own authorial 'take' on 'classic' plays by Shakespeare, Goldoni, Molière, Goethe, Calderon, Ibsen, Chekhov, and other numerous other non-copyrighted authors.

But contemporary authors and translators in the States and other English-speaking nations are "protected" by a host of copyright laws. The Dramatist's Guild's "Bill of Rights" instructs American playwrights that:

> No one (e.g., producers, directors, actors, designers, dramaturgs) can make additions, deletions, alterations, and/or changes of any kind to your script – including the text, title, and stage directions – without your prior written consent. This is called "script approval."

And:

> You have the right to mutually approve (with the producer) the cast, director, and designers (and, for a musical, the choreographer, orchestrator, arranger, and musical director), including their replacements. This is called "artistic approval."[27]

The first 'right' effectively prohibits radical interpretation or textual revision of the play without the playwright's approval; the second gives the playwright enormous artistic control over the whole enterprise of production through approval – with the producer – of the key artistic personnel. (Both clauses were operative when Arthur Miller prohibited The Wooster Group from using a twenty-minute segment from his *The Crucible*.) So, when taking on a US copyrighted play in the US, caveat emptor. For anything else, Étude away and see where it takes you.

Our earlier examples from Butusov and Krymov are exemplary here. Butusov's *The Seagull* kinda-sorta follows Chekhov's scene structure, and much of what is spoken – or yelled or whispered – is authentic dialogue directly from Chekhov's original text, if sometimes wildly recontextualized. Butusov makes each scene a separate attraction, emulating Meyerhold's "montage of attractions," enthusiastically toying with the language as he goes. Krymov, as we outlined earlier, came into his early-career rehearsals with art-studio materials – paints and brushes, sheets of canvas, puppet-making materials – making his earliest pieces with design students. But as his work advanced, he was drawn more and more to texts, rather fragments of texts, with which he plays games in gleeful abandon, as an expressionist painter might with his paints.

These are only two examples of contemporary work being done by Étude virtuosi. There are numerous others throughout the world. When it comes to the anxious text, some directors are as radical as these two – or even more: viz, Castellucci's *Inferno*. Others pursue a kind of blend between Knebel's allegiance to the author intermixed with postmodern incursions.

In this book, I decline to champion one approach to text over another, whatever my personal preference might be (which is probably pretty apparent by now). I believe that direct fidelity or radical interpretation or playing a personal game with the text must be the choice of the artists involved; excellent exciting productions can be made in any performance mode.

With that in mind we will move into the next segment, Chapter 23 *The Étude Process*, considering each of the three variants itemized above in the *Etudes Introduction* which opened this unit: the Knebel line; the Leningrad line; and our own Fusion line.

Notes

1 As supplementary reading, Sharon Carnicke's excellent twelve-page summary of Active Analysis in her *Stanislavsky in Focus* is highly recommended. Recently (2023) Carnicke came out with: Carnicke Sharon Marie. 2023. *Dynamic Acting through Active Analysis: Konstantin Stanislavsky Maria Knebel and Their Legacy*. London: Methuen Drama Bloomsbury Publishing Plc. See also James Thomas' chapter "Active Analysis in Rehearsal" in his *A Director's Guide to Stanislavsky's Active Analysis*, which uses *A Midsummer Night's Dream* as a master text.

2 Merlin, Bella "Here, Today, Now: Active Analysis for the Twenty-First-Century Actor' in White R. Andrew. 2014. *The Routledge Companion to Stanislavsky*. London: Routledge, 325–340.

3   Stanislavsky Konstantin and Jean Benedetti. 2010. *An Actor's Work on a Role*. London: Routledge p. 68.

4   З.Я Корогодский and Korogodskiĭ Z. 1996. *Начало*. Sankt-Petersburg: Санкт-Петербургский гуманитарный университет профсоюзов; Z.J. Korogodski and Korogodskiĭ Z. 1996. Beginning. Sankt-Petersburg: St. Petersburg Humanitarian University of Trade Unions, 349.

5   Korogodsky *Beginning* 345.

6   Carnicke Sharon Marie. 2009. *Stanislavsky in Focus*. 2nd ed. London: Routledge, 202.

7   https://www.larousse.fr/dictionnaires/francais/étude/31591

8   Фильштинский В.М. М. Открытая педагогика. СПб.: Балтийские сезоны, 2006; Filshtinsky V. M. M. *Open pedagogy*. Saint Petersburg: Baltic Seasons, 2006 Translation Ilya Khodosh 93.

9   Korogodsky *Beginning* 349.

10 In Filshtinsky *Open Pedagogy* 332.

11 М.М Буткевич Butkevich Mikhail Mikhaĭlovich and M. M Butkevich. 2010. *К Игровому Театру: В Двух Томах*. Moskva: ГИТИС. M. M Butkevich Butkevich Mikhail Mikhaĭlovich and M. M Butkevich. 2010. *Towards the Theater of Games*: In Two Volumes. Moskva: GITIS v1 285.

12 Knebel′ M. 1971. *О Том Что Мне Кажется Особенно Важным: Стаьи Очерки Портреты*. Moskva: "Iskusstvo"; Knebel′ M. 1971. On What Seems Especially Important to Me: Articles Essays Portraits. Moscow: "Art". 86–87.

13 Korogodsky *Beginning* 339.

14 Merlin *Here, Today, Now* 326.

15 Merlin *Here, Today, Now* 333.

16 Knebel *Important To Me* 47.

17 Станиславский К. С. Собрание сочинений: В 9 т. М.: Искусство, 1990. Т. 3. Работа актера над собой. Ч. 2: Работа над собой в творческом процессе воплощения: Материалы к книге / Общ. ред. А. М. Смелянского, вступит. ст. Б. А. Покровского, комент. Г. В. Кристи и В. В. Дыбовского. 508 с.; Stanislavsky K. C. *Collected Works*: In 9 vol. Moscow: Art, 1990. V. 3. The actor's work on himself. Part 2: Work on himself in the creative process of embodiment: Materials for the book / edited by A. M. Smeliansky, introductory article. BA Pokrovsky, commentary. G. V. Christie and V. V. Dybovsky, 508 pp. 484–485.

18 Filshtinsky *Open Pedagogy* 134.

19 Filshtinsky *Open Pedagogy* 135.

20 Korogodsky *Beginning* 372.

21 Filshtinsky *Open Pedagogy* 135.

22 Filshtinsky *Open Pedagogy* 134.

23 Author interview May 12, 2012.

24 Кнебель М. 1959. *О Действенном Анализе Пьесы И Роли. В Помощь Коллективам Театральной Самодеятельности*. Moskva: Искусствоь; Knebel M. 1959. *On Analysis through Action of the Play and the Role. In Assistance to Collectives of Theatrical Amateur Activity*. Moscow: Art. 30.

25 М Кнебель and М Кнебель. 1976. *Поэзия Педагогики*. Moskva: Всероссийское театральное общество; M Knebel and M Knebel. 1976. Poetry of Pedagogy. Moskva: All-Russian Theatrical Society, 335.

26 Knebel *Important to Me* 105.

27 https://www.dramatistsguild.com/rights

23 Études

Implementation

The Étude Process

The following is a catalog of approaches to the Étude process in rehearsal. They are listed in the order that a typical rehearsal sequence might follow, from the first day to the final dress rehearsals (and, if given the luxury, through previews). But each of our three variants – Knebel, Leningrad, Fusion – proceeds in a slightly different order and emphasis. Their contradistinctions will be noted as we progress.

But there are three fundamental articles of faith that underlie all Étude rehearsals. At the risk of echolalia, we remind the actor and director of:

The Given Circumstances: The 360-degree circumference of the play's facts, the verifiable or speculated backstory of the character, and the foremost present-tense considerations for each character which govern the character's actions and conduct in a specific Event or scene.

I in the Given Circumstances: or 'What would **I** do if...'"Let the actor not forget...that one must always live from his own being, not from the role, taking from the latter only its given circumstances" (K.S. Stanislavsky)."[1] There is no role. There is *you* in the Given Circumstances.

Here, today, now: From Merlin: "Whatever you have 'here, today, now' is enough to kick start the creative process...It is impossible to know too little."[2] As a corollary: whatever you did yesterday, today is a new day and you are a new you.

Getting Started – The First Day

Let's assume that the company and possibly even the director have little practical knowledge of rehearsing with Études. Rather than starting with the familiar reading and discussion of the play, perhaps it is best to kick off the game with a set of group improvisations. Examples of these can be found in Gob Squad's *Do It Yourself*, Complicite's *Teachers Notes – Devising*, Lecoq's *The*

DOI: 10.4324/9781003475576-29

Moving Body, or theatre games from Viola Spolin's landmark *Improvisation for the Theater* and Keith Johnstone's *Impro*.

Then, the director might split up the acting company into small groups, and assign each a three-noun sequence – e.g. *bell, haircut, forest* or *microscope, cry, tango*, and so forth. Each group must then go off for a short period of time, say ten-to-twelve minutes, and prepare a story that activates each of those words in some manner – plausible or ridiculous – and perform it.

This game can then ease into a set of improvs which, at least initially unsuspected by the group, relates to the play. Stanislavsky's pre-life list cited in Chapter 22, examples for a *Cherry Orchard*: a group waits at a train station on a cold, dark night; other people ride in a train compartment for four days; an important person who has been gone for a long time is shown room by room around their old home, with relatives recalling memories.

Then, perhaps using information from this book, the director can briefly describe the Étude process and how it will be applied in upcoming rehearsals. Then, and only then, should one do a sit-down reading of the play. No highlighters allowed; just read the play straight through, briefly gather reactions and questions afterward. (Recall Dodin's "What were your impressions?")

But here is where a major difference in tactics arises. Knebel insists:

it behooves us to remember that before etudes, we must figure out not only the large primary events, but also the smaller, secondary ones, so that the actor proceeding to etude rehearsals would not miss any external and internal challenges posed by the author for his character.[3]

Thus Knebel begins her work with dedicated table sessions:

An analysis of the major events in the play takes up a certain amount of time, approximately two or three rehearsals. Then we transition to clarification, to a more detailed analysis of the causality of events, and then begin (adhering to that same causality) to make etudes.[4]

Knebel believes that a breakdown of major Events and their analysis, then further Event clarification, all guided by the director, is obligatory "in order [for the actors] to have the right to make an étude."[5] A good portion of her first rehearsal week, perhaps all of it, would be devoted to these Event-focused table sessions. It is specific discussion about identifying Events, but it is a lot of discussion.

Bella Merlin, also seeking a gospel "dead-letter-perfect production,"[6] starts the first day with the conventional read-through of the play and design presentations, then unspecified general discussion, then "Ensemble activity" – presumably exercises and improvisations. This is followed immediately – it seems on Day 2 – with her four-step process: read the scene, discuss the scene, improvise the scene, discuss the improvisation. Thus begins "the constant interweaving of the two arteries (tablework and *études*)."[7] At the table, Merlin utilizes her rigorous pre-rehearsal text prep, with which she guides the actors through the play Event by Event. The key difference is that Merlin is "interweaving" the scene-by-scene Event analysis and resultant Études from the outset, whereas Knebel leads a meticulous Event Analysis of the full text before the actors "have the right" to make Études.

Korogodsky is unclear as to the order of things: full Event table analysis prior to initial Études or Event analyses concurrent with Études; perhaps he varied his methods. But he too is insistent that Events are the central structural element of the Étude process. "The stronger the event framework, the freer the feeling and imagination of the acting and the actor. Railroad ties and rails guarantee the speed and direction of the movement. The sequence is lined up by events, from the most particular to the most significant."[8] In Korogodsky's metaphor the 'ties' would be Events, the 'rails' the Throughline Action of the play. Without the ties – the Events – the Throughline rails cannot be laid. He continues his railway metaphor saying: "The author's text is sought as if it were a station of destination; it provokes us and it calls us, we proceed from it and strive toward it precisely in order to come to it through our own lives, through ourselves."[9]

Now, let us contrast these Event-prioritized approaches to a rather different approach of Stanislavsky's, as recorded by Boris Zon in 1933 (and cited in Chapter 2 of this book):

BZ: Do you work at the table for a long time now, and when do you move to the next period?

KS: We read the play today and it's possible to perform tomorrow. If it's not enough to read it once, we can read it a second time.

BZ: Does it mean that actors don't know anything?

KS: They don't know the words, but they know what to do. If they might forget, I would remind them. If a question arises, we would look into the text: "Something is written about that in the third act"...we find it...etc.

BZ: Does it mean that in the beginning you even don't need the text of the role?

KS: We will come to it step by step but according to a logical way through action.

BZ: Does it mean that there is no need for sitting at the table at all?

KS: Sometimes people still sit...Even with these new approaches actors could want the table...Our ardor for the table led us to indigestion. If a capon is fed too many nuts, its stomach can't digest the food anymore; so it is with the actor who is burdened by "table food" and can't use even a small part of what was done. My new method is a development of previous ones.

....

BZ: When and how are the pieces [bits/beats] and tasks [objectives/problems] set now?

KS: So we play a piece in this manner, as I said, and when it turns out that we've played a piece, a new one begins. We [you and I] have played, say, 'meeting,' and now, apparently, we are playing 'getting to know each other'. The task arises involuntarily.[10]

Stanislavsky, long known (and often ridiculed) for his interminable table sessions is here declaring that matters formerly debated lengthily at the table – events, bits and tasks – will reveal themselves through action (via Études); he is foreshadowing Merlin's notion: "it is impossible to know too little." Unlike Knebel, Stanislavsky is saying to Zon that Events are what you – the actor – discover on the floor, not by parsing them out at a table.

He expands the notion of his 'new technique' in one of the last things he wrote in the late 1930s:

"Here is my approach to a new role, "said Tortsov. "Without any reading, without any conferences on the play, the actors are asked to come to a rehearsal of it."

"How is that possible?" was the bewildered reaction of the students.

...

"Kostya, do you remember Gogol's Inspector General?" he asked suddenly turning to me. "Yes, but not very well, only in general outline."

"Good. Go up on stage and play Khlestakov's entrance in Act Two."

"How can I when I don't know what to do?" I objected in surprise.

"You do not know everything, but you know something. So play the little that you know."

...

"I can't do anything because I don't know anything!"

"How so?" Tortsov objected. "In the script it says: 'Enter Khlestakov.' Can you enter a room in an inn?"

"Yes."

"Then do it."[11]

It is Étude enthusiast Veniamin Filshtinsky, who today advocates Stanislavsky's dive-in-first methodology. Discussing Stanislavsky's notes on *Inspector General* he writes:

[T]here is no evidence that Stanislavsky suggests a separation – a reconnaissance of the mind and a reconnaissance of the body. On the contrary, he emphatically throws the body forward. He begins to boldly mix and almost simultaneously produce reconnaissance by the body and reconnaissance by the mind: reconnaissance by body – then mind – then body again, and so on. He says that his "technique" automatically analyzes the play.[12]

In short, the poles are reversed: the play is revealed at first by naive Études – "I can't do anything because I don't know anything!" – and then by analyses of those Études, each round raising more questions, thereby getting more complex and sophisticated with each Étude. It is, Filshtinsky says, ultimately a 'mix' of the two Reconnaissances, but the body leads the mind, not the reverse. The simple physical actions – Kostya entering a room at an inn – leads to a host of probing questions: where he has been, where is he going, who is behind him, who is in the room he opens the door to, what is that person doing – and so forth and so on. Crucially, each of those questions is fodder for further Études, which peel the layer of the text-onion to get to the core of the play.

Filshtinsky, like all advocates of Études, of course does not forswear Events; indeed he declares that "Études on the play's events occupy the most important place in [Stanislavsky's] final revelations."[13] By accessing and advocating the very last efforts of Stanislavsky, Filshtinsky has formulated a unique but fully defensible approach: Études first, *then* Events. (He remains faithful to the text it seems but has little to say on that subject.) We can call this method the Filshtinsky approach, derived from Zon, who noted Stanislavsky's last experiments.

Which leads us to a final methodology, the Fusion approach, developed by this author and his associates over several years of classes and rehearsals. The major innovation in this process is that (ideally) *prior* to entering the first day of rehearsal (or a studio class) the actors should have completed at least the first three of the Text Actions at home. These assignments allow the actor to study the play, not just their role. This procedure levels the playing field between director and actors as rehearsal starts.

For their pre-rehearsal preparation, the actors should finish and create notebook entries for:

Text Action 1. "The First Reading of the Play"; Chapter 12.
Text Action 2. "Novel of Life I"; Chapter 13. (If time is pressing, they should complete at least Act I or a convenient 25–33% of the first part of the play.)
Text Action 3. "The Outer Ring of Given Circumstances"; Chapter 14. (This requires going through the entire play.)

These preparatory endeavors give the actors more than enough material to hit the ground running with Études on Day One (with no discussion of big ideas or design presentations; those can come later). After ensemble exercises and improvisation, per above, the director introduces Analysis through Action, and particularly the Étude method.

Then, immediately comes the first Étude. The scene should be selected from some significant section of the play, or a major pre-life Event. It should contain many roles; the full cast should participate somehow (creating extras if needed). It is important that a crucial incident take place in the scene, preferably a climactic moment.

When teaching or directing *The Cherry Orchard*, our first day Étude is drawn from Anya's account to Varya of her trip to Liubov's Paris apartment – in fact, a tenement hovel. As the volunteer Anya and Charlotta are sent outside to trudge on nearby streets, imagining cold and muddy industrial Paris circa 1900, the remaining actors, guided by the director and associates, create the environment and the strange denizens of Liubov's fifth-floor walk-up. The two travelers return to find a dark *la vie Bohème* hellhole. Typically, Liubov must be dragged out the door by Anya and Charlotta as the occupants of the flat resist that effort. When they finally get her out, the Étude is done. Immediately we ask the (usually shaken) Anya, Charlotta, and Liubov: "What did you find out?"

The company, having all participated in an Étude, are now ready to begin work on the full play.

First Études – Setting the Stage

Whatever the Étude rehearsal procedure presented to the cast on the first day – parse Events first or parse them alternately with Études, dive in blind or concentrate on key scenes – the moment will come when it is time to begin Scenic Études. Where to begin? With the first scene is one way, or with a populous key scene, such as Anya's visit to her mother's Paris apartment, is another. Start with a simple reading of that scene (or Event if you are going Event by Event), the actors on their feet while reading.

The propellant of an Étude is Given Circumstances, so the place to start the actual investigation of the scene by the actors is the Given Circumstance of the *environment* in which the scene happens. Following Korogodsky and Knebel's recommendations, the director lures the actors into the scene by having them create *their own* appropriate physical space: Where are the necessary doors, windows, stairs, props; if the scene is in an exterior environment, what and where are the necessary features? As the actors complete their mock-up of their scenic world, the director can ask what is beyond this scenic space: where do people come from, where do they depart to, how far away is the train station, the ocean, the neighbor's house, the enemy, and so forth. Korogodsky writes:

> When you ask an actor to come out from behind the table onto the stage in order to imagine the place of the action, then he is easily absorbed into a new feeling – imperceptibly he passes from his mental attitude toward the material of the play into the state of an actor. By constructing the environment in which the event takes place, the actor includes himself in the actions and given circumstances of the role...The detailed, meticulous work of creating the environment is a provocateur of faith. Without believing in the environment, it is difficult to begin to act faithfully.[14]

It is important to add that whatever environment the actors of the first scene create, later occupants of that same space should create their own version; new actors, characters, and circumstances may well engender different configurations of the same environment. This 'playground time' (thank you, Yuri Butusov) is time well spent. It engages each actor in their own world, immediately thrusting the actor into "I in the Given Circumstances." The director may advise the actors here and there, maybe remind them of some practical necessity, but this is actor-time.

After an environment has been fabricated, Knebel asks the actors to consider simple questions:

> In what set of circumstances does the action take place? Summer or winter, cold or hot? What time of the day? How and what are their characters wearing? Where did they come from, what they have in their hands, are they tired or, on the [15]contrary, are they full of vigor and strength?...In other words, the very first étude rehearsal confronts the actor with all.the details of the physical life of the scene. As soon as he tries to put himself in the given circumstances of the role, he immediately has a complex perception of what is happening, and his internal psychological sensations become inseparable from the physical, material sensations.

Once the actors have prepared the environment and answered the director's relevant Outer Ring questions – weather, time, and so forth – it can be useful for the director to ask each actor why they are in this place right now, and (privately) what they feel about the other character(s) in the scene – here, now today.

It's time to get onstage. Here we remember bewildered Kostya's question and his maestro's simple reply:

> "How can I when I don't know what to do?" I objected in surprise.
> "You do not know everything, but you know something. So play the little that you know."

Silent (or Wordless) Études

After the stage is set and the actors have answered some simple Given Circumstances questions comes the first Étude. This is often done in *silence, no words, totally mute.* One option for starting the initial Étude is for the director to just say "Go" and see what happens; the director then ends the Étude when it fizzles out – which it might well do.

Generally no cosmic revelations arise in the frequently awkward first tries. Without words as a guide, the progression of the scene can be wobbly, repetitious, or inchoate. But the actors are now on their feet, trying to figure out what to *do* – not thinking 'what are my words?' or calling for lines. They have only each other to turn to, no scripts to hide behind, and they realize they must take ownership of the scene now – through their bodies. Even in the first round, physical actions often emerge which can momentarily expose subtextual feelings or urges. Those glimpses are to be pointed out by the director in the post-Étude download.

After brief discussion, possibly another reading of the scene (always standing up), the second pass, again mute, will reveal more. On the third go-round, it is possible to allow a few vocal sounds if they naturally come out of the body: screaming, whimpers, sighs, snorts, laughter. But as sounds enter the arena, be sure that they are emotionally based, not camouflaged words, or sound for sound's sake. The same is true for gestures; beware playing the party game 'charades'. However, if the actors are ready, the director might even move them to Stanislavsky's Ta-ta-ta exercise, substituting "Ta-ta-ta" or other sounds for words. Viola Spolin called this gibberish.

The non-verbal silent Étude step is crucial and should be done three times in a row to increasingly immerse the actors in their circumstances, possibly re-reading the scene before each round, certainly discussing their discoveries each time. The download discussion is *always* "what did you find out?" No judgments, no "keep that." The actor interrogates the play, the director interrogates the actor – and encourages them to pursue emerging sensations and actions. By the third consecutive outing, the actors' bodies will have bloomed from unease to an increasing command of time and space – and an eagerness to do more Études.

Caveat emptor: No one scene should be dwelt on for too long. The goal is to have Étuded through the entire play by Day Four or so. When the round of silent Études is completed, the first full reading of the play might take place, the actors sitting in a circle as they read, partners moving in and out of the center of the ring as their entrances and exits require. But no sitting when inside the ring, and capital 'A' 'Acting' should be curtailed. This first reading, post-silent Études, is just a reading – no lengthy discussion afterward, simply another way of getting the play in the air – and into the ensemble's soul.

Bella Merlin's Silent Étude Variant

For a silent Étude option, Bella Merlin proposes an interesting exercise. She places two actors several steps apart, with full eye contact which must continue throughout the Étude. Once they are deeply engaged optically, the actors then imagine that they are also connected gut-to-gut by a "coiled spring...dynamically charged." Once the coil is linked to both bodies – the actors will know when that is – they silently "pipette a few drops" of their individual character into their being. Then:

> Remaining on a straight line – and connected by the coiled spring – you and your partner silently begin to discover whether or not you can find a point of physical contact, attending all the time to each other's faces, bodily movements and stillnesses. The point of contact might be an embrace, a handshake, a gentle slap, a kiss, or it might not happen at all: you might find that when you truly attend to each other and to the given circumstances of the scene, no physical contact is possible. As you move across the space – either towards each other or away – you tune in to the

immense amount of information communicated through the imaginary coiled spring as it contracts and expands...The objective of the exercise is not "to make physical contact," but rather to test the given circumstances of the scene, with the suggestion of making physical contact simply being a stimulus to action.[16]

This intense and dynamic exercise will surely forge a bond between the two actors, while encouraging them to pursue the inner dynamics of the scene in a kinetic and non-narrative format. At best, this will begin to reveal to the actors the subtextual emotional forces passing between them.

Whatever approach is taken, by the end of the Silent Étude phase the actors are invariably hungry for more, eager to jump onto the floor to continue their embodied analysis of the play. The Étude process has been born. Now it is time for it to develop.

Scenic Études – Repetitions and Variants

After the silent Études have been completed, paraphrased language should be introduced while Étude-ing scenes or Events, usually in the order of the text. But the rerunning of Études is not simply "rinse and repeat." Each Étude should drill the actors deeper into the underground veins of the role and the play. During the ongoing iterations, the director will gradually become an increasingly present catalytic agent, carefully guiding and prodding the participants. But the actors are the ones inside the mine discovering the valuable ore in the veins.

The wise director is not collecting 'cool moments' for staging at this point but urging the actors to continue exploring their interior world psychophysically and imaginatively. Early on it is fine for the director to prod the actors toward extreme states and actions if everyone is safe. It is easier to cut back on excessive acting – to "put a suit on it" as genius American director Robert Woodruff says in rehearsals and classes – than to not have enough vitality in the first place. One of the goals of Études, particularly in younger actors, is to encourage *release*, to give the actor permission to go too far, for now. Early on, going too far (within the bounds of tenderness) is freeing, even exhilarating, and gives the actor permission to emotionally go anywhere they want. The wise director will know when and how to coach the actor back to earth.

In repeated Étude rounds, Knebel relies on (1) reading the scene, (2) discussing the scene, intensifying Given Circumstances, and setting the goals for the new Étude pass, (3) Étude-ing the Scene onstage with paraphrased language, (4) re-reading the scene meticulously, noting where the paraphrasing was close to the text, what was misstated or overlooked, and why, (5) discussing new goals and new Given Circumstances for the next Étude of the same scene, and (6) Étude-ing the scene again. As noted above, this sequence of steps is compacted by Merlin into (my shorthand): Read, Discuss, Improvise, Discuss.

So instead of rinse and repeat, this process is reload and reshoot, many times – but only up to a point. Knebel addresses the lifetime of Étude reiterations: "How many times should you rehearse each scene this way? As soon as the actors come close to the text and the content of the scene becomes clear in the étude…you can move on to the next part. No fixation and polishing of études is required."

She also warns of the danger of the actor memorizing their own paraphrased text; in such a case "the étude rehearsal will lose its meaning."[17] Or, if the paraphrased language of the actors strays too far from the text, or disintegrates into false emotionality or juvenile invective, Knebel, ever the text hawk, writes:

> At this time, the director faces another responsible task: to aim the actors at the iron clarification of the text according to the author, right up to interstitials, to punctuation marks, which determine the character of the author's intonation. We must not allow body vocabulary, verbal sludge, the tendency to neglect the text of the author; if such a tendency has appeared, it must be ruthlessly erased.[18]

Knebel, while accepting "primitive and vulgar" language in early Études (see above), is by the end 'ruthlessly' demanding 'iron clarification of the text according to the author.' And that stricture, along with an ever-developing sense of character and action, exemplifies the ultimate goal of Knebel's Action Analysis: a letter-perfect fully experienced performance. The letter-perfect language, she contends, will emerge through osmosis during the Étude process. "When an actor comes to the author's words in such a complicated, so deep a way, through all the wealth of their internal motions, it easily fits in his memory, in his mind, because now there is a whole series of associations, sensations, emotions."[19]

Filshtinsky proposes that as well as reiterated Études, the actor will come to the precise language of the author by re-reading the *play* (not just their scenes) many times, thereby absorbing the poetic intent of the author, and understanding how their role fits into the Throughline Action.

Iron clarification, should that be your goal, is appropriate only toward the end of the Étude phase of rehearsal. The third, fourth, or even fifth repetition of the Étude cycle should continue to yield valuable new character and conflict revelations even as the actor reports from inside the play become more succinct and purposeful. Over time the reiterations will probably produce a few psychophysical benchmarks: specific moments when physical actions or adaptations organically recur and feel energized and energizing, not just repetitious. These moments/gestures/adaptations can serve as touchstones as the Event progresses and become springboards into the next series of actions. (One of my associates calls these moments 'lily pads,' which I argue is too passive. But I get her point.)

A welcome by-product of Scenic Études is that the actors and/or the director can request Auxiliary Études: "backstory" Études (Pre-life or Inter-life), environmental Études (space, weather, time), individual characteristic Études (gait, speech, tics), genre of text Études (poetic, documentary), and the like. All of these are crucial means to bring substance and support to the Scenic Études on the Throughline Action.

As well as opening new psychophysical avenues, Auxiliary Études can be great fun to make. Usually there is no precedent text to worry about; they are completely devised by the actors on the spot, and no one knows where exactly they are going. But it should be recognized that the primary goal of the Étude method is the realization of the play, in whatever form it is ultimately going to take. It is important to use Auxiliary Études only when productive. That may be often, but the goal must always be to get out of Auxiliary Études rabbit holes and back to the Scenic Étude rounds.

When certain behavioral patterns start to emerge in Scenic Études, the director, avoiding laborious System terminology (which Dodin, Filshtinsky, and Senelick, just to name three, find stultifying) can point out to the cast that these patterns are evidence of emerging Supertasks – for individual roles or for the play or both. Just as Events can be spelled out at the table beforehand or discovered on the floor, so be it for Supertasks. Presumably the director has provisionally identified the Supertasks of the roles and the play in their tête-à-tête pre-rehearsal reconnaissance of the play. But as the rehearsal Études begin to reveal certain patterns that seem alive and instructive, it behooves the director to call attention to these. While always endorsing their unpredictable 'zig-zags,' the director should encourage the actors to understand that these oft-recurring patterns are evidencing the banks of a river – the Supertasks – within which their roles and the play should flow. (This is far more fruitful than a director calling out "Brilliant! Keep it!" thereby 'freezing' the river, soon to melt into slush.)

The Fusion Process and Études

Let us look at how our Fusion process proceeds through the Étude rounds. After the silent round, we jump right into Scenic Études in the order of the play (sometimes reversing the order, going last scene to first, or three-to-four pivotal scenes per act). But recall that ideally the actors came into rehearsal with the first three Text Actions under their belts: The First Reading of the Play, Novel of Life I, and The Outer Ring of Given Circumstances. Presumably they are ready to "dive-in." Meanwhile the next three Text Actions – Character Given Circumstances, Line of the Role, and Novel of Life II – are pursued as homework while rehearsals proceed. (In a teaching situation with a new group, casting is usually announced after the second or third day of classes, before which training improvisations and Études are cast randomly.)

It is after completion of Novel of Life II, the psycho-autobiography, that the Études inevitably begin to explode. Given the intimacy of the actor writing in the first person and rousing their own affective memories during that writing, the line between the role and the "I" begins to blur, then becomes permeable, and finally will evaporate. The actor who tip-toed into the shallow end of the ocean during early Études now launches deep dives into themselves and the role. Any timidity or hyper-excessive theatricalism that may have appeared in first Études disappears. Private secrets in public places begin to burst out of the actors; their imaginations leap to previously unknown altitudes; their access to full emotional expression from tenderness to ferocity streams into full flow; and spontaneous activation of their physical self grows exponentially.

I know this all sounds hyperbolic, but what can I say – I have seen it over and over. Actors will often surface from a deep-dive Étude in a state of elation, or preternatural calm, or frozen shock. After a particularly passionate Étude, the actor partners will often embrace. Most likely, affective memories have come into play, recognized by the actor(s) or not. This is a delicate moment for the teacher/director. The download should wait until the actors silently decompress from their mutual undersea journey. Then comes the "What did you find out" discussion, possibly with "I noticed X" from the director – but no more. As to affective memories, I sometimes ask "Did something from your own life come up for you?" When the answer is affirmative – which is frequently – I reply: "Good. I don't want to know what it is, but if it helps you, use it as you wish."

By this time, through actor pattern recognition and some director coaching, the cast have begun to recognize Events: where new Events or 'beats' arise, who is the new Protagonist, who is the new Antagonist, and what they are trying to do to each other. The actors, having written out the Line of the Role on their own, now are gaining a personal sense of what their character's goals and Actions are in each scene, and overall.

Topic Beats

As a strategy to move the actors toward the actual words of the author we have developed a plan we call "Topic Beats." Most Events of any length will have one basic conflict 'driven' by the Protagonist(s) and countered by the Antagonist(s). But within that Event, several *topics* may be brought into play. A simple example: in the first Event of *The Cherry Orchard*, the Protagonist Lopakhin deploys these broad topics:

The train and the time
Memories of Liubov
His new clothes
His wealth
His book

The actors should break down these topics together, and then choose one short phrase or key word that they feel is essential to each Topic Beat. Thus, the Protagonist Lopakhin might choose:

"You should have woken me up."
"She washed the blood off my face."
"Take a look at me now."

"I'm rich now."
"I tried reading this book."

The Antagonist, Dunyasha, would then choose a line that conflicts with Lopakhin's first key phrase.

"I thought you had left."

That is the last line Dunyasha speaks in this Event. However, in retorting to Lopakhin's other key phrases, Dunyasha might repeat "I thought you had left.' Or better yet, Dunyasha can create short rebuttals of their own such as:

"Poor baby."
"You're still a servant."
"You can't read."

These key phrases, ideally written out on a whiteboard in the room for reference, become the initial vocal weapons for conflict exchange, such as:

"You should have woken me up" →← "I thought you had left"

These twinned phrases are repeated in several serve-volley exchanges. The actors remain in that Topic Beat, always moving about the stage, fully aware of each other, repeating their serve-volley verbal exchange until they, or the director/teacher, move on to the next Topic beat found on the white board.

"She washed the blood off my face" →← "Poor baby."

And so forth, several times, each time taking a different tack.
   These exchanges, vocally encouraged and guided by the director, will necessarily change in coloration, intention, volume, physicality, and meaning as the actors repeatedly recycle them. This exercise, which we do midway in the Étude process, serves several purposes:

- It breaks long Event passages into smaller 'bits' or beats
- It gives the actors structural 'rungs' as they move through the Event
- It establishes intense awareness of the interdependency of the partners
- It ingrains the physicality of the Étude process through continual movement
- It makes the actors move up and down all kinds of physical and emotional scales
- It makes the actors eager to know what other words surround their key words or phrases
- It is a huge aid as the actors move toward full paraphrase

- It is an instrumental tool if moving toward the precise words of the author near the end of the process. (This is why we invented Topic Beats in the first place.)

Director Dmitry Krymov once observed a class in which we were doing this exercise. His admiring comment was: "You are making full plays out of only two lines."

A penultimate note on the repetition of Études: Because of the immediacy and frequent heightened theatricality of the Étude process, there is often a deadly lull as the actors struggle to move from paraphrase toward precise text. The wind goes out of the sails, the wonderful joyous work flutters into doldrums, everyone gets depressed or crabby: where'd the fun go? In this phase, it is crucial to keep rehearsing "in an Étude manner." Allow for the verbal mistakes and setbacks to become a part of the process, even a humorous part. Director/teacher: keep saying "just make something up" when they get stuck, which they will. Ultimately their joy and imaginative physicality will return. and ideally will be there for the full run of the production.

The final note: I once asked Lev Dodin, "What do you do if you find the Études more interesting than the play itself?" In his calm rabbinical demeanor, Lev Abramovich replied, "Then make a play from the Études."[20]

From Étude to Mise-en-Scène

Zinovy Korogodsky, a leading practitioner of the Étude method, writes this about the mise-en-scène:

> It is very easy to distinguish between a staged performance and a born performance. A born mise-en-scene is, first of all immediate, it seems to arise here and now...But a mise-en-scene that is imposed, ordered, or staged always suffers from efficacy, from reason, from elements of formality.[21]

This quotation prompts a fuller explication of the French-originated term mise-en-scène. Albeit rarely used in American theatre (though common in American cinematography), it is nonetheless an important idea to grasp. So far, we have been translating it as 'staging' or 'blocking.' While not incorrect – the arrangement of bodies in space is certainly a critical part of the mise-en-scène – these definitions are incomplete. Consulting the online *Larousse* French dictionary, we find this definition: "scenic or cinematographic *production* of a lyrical or dramatic work or a screenplay"[22] [emphasis added].

The noun *mise*, derived from the French word for 'put' or 'place,' signifies the action of putting or placing something'; *en scène* meaning 'in or on the stage.' So a literal translation would be 'putting (or placing) onstage.' This would of course include putting bodies in particular places onstage – what we call blocking or staging. But in France the director is often called the *metteur-en-scène*, 'metteur' meaning the 'putter' or 'placer' – the person who puts people and things onstage. This suggests a larger definition: the director is not only 'placing' bodies in space but is also (usually with designers) configuring the performance space itself and 'putting' into that space all of what we call 'production elements': scenery, costumes, lights, sound, projections, as well as stylistic or choreographic movement.

In short, the director is putting onstage everything that the audience sees and hears. (By strict definition an audience *hears*, a spectator *sees*. The director is responsible to both perspectives, using all the tools of production.)

Kama Ginkas, Tovstonogov's most renowned student, runs with this all-inclusive definition of the directorial mise-en-scène:

> If the language of writers is words and their sequence, if the painter speaks to us with a combination of colors, volumes, and lines, if the language of the composer is sounds, tones, etc., then the impudent director steals everything from everyone and uses them all at once. His language is remarkable in that it includes words, rhythm, color, melodies, gestures, pauses, and space. The only difference between the director and the other artists is that this villain also uses a living, defenseless creature called an actor.[23]

It is that 'living, defenseless creature called an actor' who is our concern here. Up to the point of moving to the stage itself, the actors have been the primary focus of the director and staff in the rehearsal room. In that room there likely is some mock-up of the set and furniture, some suggestions of costume pieces, and the full-bore mise-en-scène (minus staging) has likely been described with drawings and a set model. But the actor has not physically experienced the totality of the production's elements in the vital way they have experienced the spoken text and their partners. Thus shifting from actor-centric Études to a full production onstage can be a rocky road, possibly disappointing even overwhelming for the actors. Is there a day when the director has to say: "Well, that's that for Études; it's been fun, but now we have to move on."

That day should not exist. Étude work continues through the remaining rehearsal time and into the run; it just takes different forms.

Korogodsky proposes that "[t]he mise-en-scene is essentially the subtext materialized in space...[it] materializes all the motifs of inner life."[24] Thus, the director/teacher's subtle corralling of the late-stage Études should ideally lead to a congruency between the rehearsal hall and the production's greater mise-en-scène. In the middle Étude rounds, the director should 'place' the actors into a simulacrum of the spatial configuration they will meet onstage: the sleazy bar, the posh living room, the cold castle parapet, the empty cathedral pew, the dank prison cell, the gazebo by the lake. These specified elements become new Given Circumstances for the actors; they are new 'partners' in Études.

Instead of constrictions, these new constituents of the production can provide inspirations for new adaptations – or revisions of old ones. A scene where profound subtext was found through a spatially expansive raging argument must now adapt to the paper-thin walls of a cheap motel or a library reading room. The actors' goals remain the same, the intensity still boils, but the means of expression, aka the adaptation, must change – Robert Woodruff's 'suit' must be put on.[25] But Knebel confidently states that the Étude-rehearsed actor will adjust: "Actors, accustomed to free movement in space, accustomed to analyzing their physical behavior, intuitively and freely participate in the process of creating mise-en-scene."[26]

It is up to the director to guide the actors toward that 'intuition' and 'free participation' as new production circumstances are introduced. Korogodsky advises:

> [T]his has to be done in such a way that the actor is hardly aware of it, that there is no formal shift in his feelings, that he perceives everything as a natural process where these are not production demands, but rather a new fundamental circumstance…If all the connections we are talking about are made in such a way that they do not create a dislocation in the soul of the actor, then there is no need to fear the birth of a mise-en-scène, which is as much an action as any other action is in the process of relationships…Mise-en-scène is an action with some spatial and plastic elements.[27]

As the Scenic Études unfolded in 'Repetitions and Variants' above, the director certainly recognized the patterns the actors unwittingly created, the recurring key moments and character ideas that seemed to simultaneously feed and secure the actor. Without saying "remember the day you did such-and-such?" the director can find a way, through a Mise-en-Scène Étude in a new spatial circumstance, to test if that 'moment' can thrive in the new environment. Perhaps it dies, perhaps it mutates, but now the actor will join in a search to re-enliven that crucial moment by revising their Given Circumstances or physicality. Nothing has been lost, the search just continues. Korogodsky contends: "étude work usually leads us to a natural appearance of mise-en-scenes."[28] Or, to paraphrase Knebel's statement above, when the Given Circumstances of the production are introduced, the actor will know how to respond.

Tender shepherding of the actors into their new physical, visual, and aural environments can be one of the most intimate and collaborative parts of a joyful rehearsal process, filled with new discoveries. During this period, the director must stay fully connected to the actors, on stage and off. During 'tech' the artists and artisans sitting in the dark auditorium, their ghostly faces up-lit by their MacBooks, have lots of work to do; they don't need the director hovering over them (except when they do). The director, when not needed in the house, must maintain an 'Étude manner of rehearsing' on stage during walk-throughs, run-throughs, tech days, and previews. To repeat: 'It is very easy to distinguish between a staged performance and a born performance.' So keep giving birth. Don't "freeze" things; create new things.

Final rehearsals, tech, and even previews (should fortune smile and grant those) are where the director becomes a senior editor in the co-authorship of the production. Presumably the director has been carefully, sometimes stealthily or seductively, guiding the actors toward a goal that ultimately will release 'the scream of the production.' The work of the actors during Étude rehearsals has either reinforced the director's original intent or has altered it to something unforeseen and more exhilarating, generating a deeper and more significant scream. The production's scream, whether proven or discovered in rehearsal, will be embodied by the onstage actors; when the director departs, they become the sole authors of each performance.

FAQs about Études

We have crusaded about Études long enough. Therefore, this final section is not an attempt to get the reader to cross the Rubicon, never to return. If you've gotten this far, you are in the game or not. But there are a few dangling questions that have repeatedly arisen over the years that I will attempt to answer here.

Do Études take too much rehearsal time?

I believe Études take less time. They replace the days spent in show-and-tell and first table readings often followed by rambling discussions about the play. Then similar discussions take place about each scene and each character in the scene; then lengthy conferences about what each character wants in the scene, what are their "objectives"; then disagreements about the purpose and direction of the scene; then the actors mumbling into the script while aimlessly wandering the floor, ignoring their partners; then some blocking; then the fumbling for the exact words and calling out "Line!" All of these time-suckers disappear with Études.

Table discussion is talk about possible actions; Études *are* actions.

Will Études work with any kind of material?

I suppose one could find some medium where an Étude approach would not be beneficial. But I have used Études in narrative dramatic theatre including Shakespeare, Molière, Chekhov, and contemporary authors; post-dramatic texts by Muller, Churchill, and Jelinek; musical theatre and opera; adapting from other media: fiction, film, paintings; and company devised work. While originated for dramatic realism – that was the *nouvelle vague* then – Études are flexible instruments that easily migrate to other forms of artistic expression. In the end, all the Text Actions may not readily apply to all texts; there is an admittedly Aristotelian bent to some of them. But attempting to apply them will lead to certain pattern recognitions, will reveal certain structural operatives that may be elusive at first. And any portion of any piece can be fodder for

Études, even if the text intentionally defies coherence. Rembrandt did numerous sketches – Études – of the characters in his painting *Night Watch*, Mozart wrote Études for piano. Étude rehearsing is commonplace in Russian and Eastern European avant-garde theatre. Western theatre has been a late arriver, but the time has come.

Any more tips about the memorization thing?

This remains a tough area; even Stanislavsky admitted he hadn't solved it, nor did Knebel. The learning of the spoken text through Étude repetition and osmosis, while common, does not work for everyone. If an actor is continually holding up improvisational Études with deer-in-the headlights paralysis or just plain resistance, it may be best to allow them to revert to their customary mechanical memorization. Of course their partner(s) must continue to invent and paraphrase, which often loosens up the recalcitrant actor, who, now that they know their lines, feels freer. (This has only happened once in my time using Études.)

Following Filshtinsky, encouraging the actor to read the play, *not the scene but the play*, will also help. Additionally, the night before a scene will be rehearsed I ask the actors involved to read the scene once (only) at home. Then it is re-read with the partner(s) just before doing the Étude. That seems to help memorization without pushing for 'iron clarification.'

Finally, this problem is why we invented Topic Beats (hijacked from text analysis of Shakespeare, where topic shifts are usually evident). The actors use those key phrases – which may change when they know more about the scene and their role – as 'rungs' to guide them through the scene. Naturally, after the key-phrase Études, they are eager to know what else is in each Topic Beat and begin to paraphrase from there. So the key-phrase Études are a mnemonic trick which leads to fuller paraphrase and onto the author's words.

What to do when an Étude goes off the rails?

This will happen – maybe a lot, particularly early on with actors who are not used to the Étude process. If things get really off-course, it is up to the director/teacher to call time. Then, review the Given Circumstances of the scene: the prior relationship between the characters, what is new in this scene, who is driving the scene forward and how, who is trying to alter the Protagonist's behavior and how. Possibly a re-reading of the scene, but then go back at it, right away. A dud Étude is a kind of gift: now we know *that* doesn't work, let's try something else. The only mistake one can make in an Étude is laziness.

What are other pitfalls of Études?

For an actor who has never worked this way before, for example, most actors in the US, the first Études can be daunting. Self-consciousness based on fear of judgment oozes from their egos. Therefore having each set of scene partners initially construct their own floor plan is very useful, as is Bella Merlin's 'coil' exercise. But early on, no one in the room should expect genius Études. Those will come later. I regularly say to the actors before or during an early Étude: "Be Stupid!" – if necessary, followed by "No, be *really* stupid!" (This is the best director phrase I know: "Be stupid!" I say it all the time – to my actors and to myself.)

Another pitfall is that sometimes an Étude can overwhelm an actor. As discussed earlier, this is usually because some very powerful affective memory suddenly flooded over the banks of their personal river (or sometimes there is something going on between the two actors). Panic, crying, rage, or running out of the room might rarely occur in extreme cases. (Of course this reaction has happened in non-Étude classes and rehearsals as well.) The director must act quietly but clearly, not probing or pushing the actor, but giving them time to calm down; perhaps advising the 3-4-5 breath exercise and/or possibly asking the scene partner or a close friend of the actor to lend their support.

The final pitfall is preventable. Actors and director/teachers tend to fall in love with Études and the Étude process. It can be difficult to 'set' anything, whether it be the exact words of the text or newly invented text that emerged from riffing on the original text. Certainly moving to set language and physical mise-en-scènes can feel confining after the frolic and freedom of open Études.

This is where the difference of the 'born' performance and the 'staged' performance is pivotal. The born performance will, with encouragement, keep its feel, its atmosphere alive even during a long run. If the performances start to flag, someone must call attention to this problem. If the director is unavailable, someone qualified should lead wake-up Études for the company to rejuvenate itself.

Stealing from Krymov and Butusov I always leave certain moments open to the actors' nightly whims. In effect I say "You must hit your marks on A and C. But for B, do whatever you want (just stay in the light)." After a while, the actors tend to fall into the same pattern for B every night. But just knowing that they are free to improvise periodically is a great stimulant to keeping the Étude process alive, thereby birthing a born performance every night.

Closing Thoughts

On page 609, the last page of his magnum opus, *An Actor's Work*, Stanislavsky tells us "There is no system, there is nature."[29] When asked what is the essence of Analysis through Action, Maria Knebel replied: "I don't know. No one does."[30]

I certainly don't claim that what you have read here *is* Analysis through Action. This is only one variant offered in part to create more variants – say, yours – and to challenge the shopworn routine of teaching and rehearsing in the American theatre. As I said in the Introduction, hopefully Analysis through

Action helps shake the American theatre's conscience and disrupt the all-too common lassitude of that American theatre.

As I finish this book it is well-known that our theatres are in "freefall."[31] Perhaps replacing our conveyor belt progression – read, talk (too much), block, tech, dress, open – with a creative and communal new rehearsal method will be a restorative for our weary and struggling theatre. I believe Analysis through Action *can be* that restorative.

Let me know how it works out!

Notes

1 К.С Станиславский Konstantin Stanislavsky and Vinogradskaya I. N. 1991. *Работа Актера Над Ролью: Материалы К Книге*. Moskva: Искусство; K.S Stanislavsky Konstantin Stanislavsky and Vinogradskaya I. N. 1991. *The Actor's Work on the Role: Materials for the Book*. Moscow: Art, 59.

2 Merlin, Bella "Here, Today, Now: Active Analysis for the Twenty-First-Century Actor' in White R. Andrew. 2014. *The Routledge Companion to Stanislavsky*. London: Routledge, 326, 333.

3 Knebel' M. 1961. *О Действенном Анализе Пьесы И Роли; В Помощь Коллективам Театральнои Самодеиательности* [2. Rasshir. izd.] ed. M: Iskusstvo; Knebel' M. 1961. *On the Analysis through Action of a Play and a Role; In Assistance to the Collectives of Amateur Theatre Activities* ed. M: Art. Translation Ilya Khodosh, 28.

4 М Кнебель and М Кнебель. 1976. *Поэзия Педагогики*. Moskva: Всероссийское театральное общество; M Knebel and M Knebel. 1976. *Poetry of Pedagogy*. Moskva: All-Russian Theatrical Society. Translation Ilya Khodosh, 328.

5 М Кнебель and Knebel' Mariâ Osipovna. 1971. *О Том Что Мне Кажется Особенно Важным: Статьи Очерки Портреты*. Moskva: Искусство. M Knebel and Knebel' Mariâ Osipovna. 1971. *On What Seems Especially Important to Me: Articles Essays Portraits*. Moscow: Art, 65.

6 Merlin "Here, Today, Now," 325.

7 Merlin "Here, Today, Now" 325.

8 З.Я Корогодский and Korogodskiĭ Z. 1996. *Начало*. Sankt-Petersburg: Санкт-Петербургский гуманитарный университет профсоюзов. Z.J. Korogodski and Korogodskiĭ Z. 1996. *Beginning*. Saint Petersburg: St. Petersburg Humanitarian University of Trade Unions 355.

9 Korogodsky *Beginning* 363.

10 составитель В and В Львов. 2011. *Школа Бориса Зона: Уроки Актерского Мастерства И Режиссуры*. Санкт-Петербург: Мастерская СЕАНС; Compiled by V and V Lvov. 2011. *The School of Boris Zon: Lessons of Acting and Directing*. St. Petersburg: Workshop SEANS, 461–462.

11 Stanislavsky Konstantin and Jean Benedetti. 2010. *An Actor's Work on a Role*. London: Routledge, 47–48.

12 Вениамин Фильштинский and Fil'shtinskiĭ V. M. 2014. *Открытая Педагогика* 2-Е izd ed. Sankt-Peterburg: "Baltiĭskie sezony"; Veniamin Filshtinsky. 2014. *Open Pedagogy* 2-E ed. Saint Peterburg: "Baltic Seasons" Translation Ilya Khodosh 66.

13 Filshtinsky *Open Pedagogy* 69.

14 Korogodsky *Beginning* 353.

15 Knebel *Important to Me* 65–66.

16 Merlin "Here, Today, Now" 332.

17 Knebel *Important to Me* 75.

18 Knebel *Important to Me* 107.

19 Knebel *Important to Me* 105.
20 Author interview June 10 at Brooklyn Academy of Music (BAM).
21 Korogodsky *Beginning* 392.
22 https://www.larousse.fr/dictionnaires/francais/mise/51755#:~:text=Mise%20en%20 sc%C3%A8ne%2C,ou%20pour%20obtenir%20quelque%20avantage
23 Kama Ginkas interview with Marina Davydova, May 4, 2012: Что такое мизансцена; "What is mise-en-scène?" https://os.colta.ru/theatre/events/details/ 36786/
24 Korogodsky *Beginning* 390.
25 After a particularly passionate actor exercise, director/teacher Robert Woodruff would often say "That was great. Now put a suit on it."
26 Knebel *Play and Role* 58.
27 Korogodsky *Beginning* 391.
28 Korogodsky *Beginning* 390.
29 Stanislavsky Konstantin and Jean Benedetti. 2008. *An Actor's Work: A Student's Diary*. London: Routledge, 612.
30 Author interview with Valery Galandeev, Saint Petersburg, May 18, 2012; live translation by Dina Dodina.
31 Peter Marks, *Washington Post*, July 6, 2023.

Acknowledgments

As described in the Introduction to this book, I more or less stumbled onto Analysis through Action while co-producing a Yale School of Drama/Saint Petersburg Theatre Arts Academy collaborative project focused on Meyerhold. But in my early trips to "Piter" and the Academy I took note of some novel (to me) ways of training and rehearsing there, something that had to do with Georgii Tovstonogov and his contemporaries whom my Russian peer colleagues had studied with. But it was not until a few years later in Galati, Romania, that I met Professor Maria Ganeva, a wonderful teacher and director. Maria had spent eight years studying with Tovstonogov, the last four for her PhD. It was she who tutored me on Tovstonogov's version of Analysis through Action and enthusiastically introduced me to the Étude Method of Maria Knebel. I was hooked.

Soon, steered by my fellow producer on the Meyerhold Project Academy, Professor Nikolai Pesochinsky, I received a Likhachev Fellowship which afforded an extensive stay in Petersburg and a side trip to Moscow. What began then with a simple idea turned into years of research and writing.

At the Petersburg Academy (since 2015, RGISI – the Russian Institute of Performing Arts) I was tutored by my friend Professor Sergei Tcherkasski, a Stanislavsky/Strasberg expert, author, and master acting teacher; Assistant Professor in the Department of Foreign Arts Yulia Kleiman, who was crucial in my early stages of research and translation; and of course the brilliant, wise, and humorous Pesochinsky, who among his many notable achievements is the godfather of my son Dmitri. Also at the Academy/RGISI I wish to thank former Rector and current Deputy Director of the Alexandrinsky Theatre, Alexander Chepurov. From both offices he has invited me to speak at various conferences during which times I was able to continue my in-country research.

It was early on at this renowned theatre school that I had an extended interview with Professor Irina Malochevskaya, the former teaching associate of Tovstonogov and author of *The Directing School of Georgii Tovstonogov*. This pivotal interview was also attended by her PhD student Andrei Smolko, with whom I stayed in touch and exchanged numerous e-mails about the implementation of Analysis through Action. It was Andrei who delineated the important distinctions between the methods of Tovstonogov and Knebel – and their radically differing temperaments.

The delightful and determined Elena Vitenberg, Program Coordinator of Petersburg's Likhachev Foundation, immediately set me up with Dina Dodina, deputy director, literary manager, and dramaturg at Lev Dodin's Maly Drama Theatre (MDT) in Petersburg. Along with her wicked humor and fluent English (she is a graduate of City University of London), Dina became an invaluable resource, introducing me to her uncle, world-renowned director Lev Dodin; Dina translated many times for the two of us in Petersburg and in Brooklyn when MDT toured to BAM. In addition, Dina hosted several interviewees for me, including warm and sage Valery Galandeev, a director at the MDT, a teacher at RGISI and, because his teaching field is vocal expression – a specialty of Knebel's – has boundless wells of knowledge about Analysis through Action.

Certainly not to be overlooked in my Petersburg research stints was my extensive and laughter-wracked interview a couple of years later with self-proclaimed "theatre hooligan" Yuri Butusov, then artistic director of Petersburg's Lensovet Theatre and a teacher at RGISI. This inspiring meeting was arranged and translated by Yulia Kleiman; I still listen to the tape of that interview for fun and wisdom.

In Moscow and later also at Harvard, I had numerous meetings with the brilliant academician, author, former Rector of the Moscow Art Theatre School, and Stanislavsky authority Anatoly Smeliansky. Tolya, who is perhaps the best and wittiest public speaker I have ever seen, remains a friend to this day due to his longtime relationship with Harvard University and our residences in Massachusetts. Although my connection with him pre-dated my interest in Analysis through Action, Tolya was instrumental in connecting me with Inna Soloviova, the venerable house historian at The Moscow Art Theatre, who first opened my eyes to alternative ways (i.e., not American) of looking at Stanislavsky. Also in Moscow, I had several coffee chats about more or less everything with John Freedman, then the theatre critic of the English-language *Moscow Times*. John's long view of the Russian theatre from Soviet times to the Putin era was instrumental to my initial understanding of the ever-evolving Russian theatre. Finally, in Moscow I had personal and e-mail conversations with translator Maxim Krivosheyev, who introduced me to the radical Theatre of Games theories of Mikhail Butkevich, a Knebel protégé. More needs to be known in English about this brilliant thinker who has influenced Butusov, Krymov, and many others.

In the States, I have had continuing collegial, academic, and financial support from Yale University. It was at the Yale School of Drama that I first began researching and teaching Analysis through Action (see Introduction). My esteemed Directing Department Chair, Elizabeth (Liz) Diamond encouraged me to keep pushing forward on this long journey and urged me to use the process in my teaching. Later I was joined by Ron van Lieu, then Chair of Acting at YSD for the first workshops between Yale MFA actors and directors. Liz and

Ron, I hope you read this book with pleasant memories; your early support, questions, and input were invaluable. Jumping ahead a few years, I want to thank Professor Emeritus of Yale College Joseph Roach for encouraging me to take the course to the undergraduate Theatre Studies program, where I remain today. My thanks also to faculty leaders Nathan Roberts and Shilarna Stokes for encouraging me to teach Analysis through Action to the Yale undergraduates. Finally, I am grateful to the Griswold Fund of Yale University, which underwrote three of my research tours to Russia.

In the time between leaving the School of Drama and returning to Yale College, I was fortunate to teach Analysis through Action in the inaugural years of Harvard's Theatre, Dance, and Media concentration. For this opportunity I remain deeply grateful to Martin Puchner, the founder and first Chair of that program. I fondly recall the wonderful students there who detonated the Analysis through Action classes with their commitment – they did *all* the Text Actions, on time! – and for their theatrical passion.

Also during this period, I also began teaching at the MFA level New School of Drama. I thank former Dean Pippin Parker for bringing me there, and especially acting teacher Cotter Smith, who welcomed me to his classes (which I later inherited). Cotter: *finally*, here is the book you have been asking about for years! My last cohort of New School graduate actors, self-titled The Elephants for reasons of their own, were as good as any MFA group I have seen anywhere.

At the New School for Drama, as well as at Yale I have had the rare and joyful privilege of co-teaching with a true genius, Dmitry Krymov. who pours his boundless improvisational enthusiasm into each class and every student. Their lives are changed, as has been my life, for which I am eternally grateful to my dear friend Dima.

Along the way I had enormous help from Laurie Vincent, the first reader and first editor of this book. A prize-winning writer herself, Laurie gave influential input throughout the first draft. My early translators, the superlative bilingual writer Ilya Khodosh, a former student at Yale, and the already-mentioned Yulia Kleiman at RGISI, were crucial to converting numerous Russian books and articles into English. Necessary collegial support for this new writer came from Professor Bella Merlin of UC Riverside and my colleague-companion Professor Dassia Posner of Northwestern. It was Dassia who introduced me to the prodigious polymathic scholar Laurence Senelick, who gave me keen insights and criticism for the Stanislavsky System chapter (Chapter 1). Laurence and Maria Shevtsova – she encouraged me to write this book long, long ago – are probably the most-cited living authors on the previous pages. They dwell on the Olympian heights of Russian and Soviet theatre scholarship (and many other matters) and I am honored to be able to visit them there.

And speaking of passionate investigators of modern Russian theatre, Stanislavsky, and consequent American methodologies, I want to extend my awe and thanks to Robert Ellerman, an instructor of acting at the Lee Strasberg Institute of Film and Theatre in New York. Robert is an inexhaustible researcher and a passionate advocate for Stanislavsky, Robert Lewis, and Lee

Strasberg. I have an enormous file of informative e-mails from Robert and I hope he finally gets *his* book written!

Although I mentioned them in the Introduction I must again thank the outstanding teaching associates who have made such important contributions over the years. Once again in chronological order, they are: Angie Tennant (The New School for Drama); Aida Rocci (Harvard College); Annelise Lawson (The New School for Drama and The Stella Adler Studio); Sara Holdren (The New School for Drama); Mikaela Boone (Yale College); and Evelyn Giovine (The Stella Adler Studio). And I would be remiss not to extend warm thanks to Tom Oppenheim, Artistic Director of The Stella Adler Studio for the Arts. Tom was an enthusiastic reader of early parts of the book and has regularly invited me and a TA to teach Analysis through Action at the Adler Studio.

All-time nice guy Lucian Burg of Lu Design Studios, Portland, Maine put his expertise to work on three key graphics – Three Rings of Given Circumstances, The Plan of the System 1935, and the Analysis through Action Flowchart – and consulted on the cover. Lucian was also a giver of great encouragement and my consultant on the process of putting a book together. https://www.ludesignstudios.com/

Finally, all these years later, I want to thank editors Ben Piggott and Talia Rodgers, both then at Routledge, for initially taking on this project swiftly and with enthusiasm. Ben and Talia, I regret that it has taken so long to get there (I'm an experienced director but a first-time author), but both of you gave me the permission and inspiration to dive into this ocean. Thank you, thank you. And my gratitude to the current Routledge editorial assistant Steph Hines for shepherding the book down the final stretch.

Finally to my beloved family, especially Christine, Jessica, and Dmitri: it ain't over yet, there is still production to go, but it will be. Thanks for sticking through this with me. Now we can spend more time together!

David Chambers
Cambridge, Massachusetts
January 2024

Index

Pages in *italics* refer to figures.